T4-ALB-183

# SOCIOLOGICAL INSIGHTS OF GREAT THINKERS

# SOCIOLOGICAL INSIGHTS OF GREAT THINKERS

## Sociology through Literature, Philosophy, and Science

Christofer Edling and Jens Rydgren, Editors

AN IMPRINT OF ABC-CLIO, LLC
Santa Barbara, California • Denver, Colorado • Oxford, England

**Library of Congress Cataloging-in-Publication Data**

Sociological insights of great thinkers : sociology through literature, philosophy, and science / Christofer Edling and Jens Rydgren, editors.
p. cm.
Includes bibliographical references and index.
ISBN 978–0–313–38470–7 (hard copy : alk. paper) — ISBN 978–0–313–38471–4 (ebook)
1. Sociology. 2. Sociology in literature 3. Sociology—Philosophy. 4. Literature and science. I. Edling, Christofer. II. Rydgren, Jens.
HM585.S593 2011
306.4′2—dc22 2010032470

ISBN: 978–0–313–38470–7
EISBN: 978–0–313–38471–4

15 14 13 12 11 2 3 4 5

This book is also available on the World Wide Web as an eBook.
Visit www.abc-clio.com for details.

Praeger
An Imprint of ABC-CLIO, LLC

ABC-CLIO, LLC
130 Cremona Drive, P.O. Box 1911
Santa Barbara, California 93116-1911

This book is printed on acid-free paper ∞

Manufactured in the United States of America

# Contents

*Preface* ix

CHAPTER 1. Introduction 1
*Christofer Edling and Jens Rydgren*

**PART I. SOCIOLOGICAL ILLUSTRATIONS** 21

CHAPTER 2. William Shakespeare: On Social Stratification 23
*Hiroshi Ono*

CHAPTER 3. Plato: Seven Sociological Ideas for the Happy Life 31
*Guillermina Jasso*

CHAPTER 4. Franz Kafka: Bureaucracy, Law, and Abuses of the "Iron Cage" 45
*Joachim J. Savelsberg*

CHAPTER 5. Marcel Proust: On Social Status and Capital Forms 55
*Jens Rydgren*

CHAPTER 6. George Orwell: From Democratic Revolution to Authoritarian Rule 65
*Karl-Dieter Opp*

CHAPTER 7. Robert Musil: State, Nation, and Nationality 75
*Helmut Kuzmics*

CHAPTER 8. August Strindberg: Forms of Interaction 85
*Christofer Edling*

CHAPTER 9. Henrik Ibsen: The Power of Charisma 95
*Fredrik Engelstad*

CHAPTER 10. Chinua Achebe: Colonial Anomie 105
*Wendy Griswold*

**PART II. SOCIOLOGICAL CONCEPTS** 111

CHAPTER 11. Ernst Cassirer: Science, Symbols, and Logics 113
*John W. Mohr*

CHAPTER 12. Cicero: Persons and Positions 123
*Lars Udehn*

CHAPTER 13. Charles Darwin: Selfishness and Altruism 133
*Wendelin Reich*

CHAPTER 14. François Rabelais: Materiality and Culture 141
*Emily Erikson*

CHAPTER 15. Émile Zola: Seductions and Emancipations of Consumption 149
*Helena Flam*

CHAPTER 16. Fyodor Dostoevsky: On Extreme Political Violence 159
*Eva M. Meyersson Milgrom and Joshua Thurston-Milgrom*

CHAPTER 17. Goethe: The Ambivalence of Modernity and the Faustian Ethos of Personality 169
*Hans-Peter Müller*

**PART III. META SOCIOLOGY** 177

CHAPTER 18. Pearl Sydenstricker Buck: At the Intersection of Sociocultural Worlds 179
*Karen A. Cerulo and Janet M. Ruane*

CHAPTER 19. Dante Alighieri: The Afterworlds Are Hell for Sociologists 189
*Peter Bearman*

CHAPTER 20. Galileo Galilei: Which Road to Scientific Innovation? 197
*Roberto Franzosi*

CHAPTER 21. Jorge Luis Borges: Reduction of Social Complexity 207
*Filippo Barbera*

CHAPTER 22. Isaac Asimov: Impacting and Predicting Sociocultural Change 217
*Kathleen M. Carley*

CHAPTER 23. Alfred North Whitehead: From Universal Algebra to Universal Sociology 227
*Thomas J. Fararo*

CHAPTER 24. Kurt Vonnegut: From Semicolons to Apocalypses 237
*Barry Markovsky*

CHAPTER 25. Jonathan Swift: Political Satire and the Public Sphere 245
*Gary Alan Fine*

PART IV. SOCIOLOGICAL FOUNDATIONS 253

CHAPTER 26. Baruch Spinoza: Monism and Complementarity 255
*Ronald L. Breiger*

CHAPTER 27. Isaiah Berlin: On the Sociology of Freedom 263
*Margareta Bertilsson*

CHAPTER 28. Bertrand Russell: Insights on Power 271
*David Willer*

CHAPTER 29. Immanuel Kant: An Analytic Grammar for the Relation between Cognition and Action 279
*John Levi Martin*

CHAPTER 30. John Dewey: The Sociology of Action 289
*Christopher Muller and Christopher Winship*

CHAPTER 31. Charles Sanders Peirce: On the Sociology of Thinking 299
*Richard Swedberg*

CHAPTER 32. Thomas Hobbes: On Generating Social Order 307
*Mohammed Cherkaoui*

CHAPTER 33. Jean Piaget: Sociology Beyond Holism and Individualism 315
*Omar Lizardo*

*Bibliography* 323

*Index* 345

*About the Editors and Contributors* 363

# Preface

The idea for this project came to us on a beautiful spring day in Florence several years ago. It was the focus of a light dinner conversation, which later that same evening evolved into a fantasy multi-volume encyclopedia, spanning the history of humankind from Aristotle to Zola. As time passed we would occasionally return to the idea, and to our great surprise it began to shape into something that we actually thought we would like to pursue even in the light of day. One of us (Edling) enjoyed a highly stimulating spell at the *Wissenschaftskolleg zu Berlin* at this time, and that also provided fuel for the idea. Finally, in late 2007 we began to seriously plan for the project, and some months later we tried our bearings on a few colleagues and mentors.

Our invitation to join the project was extended to a number of sociologists from across the world. We suggested interesting thinkers to consider, but by and large we left it to the contributors to decide on whom to write. We regret that we failed to convince everyone that we contacted and that we lost a few unnamed contributors at a late stage. Perhaps you will join us for volume two? Of course there are a few grumpy exceptions to the rule, but from the very first moment we felt that the invitation was met with genuine support, and that feedback truly gave us all the motivation we needed to see the project through to this point.

We wish to extend our deep and sincere gratitude to all the contributors, both for writing stimulating texts on original topics and for infecting us with enthusiasm and commitment. We also wish to thank Valentina Tursini of Praeger/ABC-CLIO, who has been our very reliable supporter from proposal to print. Pär Benz set aside time at a very late stage to assist in the preparation of the final manuscript. Many thanks!

Bremen and Stockholm, August 2010
Christofer Edling and Jens Rydgren

# CHAPTER 1

# Introduction

*Christofer Edling and Jens Rydgren*

This book is about probing the limits of our sociological understanding and testing the borders of the discipline by confronting sociologists with "non-sociological" originators. We know of few books that have pondered a similar theme, but three titles immediately spring to mind. As an experimental introduction to sociology, Coser (1963) edited a selection of literary texts ranging from Shakespeare to Mark Twain, in which the original texts where intended to speak for themselves without much sociological commentary. In his chronicle on the rise of sociology, Lepenies (1988) suggested that sociology has a problem of demarcation, inherently positioned as it is between literature and science that goes back to its foundation.

More recently, Kuzmics and Mozetič (2003) took on a thorough exploration of the relationship between literature and sociology, with the first part of the book devoted to the relationship between literary and sociological analysis and the second part focused on extracting sociological insights from selected literary texts. These three books all relate sociology to literature in one way or the other. Positive accounts on the role of literature in sociology can also be found in methodological discussions, such as in Runciman (1983) and in Elster (2007), who likes to refer to literary texts in many of his works.

The other interface that Lepenies alluded to, that between sociology and science, frequently surfaces in the methodological debates and mostly ends in the lame conclusion that sociology is not natural science, although Coleman (1964), Fararo (1989), White (1997), and others could be counted upon for seeing productive outcomes emerging from this interface too, at least as far as formal theory goes. For the current volume, we have in mind the broadest possible interaction with literature, philosophy, and science, but as will become evident the majority of the contributors have chosen to go down the alley of literature rather than science.

Our chief ambition is to reclaim the sociological imagination for all of sociology. Since the publication of C. Wright Mills's landmark book, the concept of *sociological imagination* has been reserved for the idea that sociology can and should be put in the service of ordinary men, to carry out the "cultural tasks of our time" (Mills 1959:18). Mills wrote his text as a reaction to a bureaucratization of the social sciences that he believed was ongoing. To counter that trend, Mills forcefully argued for bringing sociology back on the "classic social analysis" track by insisting that sociology deals with the problems that "are of direct relevance to urgent public issues and insistent human troubles" (Ibid.:21).

Even if his claim that he has found the answer for how to fix social science is a display of bravery that borders stupidity, it is hard to argue with Mills's basic assumption that a social science that offers no relevant keys for understanding contemporary social life and that is completely devoid of any practical ambitions is heading in the wrong direction. Looking at where social science is today, many would claim that Mills's critique is still valid, and perhaps even more so today than 50 years ago. Still, and in defense of all those scholars who stood in the line of fire as Mills put his sharp pen to action, we cannot rid ourselves of the fear that by following Mills there is a huge risk that we will be throwing the baby out with the bath water. In contrast to Mills, we do not use sociological imagination as a means to streamline sociology or to point out the way of the future.

We believe that sociologists of all camps need imagination, regardless of methodological convictions, theoretical schooling, or methods training, regardless of the degree of abstractness, applicability, and policy relevance, and regardless of what topics, time-scales, and social phenomena they are interested in. There are many ways to find this imagination, and at the personal level it is likely that it will not emerge from scholarly work or research. Also within the discipline, however, we should allow ourselves once in a while to move beyond the borders that usually constrain us in class, in the seminar room, and in journal articles and academic books, and try to tease our sociological imagination.

To be imaginative is generally considered a good trait. Merriam-Webster Online offers three definitions of imagination, a word dating back to the fourteenth century. First, imagination is "the act or power of forming a mental image of something not present to the senses or never before wholly perceived in reality." Second, imagination is "creative ability," and third, "a creation of the mind." Our printed copy of Webster's College Dictionary, third edition, also has "foolish notion" and "evil plan" to offer. Although the latter definitions might be considered by critics of Mills, for the present discussion we stick to the first three. Our intuitive understanding of sociological imagination is that it is an ability that a sociologist can have for taking on social analysis or for presenting a sociological idea in a creative and novel way.

What we propose is that we can feed our sociological imagination by searching for sociology outside of sociology, and by doing so we can potentially learn something new about sociology or about our understanding of sociology. And we would like to suggest that there is a lot of sociology outside of sociology. We do not argue that this is *the* way to do sociology; in fact, we believe it is not at all the way to do sociology proper. But even though we want to remain lighthearted about the whole project, it is not all about fun and games. To feed our sociological imagination is an important intellectual task, and this volume is meant to show a way of feeding it.

In this short introduction we briefly outline the rationale for editing this volume and introduce the content and structure of the book. In the next two sections we further discuss how we conceive of sociology and what sociology outside of sociology is. The key question, of course, is what sociologists can learn from finding inspiration from outside the confines of disciplinary sociology. In the third section we argue that the works of great thinkers outside of sociology can provide not only new concepts but also figures of thoughts, qualitative simulations, and thought experiments, which will potentially enrich sociologists' thinking by stimulating their imagination. In the last sections we introduce the chapters, which have been divided into four different categories depending on what kind of insights they can offer sociologists and students of sociology: sociological illustrations, sociological concepts, meta sociology, and sociological foundations.

## WHAT IS SOCIOLOGY?

The question "what is sociology?", is as old as the discipline itself. It is not our ambition to make a contribution to this discussion; however, since we make the argument that there are sociological insights outside of (disciplinary) sociology that sociologists could and should learn from, we need to say something about what sociology is.

We will claim that sociology is the systematic study of the social aspects of reality. This may appear as a tautological definition, but it is not. What this definition does, however, is to switch the crux of the matter to the definition of the social. According to Max Weber, a situation is social to the extent that people orient their actions toward one another; and the web of meanings, expectations, and behaviors resulting from such reciprocal orientations are material for sociological analyses. This is a broad definition, and it is evident that sociologists are less constrained by specific empirical focus areas than many other social scientists: most things in life have a social dimension and can be studied sociologically. Even though it is broad, the definition also excludes important aspects of reality by deeming them irrelevant for sociological study. We can distinguish between a harder and a softer line on what sociologists should stay away from. According to the softer line, which we concur with, a study is not sociological if neither explanans nor explandum contain social elements, in the sense given above. According to the harder line, both explanans and explandum should be social in character.

This definition, of course, is only a partial answer to what sociology is about. Sociology is the systematic study of the social aspects of reality. For us, this means two things in particular. First, sociology is empirical in orientation in that it is about explaining and understanding empirical reality. Second, it is not the case that everything goes in explaining and interpreting this reality and there are certain rules that must be followed: explanations should be coherent and consistent, observations should be systematic, data should be reliable, and inferences should be valid, and so on. As a consequence, we need methods and theory to do sociology.

We need theory to help us distinguish between pertinent and non-pertinent aspects of the object of study. All sociological analyses are about simplification—although they differ greatly in the style and level of simplification—and theory provides models for simplifying social reality systematically in ways that satisfy the conditions of internal consistency. We need methods to make sure that empirical observations are reliable and that inferences based on them are valid. In other words, in our view sociology is a scientific enterprise and you need almost by definition to be trained as a sociologist—or at least a social scientist—at a university to be able to do it.

However, this does not preclude the existence of sociological insights outside of disciplinary sociology that sociologists can learn a lot from. Sociology exists both in embryonic and fulfilled form. Here it is useful to keep in mind the distinction between the context of discovery and the context of justification (Reichenbach 1938; Popper 1959). Its fulfilled form, as discussed above, entails by necessity a scientific approach to the context of justification; that is, the systematic and rule-based ways in which observations are made and inferences are drawn. Yet, good sociology should be problem-driven, which means that sociologists need to identify important and creative questions to ask about social reality. The formulation of hypotheses, belonging to the context of discovery, is a fundamental part of sociology, and here sociologists can find great inspiration from thinkers and observers outside of sociology.

## SOCIOLOGY OUTSIDE OF SOCIOLOGY

As have so many sociologists before us, we take the answer to the straightforward question of what sociology is to be non-trivial. Nevertheless, as sociologists tend to do, we have settled on an answer that is as wide-ranging as possible and with which we can still identify. The main implication from trying to answer the question in the first hand is that we clearly do not think that sociology is everything and that everything is sociology. At the same time, however, we also argue that sociological insights—at least in embryonic forms—prevail also outside of what is taken to be sociology. In this section we further discuss what sociology outside of sociology is.

One essential component of our answer to the question of what sociology is includes the idea that there exists something real, something social, that we can observe and make sense of. Of course, this social reality is there for all who form part of society; in other words, this is the reality of all humankind across time and space. Making sense is not only an important aspect of all sciences, among which we regard sociology to be one, but sense-making is also part of what it is to be human. In this respect, every endeavor to make sense of social reality carries a sociological embryo. Consequently, in a naïve sense of the word, we all become sociologists as soon as we enter society (Edling and Rydgren 2007:15).[1]

The wide range of sophisticated ethnography, survey, and interview studies are all evidence that sociologists take the everyday sense-making of people very seriously. In fact, the data we analyze most often consist of what people told us, in one way or the other. As sociologists we usually insist that all such accounts are equally valid, regardless of whom they come from. For the purpose of the current volume, however, we attach a higher value to some sense-making than the other. In particular, it is in the sense-making that manifests itself in scholarly work and in art that interests us here. As we see it, pieces of art or a treatise on philosophy are materialized products emanating from someone trying to make sense of reality. More precisely, we want to explore the work of literary authors, philosophers, and scientists from a sociological point of view.

The proposal that there are not only thinkers—in other words, all of us—but also "great thinkers," those whose sense-making is superior to the sense making of most of us, might be regarded as elitist. However, to level this charge we believe is to miss the point. What we simply suggest is that we should take seriously all the effort that went into these works. It might very well be that we all carry the capacity to produce them, but due to the great variation in individual beliefs and opportunities only some have been able to make the contribution. However, the fact that some works of art, science, and philosophy stand the test of time better than others also suggests to us that some manifestations of sense-making carry a higher value than others. This is a difficult discussion that we neither can nor wish to pursue here.

In this volume we want to learn from those great thinkers who we do not generally consider to be sociologists. We wish to see in what way their sociological insights harmonize with the "accepted" insights of sociology and to what extent we can incorporate their insights into sociology and learn from them, either by shedding new light on key ideas, illustrating main points, or opening our eyes to aspects that we have overlooked.

We would be the first to accept that we deal here with a fuzzy set and that the definition of sociology as well as the distinction between that which falls within and outside sociology is problematic. There simply are no crisp and clear-cut borders between sociology and other approaches to sense-making. And perhaps Runciman (1983:21) has a point when he says that "[n]ovels *are* sociology to the extent that their authors make them so," meaning that if we want to understand "what it was like for the agent," novels can provide that understanding. (In Runciman's terminology this is sociological understanding in the tertiary sense, Ibid.:20.) Still, we need to insist on some borders in order to uphold our intuitive understanding that sociology has a unique essence.

We do not wish to imply that literature, philosophy, and science are the same as sociology. Rather, we believe that sociology lies between these disciplines, and that a sociology that drifts too close to any of the others will compromise its soul. The usual approach to define the essence of sociology is to look at the canon. Introductory sociology texts refer to a core of classical texts that tend to be more or less the same across textbook authors, publishers, languages, and countries. This set is also relatively stable across time, at least for the last 50 years. There will be differences in emphasis and in the inclusion, of course, but by and large all sociologists recognize the same sociological canon.

Thus, for the sociological identity the canon plays a crucial role. But a canon can also be both conserving and reifying. As we reproduce the canon we tend to reproduce our understanding of sociology, the meaning of our core concepts, the rational for our key assumptions, our methodological predispositions, and so forth. We believe it is a useful exercise to step outside the canon and look for sociological insights outside of sociology, both as a reality check and to stimulate our sociological imagination.

## FIGURES OF THOUGHT, SIMULATIONS, AND EXPERIMENTS

Let us briefly continue our speculation on the possible usefulness of the present project, suggesting how non-sociological work feeds into sociology. Sociological texts are afloat of figures of speech and metaphors. Consider, for instance, the title of Hedström's (2005) *Dissecting the Social*, and picture for yourself the sociologist cutting through the delicate textures of society with her razor-sharp scalpel, laying bare the basic workings of social nature—just like any other naturalist. Some will be tempted by this image and the potency it ascribes to sociology; some will no doubt shed away.

The important point here is just to take note of the title as a powerful figure of thought. In fact, we believe that this is a good illustration of how literature, philosophy, art, and science normally inspire sociology, often moving it in a rhetorical direction by suggesting powerful images. In contrast, we propose that literature, philosophy, and so forth can influence sociology in a much more profound way than supplying it with simple figures of speech. We like to call it "figures of thought," although it is important to note that we use the concept in a way that differs somewhat from how it is usually used in linguistics and philosophy (see Lakoff 1986 for an interesting position).

We conceive of a figure of thought in a fairly literal sense, as a representation or an image, which is for instance much closer to the way in which a professor uses graphs and other drawings to illustrate sociological concepts and theories (e.g., Toth 1980). In other words, the figures of thought that we have in mind share many of the properties of the Weberian ideal-type and are much closer to what Max Weber had in mind when he wrote about *Gedankenbilder*. For Weber, however, a figure of thought is a sort of theoretical aggregate "formed by a one-sided *accentuation* of one or more points of view and by the synthesis of a great many diffuse, discrete, more or less present and occasionally absent *concrete individual* phenomena, which are arranged according to those one-sidedly emphasized viewpoints into a unified *analytical* construct" (Weber 1949:90). Thus, an ideal-type can only be formed at a fairly advanced stage of the research process, and it is rather the (theoretical) outcome of sociological work than the input.

A figure of thought, brought in by the sociologist from the outside, serves a completely different purpose. Such a figure of thought can trigger the sociological imagination by suggesting new questions to work on, and it can serve to illuminate certain social processes, phenomena, or situations. This book contains many examples of such figures of thought that clearly show how they can be evoked in both quantitative and qualitative reasoning and in narrative as well as lyrical sociology (see Abbott 2007 on this distinction). Figures of thought bring matters to a head in just the same way as an ideal-type. However, what is essential to keep in mind is that despite their resemblance to ideal types these figures of thought are not the product of sociological observation and analysis.

The term qualitative simulation is used in science and engineering to refer to the attempt to assess the behavior of a dynamic system as a complement to numerical simulation or, in lack of qualitative indicators, as a substitute. It provides the analyst with an intuitive feeling for the system dynamics and indicates the range of behaviors that can be expected to arise. In other words, qualitative simulation is a technique to shed light onto processes where we have incomplete knowledge about some aspects of the system. Qualitative simulations do not produce point predictions; they only suggest possible outcomes.

We propose that literature could serve the same purpose for sociological reasoning. Autobiographies would be a particularly clear case in mind where, for instance, one could read recollections from a selection of persons who grew up at a particular intersection of space and time. Each biography can be regarded as one simulation run, and taken together the stories could give some insight into the opportunities and constraints that form social life or of the different moods that are triggered in different individuals by some common experience. Also, works of fiction may provide "models of man" and of situations and provide detailed scenarios—or thick descriptions (Geertz 1973)—of the ways in which people are likely to act in specific situations.

Such accounts can be seen as "as if" models and are potentially very important for generating new hypotheses. In contrast to quantitative agent-based simulation, qualitative simulation is unlikely to provide information about how likely it is that scenarios can be generalized. Instead they "ring true" (or not); that is, they are seen as plausible given the reader's more or less articulated preconceptions. Such an approach to qualitative simulation can inform not only theoretical assumptions and methodological approaches but also serve to remind the sociologist that most social phenomena can be viewed from a great many different angles. It should be emphasized, however, that hypotheses generated by simulation (whether of the qualitative or quantitative kind) must be checked against real-world data in order to qualify as sociological accounts of reality.

Simulations can be regarded as experiments, and another way to see how sociology can put to use the sense-making efforts done outside of the field is to think about the structure of experiments, as suggested in Engelstad's concluding remark in his chapter in this volume. An experiment, just as a simulation, is a means to try out something in a very rigorous way. Leave out the rigor and consider only the structure of an experiment and it appears that one of the crucial aspects is that some (few) conditions are varied while (many) others are held constant. The experiment is repeated at least once for each (slight) variation to produce a set of experimental sequences.

Writing on the works of the great Norwegian playwright Henrik Ibsen, Engelstad claims that in contrast to writers that tell the same story over and over again "Ibsen had an uncommon ability to explore a few general themes from ever new angles, with the result that his total *oeuvre* may be regarded as analogous to a series of experiments, each with a different focus and different outcome." In such bodies of work, for instance, the same type of individual appears across stories but each time in a different social situation. The novelist here is not completely dissimilar from the experimenter in altering some fundamental conditions while holding other key parameters constant. Obviously, the sociologist need not be confined to works by the one and same author when using literary texts as a form of experiments.

Early on in this chapter we said that we do not believe that stimulating sociological imagination by going after the "sociology outside of sociology" is sociology proper. Now, that is a strong statement, and who are we to say so? What we mean is that feeding the sociological imagination is not the same thing as putting it to work. It would be like equalizing a display game with a game in the actual championship. We maintain that sociology is professional in the sense that sociology does posses a unique sociological intuition as well as sociological skills and tools that are quite distinct from the intuition, skills, and tools of a novelist for instance.

It is when those skills and tools are put to work on challenging questions that we produce sociology. Consequently, we categorically object to the image of the "novelist as a researcher" (Brinkmann 2009) that can be equated with the sociologist as a researcher. As Runciman suggested (1983: Ch. 4), the novelist can play a role in descriptions of what something is or was actually like for those involved. Indeed, some of us who had literary texts inspire us for the contributions to this volume use them for such understanding, but that descriptive aspect remains just one of many pieces in the sociological jigsaw puzzle.

## STRUCTURE AND CONTENTS OF THE BOOK

Taken together, the chapters in this volume demonstrate the scope and insight of sociology. Standing on the shoulders of giants outside our own field we wish to provide glimpses of the relevance and vigor of sociological thinking across time and space. We have organized the book into four parts: sociological illustrations, sociological concepts, meta sociology, and sociological foundations. Some chapters certainly overlap two or even all of these headings, but by and large we felt that this structure emerged quite naturally when going over the contributions.

In the first part we find a set of chapters that draw upon the work of a great thinker to illustrate a fairly delimited sociological process or an important sociological idea. These chapters take the sociological concepts as given and use (predominantly) world literature to show that a sociological reading of these texts can serve as introductions to sociological thinking on social structure and social action. The second part, on sociological concepts, takes a slightly different approach, where the main task is not to illustrate but to discuss key sociological concepts. Here the authors use great thinkers to demonstrate how works outside of sociology can further our understanding of particular concepts, such as culture or modernity.

Chapters in the third part, which we have called meta sociology, deal with the nature of society and sociology and with the role of the sociologist. From the American novelist and Nobel Laureate Pearl Buck, for example, sociologists are advised "to observe and understand rather than to rank and moralize." In this part we also find methodological discussions ranging from complexity reduction to satire. Whereas the first and the second parts are concerned primarily with relating sociological thinking to sense making outside of sociology, the fourth part, called sociological foundations, includes chapters where the authors are entangled in ongoing and central sociological discussions.

The chapters in part four are the most intra-disciplinary chapters in the volume. Here the contributions of great thinkers are used to reconsider the fundamental assumptions of sociology in a fairly provocative way, as in David Willer's case, for instance, who asks if Max Weber really gave sociology the most adequate concept of power. In a way these chapters close the circle, and we are brought back to where we took off, with a set of sociological concepts that need to be illustrated.

Having toyed with the idea for quite some time, we certainly had a firm conception of which thinkers to include in the volume. Not all of these ideas caught on with the invited authors, and several new suggestions were made. As a result, the thinkers that are included are selected based on the curiosity and interest of the respective author(s). As already mentioned, many of the great thinkers that inspired the contributors to this volume are novelists or playwrights. As is evident from Table 1.1, however, there are also a fair number of philosophers and a few scientists and polymaths—but again, these borders are not clear cut.

Of course, the list of thinkers that grew out of this process hinges upon who we asked to contribute and who eventually decided to write a chapter. A quick glance at the list of contributors reveals our U.S.-Western European bias. Nevertheless, we think the mosaic of thinkers that has emerged is an artifact that in itself says something interesting about sociology.

Time prevents us from any analysis of the essence of this mosaic. As the reader will experience when reading the book, however, there is no shortage of parallel lines of thought as well as explicit and implicit cross-references between what might at first sight appear to be a highly unsystematic arrangement of chapters. We think of this mosaic of authors, thinkers, and insights as a "self-organized" image of sociology, reflected in great thinkers. It remains an open question as to what sociological mosaic a scaled-up version of the same exercise would produce.

As illustrated by the citation ranking provided in Table 1.1, some of the thinkers have a reasonably strong presence in contemporary sociology, and it would not surprise any sociologist that in this list of thinkers Dewey is the most cited, followed by Kant, Piaget, and Hobbes. Still, almost one-third of these thinkers have been cited less than 50 times during the last 20 years. Just by looking at which of the great thinkers are cited the most we come away with yet another image of sociology, produced by sociologists themselves. Again, a systematic scaled-up version of this project would certainly provide an interesting picture of sociology's self-image.

It is the philosophers that score high on the ranking. The novelists rank low, Buck having been cited only once in the last 20 years, followed by Strindberg (three times) and Dostoevsky (four times). The authors that would presumably be relevant because they where around when modern sociology was born and in a way wanted to be part of sociology—Ibsen, Strindberg, and Zola—all rank low or fairly low. The ranking within sociology largely correspond to the overall-ranking within the whole Social Science Citation Index database, with a spearman rank correlation of .91. Piaget is an outlier with almost 14,000 citations, followed by Dewey (8,000), Kant (7,000), and Darwin (4,500). As evident from the table, giants like Goethe and Shakespeare, who are not widely cited in sociology, are pretty well cited in the social sciences at large.

Needless to say, the citation ranking of great thinkers tells us nothing about what these thinkers can do for our sociological imagination. We do not like to completely dismiss the ranking because both the compilation of the list and the citation trend was produced by sociologists in a bottoms-up fashion, and therefore we think it tells us something interesting about sociology. To find out the real potential that the great thinkers listed in the table have for sociology, however, you will have to go to the chapters.

## Sociological Illustrations

The chapters in the first part of the book all discuss sociological insights that illustrate sociological ideas that are already common knowledge in sociology. Yet, these illustrations provide important contributions to sociology in two different ways. First, some of them were formulated, in literature or

**Table 1.1**
**Great Thinkers Citation Ranking in SSCI, 1990–2010**

| Thinker | Subject Area Sociology | Articles | Total SSCI |
|---|---|---|---|
| Buck | 1 | 1 | 53 |
| Strindberg | 3 | 3 | 36 |
| Dostoevsky | 4 | 3 | 145 |
| Galilei | 4 | 3 | 152 |
| Rabelais | 5 | 5 | 33 |
| Ibsen | 6 | 5 | 85 |
| Dante | 8 | 4 | 102 |
| Vonnegut | 8 | 5 | 134 |
| Proust | 9 | 7 | 315 |
| Asimov | 10 | 8 | 184 |
| Goethe | 10 | 7 | 755 |
| Cicero | 12 | 8 | 415 |
| Swift | 12 | 9 | 241 |
| Musil | 13 | 11 | 135 |
| Shakespeare | 14 | 12 | 648 |
| Zola | 19 | 15 | 110 |
| Kafka | 20 | 13 | 350 |
| Achebe | 23 | 14 | 251 |
| Spinoza | 27 | 25 | 349 |
| Borges | 28 | 22 | 415 |
| Whitehead | 59 | 40 | 1207 |
| Cassirer | 62 | 47 | 815 |
| Russell | 77 | 51 | 2172 |
| Orwell | 87 | 64 | 895 |
| Peirce | 98 | 75 | 1620 |
| Plato | 112 | 86 | 1766 |
| Berlin | 142 | 90 | 1964 |
| Darwin | 144 | 98 | 4567 |
| Hobbes | 163 | 117 | 2243 |
| Piaget | 233 | 189 | 13958 |
| Kant | 341 | 251 | 7172 |
| Dewey | 414 | 286 | 8148 |

*Note*: Compiled from *Web of Science* in March 2010.

philosophy, long before they were known in sociology—or, in fact, before sociology even existed. This anticipation of sociological ideas in literature and philosophy, which is often left unrecognized by sociologists, is highly interesting from the perspective of the discipline's history.

Second, many of the illustrations discussed in this part of the book add vivacity and elegance to the sociological ideas that are often missing in sociological writings, and sometimes they also add clarity by helping us see the ways in which social mechanisms operate in realistic settings. As discussed above, literature in particular potentially functions as qualitative simulation—as simplified "as if" or "what if" models—that help us get ideas about how the real world functions.

In Chapter 2, Hiroshi Ono discusses Shakespeare's insights into the workings of social stratification. He shows that the greater part of sociological theory on stratification can be found, in condensed form, in a single verse in Shakespeare's *Twelth Night* ("Some are born great, some achieve greatness, and some have greatness thrust upon 'em"), and he provides several examples of the ways in which Shakespeare showed great insights on how social stratification is produced and reproduced and how it affects people's lives and their relations with others.

In Chapter 3, Guillermina Jasso extracts seven sociological ideas for a happy life from the writings of Plato. She shows that Plato provided exact measurements of inequality, which were highly sophisticated for his time, and that he distinguished between numerical and proportional equality. Among other things, Plato also voiced detailed ideas about gender equality and the ways in which marriage and mating patterns influence social inequality at the aggregated level. In Jasso's reading, Plato emerges as an important source of inspiration for the contemporary literature on distributive justice.

In Chapter 4, Joachim Savelsberg discusses the sociological insights of Franz Kafka. Kafka is one of the few authors of fiction who is relatively often cited in social science writings, predominantly in law journals. The value of Kafka is his vivid descriptions of the malfunction of what Max Weber called the iron cage of bureaucracy and formal-rational law. In his novels and short stories, people find themselves in situations where bureaucratic forces determine their lives in ways that are opaque and that appear meaningless for everyone except the specialists inside of the system. Kafka also demonstrates how fleeting and transitory—yet absolute—power may appear to the people who lack access to it.

In Chapter 5, Jens Rydgren writes about the sociology found in Marcel Proust's novel, *Remembrance of Things Past*. He shows that Proust anticipated many of the key ideas found in Bourdieu's theory of habitus, taste, and social distinction. More specifically, Proust provides detailed scenarios of the ways in which people are driven by a will to status distinction, and how access to high-status groups combines with dissociation from members of low-status groups as the main strategy for status climbers. Without using the terms, Proust shows how important cultural capital and social capital are for understanding social action and inter-group behavior in particular.

In Chapter 6, Karl-Dieter Opp discusses the deep insights into the sociology of revolutions to be found in George Orwell's fable *Animal Farm*. From this book a number of general propositions about the different stages of revolutions can be identified. The propositions cover both the emergence of a revolution, critical events and the success of rebellion, the origin of a democratic post-revolutionary regime, and how such a regime might be undermined or even overhauled by authoritarian fractions within the (post-)revolutionary party. Even if most of the insights are well known within the sociology of revolution, when seen in isolation, the great contribution of Orwell was to forge them together into a comprehensive stage model.

In Chapter 7, Helmut Kuzmics provides a sociological reading of Robert Musil's novel *The Man Without Qualities*, which he argues is a valuable text to read for sociologists interested in the formation of nation states, and in particular the transformation from dynastic states to nation states. In this reading, Musil offers a bridge between different strands within the sociology of nationalism that focuses on emotional or rational aspects of national attachments.

In Chapter 8, Christofer Edling turns to the short but widely played drama *Miss Julie*, written by August Strindberg. This one-act drama, which was a contribution to the Naturalist movement of the late nineteenth century, is about the struggle between the two sexes and between social classes evolving around two leading actors. Inspired by Georg Simmel's sociology, the drama is presented as an illustration of interaction forms and about the crucial role of social structure in understanding social processes.

In Chapter 9, Fredrik Engelstad discusses how Henrik Ibsen's plays can deepen our understanding of Max Weber's concept of charisma. Whereas charisma for Weber is a way out of the iron cage of rationalization, as something that brings an element of spirit into the machine, Ibsen illustrates the destructive force in charisma and the longing for purely ideational power.

In Chapter 10, Wendy Griswold discusses how Chinua Achebe's novels provide great sociological insights of the ways in which anomie works, and the effects of anomie on individuals, villages, and societies. Achebe has written about pre-colonial, colonial, and post-colonial experiences in African societies and what happens—sociologically as well as psychologically—when traditional society suddenly breaks apart. In common with Durkheim, one of the founding fathers of sociology, Achebe has tried to find the answer to the question of what holds society together in those situations of unpredictability that characterize modern society in general and the transition from traditional to modern society in particular.

## Sociological Concepts

The second part of the book has chapters about central concepts in contemporary sociology. Even though various examples are used to shed light on these concepts, the main concern is not illustration but conceptual discussion. As demonstrated in these six chapters, the role of the great thinkers can be to anchor a key concept in very early contributions or in parallel fields and to study the concept from another "non-sociological" perspective.

In Chapter 11, John Mohr discusses Ernst Cassirer's contribution to the modes of scientific thought, institutional logics, and cultural analysis. These are all interrelated aspects of Cassirer's thinking, and these questions span several sections of this volume. We decided to place the chapter in the section on concepts because, as Mohr suggests, Cassirer's work on the logic of symbols that make up "the tangled web of human experience" is profoundly linked to what was later to become modern structuralism. Taken together with his relational philosophy of science, Cassirer's analysis of symbolic forms, Mohr points to a novel and largely untried approach to cultural sociology.

In Chapter 12, Lars Udehn goes to the Roman statesman Marcus Tullius Cicero, who was an influential thinker in the Enlightenment but is largely forgotten today. However, not only does Cicero offer an early account of the duality of individual and society, claiming that humans are social by nature, but he also writes upon exchange in a way that forestalls modern ideas on the utility of friendship for instance. Udehn's reading of Cicero further suggests that the Roman had a very clear conception of structure and might have been the first to clearly separate person from position.

In Chapter 13, Wendelin Reich takes a fresh look at what he calls Charles Darwin's puzzle, namely the occurrence of purely altruistic behavior, or costly cooperation. Although Darwin did not have the tools to solve the puzzle, it is argued that his contribution was fundamental in posing the right question. Drawing on recent advances in research on genetic inheritance, Reich gives two examples that illustrate how sociology can deepen and broaden its understanding of costly cooperation.

In Chapter 14, Emily Erikson reads François Rabelais's mid-sixteenth-century novels about the giants *Gargantua and Pantagruel*. Moving beyond the racy narrative, which most modern readers present itself as an insurmountable obstacle, Erikson presents Rabelais as an exemplary reminder about the power that context has on our cultural perception. Drawing on the work of cultural historians

Bakhtin and Febvre, she reminds us that the role of laughter in society has changed profoundly over 500 years, and that to understand the significance of Rabelais work we need to overcome the solid boundary between the modern and the medieval. Erikson argues that a similar type of boundary spanning is essential in all cultural sociology.

In Chapter 15, Helena Flam discusses the sociology of consumption through the lens of Émile Zola's novel *The Ladies' Paradise*. Zola researched his novel in pretty much the same way as a sociologist would prepare ground for her analysis, by means of interviews, observations, and statistics, and in many ways the novel is indeed a data source for historical sociology. However, Flam argues that what makes the novel particularly interesting is the insightful comprehension of the roles that consumption play in modern society. The one-sided treatment on consumption found among some of the classics of sociology is effectively challenged by Zola.

In Chapter 16, Eva Meyersson Milgrom and Joshua Thurston-Milgrom discuss Fyodor Dostoevsky's novel *Daemons* in the context of political violence. In Dostoevsky they find several underlying ideas that translate to sociological theory, such as the assumption that people across different situations and classes are generally driven by status comparisons and the dynamics of group identity. The authors suggest that, pieced together, Dostoevsky's novel provides a key to a sociological understanding of the emergence of extreme political violence that can also shed light on contemporary events.

Chapter 17 concludes the section on sociological concepts with the intellectual giant, Johann Wolfgang von Goethe. Hans-Peter Müller turns to *Faust* to see what the great anti-sociologist has to tell contemporary sociology and shows that Goethe has both epistemological, analytical, and substantial lessons to teach. Müller's reading is centered on the idea of modernity, a fundamental concept for sociology on which Goethe's insights are highly valuable because of his historical position on the verge between traditional society and modern society. Müller argues that there is indeed more to Goethe's vision on modernity than the doomsday prediction one would derive from *Faust*.

## Meta Sociology

The chapters in the third part of the book use the insights of great thinkers outside of disciplinary sociology to discuss meta sociological questions and to find inspiration in how good sociological research should be conducted. It involves questions of methodology and theory, but also of more general approaches to the sociological enterprise, such as which questions that should be asked.

In Chapter 18, Karen Cerulo and Janet Ruane discuss what sociologists can learn from the writings of Pearl Sydenstricker Buck. Buck was born American but spent most of her first 42 years in China, which made her deeply acquainted with two rather different cultures. According to Cerulo and Ruane, Buck's position at such a sociocultural intersection made her especially well positioned to explain social worlds. By being in a community, but not of it, she was able to observe and spotlight things that others would have left out as everyday and routine. Buck's novels are sociological in the sense that she sees the social in human biographies, and many sociologists could learn from her sociological approach to observe and understand rather than to rank and moralize.

In Chapter 19, Peter Bearman presents Dante as the first ethnographer of hell. Like other ethnographers, Dante uses his study of another world to reflect the workings of the world of the readers. Revealing the structure and logic of the worlds of the afterlife is important in explaining how the ordinary world functions sociologically. As Bearman notes, the afterworlds are hell for sociologists. Contrary to the world we know, there is no competition over scarce resources, no status mobility, no way to understand action by referring to either identity or interests as motivational forces, and no actors living in the afterworlds who are able to shape these afterworlds.

In Chapter 20, Roberto Franzosi discusses Galileo Galilei and the road to scientific innovation. The telescope was invited in 1608, and shortly afterwards both the English astronomer Thomas Harriot and Galileo Galilei pointed a 6X telescope towards the moon and made a drawing of what they saw. Whereas Harriot's painting revealed no understanding of what he saw, Galileo's drawing correctly interpreted the spottedness of the moon as craters and mountains—which made Galileo determined to go on developing more powerful telescopes and evolving his path-breaking astronomic theories. Why this difference, and what can sociologists learn from it? First, new methods are very important, but they do not explain everything; second, theoretical understanding is important, which helps sort incoming data; and third, knowledge and education outside of scientific training is important—in this case the fact that Galileo had studied art and had a feeling for perceptions.

In Chapter 21, Filippo Barbera finds inspiration in Jorge Luis Borges for an argument against "senseless completeness" in sociological analysis; that is, that a greater amount of information does not necessarily provide better knowledge. The inability to remove complexity by categorizing things into larger categories and by distinguishing between pertinent and non-pertinent aspects of reality creates an absurd situation in which it takes a whole day to remember what happened yesterday (to take just one example from Borges). In order to describe phenomena and to interpret or explain them, we have to choose and select, and we should do this systematically based on an explicit strategy.

In Chapter 22, Kathleen Carley writes about Isaac Asimov and the sociological inspirations to be found in his science fiction writings. Asimov coined terms such as positronics, psychohistory, and robotics, and Carley shows how he inspired contemporary research in computational modeling—in particular computational models of complex socio-cultural systems and how they can contribute to social forecasting.

In Chapter 23, Thomas Fararo provides a sociological reading of Alfred North Whitehead, showing Whitehead's importance for process-oriented sociology in general and system theory in particular. Talcott Parsons in particular, but also George Homans, were influenced by Whitehead's ideas of universal theory and looked for ways to develop key concepts into a universal sociology.

In Chapter 24, Barry Markovsky finds inspiration in Kurt Vonnegut's science-fiction novels for a multilevel sociology. For Markovsky, Vonnegut's narratives are zooming in and out between multiple levels of aggregation and are unpacking little stories inside big stories as well as establishing critical points of connections between them. This jump between different levels not only adds interest and complexity to the stories, but also provides greater insights into the mutual impact and interaction of society's micro and macro components.

In Chapter 25, Gary Alan Fine writes about the political satire of Jonathan Swift. To write satire, Fine notes, is to balance a fine line: having to write what you do not believe or think, but with a twist in that you need to trust that the audience will get the joke. This trust is facilitated by the existence of a public sphere, making it easier for authors to know what to expect of their readers. Sociologically, therefore, Swift's importance should be seen in relation to the emergence of the public sphere.

## Sociological Foundations

The fourth and last part of the book closes the circle and takes us back to the starting point. These chapters deal with absolutely fundamental assumptions about the social. The great thinkers are used here to ask why some of these assumptions disregard aspects that seem quite central to the discussion and to indicate new solutions to old problems that sociology has not yet been able to solve. Compared to the other parts of the book, these chapters might require that the reader have more of a sociological background. In other words, these chapters will eventually produce the sort of concepts and ideas that we aimed to illustrate in the first part of the book.

In Chapter 26, Ronald Breiger discusses Spinoza's influence on the theoretical thinking of two of sociology's classic authors, Durkheim and Simmel. Specifically, Breiger shows how Spinoza's spirit is present when both of these authors address the problem of singularity and complementarity. In their theories both Durkheim and Simmel would view the individual and society not as two casually connected entities but rather as belonging to the same content, a thought that Breiger sees emerging as if directly inspired by the great thinker. Thus, by tracing central themes in both classical and contemporary sociology back to Spinoza, Breiger adds to the sociologist's awareness of the origin and development of central theoretical constructs.

In Chapter 27, Margareta Bertilsson turns to Isaiah Berlin and proposes that sociology needs to take seriously the issue of freedom in order to remain a vigorous critical discipline. Focusing on Berlin's concepts of negative and positive freedom, Bertilsson argues that sociology has reached an impasse by stressing the latter while largely disregarding the implications of the former. A sociological contribution to current social debate, Bertilsson claims, would be much better served by subscribing to the vision of the "sacred individual," a theme closely related to Berlin's discussion of negative freedom.

In Chapter 28, David Willer discusses Bertrand Russell's potency for the sociological analysis of power. Willer argues that Russell's writing is original in relation to the two preceding sociological authorities on power, Karl Marx and Max Weber, suggesting that Russell's contribution exceeds that of both the others. Russell argued that power was *the* fundamental concept of social science, and while Willer does not take that claim literally, he demonstrates the wide applicability of Russell's analysis of power, including the question of how power in society is tamed.

In Chapter 29, John Levi Martin explores the thinking of Immanuel Kant and the idea of grammar for sociological theories of action. Drawing on Kant's critique of the human ability to understand, reason, and judge, Martin proposes that a missing link in sociological theory is an understanding of the role of judgement in social action. With reference to Bourdieu's theory of habitus, Martin suggests how a grammar based on Kant's critique of judgement can enrich the sociological treatment of taste and other qualitative experiences.

In Chapter 30, Christopher Muller and Christopher Winship revisit John Dewey's theory of action and its contribution to the ongoing discussion on linking sociology and American pragmatism. Muller and Winship argue, pragmatically, that Dewey's theory of action should not be thought of as a replacement of all other action theory, but rather that its combined experimental, contextual, and habitual themes make it particularly useful as a bridge between advances in psychology and sociological theories of action.

Dewey's insistence on theoretical pluralism and on fallibility is also put forward as the recommended guiding principles for sociological research.

In Chapter 31, Richard Swedberg suggests how Charles Sanders Peirce, another of the great American pragmatists, can lead the way to a sociology of thinking. He claims that applying Peirce's pragmatic analysis of thinking is facilitated by the fact that many of Peirce's concepts are essentially social, such as habit or community. Swedberg argues that Peirce's ideas about signs can provide the missing link in a sociological theory of thinking because in Peirce's theory it is via signs and language that meaning and thinking become directly related to social action.

In Chapter 32, Mohammed Cherkaoui discusses Thomas Hobbes and the problem of order. Cherkaoui surveys the profound influence of Hobbes on Western social thought about interest and rationality, and on the hypothetical deductive method widely adapted in sociology and social science in general. The chapter highlights the actuality of Hobbes in contemporary debates and research programs on social order, on challenges to collective action, and on the relation between micro-motives and macro-behavior.

In Chapter 33, the final chapter of the book, Omar Lizardo reinstalls Jean Piaget among the classics of sociology. Although Piaget is widely read and cited in contemporary social science (see Table 1.1), at face value he plays a very marginal role in sociological theory. Lizardo has chosen to display Piaget's contributions to the ontology of the social and to sociological explanation and demonstrates a range of parallels between Piaget and other social thinkers. Piaget believed that psychology and sociology contributed two unique understandings of the same phenomenon, and in Lizardo's reading of Piaget the unique role of sociology is to study and understand interaction-linkages and the emergence of higher order social organization.

## NOTE

1. Closely related to this idea is the insight that the sociologist herself is part of the reality she is studying.

# PART I

# Sociological Illustrations

# CHAPTER 2

# William Shakespeare: On Social Stratification

*Hiroshi Ono*

All modern societies are stratified and layered hierarchically. The allocation of resources is a finite zero-sum game and invariably generates an unequal distribution of wealth, with societies consisting of the haves and the have-nots. In this stratified society, individuals sort themselves into classes, or groups of people who occupy similar socioeconomic status. Determinants of class, and the extent to which individuals move between classes, have fascinated sociologists for centuries. Indeed, the study of social stratification lies at the very core of sociological inquiry and has provided "the major concepts and independent variables for theory and research both at the individual and at the societal level" (Sørensen 1996:1333–1334).

This chapter concerns the topic of social stratification and social mobility, but it is less about the classic sociological perspective and more about William Shakespeare, and his insight into the field. The very same topic—the process of generating inequality—that occupied the minds of Karl Marx and Max Weber were inherent also in Shakespeare's writings, which preceded the works of the master thinkers by well over two centuries.

Shakespeare is one of those rare figures who require no introduction: Playwright, poet, dramatist, master of prose . . . his works have been read and studied across generations, across class boundaries, and across national boarders. During his lifetime, he wrote 38 plays, 154 sonnets, and a large number of poems. His writings have inspired generations of writers, actors, and artists. His work is not simply confined to the art and literary world but transcends it, which makes him truly one of the greatest writers and greatest thinkers of all time.

Let us start with the following quote taken from the second act of the comedy *Twelfth Night*:

"In my stars I am above thee, but be not afraid of greatness.

Some are born great, some achieve greatness, and some have greatness thrust upon'em."

(a) (b) (c)

This passage appears in a phony love letter addressed to the egocentric character Malvolio, who believes that the letter was written by Olivia, the woman he desires. Without loss of generality, we lift this quotation from its original context for the sake of our current heuristic exercise. Hereafter, I refer to parts a, b, and c of this quote as the elements of greatness.

Like the formal elements of fiction—character, plot, setting, theme, and style, which Shakespeare perfected in his plays—there also exist the core elements of greatness. When formally defined and specified into quantifiable terms, these elements can then be placed into some kind of a "greatness generating equation" to assess how much of an impact these elements have in predicting greatness.

Greatness itself comes in many forms, and Shakespeare cleverly leaves this open to interpretation. In the sociology tradition, greatness may be occupational prestige or status, which can then be expressed as a status attainment model. In economics, greatness may be captured by wealth or income, which can be specified by an earnings function or a human capital production function. In political science, it may be some measure of bargaining power or the ability to mobilize resources. Here we interpret greatness loosely and assume that greatness encompasses all of these concepts.

In its most general form, the formula that generates inequality can be expressed as:[1]

$$Y = \alpha + \mathbf{Xb} + \varepsilon \qquad (1)$$

where $Y$ is some arbitrary measure of outcome, $\mathbf{Xb}$ is the vector of attributes that generates inequality in Y, and $\varepsilon$ is the error term associated with this equation. Here, $\alpha$ is the intercept, which, for our purposes, corresponds to what human capital theorists refer to as natural (or genetic) endowments, such as IQ or native ability.[2] By definition, endowments are given and determined at birth and cannot be manipulated through effort. Endowments are not regarded as investments by the individuals involved but are rather considered to be gifts or "assets" that are acquired at birth (Grusky 1994).

A variant of the general equation, which distinguishes ascription from achievement, can be expressed as:

$$Y = \alpha + \Sigma\delta D + \Sigma\beta Z + \varepsilon \quad (2)$$

Here, $D$ consists of measures that capture individuals' ascriptive characteristics. These consist of demographics such as sex, race, and ethnicity as well as acquired traits such as parental wealth and nationality (Grusky 1994). The symbol $\delta$ is the coefficient associated with each ascriptive characteristic, and it can be positive or negative depending on the attribute. By definition, ascriptive measures are traits that an individual is born into and are not subject to choice. One cannot choose her parents, and one cannot choose the color of her skin.

In contrast, $Z$ represents the variables relating to achievement, which can be enhanced through investments. People are free to choose the level of investment, although they are subject to constraints. Education is a prime example of an investment activity that enhances productivity. The coefficient $\beta$ corresponds to the rate of return for each investment activity, with the necessary condition that $\beta > 0$ for all $Z$; otherwise there would be no incentive to invest. Now let us decompose the quotation into three components and examine each in turn.

## (A) SOME ARE BORN GREAT

There are two ways to interpret this statement. First, some persons are well endowed with natural ability and talent at birth, that is $\alpha$, and these natural endowments propel them into greatness. Second, some persons are born *into* greatness. They possess all the ascriptive traits that are associated with greatness (i.e., their attributes are associated with high levels of $\delta$). An obvious example is where an individual simply inherits greatness by being born into great families or dynasties. Likewise, some persons may be born greater than others by virtue of her sex and race, as opposed to others who are less fortunate for the same reasons.

These words point to the great insight that much of inequality is generated at birth, oftentimes beyond the control of the individuals involved. With regard to genetic endowments, Hamlet speaks of the "mole of nature," where he speaks not of greatness but of weakness and how some men have a genetic propensity to drink: "In their birth—wherein they are not guilty; Since nature cannot choose his origin" (*Hamlet*, Act I). One could also argue that Shakespeare's treatment of demographic characteristics—race in *Othello*, gender in the *Taming of the Shrew*, or religion in the *Merchant of Venice*—provides examples to illustrate how ascription can influence individuals' life chances and outcomes.

Shakespeare's plays are ripe with stories of feuds between families and dynasties. In *Romeo and Juliet*, the quote, "What's in a name?" expresses Juliet's despair and frustration with her destiny. She and Romeo are lovers, but they are cursed by their "prodigious birth." They are born into two warring families, not by choice but by ascription. Juliet can be united with Romeo if only he could "doff" the Montague name that he inherited.

On the topic of endowments, we are reminded here that natural talent is a gift. Some have them, some do not, and still others may be unaware of their talents. Consider the following quote by *Ophelia* in Hamlet: "Lord, we know what we are, but know not what we may be" (Act IV). And herein lies another cruelty of human nature: that many of us live out our lives without knowing what we were meant to be great in. Natural endowments or talents come in many shapes. Some are fortunate to discover their talents.

Clearly, Mozart was an exceptional composer. He was well endowed with musical talent, and evidence suggests that he was well aware of his natural abilities during his lifetime. However, most of us are less fortunate. We do not know what our $\alpha$ is, and natural talents, if any, go undiscovered. And so we rely on achievement and effort, which we turn to next.

## (B) SOME ACHIEVE GREATNESS

These words are self-explanatory and correspond to the achievement characteristics (Z) in equation (2). If one is not born with greatness, then one still may achieve greatness through the conventional channel of hard work and effort.

Let us note here the interplay between natural endowments and achievement. The two are generally complementary, i.e. Corr $(\alpha, \beta) > 0$. For example, Becker's view of elite formation posits that abler persons have a higher capacity to benefit from investments in human capital (Becker 1993). In other words, those that are born great are also more likely to achieve greatness. This phenomenon, which is another manifestation of the rich pulling away from the poor, is widely observed in stratification research, such as the Matthew effect in science (Merton 1968).

The pertinent question for stratification theorists is this: which component is more important in determining greatness, ascription or achievement? Many of us would like to believe that it is achievement, and we may in fact live our lives under this assumption. In the words of Turner (1960), a system that encourages mobility through hard work and effort corresponds to contest mobility, where the prize in the contest is open to all participants who are willing to compete. Success is attained solely by one's own efforts, with the most satisfactory outcome earned by the most deserving. In contrast, sponsored mobility is characterized by early selection and induction into elite status, a notable example of which is selection through social class and family affiliation.

Particularly in the United States, individuals believe strongly in the American dream of achieving upward mobility through contest mobility. In a country that upholds meritocracy as its very foundation, sponsored mobility is downplayed. The empirical findings that have come out of this debate are too many to name in this chapter, but the question of how one gets ahead has been a core concern for generations of sociologists, and it remains central to the social mobility debate in both the theoretical and empirical literature.[3]

Related to the topic of achievement, Shakespeare reminds us that greatness, once achieved, can be easily destroyed or taken away. Hamlet is upset by his uncle's proclivity for wine and boisterous drinking. Because his uncle is the King of Denmark, Hamlet is embarrassed that this man's behavior has brought shame and a reputation of drunkenness to the entire nation: "Soil our addition, and indeed it takes from our achievements, though performed at height, the pith and marrow of our attribute" (*Hamlet*, Act I). Although the Danes have achieved greatness, their accomplishments have been overshadowed by their reputation for drunkards and swinish men.

## (C) SOME HAVE GREATNESS THRUST UPON 'EM

Shakespeare's third way of achieving greatness comes down to luck and fortune. The use of the expression "thrust" suggests that individuals may not have a choice in the matter and that chance plays a role in greatness. So Shakespeare offers a way out; if one cannot achieve greatness through ascription or achievement, all is not lost, for there is always luck. For example, one may become rich by winning the lottery. In statistical equations, such matters conventionally are relegated to the error term ($\varepsilon$). Stated differently, luck and fortune are the residual part of greatness that cannot be explained by ascription or achievement, or by **Xb** in equation (1).

Others may be more strategic in their pursuit of greatness, as in the case of marriage. In the sixteenth-century setting of the comedy *The Taming of the Shrew*, marriage was in fact a business arrangement. As suggested by the quote, "I come to wive it wealthily in Padua," the male character Petruchio unashamedly pursues Katharina for her wealth. In *King Lear*, the Duke of Burgundy requests Cordelia's hand in marriage, but he turns her down when he discovers that she is without dowry.

However, what is also implied in Shakespeare's words is that one cannot rely on fortune to achieve greatness, for fortune is beyond one's control. Shakespeare's use of the expression, "fortune's fool" (e.g., *Romeo and Juliet*) suggests a situation in which persons become powerless because of their overreliance on fortune to determine their fate.

## DISCUSSION

When they are specified in a statistical model, the elements of greatness as formulated by Shakespeare can explain a great deal of variance in predicting inequality.[4] As implied by the expression, "In my stars I am above thee," greatness (or rank in this context) is maximized when the stars are aligned just so. Here again is Shakespeare's flirtation with chance and fortune, for we do not know precisely which constellation of the stars (i.e., which combination of the elements) elevates us to greatness.

At the aggregate societal level, history tells us that a system of mobility that rests entirely on ascription (as in sponsored mobility) is prone to civil unrest. Luck, insofar as it brings hope and aspiration, is not a bad thing, but a society cannot thrive by relying solely on luck. As idealized in the notion of meritocracy, a well-functioning society must have in place a system of rewards and incentives that enables individuals to achieve upward mobility through their talents and effort. Shakespeare's famous sentence bringing together the elements of greatness captures the idea that stratification and mobility are best understood through an integrated approach that examines all three elements as a whole.

This chapter looked at Shakespeare's insights on sociology, with specific focus on the process of stratification and mobility. We could extend the exercise to frame other areas of sociology. Perhaps the most obvious connection is dramaturgy. The famous quote, "All the world's a stage, and all the men and women merely players" (*As You Like It*, Act II), is but the genesis of dramaturgy itself and has inspired great thinkers, such as Kenneth Burke and Erving Goffman. Gender inequality and Shakespeare's treatment of women in his plays (e.g., *Merchant of Venice*) has had its share of attention from feminist scholars and literary critics (e.g., Callaghan 2000). Loyalty is another persistent theme in his plays.

In closing, I want to point out that Shakespeare teaches us sociologists another valuable lesson: brevity. The elements of greatness not only capture the essence of stratification, but they do so in merely 14 words. Shakespeare said it best with the quote, "Brevity is the soul of wit" (*Hamlet*, Act 2). All would agree that sociologists need to work on our brevity.

## NOTES

1. The simple statistical equations that are stipulated here do not account for complications such as endogeneity and selection bias.

2. This is a simplified interpretation of the endowment. Other formulations include, for example, Becker's version (1993) of the endowment, which takes the following form of a Markov equation: Endowment ($E_t$) depends on her parent's endowment ($E_{t-1}$) such that $E_t = \alpha + hE_{t-1} + v_t$ where $\alpha$ is the social endowment that is common to all members of a given cohort in the same society, $h$ is the degree of inheritability of these endowments from her parents, and $v$ measures luck in the transmission process (Becker 1993:261).

3. For example, the large-scale *New York Times* (2005) project, *Class Matters*, investigated social mobility in the United States through a number of interviews and case studies. Citing a number of academic studies and results from empirical research, the project concluded that the American dream of upward social mobility through hard work has declined over time: "Americans are arguably more likely than they were thirty years ago to end up in the class into which they were born" (*New York Times* correspondents 2005:4).

4. For example, Mincer (1974) explains that accounting for schooling and work experience can explain 50 percent of the variance in a logged earnings equation.

# CHAPTER 3

# Plato: Seven Sociological Ideas for the Happy Life

*Guillermina Jasso*

Follow me then, and I will lead you where you will be happy in life . . .
Socrates, in *Gorgias*, 527

## PLATO AND SOCIOLOGY

Reading Plato is an endless source of pleasure. For sociologists, it is also an endless source of deep, rich insight into human nature and the social worlds that humans build. Pronounced by Popper (1968), who had more than a little disagreement with him, "the greatest thinker of all times" and the "founder of political theory . . . and of sociology," Plato was born in 427 BCE and died at the age of 80 in 347 BCE. His formative years combined the upheavals of the Peloponnesian Wars and the invitation to think with his teacher Socrates. Though only about 30 when Socrates died in 399 BCE, Socrates survives as the commanding presence in Plato's (1952) *Dialogues*—part engaging thinker, part literary hero.

Every reader of Plato, and every sociologist who reads Plato, will find distinctive ideas that impress and resonate. Here we collect seven of those ideas. Along the way we will meet inequalities of various kinds, status, principles of justice, the optimal city size, love, and even two new paradoxes. But a single theme unifies them: happiness.

## INEQUALITY MEASUREMENT

> [The law] will permit a man to acquire double or triple, or as much as four times the amount of [the minimum lot]. But if a person have yet greater riches, . . . if he give back the surplus to the state, and to the Gods who are the patrons of the state, he shall suffer no penalty.
>
> Athenian Stranger, in *Laws* V, 744–745

It is easy for us in the early twenty-first century to measure inequality. We have many measures of inequality, from the Gini, Theil, and Atkinson measures for personal inequality to difference and ratio measures of racial, ethnic, and gender gaps. But in the context of the fifth century BCE, without benefit of Arabic numerals, the inequality measure embedded in the *Laws*—the ratio of the maximum to the minimum—seems like a miracle. Representing the persons in a population by the order statistics from 1 to $N$, where 1 denotes the poorest person and $N$ the richest, and denoting wealth (or income) by $x$, Plato's ratio, denoted $P$, is written as follows:

$$P = \frac{x_N}{x_1}. \tag{1}$$

Plato's ratio is simple, beautiful, elegant, and dimensionless. It is applicable to all monetary currencies and to almost all situations. It satisfies, besides scale invariance, the property that adding a constant reduces inequality while subtracting a constant increases it. However, it satisfies only an extreme version of the principle of transfers, namely, that a transfer from the maximum amount to the minimum amount reduces inequality. Moreover, by modern standards, it has another flaw; it cannot be used in mathematically specified distributions whose upper extreme value tends to infinity.

Substantively, we may distinguish two parallel worlds of inequality (Jasso 2008). The first is the world of goods and bads (like income and taxes); the second is the world of primordial sociobehavioral outcomes (like status and power). The two worlds are connected because the goods and bads generate the primordial sociobehavioral outcomes; the primordial sociobehavioral outcomes, in turn, generate identity and happiness. In each of the two parallel worlds, two types of inequality—inequality between persons and inequality between subgroups—are at work (Jasso and Kotz 2008). Thus, there are four special realms of inequality, with two types of inequality in two parallel worlds. Plato's ratio takes pride of place as historically the first measure of inequality between persons, applicable in both parallel worlds.[1]

## PRINCIPLES OF MICROJUSTICE: JUSTICE IS EQUALITY

Then not only custom but nature also affirms that justice is equality . . .
Socrates, in *Gorgias*, 489

The first of the four central questions in the scientific study of the sense of justice asks, "What do people think is just, and why?" The question of what is just pertains to many domains, from the just war to the just procedure to the just minimum income to the just reward for an individual. It is remarkable that with respect to microjustice—the just reward for an individual—Plato answers both parts of the question in a single sentence. And though his answers are incomplete, the achievement is great.

It is by now well established that ideas of justice differ substantially across persons—as expressed in the Hatfield principle, "Equity is in the eye of the beholder" (Walster, Berscheid, and Walster 1976:4). Yet, it is often the case that the justice repertoires include equality, and that for most persons reflecting on the natural or social goods (and bads), justice is equality.

Plato (*Laws* VI, 757) later distinguished between "numerical" and "proportional" equality, observing that proportional equality, which gives more to the more deserving, is the higher kind of justice. Yet from the vantage point of contemporary scientific frameworks, the "justice is equality" formulation is preserved intact; what changes is the population within which the equality is calculated. Thus, a person may think that, as in the first sense, the just wage is the same for everyone, or that, as in the second sense, the just wage is the same for all persons identical in relevant respects, such as to all workers of equal ability and effort.

## PRINCIPLES OF MACROJUSTICE: THE JUST MINIMUM, THE JUST MAXIMUM, AND THE JUST INEQUALITY

[T]here should exist among the citizens neither extreme poverty, nor, again, excess of wealth, for both are productive of both these evils [faction and distraction]. . . . [The minimum lot] ought to be preserved, and no ruler, nor any one else who aspires after a reputation for virtue, will allow the lot to be impaired in any case. . . . [The law] will permit a man to acquire double or triple, or as much as four times the amount of this [minimum lot]. But if a person have yet greater riches, whether he has found them, or they have been given to him, or he has made them in business, or has acquired by any stroke of fortune that which is in excess of the measure, if he give back the surplus to the state, and to the Gods who are the patrons of the state, he shall suffer no penalty or loss of reputation.
Athenian Stranger, in *Laws* V, 744–745

Across history, ideas of justice include not only ideas of microjustice—such as St. Antoninus's idea of the just wage—but also ideas of macrojustice, pertaining to the distribution as a whole. These most often highlight the minimum income (as in Rawls 1971) or the amount of inequality. Plato provides ideas of justice for three distinct distributional features.

## The Just Minimum

Plato's description of the minimum lot is quite detailed, including a parcel of land in the city and another in the countryside and attentive to the quality of the soil. Moreover, the property must be registered. Importantly, he stipulates that this property is inviolable.

## The Just Maximum

Twenty-five hundred years ago, as now, effort, cleverness, and luck could transform a small holding into a giant one. Plato lists the major ways in which the lot can be parlayed—to use a word emblematic of modern business and politics—into vast holdings. However, he will not permit the riches to be kept. For Plato, the just society has a rigid maximum.

## The Just Inequality

The passage in the epigraph suggests that for Plato, the zone of justice extends from perfect equality to a society in which the maximum is five times the minimum. Beyond that, the inequality becomes unjust. This is a remarkably crisp answer to the question, "How much inequality is too much?"[2]

Of course, others have reached different conceptions of the just inequality, and these limits also vary over time. For example, not too long ago—16 years ago, to be precise—a U.S. newspaper profiled a firm which announced that it was abandoning its policy that the salary of the highest paid individual, such as the chief executive officer (CEO) or managing director, not exceed seven times the salary of the lowest paid individual (Feder 1994). That was before the explosion in CEO compensation.

Today, even after the overall decreases in CEO compensation of 2007 and 2008, the annual pay of top CEOs, as well as that of entertainers and athletes, easily exceeds $200 million. For example, in 2008 the top earnings among entertainers and athletes was $300 million (to an author), and in 2009, the top earnings among CEOs was almost $557 million (www.forbes.com).

As a simple calculation, consider the value of Plato's ratio if (1) the minimum income is in fact the U.S. federal minimum income of $7.25 an hour

**Table 3.1**
**Plato's Ratio in the U.S. Earnings Distribution in 2009 for Given Federal Minimum Pay and Hypothetical Amounts of Maximum Pay**

| Minimum Pay | Maximum Pay | Plato's Ratio |
|---|---|---|
| $15,080 | $100,000,000 | 6,131.30 |
| $15,080 | $200,000,000 | 13,263.60 |
| $15,080 | $300,000,000 | 19,894.90 |
| $15,080 | $400,000,000 | 26,525.20 |
| $15,080 | $500,000,000 | 33,156.50 |

*Notes*: The federal minimum pay in the United States, effective July 24, 2009, is $7.25 an hour. Accordingly, a person who works 40 hours a week for 52 weeks earns $15,080. Some kinds of work, however, are exempt from the minimum pay. Meanwhile, the top earnings reported in 2009 for 2008 were $556,980,000 for a CEO and $275,000,000 for an entertainer (www.forbes.com).

and the bottom earner works 40 hours a week for 52 weeks a year and (2) the maximum income is set at hypothetical amounts from $100 million to $500 million. Table 3.1 shows the values of Plato's ratio. When the maximum income is $100 million, Plato's ratio registers 6,131; and when the maximum income is $500 million, Plato's ratio reaches 33,157—a far cry from the halcyon 7 of the ice cream makers.

A question that has arisen recently is whether inequality in a primordial sociobehavioral outcome is larger or smaller than in the good which generates it (Jasso 2008). For example, the Gini coefficient in the distribution of status in the case of one valued good (or *k* perfectly positively associated goods) is equal to .5—larger than in most real-world distributions of wealth or income (Jasso and Kotz 2007).

To address this question, consider the magnitude of Plato's ratio in status distributions in groups of finite size N. Applying the formula proposed by Sørensen (1979) for status (Jasso 2001):

$$\ln\left(\frac{1}{1-r}\right), \tag{2}$$

to the highest- and lowest-ranking individuals, where the relative rank $r$ is expressed in terms of the absolute rank $i$ and the group size $N$ ($r$ equals $i/(N + 1)$), yields the formula for Plato's ratio in a status distribution:

$$\frac{\ln(N+1)}{\ln(N+1)-\ln(N)}. \tag{3}$$

Plato's ratio is 4.82 when the group size is 3, and it registers 7.21 when the group size reaches 4. Indeed, one can calculate Plato's ratio for all the groups

**Table 3.2**
**Plato's Ratio in the Status Distribution in Small Groups, for One-Good and Two-Perfectly-Negatively-Associated-Goods Regimes**

| | Plato's Ratio in the Status Distribution | |
|---|---|---|
| Group Size | One Good | Two Goods Perfectly Negatively Associated |
| 2 | 2.71 | 1 |
| 3 | 4.82 | 1.21 |
| 4 | 7.21 | 1.28 |
| 5 | 9.83 | 1.42 |
| 6 | 12.62 | 1.49 |
| 7 | 15.57 | 1.60 |
| 8 | 18.65 | 1.66 |
| 9 | 21.85 | 1.74 |
| 10 | 25.16 | 1.79 |
| 11 | 28.56 | 1.86 |
| 12 | 32.04 | 1.90 |

*Notes*: The formulas for Plato's ratio are as follows: In the case of one good,

$$\frac{\ln(N+1)}{\ln(N+1)-\ln(N)}$$

In the case of two perfectly negatively associated goods, for even group size,

$$\frac{\ln\left(\frac{(N+1)^2}{N}\right)}{\ln\left(\frac{(N+1)^2}{N}\right)-\ln\left(\frac{N+2}{4}\right)}$$

In the case of two perfectly negatively associated goods, for odd group size,

$$\frac{\ln\left(\frac{(N+1)^2}{N}\right)}{2\ln 2}$$

represented in the *Dialogues*. To illustrate, Table 3.2 reports in the middle column the magnitudes of Plato's ratio for groups of size 2 to 12. As shown, Plato's ratio in the status sociobehavioral world is quite large. Whether it exceeds Plato's ratio in the underlying good—for example, income—depends on the income distribution in the group. If the group includes a cross-section of earners (as may happen in a jury, say), Plato's ratio in income would exceed Plato's ratio in status.

One can also speculate about the social situations portrayed in the *Dialogues*. In modern terms, we might speculate that the participants in the

*Dialogues* did not care about status; they may have cared about justice or about power. Thus, it would not occur to anyone that status inequality would quickly cross the threshold of 5 on Plato's ratio and, depending on the group's composition, might far outstrip wealth inequality.

Alternatively, perhaps when status was activated in Athens, so were several goods simultaneously, such as beauty, intelligence, and musical skill—and the goods were not perfectly positively associated. In such a situation, status is substantially attenuated, as discussed in the pioneering work of Berger, Cohen, and Zelditch (1966) and more recently investigated by Jasso and Kotz (2007). Table 3.2 also reports (in the far right column), the values of Plato's ratio for the case of two perfectly negatively associated goods. For example, in a six-person group that values two perfectly negatively associated goods (say, intelligence and military skill), Plato's ratio would be only 1.49.

Exploring more deeply the case in which a group or population values status and generates status from two perfectly negatively associated goods, we find that Plato's ratio does not reach 5 until the population size exceeds 1,022, registering 5.001 when $N$ equals 1,023.

Of course, a deeper question is whether anything can be done about a person's "surplus" of status. A citizen of Athens could not become less handsome or less adept in the arts of disputation or of war. Moreover, if the population size remained the same, Plato's ratio in the status distribution would remain the same. There would be only two remedies: (1) restriction of status hierarchies to subdivisions of the city; and (2) expulsion of individuals, through emigration, exile, or execution. Below, we return to the idea of subdividing the city. Plato (*Laws* V, 740) mentions emigration as a tool for maintaining the ideal city size of 5,040 (to be discussed below), so that expulsion by emigration would seem natural as a tool for maintaining low levels of Plato's ratio in status. As for expulsion by execution, Socrates himself may have been a case in point.

## NEGATIVE ASSORTIVE MATING AS A CURE FOR SOCIAL INEQUALITY

> Every man shall follow, not after the marriage which is most pleasing to himself, but after that which is most beneficial to the state. For somehow every one is by nature prone to that which is likest to himself, and in this way the whole city becomes unequal in property and in disposition; and hence there arise in most states the very results which we least desire to happen. . . . [T]he rich man shall not marry into the rich family, nor the powerful into the family of the powerful.
>
> Athenian Stranger, in *Laws* VI, 773

Plato's idea that positive assortative mating perpetuates social inequality while negative assortative mating reduces it is a powerful early insight and one that is well known today (Jencks 1972:74, 212, 233–234, 271–273; Becker 1991:228). For example, it is straightforward to show how perfect negative assortative mating reduces the variance in the couple's income distribution.

To illustrate, consider the simplest case. Let the husband's and wife's income distributions be identical with variance $Var(X)$. By well-known theorems on the variance of a sum or difference of random variables, we obtain the variance of the married-couple's income distribution for three special cases. If the husband's and wife's income distributions are independent, the variance of the married-couple's distribution is $2Var(X)$. If the two spouses' distributions are perfectly positively associated, the variance of the married-couple's distribution is twice as large as in the independent case—$4Var(X)$. If the husband's and wife's distributions are perfectly negative associated, however, the variance of the married-couple's distribution is smaller than in any other case, namely, $[2Var(X)](1 + \rho)$, where $\rho$ denotes the correlation between the spouses' distributions.

Correlation is delicate and demanding, and so it is that the correlation between two perfectly negatively associated distributions is not necessarily –1. However, the correlation is always negative, and thus the variance of the married-couple's distribution is always smallest in the negative-association case. Moreover, if the two spouse-specific distributions do indeed have a correlation of –1, then the variance reduces to zero and the married-couple's distribution is perfectly equal (or, equivalently, degenerate).

Although it might have gone unnoticed in fifth century BCE Athens, negative assortative mating also generates marital inequality. Plato (*Laws* VI, 757) quotes the saying, "equality makes friendship," but it was Aristotle (*Nicomachean Ethics*, Book VIII) who would note more trenchantly that love is possible only to equals, thus signaling the price of negative assortative mating. Representing marital inequality by the log of the ratio of one spouse's income to the other's, it is straightforward to show that under perfect positive assortative mating, husband and wife are equals, but in the other cases there are varying amounts of marital inequality.

The variance of the marital inequality distribution shows these effects. Continuing with the example in which the two spouses' distributions are identical, if they are perfectly positively associated, the variance of the marital inequality distribution is zero. If the two distributions are independent, the variance of the marital inequality distribution is $2Var[\ln(X)]$. The variance of the marital inequality distribution under perfect negative assortative mating is even larger—$\{2Var[\ln(X)]\}(1 - \rho)$. If the correlation is a perfect –1, then the variance of the marital inequality distribution becomes $4Var[\ln(X)]$.

**Table 3.3**
**Variance in the Married-Couple Income Distribution and in the Marital-Inequality Distribution Under Three Assortative Mating Regimes, for the Case of Identical Spousal Distributions**

| $X_H$ and $X_W$ Identical | Association between $X_H$ and $X_W$ | | |
|---|---|---|---|
| | Perfect Positive | Independent | Perfect Negative |
| Married Couple | $4Var(X)$ | $2Var(X)$ | $[2Var(X)] \times (1 + \rho)$ |
| Marital Inequality | 0 | $2Var[\ln(X)]$ | $\{2Var[\ln(X)]\} \times (1 - \rho)$ |

*Notes*: The correlation between the $X_H$ and $X_W$ distributions is denoted by $\rho$. The correlation $\rho$ is always negative in the perfect negative association case, so that the right-hand factor attenuates the variance in the married-couple distribution and increases it in the marital-inequality distribution. The ordering of the variances across the row is opposite for the two distributions, decreasing in the married-couple distribution and increasing in the marital-inequality distribution, as the association between the two spouses' distributions goes from perfect positive to independent to perfect negative.

Table 3.3 summarizes these results, reporting the variances for the married-couple and marital-inequality distributions in this simplest case of identical husband's and wife's distributions, under three assortative mating regimes. As shown, the orderings of the two sets of variances are exactly the reverse of each other. While the married-couple variance decreases as the association between the two spouses' distributions goes from perfect positive to independent to perfect negative, the marital-inequality variance increases.

Social inequality and marital inequality are thus on a collision course. If Plato was right and social inequality destroys the social fabric, and if a long line of thinkers stretching from (a somewhat unconscious) Aristotle to modern social scientists are right and marital inequality destroys the marital bond, then there is indeed a harsh reality. What is good for society is bad for marriage, and what is good for marriage is bad for society.

This may be a new Plato's Paradox to add to the canon. Marital sorting produces opposite effects on social inequality and marital inequality.[3]

## GENDER EQUALITY

> Then both men and women, if they are to be good men and women, must have the same virtues of temperance and justice?
>
> Socrates, in *Meno*, 73

> The law which we then enacted [that men and women would be governed by the same laws and have the same pursuits] was agreeable to nature, and therefore not an impossibility or mere aspiration; and the contrary practice, which prevails at present, is in reality a violation of nature. . . . You will admit that the same education which makes a man a good guardian will make a woman a good guardian; for their original nature is the same? . . . [T]he guardians of either sex should have all their pursuits in common . . .
>
> Socrates, in *Republic* V, 456–457

Throughout history, whenever human beings differ in some respect, the question arises whether they should be treated differently. Of course, humans differ in infinitely many ways—from handedness to a wide variety of skills and aptitudes to the color of the eye and the timbre of the voice. The process by which some of these differences are selected as pertinent to social organization is a perennial theme in social science. There is much at stake, not only in terms of opportunities and rewards but also in terms of personal freedom. Thus, across space and time, we observe one subset making laws to govern the behavior of everyone; examples include property owners, the physically or militarily powerful, clerics, and men.

Plato provides the earliest careful analysis of differential treatment of men and women. Others had proposed gender equality (e.g., Pythagoras), but it is in Plato that we find two pivotal insights, as modern analysts observe. (For an overview of modern scholarship and a provocative analysis, see Forde 1997.)

The first insight is that analysis of the problem of discerning which human differences are relevant for differential treatment quickly reveals that sex is not one of them. Whether the analysis is couched in terms of "rational beings" or "higher and lower traits" or "body and soul," sex, says Socrates, is not in the pertinent set. As Forde (1997:669) notes, Plato explores the "elements that can form the basis of a nongendered human perfection."

This theme recurs in all analyses of gender equality. Even St. Paul, not averse to prescribing headwear for women in church (1 Corinthians 11:1–16), asserts, "There is neither Jew nor Greek, slave nor free, male nor female, for you are all one in Christ Jesus" (Galatians 3:28).

The second insight is that the fundamental problem underlying gender equality is sexuality, not sex. If persons do not operate as sexual beings, a full and uncompromising gender equality is substantially easier.

This theme, too, recurs. Thus, St. Jerome, for whom the evils of gender inequality are most visible in marriage, catalogs the *molestias nuptiarum*, or vexations of the married state (for example, in the famous Letter XXII, to Eustochium, written in AD 384)—chief among these vexations, the *dominatum maritorum*, or rule by husbands—and concludes with his celebrated and simple advice, "Don't marry." More than eleven-hundred years later, another practical psychologist, the humanist Juan Luis Vives (1947–1948 [1522–1540]), writing on "the duties of a husband" (in the *De Officio Mariti* of 1528) and noting the woman's rational soul and her heirship to the City of God, proposes the ingenious idea that once the reproductive years have passed—and, presumably, true blindness to sexuality is possible—women be granted full freedom and rights completely equal to those of men.

Plato's insights on gender equality lead to a second Plato's Paradox. Gender equality is fully possible only by eliminating sexuality, but love is possible only to equals. Unlike the first paradox (reported in the section "Negative assertive mating as a cure for social inequality" above), this one has an immediate solution: Platonic love.

## GROUP SIZE AND SOCIAL DYNAMICS

> The number of our citizens shall be 5,040—this will be a convenient number; and these shall be owners of the land and protectors of the allotment. The houses and the land will be divided in the same way, so that every man may correspond to a lot. [W]e are going to take that number which contains the greatest and most regular and unbroken series of divisions. The whole of number has every possible division, and the number 5,040 can be divided by exactly fifty-nine divisors, and ten of these proceed without interval from one to ten; this will furnish number for war and peace, and for all contracts and dealings, including taxes and divisions of the land.
>
> Athenian Stranger, in *Laws* V, 737–738

Following Pythagoras, Plato loved numbers and saw their operation everywhere. His love of the number 5,040—which is 7 factorial—is boundless. The Athenian Stranger, exhorting others to honor equality, adds, "And, above all, observe the aforesaid number 5,040 throughout life" (*Laws* V, 741). Plato may have been the first to notice that group size affects social dynamics. The idea of fixing the number of households so that there will be natural subdivisions for every possible civic activity is splendid. Any child who has suffered through odd-numbered classroom sizes (such as the ubiquitous 25 and 35) will find in Plato an understanding friend.

To examine more carefully the number 5,040—and mindful that it represents households rather than individuals—let us take some poetic license and calculate Plato's ratio for the ensuing distributions of status in the case of two perfectly-negatively-associated valued goods. It turns out to be 6.15, not that much larger than Plato's maximum of 5, but nevertheless larger.

**Table 3.4**
**Plato's Ratio in the Status Distribution in Subgroups of the Ideal City (N = 5,040), for One-Good and Two-Perfectly-Negatively-Associated-Goods Regimes and by the Subgroup Size That Emerges When the City Is Subdivided into 2 to 10 and 12 Subgroups**

| | | Plato's Ratio in the Status Distribution | |
|---|---|---|---|
| Number of Subgroups | Subgroup Size | One Good | Two Goods Perfectly Negatively Associated |
| 1 | 5,040 | 42,972.08 | 6.15 |
| 2 | 2,520 | 19,741.59 | 5.65 |
| 3 | 1,680 | 12,481.32 | 5.36 |
| 4 | 1,260 | 8,999.54 | 5.15 |
| 5 | 1,008 | 6,975.51 | 4.99 |
| 6 | 840 | 5,660.42 | 4.86 |
| 7 | 720 | 4,741.35 | 4.75 |
| 8 | 630 | 4,065.03 | 4.65 |
| 9 | 560 | 3,547.81 | 4.57 |
| 10 | 504 | 3,140.29 | 4.49 |
| 12 | 420 | 2,540.93 | 4.36 |

*Notes:* The formulas for Plato's ratio are given in Table 3.2.

If, following Plato, we wish to prevent Plato's ratio from exceeding 5, then it will be necessary to prevent a status hierarchy from developing in the entire city, confining it to subdivisions of the city. Accordingly, we calculate Plato's ratio for all the subgroups that arise when the city is divided into 2 to 10 subgroups, as well as 12 subgroups.

Table 3.4 collects these results. As shown, when there are two subgroups, their size is 2,520; when there are three subgroups, their size is 1,680, and so on. For each of these subgroup sizes, Table 3.4 reports Plato's ratio for the status distribution in the case where there is one valued good (or $k$ perfectly positively associated valued goods) and in the case where there are two perfectly negatively associated valued goods.

Earlier we saw that in the case of one good (or $k$ perfectly positively associated valued goods), Plato's ratio in the status part of the sociobehavioral world exceeds 5 when the group size exceeds 3. Accordingly, the only hope for constraining Plato's ratio is for the population to value goods that are independent or negatively associated. In the case of perfectly negatively associated goods, Plato's ratio exceeds 5 when the population size exceeds 1,022.

In the equal subdivisions envisioned by Plato, Plato's ratio exceeds 5 when the number of subgroups is less than 5. When the number of subgroups is 5, and each of the five subgroups has a population of 1,008, Plato's ratio is safely contained at 4.99.

## INDIVIDUAL AND SOCIETY, PERSONALITY AND CULTURE

> [G]overnments vary as the dispositions of men vary, and . . . there must be as many of the one as there are of the other. . . . [T]he States are as the men are; they grow out of human characters. . . . [I]f the constitutions of States are five, the dispositions of individual minds will also be five.
>
> Socrates, in *Republic* VIII, 544

Sometimes two ideas come together in a way that instantly impresses. Alone they might appeal, but together they amaze. So it is with these ideas of Plato. The first provides the foundation for the study of the micro-macro link and of the micro foundations of macro phenomena. Personal dispositions, deep in human nature, generate social forms. The second quietly observes that there are five types of personalities and thus five types of societies.

There are no doubt many ways to make a list of five types of persons and link it to a list of five types of societies. And this is a straightforward path to focused thinking. Sometimes this is how secrets are found. Other times, however, reasoning along very different lines, a new vision emerges, and it turns out to evoke the old insights.

The new unified theory of sociobehavioral forces provides an example (Jasso 2008). The goal of the new unified theory (NUT) is to integrate theories describing five sociobehavioral processes—comparison (including justice and self-esteem), status, power, identity, and happiness. The integration (partial, in the case of happiness) is made possible by the remarkable similarity of the internal core of the theories. The core consists of three elements: personal qualitative characteristics, personal quantitative characteristics, and primordial sociobehavioral outcomes. The theory posits the operation of three sociobehavioral forces (i.e., comparison, status, and power), each associated with a distinctive way of generating a primordial sociobehavioral outcome from a personal quantitative characteristic—notably, a distinctive rate of change of the outcome with respect to the quantitative characteristic. Each combination of elements—for example, justice-wealth-city or status-beauty-classroom—generates a distinctive identity and a distinctive magnitude of happiness.

Because in nature there are only three rates of change—constant, increasing, decreasing—there can only be three sociobehavioral forces. It turns out that the scientific descriptions of the three forces indicate that two of them (comparison and power) distinguish between cardinal and ordinal quantitative characteristics (between, that is, materialistic and nonmaterialistic goods and bads), while status notices only relative ranks. Thus, there are five types of operations and five ensuing types of societies, known as justice-materialistic, justice-nonmaterialistic, status, power-materialistic, and power-nonmaterialistic (Jasso 2008:418, 420, Tables 2 and 3)—a great Platonic surprise.

Predictions obtained from the theory show the importance of the Platonic dispositions. For example, while in a status society intersubgroup conflict is predicted to increase as the proportion in the disadvantaged subgroup increases, in a justice-nonmaterialistic society it decreases. Similarly, predictions about how individuals become attached to themselves (Selfistas) or their racial or gender subgroups (Subgroupistas) indicate that Selfistas are always in the majority in a justice-nonmaterialistic society but in the minority in a status society (Jasso 2008:428–429). Of course, there are other finer distinctions; in materialistic societies the distributional form of the material goods also affects the outcome. Nonetheless, the main result—five kinds of dispositions and five kinds of societies—is deeply evocative of Plato and his far-reaching insights.

## ACKNOWLEDGMENTS

I am grateful to Joseph Berger, Bernard P. Cohen, Thomas J. Fararo, Samuel Kotz, Jui-Chung Allen Li, Stefan Liebig, Eva M. Meyersson Milgrom, Kjell Törnblom, Murray Webster, Bernd Wegener, and Morris Zelditch for many valuable discussions. I also gratefully acknowledge the intellectual and financial support provided by New York University.

## NOTES

1. In the sociobehavioral world, Plato's ratio is applicable to two of the three primordial sociobehavioral outcomes—status and power. The third—justice, including self-esteem and the other comparison outcomes—spans negative magnitudes and zero and is thus not amenable to calculation of Plato's ratio.

2. Historically, there are three riveting questions about inequality. First, how does inequality arise? Second, how much inequality is too much? Third, how long does it take for inequality to reach destructive levels? Plato begins to answer the first question when he enumerates the ways that riches are acquired and the lot grows (e.g., by gift or business profit). As for the third question, *Leviticus* 25 offers a simple answer: less than 50 years.

3. Marital inequality may also harm the childrearing environment. If so, negative assortative mating is bad not only for marriage but also for the family. To the extent that family is foundational for society, negative sorting may have mixed effects on society.

# CHAPTER 4

# Franz Kafka: Bureaucracy, Law, and Abuses of the "Iron Cage"

*Joachim J. Savelsberg*

## INTRODUCTION

Almost a half a century ago, Lewis Coser (1963) published a reader that presented basic sociological concepts such as culture, socialization, and domination and provided samples of great fiction to illustrate the social reality to which those concepts refer. Included in Coser's selection are "bureaucracy" and an excerpt from Franz Kafka's *The Castle*. Coser comments: "By stressing the pathology of bureaucratic behavior, he [Kafka] aimed at representing in emblematic forms the nightmare of a fully rationalized world. Kafka's work can be read at many levels; the interest here is in his acute comprehensions of the dysfunctional aspects of bureaucracy and in his realization that, to paraphrase Robert K. Merton, rules originally conceived as a means may become if rigidly adhered to, transformed into ends in itself, so that an instrumental value becomes a terminal value" (Coser 1963:177).

Kafka indeed has much to tell us about the "iron cage" or "steel-hard casing" (Stephen Kalberg's translation of Max Weber's *stahlhartes Gehäuse*) of bureaucracy and formal-rational law as well as about subjects such as identity, guilt, punishment, and shame (Heller 1974). However, some of *The Castle's* lessons and those from Kafka's *The Trial* are exactly about situations where the iron cage does not function in the prescribed form, even with its systemic dysfunctions, but where it becomes a tool in the hands of negligent, corrupt, or repressive regimes.

Have sociologists indeed drawn inspiration from great literary work such as Kafka's? Or did an ever specializing discipline, seeking to secure its place at the table of respected sciences and recipients of national funding programs, shy away from all that appears too close to the arts? References to great writers in *Sociological Abstracts*, the well-established search index, give some preliminary indication of sociology's fertilization by fiction. Limiting the search term to the author's last name, and specifying that the name appear in the abstracts of articles, the search for "Kafka" yielded more than 100 results—many compared to other famous writers. Using other criteria and indices yields other results, of course (see, e.g., Ch. 1, Table 1.1).

Allowing for all entries with the word "Kafka" anywhere in the text, *Sociological Abstracts* shows 216 published works. The *Social Sciences Citation Index*, casting a wider net, shows 717 publications containing the word "Kafka," and many of these entries are from law reviews. While the value of such indicators may be limited, they show that social scientists make at least some use of fiction, and that Franz Kafka's work is referred to *relatively* frequently.

## LOCATING FRANZ KAFKA—HISTORICALLY AND SOCIOLOGICALLY

Franz Kafka was born on July 3, 1883 into a middle-class Jewish family in Prague, capital of the Bohemian Kingdom within the Austro-Hungarian Empire. He died of tuberculosis on June 3, 1924, six years after the end of the Empire, in a sanatorium near Vienna. About two decades later the Shoah would take the lives of his three sisters.

Kafka is in many respects Georg Simmel's "stranger" or Robert Park's "marginal man." He was estranged from his father, having suffered deeply from overbearing and emotionally abusive parenting. Yet, he was also a devoted son, caring enough about his relationship with his father that he described his suffering in a long "letter to his father" (Kafka 1994). He was a Jew in a society of growing anti-Semitism that impeded his professional career; as a boy he only reluctantly followed his father to the synagogue for high-holiday services. He was an intellectual, but when his engagement with Judaism grew, he was primarily taken by the affectively loaded current of Eastern European Jewry, Yiddish literature, and theatre. He lived in the ethnically diverse Prague with its German and Czech cultural and nationalist currents and domination by Austria Hungary, attending the German *Gymnasium* and writing in German, but he was also fluent in Czech.

As a law student, Kafka simultaneously attended courses in German studies and art history and joined a literary club, the *Lese- und Redehalle der Deutschen Studenten*. Later he became a crucial contributor to the Prague

Circle, a group of German-Jewish writers. At that time he earned his living working in insurance, immersing himself in probability mathematics and risk calculations, while spending nights in literary circles and on his writings, in which he bemoaned what he perceived to be the hopelessness and absurdity of modern life. Clearly, Kafka lived in several overlapping fields of tension.

While much attention has been paid to Kafka's marginal status and his life in a multi-cultural world, the importance of his work life has only recently been recognized, culminating in the argument that the "world of Kafka's writing, both literary and official, is a single institution, in which the factor of bureaucracy is ever present . . . " (Corngold, Greenberg and Wagner 2009:xv).

After earning his JD, Kafka was briefly employed with a large Italian insurance company and discovered that "the whole world of insurance itself interests me greatly" (Wagner 2009:21). Yet, as his work schedule impeded his literary production, Kafka underwent additional training to qualify for employment at the Workmen's Accident Insurance Institute for the Kingdom of Bohemia in Prague, where he worked, with great engagement, from 1908 until 1922.

Kafka, the lawyer, had thus entered a world that weakened the liberal legal norm of responsibility, supplementing the principle of guilt by that of risk, and the judge by the expert. Central to his work was the Austrian Workmen's Accident Insurance Law of 1887, an attempt to pacify increasingly restless working classes. Yet, the law and the bureaucracy it created came with massive weaknesses that weighed on Kafka's work, including the lack of reliable statistics on industrial accident risks; a decentralized network of unwieldy arbitration courts consisting of judges, experts, employers and employees, verdicts of which could not be appealed (evoking images of the mysterious "attic courts" in *The Trial*); organizational confusion resulting from the conflict between a rigid imperial bureaucracy and aspirations of ethnic groups that were granted regional self-government (reminiscent of the confusions between village and castle authorities in *The Castle*); and a rampant and incessantly growing bureaucracy, complicated by nationality conflicts that cut across the lines of omnipresent class strife. When Kafka joined the Prague institute in the summer of 1908 it employed "more than 200 mathematicians, lawyers, engineers, clerks, typists, and office assistants, a number that had been growing annually" (Wagner 2009:35).

Kafka's place, after a short period in the accident department had confronted him with the suffering of injured workers, became the actuarial unit where his primary tasks were accident prevention, risk classification, and setting premiums. Familiarity with neo-Taylorist ideas about breaking down risks not just to the level of firms but further to stages and phases of work and to separate motions made Kafka an expert in modern state power in the Foucauldian sense, with its norms of discipline and regulation. Elias Carnetti, in fact, noted, "Of all writers, Kafka is the greatest expert on power" (after Wagner 2009:41).

Inspired and haunted by the worlds he inhabited, Kafka produced his literary oeuvre. Yet, little was published during his lifetime and with his consent, including *A Report to an Academy*, *In the Penal Colony*, *The Judgment*, and *Metamorphosis*. All of it fits into one small 278-page volume (Kafka 1978). His closest friend, Max Brod, overrode Kafka's wishes that his other writings be destroyed after his death, having received verbal messages to the contrary from Kafka during his lifetime. Today's readers, including social scientists, can thus draw insights from Kafka's novels, albeit unfinished, and a multitude of additional short stories.

First translations of Kafka's work into English appeared in the 1940s and 1950s, spurring a surge in his popularity in the United States. (For the most recent translations of his novels see Kafka 1998a, 1998b, and 2004.) Famously, *The Trial* tells the story of Joseph K., his accusation by legal authorities, and his desperate and vain attempts at seeking justice and clearing his name. Similarly, *The Castle* depicts K.'s failure at gaining access to the bureaucracy of the *Schloss* and the position of land surveyor for which he had come to town. Both protagonists are outsiders to law and bureaucracy, failing to enter their gates or master their labyrinths.

How then can Kafka's literary production inform social science? What has been missed and what materialized? Social scientists use fiction as a source of illustrations for sociological arguments; as empirical evidence, especially where—for historical or political reasons—solid social science evidence is missing; finally, as analytic description and interpretation of social conditions, illustrated by anticipations of the "self-fulfilling prophecy" by T. S. Eliot and the Protestantism thesis by Thomas Mann (Kuzmics and Mozetič 2003). The realist tradition in literature has long been a rich source, doing the ethnographic work for sociologists before the latter had even begun their systematic accounting of social reality. Balzac's novels offer but the most famous illustration.

Which of these applications work for Kafka's oeuvre, existentialist in its philosophical orientation and a precursor of magical realism, a literary genre that interjects magical elements or illogical scenarios into the depiction of otherwise realistic settings? If inspiration may be drawn from realist elements in Kafka, as suggested by Kuzmics and Mozetič, how can the social sciences gain from "magic" or "fantasy" in his texts? I borrow the latter term from Burgum (1965) who contrasted naturalist and realist fiction with "fantasy novels" of authors such as Cervantes, Joyce, and Kafka, invoking Freud to liken their depictions to dream images.

The cue is obvious: Just as dreams provide access to a deeper reality, hidden behind the surface of outer appearance, might not dream-like—or nightmarish—elements in the work of magical realists allow for insights that reach far below the surface of appearance, revealing latent functions, hidden motives, secret structures, and the back stages of social life? Such strategy would certainly be consistent with the demystifying and ideology-critical agenda of sociology. Consider the case of law and bureaucracy.

## INSIGHTS MISSED: LAW AND BUREAUCRACY IN KAFKA—THE "IRON CAGE" AND ITS ABUSES

Coser's linking of Kafka's *The Castle* to Max Weber's dark "iron cage" prophesy of modernity can easily be extended to *The Trial*—frighteningly well captured in the modernist images of Orson Welles's film depiction of the latter book. For the protagonists, bureaucracy and the legal process appear radically divorced from the world of real human subjects. Access is blocked, and the citizen stays "Before the Law." Law here constitutes, in Luhmann's terms, a hermetically sealed autopoietic system—as does bureaucracy, illustrated by Kafka for *The Castle*.[1] In addition, bureaucracy—as Weber pointed out—erodes—or, at least, channels—meaning into narrowly conceived forms, meaningful only to the "specialist."

Kafka's novels tell us about the efforts with which people nevertheless attempt desperately to gain access to and locate meaning in impersonal systems. Yet, his message has not reached social scientists. They have not been sufficiently attentive to the despair of the person before the gates of law or bureaucracy. Having developed good theories of bureaucracy and of state power, social scientists showed little interest in how people feel in the face of these institutions or try to make sense of them. There is a gaping hole where good ethnographies might tell us about citizens' experiences—strangely so, as the broad reception of Kafka and his iconic status suggest a widely shared social need. In one rare exception, *The Trial* is used to depict "possessed" states as one coping mechanism in the face of alienation (Horton 1978).

Also for those on the inside, the execution of bureaucratic tasks or legal judgment is separated from their moral selves and life worlds. A late Soviet-era contribution articulates—historically adequately—the conflict between bureaucratic mentality and liberal democracy with reference to *The Trial*. In the extreme, the concentration camp commander, after his work is done, writes loving letters to wife and children. Hannah Arendt (1961) quotes Kafka's words that "Man found the Archimedean point, but he used it against himself; it seems that he was permitted to find it only under this condition."

Two years later her *Eichmann in Jerusalem* appeared, bringing into plain sight what constitutes, at least in part, the "banality of evil." Here is "The Civil Servant," "The Official," or "The Functionary" at work, just like *In the Penal Colony*, fulfilling his duty and proudly presenting his torture instrument to the visitor. Here appears the model of the modern bureaucrat, which Alfred Weber described in *Der Beamte* in 1910, four years before Kafka first drafted his story, an example of potential scholarly inspiration of fiction (Harrington 2007). Kafka thus also finds himself in the intellectual lineage of Zygmunt Bauman with his insights into the apparatus of the modern state as a precondition of the Shoah.

It is not surprising that in light of the American climate of the "war on terror," institutions it inspired such as Guantanamo Bay, and practices such as those publicized from Abu Ghraib, themes of brutal bureaucracies and unresponsive law are regaining scholarly attention, accounting for much of the recent references to Kafka in law-related articles. For example, Khanna (2008) questions even the use of "dignity" with reference to *In the Penal Colony*. Earlier Curtis (1999) linked Kafka to Lyotard's arguments about law's violence against the body.

Kafka's writings thus speak to both the expected dysfunctions of well-functioning bureaucratic and legal machines and their uses toward evil ends. In addition, Kafka's texts sensitize us to simple malfunctions, "Kafka circuits" (Singer 1980), instances in which bureaucratic machines do not follow their own rules. Misdirected files in *The Castle* (Kafka 1998a:59ff.) illustrate that point. Further, while the "Urban Villagers" in Herbert Gans's classic ethnography may not have learned the code that allows for effective communication with public administrations, at least those familiar with the code should be able to gain access. Yet, many remain "before the law."

Finally, there is abuse of law and bureaucracy by corrupt and cruel actors. Here, too, potential for sociological inspiration is entailed in many of the nightmarish images we encounter in *The Trial* (Kafka 1998b) and *The Castle* (Kafka 1998a). References to just a few of these images as signposts toward future inspiration must suffice here: intrusion of privacy by law enforcement in the arrest scene: "What sort of men were they? What were they talking about? What office did they represent?" (Kafka 1998b:6); withholding of charges: "I asked the inspector why I had been arrested. . . . [H]e really had no reply at all, perhaps he actually knew nothing, he had arrested me and that was enough for him" (p. 48); unresponsive and "corrupt" courts (pp. 41–53); use of personal ties to court officials (p. 116); the breach between private and public exemplified by the abuse of women by their male superiors: "Klamm is like a commander over women" (Kafka 1998a:196); and the submission of community to the corrupt practices of the bureaucracy, a colonization of the life world in which the colonized appear as willing collaborators, best exemplified in the Sortini story in *The Castle* (p. 187ff.).

Sortini, the reader of the novel will remember, demanded the customary sexual submission by one of the village's young women (Amelia). Her decisive refusal did not only draw the ire of the bureaucrats, but of the villagers themselves—with catastrophic consequences: the father's loss of his dignity, health, and business and the family's stigmatization and condemnation to outcast status in the community.

And yet, Kafka does not just tell us about passive suffering and exposure to the dysfunctions and abuses of law and bureaucracy. Social scientists have also been inspired by Kafka's insistence that there can be enchantment (Bennett 1997) and resistance in the modern world. Kafka is grouped with other members of the Central European (Jewish) intelligentsia as exemplifying "elective affinity" between Jewish messianism and anarchist utopias (Lowy 1998). With T. S. Eliot he appears as a model of someone who is simultaneously a productive worker and savage critic of the organizational culture in which he toils (Schoneboom 2007).

Again, Kafka has much to tell social scientists about law and bureaucracy. Even if he uses these worlds only metaphorically to address the Faustian struggle of human beings, as Max Brod (2006) suggested (albeit not for ultimate knowledge but for securing basic livelihood and belonging in a community), the metaphors also speak to the concrete spheres and levels of experience from which Kafka drew inspiration.

Some social scientists have picked up on these themes. Those at the mainstream, however, have yet to take seriously common people's desperate attempts to gain access to and make sense of the worlds of law and bureaucracy, with which they interact with increasing frequency. Their perceived needs and sense of justice and morality do not seem to matter. Reading Kafka should be a remedy, as even the structure of his novels encourages a focus on personal experience. The reader easily identifies with the protagonists, following their story of attempted discovery. With Kafka she steps into their shoes. Thus, Franz Kafka clearly sought to make experience in the face of the "iron cage" central to his texts, for all concerned and specifically for those at the margins of society who are subject to abuses of law and bureaucracy.

## INSIGHTS MATERIALIZED: KAFKA READ BY SOCIAL SCIENTISTS

Despite gaping omissions in themes and perspectives, Kafka's work has delivered inspiration to social scientists. Returning to *Sociological Abstracts* one more time tells us how and when Kafka's themes have been used and by whom. While Anglo-American sources and authors clearly dominate (partially an artifact of the index), we find almost no concentration in terms of journals. Only one holds three references to Kafka, and a few hold two. Noticeably, most dominant disciplinary journals, including those affiliated with major sociological associations, are missing.

Further, most abstracts contain only a general reference to Kafka, or they list him among other authors with no reference to specific publications. Authors we encounter in Kafka's referential neighborhood include especially existentialist philosophers, prophets of dark visions of modernity, post-modern thinkers, and post-colonial writers, among them Samuel Beckett, James Joyce, Robert Musil, Gustave Flaubert, J. M. Coetzee, Salman Rushdie, Jean-Paul Sartre, Albert Camus, Søren Kierkegaard, Jacques Derrida, Jean-François Lyotard, Walter Benjamin, Georg Lukacs, Theodor W. Adorno, Zygmunt Bauman, Francis Fukayama, Sigmund Freud, and Alfred and Max Weber.

Finally, across time, the seemingly stable use of Kafka's work with 15 (1960s), 13 (1970s), and 14 (1980s) cases per decade actually indicates decreasing interest considering the massive growth of the social sciences during the 1960s and 1970s. Yet, references picked up during the past two decades, with 27 "hits" in the 1990s and 30 in the not-quite-completed first decade of the twenty-first century. This increase is concentrated in the study of law and punishment. For *The Trial*, 6 out of 11 references are from the current decade, as are 4 out of 7 for *In the Penal Colony*; and the two references to *Before the Law* are from 1998 and 2007.

Using the substantive categories offered by *Sociological Abstracts* confirms that the recent increase in interest is inspired particularly by Kafka's writing on law and punishment. While the 35 entries categorized under "sociology of language and the arts/linguistics," are relatively evenly distributed over time, 9 out of 10 entries in the "sociology of law/control" or the "study of violence and terrorism" are from the current decade. In contrast, the last of only four references to *The Castle* is from 1970. The latter finding is as surprising as the fact that the recent rise of interest in the body and Bauman-type social theory on the critique of modernity did not bring Kafka more into social science discourse than it did.

In sum then, while some specialty areas draw continued inspiration from Kafka and while there are gaping and surprising gaps in others, interest in his writings about law has only recently grown.[2] Apart from the potential Kafka's themes hold for the social sciences, sociologists can gain profound insights if they dare to follow Kafka into the shoes of those waiting before the gates of law and bureaucracy or those caught and lost within their labyrinths, if they take seriously their search for meaning and their attempts toward an interpretive understanding of worlds that appear to be thoroughly sealed against intrusions from the life worlds we all inhabit.

## ACKNOWLEDGMENTS

I thank Pamela Feldman-Savelsberg, Stephen Kalberg, and Philip Smith for their input.

## NOTES

1. Luhmann's use of the labyrinth metaphor was apparently inspired by Kafka's work (Soentgen 1992).

2. Other entries across all decades are on: sociology: history and theory (12); sociology of knowledge (10); complex organizations (5); political interaction/political sociology (5); radical sociology (4). Areas with three or less entries include social psychology, family and socialization, group interaction/ identity, and sociology of religion. Where two categories were listed I noted the first.

# CHAPTER 5

# Marcel Proust: On Social Status and Capital Forms

*Jens Rydgren*

Marcel Proust was born in 1871 in Auteuil outside of Paris, and he died in 1922. The first volume of his monumental novel *À la Recherche du Temps Perdu (Remembrance of Things Past)* was published in 1912, and the seventh and last volume was published posthumously shortly after his death. Proust was thus contemporary with the great founding fathers of sociology: Max Weber, Georg Simmel, and Emile Durkheim. Like them, he found inspiration in living through an "unsettled time" (Swidler 1986) during the transition from traditional to modern society. During such times, old take-for-granted traditions, institutions, and social practices were made more visible, and at the same time new ones had not yet coalesced into hidden structures. In such a situation it was natural for intellectuals with a sensitive eye to the social world to turn into sociologists, if by sociologist we mean someone who asks and tries to answer sociologically relevant questions. With this broader definition, it would be a mistake to confine the space for sociology during these formative years to disciplinary sociology only.

Many relevant insights were offered by sociologically inclined writers, such as Proust—who himself spoke of having presented in his novel a *sociology* of Combray—whom we cannot ignore if we want to understand the "third culture" of sociology emerging between science and literature (Lepenies 1988). Sociologists should not only read Proust because of his role in sociology's history of ideas, but also because of his contemporary relevance: like all good sociology Proust offers insights into the workings of the social world of relevance across time and space.

Proust is not particularly well cited in sociology, which is not surprising since this absence only reflects the fact that sociologists in general are not especially keen to cite fictitious works. According to the Social Science Citation Index (ISI), Proust has been cited 22 times over the years in the category "sociology" and 43 times in the category "social science interdisciplinary."

A glance through these 65 publications reveals that Proust has been referred to for numerous reasons. The two most common aspects are his writings on the Jewish issue and the Dreyfus affair and on homosexuality. On both of these themes Proust offers insightful, detailed ethnographic accounts of the social role of outsiders in society. However, in this short chapter I will focus on other aspects, which so far have received less attention in sociology: Proust's insights into the workings of status groups and the role of cultural and social capital and social distinction, which not only foreboded modern sociological theories but also complement them in important ways—not the least by providing detailed scenarios of how these sociological mechanisms work in realistic settings.

I will make a distinction between "Proust" and "Marcel": Proust refers to the author of *Remembrance of Things Past*; Marcel refers to the leading character in the novels. Although *Remembrance of Things Past* is partly based on autobiographical material, it is even more a work of fiction—and I have no ambitions in this chapter to tell the former from the latter. It simply does not matter for the sociological readings of *Remembrance of Things Past* that I will offer.

## STATUS AND STATUS GROUPS

For Robert Frank (1985:17), "people come into the world equipped with an inner voice urging them to rank as high as possible in whatever hierarchy they belong to." Proust shares this view; for him the will to status and social prestige is the key driving force determining social action. This driving force works independently of social class. Even if it is manifested differently in the higher and the lower classes, the mechanism is the same. Yet, in *Remembrance of Things Past* Proust is principally preoccupied with the nobility and the upper bourgeoisie, and he says relatively little about the working classes.

As Max Weber observed, status groups only overlap partly with social class. More specifically, a status group is seen by Weber (1978:306) to be a "plurality of persons who, within a larger group, successfully claim a special social esteem." This social esteem can be based on economic capital, but also on symbolic, cultural, or social capital. Heralding Pierre Bourdieu, Proust stresses the role of the non-economic capital forms. At the same time he makes an interesting distinction between how status groups achieve social prestige within the nobility and the bourgeoisie. For the bourgeoisie, economic capital is the principal asset for judging status and prestige, whereas it is relatively unimportant for the nobility, which put more stress on cultural and social capital:

> in that [bourgeois] Combray world in which everyone is classified for ever, as in an Indian caste, according to the income he is known to enjoy, no one would have been capable of imagining the great freedom that prevailed in the world of the [aristocratic] Guermantes, where no importance was attached to wealth and where poverty was regarded as being as disagreeable as, but no more degrading, having no more effect on a person's social position, than a stomach-ache. (Proust 2003c:867)

For Proust, the status groups within high society are partly what Weber (1978:306) calls hereditary status groups, in which status is derived "by virtue of successful claims to higher-ranking descent." Moreover, it should be emphasized that for Proust it is the higher-ranking descent of roles or positions—that is, titles—that yield social prestige, not necessarily that of individuals. For the nobility, "there is no real social importance in the fact that the daughter of a Jew becomes Duchesse de Guermantes or that a bourgeoisie takes the title of Princesse de Guarmantes," through marriage, for the social prestige derived from these titles (Kopp 1971:135).

However, being able to claim a higher-ranking descent is far from sufficient to maintain a high status position within high society; it is also necessary to follow the social codes, which will be the topic of the remainder of this chapter. Social codes consist in showing appropriate cultural and social capital and, in particular, following the rules of social distinction and exclusiveness.

## CULTURAL CAPITAL AND SOCIAL DISTINCTION

As noted by Philip Smith (2004:109), there are "remarkably strong Bourdieuvian themes" in *Remembrance of Things Past*—or maybe we should say Proustian themes in Bourdieu's writings. Like Bourdieu, Proust pictures society as a space of "contending but overlapping social circles among aristocratic, military, artistic, intellectual, and bourgeois spheres. These are arranged hierarchically and are maintained by systems of difference and distinction, taste, and refinement" (Smith 2004:108). In addition, Proust shares with Bourdieu the idea of "the self as imprisoned by habit. . . . This self, habituated and embodied, is also shaped by" the position in the social world

(Smith 2004:109; see Bourdieu 1984). I would also like to add that Proust anticipated Bourdieu's idea of social capital.

For Proust, people's predispositions are shaped by practice as experienced in the social milieu of which they are part. It is the habits and not the ideas that constitute the real differences between groups in society (Kopp 1971:104). In discussing the way in which his beloved Albertine talks, for instance, the narrator Marcel reflects on the social origin of behavior:

> expressions dictated in such cases by a sort of bourgeois tradition almost as old as the *Magnificat* itself, which a girl slightly out of temper and confident that she is in the right employs, as the saying is, "quite naturally," that is to say because she had learned them from her mother, just as she had learned to say her prayers or to curtsey. All these expressions Mme Bontemps had imparted to her at the same time as hatred of the Jews and a respect for black because it is always suitable and becoming, even without any formal instruction, but as the piping of the parent goldfinches serves as a model for that of the newborn goldfinches so that they in turn grow into true goldfinches also. (Proust 2003a:487)

Although Proust conceives of real differences between social groups, manifested through embodied habits, these differences are relatively small. The principal differences between status groups are socially constructed in order to distinguish the own group against outsiders and in order to enhance the social esteem associated with the in-group. This process of social distinction is partly executed through taste (and distaste) and by displaying cultural capital. In such a way, for example, Baron de Charlus is patronizing the bourgeois Marcel (who at this stage is still an outsider to high society circles) for breaking appropriate social etiquette by saying that nothing more was expected from a person who "could all too easily mistake a piece of Chippendale for a rococo chair" (Proust 2003a:763).

The real differences between social groups are relatively small in contrast to the considerable differences that are attributed to them, and this becomes evident as soon as an epoch is seen at some distance, when "social, and even individual, differences are merged":

> The truth is that similarity of dress and also the reflexion of the spirit of the age in facial composition occupy so much more important a place in a person's make-up than his caste, which bulks large only in his own self-esteem and the imagination of other people, that in order to realise that a nobleman of the time of Louis-Philippe differs less from an ordinary citizen of the time of Louis-Philippe than from a nobleman

> of the time of Louis XV, it is not necessary to visit the galleries of the Louvre. (Proust 2003b:110–111)

It should also be emphasized that the *content* of cultural capital need not be especially exclusive in highly ranked status groups; the important thing is to follow the social code (doxa) and to appear exclusive to (excluded) outsiders. Because social distinction generally works effectively, social groups are relatively detached from one another and the knowledge about the internal working of out-groups are often scarce. Marcel cannot hide a deep disappointment the first time he was invited to the Guermantes, to a dinner party that "differed in essence from those that are given elsewhere than in the Faubourg Saint-Germain no more than one feels oneself at Balbec to be in a town that differs from what one's eyes are accustomed to see," and he cannot help asking himself:

> Was it really for the sake of dinners as this that all these people dressed themselves up and refused to allow middle-class women to penetrate into their so exclusive [salons]—for dinners such as this . . .? The suspicion flashed across my mind for a moment, but it was too absurd. Plain commonsense enabled me to brush it aside. And then, if I had adopted it, what would have been left of the name Guermantes . . .? (Proust 2003a:745–746)

Yet, because of defective knowledge between groups, individuals belonging to high-status groups sometimes fail to signal their high status to outsiders. By putting so much stress on economic wealth and moral conduct for judging people's status, members of the bourgeoisie look for the same traits in the nobility, for whom this is relatively unimportant compared to heredity and social capital. As a result the bourgeoisie in Balbec disparage of the Princess de Luxembourg because they think she is a cheap prostitute (who else would wear such eccentric cloths and use too much perfume), and "from M. de Charlus morals," the bourgeois salon around Verdurin concluded that:

> the Baron's social position must be equally low, since [they] had no information whatsoever about the family to which M. de Carlus belonged, his title or his name. Just as Cottard imagined that everybody knew that the title of doctor of medicine meant nothing and the title of hospital consultant meant something, so people in society are mistaken when they suppose that everybody has the same idea of the social importance of their name as they themselves and the other people of their circle. (Proust 2003b:410)

## SOCIAL CAPITAL

Within sociology, social capital is commonly seen as a range of resources available to people through their social network contacts (Bourdieu 1986; Lin 2001), or more broadly as aspects of the social structure that facilitate certain actions for actors embedded within these structures (Coleman 1988). Proust was clearly a forerunner to the former way of understanding social capital. For him, status is the principal resource embedded in people's networks, and he shared a radically instrumental view of social friendship and acquaintance.

As Kopp (1971:110) puts it, Marcel "appears thoroughly convinced that social friendship is a meaningless expression. It is a social standard. One must have 'friends' in order to be accepted into the various salons." And in *Remembrance of Things Past* Proust echoes modern management theories in proclaiming that there are no "personal relations, from which we can be certain that we shall not one day derive some benefit" (Proust 2003a:752).

Hence, one of the principal functions of social capital is that it opens and closes the doors to high-status positions. To be accepted into high society, if you cannot claim heredity, you need to have friends on the inside. Moreover, knowing high-status persons is also likely to enhance your social prestige in the eyes of members of less prestigious status groups—even if you are not a permanent member of high society. However, Proust also emphasized the role of bad social capital: it is at least as important *not* to know the wrong people as it is to know the right people because too close and too many contacts with members endowed with less status may lead to social degradation.

*Remembrance of Things Past* gives numerous examples of this process. The most notorious is Oriane de Guermantes. When she was on the top of the status ladder as the most prestigious salon hostess, she "had the knack of attracting to her salon [unaristocratic] men who were in the public eye, in a ratio that of course never exceeded one in hundred, otherwise she would have lowered its tone" (Proust 2003a:589). Later, however, she declined socially because she "had neglected the rule by accepting too many actors into her salon" (Kopp 1971:111). The social fate of Gilberte de Saint-Loup took a similar process:

> The Marquise de Saint-Loup said to herself, "I am the Marquise de Saint-Loup," and she knew that, the day before, she had refused three invitations to dine with duchesses. But if to a certain extent her name aggrandised the very unaristocratic people whom she entertained, by an inverse process the people whom she entertained diminished the name that she bore. Nothing can hold out against such trends; the greatest names succumb to them in the end. Had not Swann known a

> princess of the House of France whose [salon], because anyone at all was welcomed there, had fallen to the lowest rank? (Proust 2003c:909–910)

As a result of this risk of social degradation, social interaction is characterized by a certain amount of insecurity and wariness. Since it may be costly for one's social status and prestige to know the wrong people, people are careful not to engage socially with people whose status is undetermined for them (or whose status in the eyes of others are unsure). When Marcel asks Mme. de Souvré to present him to the Prince de Guermantes, for instance, "the lady is afraid that she may be presenting someone of no social significance, and that the prince will take offence"—and refuses (Kopp 1971:105). At another moment Baron de Charlus scolds Marcel for, while being an outsider to the nobility, daring to say in public that he is a "good friend" to the baron (Proust 2003a:617).

As the last example indicates, there is a risk associated with showing off one's social contacts with higher-status persons: the risk of being considered a snob. In *Remembrance of Things Past* we can extract a fragment of a sociological theory of snobbery, in which Proust argues that snobs are predominantly found among those "not yet socially secure" (Proust 2003a:691), those whose place in the status hierarchy is undetermined—in particular "the social climbers of the world" (Hindus 1962:72)—whereas high nobility, whose status position is secure, have no need for snobbery.

Hence, for Proust social capital is intimately related to status distinction. However, he also suggests other functions of social capital, which anticipated contemporary discussions within sociology. Most important, he shows insights into the workings of information diffusion. Baron de Charlus, for instance, gives the following lesson about how to proceed in order to create an audience and to build a positive reputation:

> It's all very well, don't you agree, to have the finest music played by the greatest artists, but the effect of the performance remains muffled, as though in cotton-wool, if the audience is composed of the milliner from across the street and the grocer from around the corner. You know what I think of the intellectual level of society people, but there are certain quite important roles which they can perform, among others the role which in public events devolves upon the press, and which is that of being an organ of dissemination. You understand what I mean: I have for instance invited my sister-in-law Oriane; it is not certain that she will come, but it is on the other hand certain that, if she does come, she will understand absolutely nothing. But one doesn't ask her to understand, which is beyond her capacity, but to talk, a task for which

> she is admirably suited, and which she never fails to perform. The result? Tomorrow as ever is, instead of the silence of the milliner and the grocer, an animated conversation at the Mortemarts' with Oriane telling everyone that she has heard the most marvellous music, that a certain Morel, and so forth, and indescribable rage among the people not invited, who will say: "Palmède obviously thought we were not worth asking; but in any case, who are these people in whose house it happened?"—a counterblast quite as useful as Oriane's praises, because Morel's name keeps cropping up all the time and is finally engraved in the memory like a lesson one have read over a dozen times. (Proust 2003c:286–287)

## CONFORMITY

In common with the great founding fathers of sociology—Weber, Simmel, and Durkheim—and with philosophers such as Nietzsche, Proust shared the belief that modern society is limiting the room for individual self-fulfillment and originality. For Proust the reason for this lays, paradoxically, precisely in the will to status and social prestige as the key driving force for people's aspirations. With this aspiration, according to Proust, follow cowardice and "the fear that a certain action will harm one's social prestige" (Kopp 1971:105). This, in turn, leads to conformity since the only way to enhance and maintain one's prestige is to follow the social conduct considered appropriate within the group where one finds oneself.

Hence, with aspiration for social success comes the "willingness to please in order to find acceptance in almost any social situation" (Kopp 1971:107). The result will be a loss of spontaneity and of individuality—in short, mediocrity. This pessimistic view is not without moral implications, and the main message of *Remembrance of Things Past*, if there is one, is that people should stop seeking immediate status recognition for insignificant things; instead "they should be seeking recognition of much greater scope in Time":

> Like Swann, these people are forgotten after a while and the enduring deeds they may have created never come to light because their would-be creators spend their time in the pursuit of a meaningless goal called social success. The individual's struggle for social acceptance according to an impossible, and therefore meaningless, code illustrates, in effect, the concept of *temps perdu* in the novel's title. (Kopp 1971:138)

The tragedy, of course, is that there are compelling reasons keeping people captivated in the social games of conformity and status distinction. Most important, people fear social ostracism and isolation. However, it is also hard to impossible to step outside of the social world of which one is a part, which is arguably necessary for fully seeing through the illusory surface level into the more hidden mechanisms of social behavior. For Marcel it took many years of social isolation due to sickness and convalescence to come to these insights.

# CHAPTER 6

# George Orwell: From Democratic Revolution to Authoritarian Rule

*Karl-Dieter Opp*

## INTRODUCTION

George Orwell is certainly one of the writers whose work, especially his novels *Nineteen Eighty-Four* (1961 [1949]) and *Animal Farm: A Fairy Story* (1996 [1945]), could yield insights that may be new to social scientists and sociologists in particular. Due to space limitations, this chapter will concentrate on the latter work. How could this novel yield new scientific insights? This question can be answered by looking briefly at Orwell's biography (for details, see Bowker 2004). Born in 1903, Orwell attended several schools in Britain, the last one being Eton, which he attended from 1917 to 1920. He then joined the Indian Imperial Police in Burma (now Myanmar) for five years because he was not able to secure the financial means for a scholarship.

The following years in London and Paris were characterized by poverty and bad health. In 1936, Orwell joined the Republicans in the Spanish war against Franco's uprising. He also joined the anti-Stalinist Spanish Trotskyist Partido Obrero de Unificación Marxista or POUM, the Workers' Party of Marxist Unification. Being wounded and persecuted by the communist police, he returned to England.

In his essay *Why I Write*, Orwell indicates that the years in Burma and his life in poverty increased his aversion to authority and made him fully aware of the existence of the working classes. His firm political conviction of being against totalitarianism and for a democratic socialism was formed after the Spanish war and other events in 1936 and 1937. Back in England he became a freelance writer. In 1949 he was admitted to a hospital for tuberculosis, of which he died in London on January 21, 1950 at the age of 46.

As this brief biographical sketch indicates, Orwell's political persuasion implied that he was a strong adversary of Stalinism and any kind of totalitarianism. In *Animal Farm*, the actors are animals who mimic developments in the Soviet Union after the Russian Revolution (see, for example, the preface by Russell Baker in Orwell 1996). Due to his biography we can assume that Orwell had a firm knowledge of the ideologies and societies of his time. This knowledge will presumably be integrated into his work. Thus, it is likely that we find interesting ideas that explain the phenomena Orwell is concerned with.

Of particular interest here is not so much *descriptions* of what different actors do but Orwell's *causal statements* about the effects of certain actions of individuals on the actions of others. If writers (including social scientists) make causal statements they apply—mostly implicitly—general hypotheses (i.e., theories). To illustrate, if a person P gives an order that Q follows, although Q does not like the order, the implicit general proposition may be that orders are followed if the advantages of doing so are greater than the disadvantages.

The question addressed in this essay is to what extent we can find such general theoretical statements in *Animal Farm* that might be new. We further ask and show how Orwell applied general hypotheses to explain a specific political process that starts with a democratic revolution and ends with a stable authoritarian regime. In other words, Orwell proposes a theoretical model about a specific political process that cannot be found in the literature. We will suggest a reconstruction of the general propositions and the theoretical model implicit in Orwell's novel.

## THE START OF A REVOLUTION

Mr. Jones is the owner of Manor Farm and an alcoholic. Although one night he locked the hen-houses, he was too drunk to remember to shut the popholes. This oversight provided the opportunity for the animals to meet. They informed each other that old Major, the prize Middle White boar, had a strange dream that he wished to share with the other animals. This was a reason for the animals to come to the meeting; the boar was highly regarded, so everybody was curious to hear what he had to say. Furthermore, there was a natural meeting place: a room where enough animals could gather. This was the old barn. The time of the meeting was "as soon as Mr. Jones was safely out of the way" (Orwell 1996:4).

The long speech of old Major is about the life of the animals at the farm. He first addresses their grievances: "We are born, we are given just so much food as will keep the breath in our bodies, and those of us who are capable of it are forced to work to the last atom of our strength; and the very instant that our usefulness has come to an end we are slaughtered with hideous cruelty. No animal in England knows the meaning of happiness or leisure after he is a year old. No animal in England is free. The life of an animal is misery and slavery: that is the plain truth" (pp. 6–7). This is the general outline of a situation of an oppressed people with severe grievances.

Grievances alone are not enough for a revolution to arise. Another condition is that the situation is perceived as unjust, which is precisely what Major claims: the situation of the animals is not "part of the order of nature" (p. 7). ". . . nearly the whole of the produce of our labour is stolen from us by human beings. There, comrades, is the answer to all our problems. It is summed up in a single word—Man" (p. 7). The speech thus identifies the situation as against the natural order and the perpetrator of all the misery.

A third part of the speech addresses the technology of change: "Only get rid of Man, and the produce of our labour would be our own" (p. 9). The means is "rebellion" (p. 9). In addition, there is a prophecy that rebellion will come. But what exactly should the oppressed subjects do to bring about a rebellion? The recipe suggested is not very specific: "Above all, pass on this message of mine to those who come after you, so that future generations shall carry on the struggle until it is victorious" (p. 9). Major further appeals to the "duty of enmity toward Man" (p. 11). "Whatever goes upon two legs is an enemy. Whatever goes upon four legs, or has wings, is a friend" (p. 11). Major's speech ends with a song that outlines a rosy future and that "threw the animals into the wildest excitement" (p. 13).

What could be the general propositions that underlie this initial stage of a revolution? There is strong *discontent* with a dictatorial regime (Mr. Jones's rule); there is a power vacuum (the drunk owner) and an *opportunity for the initiation of a rebellion* (the drunk farm owner and a meeting place, the barn); there is a *political entrepreneur* (some leader or high-status person or group)—in this case old Major—who delivers arguments for the injustice of the grievances, who identifies the perpetrators, who sketches the technology of change (rebellion), and who predicts the success of the rebellion in the future. This may be called the *revolutionary ideology*.

In regard to the initial stage of a revolution it is striking that the recipes are relatively vague and that there is not even a blueprint of the new order. Is this sufficient for bringing about a revolution? Orwell's answer seems to be "yes," which seems plausible (and is in line with what social scientists know). Indeed, the Russian revolution illustrates this: the revolution arose even though it was not clear how exactly a centrally planned economy and the "dictatorship of the proletariat" would work.

## THE EMERGENCE OF THE REVOLUTION

The singing of the animals' freedom anthem (as one may call it) awoke Mr. Jones, who entered the scene and ended the meeting. Nevertheless, the revolutionary process continued. The "more intelligent" animals were aware that it could take a long time until the revolution would arise, but they saw it as their duty to prepare for it. The pigs were recognized as the cleverest animals. Among them three young boars stood out: Snowball and Napoleon were the leaders, and Squealer acted mainly as their mouthpiece. They created an ideological system based on old Major's ideas: Animalism.

Like every human population, the animal population is heterogeneous. First, there is an intellectual elite, in this case the pigs. Adherence to the ideas of the revolution differed. At the one extreme, the "most faithful disciples were the two cart-horses, Boxer and Clover" (p. 18). At the other extreme, there were opponents (the representatives of the old order), such as the tame raven Moses who tried to spread lies. There were further differences with regard to physical strength—the two horses could not be surpassed.

The implicit proposition here could be that *differences in regard to intellectual and physical resources* are important for the start and success of a revolution. This idea is compatible with social science theory. Orwell seems to address the *free-rider problem* without mentioning the term when he lets animals ask questions such as: "If this Rebellion is to happen anyway, what difference does it make whether we work for it or not?" (p. 17) In other words, the revolution provides benefits to all (i.e., public goods are produced) whether one contributes or not. The "free rider" lets the others do the work because their activities are sufficient to bring about the collective good (see, in particular, Olson 1965).

Assuming that Orwell as a socialist accepts historical materialism, however, those utterances can also be interpreted in the following way: the actors could mean that a revolution of the working class will happen anyway because this is the course of history. There is thus no point to do anything to contribute to the origin of a revolution. The conclusion from the perspective of the individual is the same: there is no motivation to participate.

However, there is a difference whether the free rider problem exists or whether historical materialism's deterministic view of history is adopted: if the former mechanism holds that there are possibilities to evade the trap of the free rider problem, then there may be political entrepreneurs who provide selective incentives, as Olson argues. Thus, taking the perspective of the theory of collective action, the free rider dilemma can be resolved. If everybody believes in historical materialism, however, then nobody will ever participate. We must leave it open what Orwell really means, but his writing is at least compatible with a more modern theoretical view based on the theory of collective action.

Finally, Orwell describes at least some expected (selective) *benefits* that may lead to participation in revolutionary action and thus solve the free-rider problem. As theorists of revolution have emphasized, expected material incentives are relevant. This type of incentive is exemplified by the white mare Mollie, who asked Snowball whether there will be sugar after the rebellion and whether she will be allowed to wear ribbons in her mane.

## CRITICAL EVENTS, THE WEAKNESS OF THE OLD REGIME, AND THE SUCCESS OF REBELLION

The animals did not need to engage in a battle with many casualties, and it did not last as long as old Major had expected until a successful rebellion occurred. Instead, the "old regime" was so weak that a successful revolution was achieved soon and very easily: Mr. Jones was drunk, and his four men did not care to feed the animals. When the animals could not stand this anymore, they began to help themselves from the bins. Mr. Jones woke up and he and his four men "were in the store-shed with whips, lashing out in all directions" (p. 19). The animals "flung themselves on their tormentors," who "took to their heels." In other words: there were *critical events:* the increased negligence of the old regime and, as a consequence, a sudden increase of deprivation (hunger). This led to a riot, which expelled the rulers and cleared the way for the animals to seize power.

## ORIGIN OF A NEW DEMOCRATIC ORDER

After the toppling of the old order there was no vacuum: there were foresighted animals who had taught themselves the necessary skills for running the new "state" and who had devised a first blueprint of the new order: the pigs Napoleon and Snowball. Among other things, they reduced the principles of Animalism to Seven Commandments (pp. 24–25) and, finally, to one: "four legs good, two legs bad." This was understood by everybody. The pigs also organized the work on the farm and decision making in several committees. They were the leaders. Everybody worked according to his abilities.

There was no crime. "The animals were happy as they had never conceived it possible to be" (p. 28). The produce was equally distributed, and only the pigs got more because, as they argued, they needed this (pp. 37–38). And this was accepted. Work did not take place on Sundays, and there was a ceremony with the hoisting of a flag. Work was planned at the meetings, which always ended with the singing of the anthem "Beasts of England," which was first sung when old Major gave his speech.

What could be the underlying assumptions that explains the new order? One hypothesis could be that the new order tries to avoid the particularly frustrating features of the old order (i.e., a dictatorship). The detailed rules of the new order depend on the preferences of the leaders. They were the reference persons whose demands were followed. But not everything a leader suggests is accepted, as will be seen below. The leader must always find the balance between what he or she wants and what his or her "clientele" is satisfied with and willing to bear. This will be any decision that can be justified as being in the confines of a democratic order. Accordingly, the justifications for the decisions of the pigs always pointed in this direction, which indicates that Orwell applies these hypotheses about leadership.

## HOW TO INSTALL AND MAINTAIN AN AUTHORITARIAN REGIME

It is unlikely that, given the new order, a dictatorship could be established in a nonviolent way. A single animal or a group of animals would certainly not get the vote for such a change. To seize power one has to organize a task force that is able to suppress any resistance to the goals of the group. Napoleon proceeded in this way: Jessie and Bluebell had given birth to nine puppies. Napoleon took them away, saying that he would educate them. He hid them so that the other animals soon forgot their existence.

The democratic order was overturned after a conflict about the construction of a windmill. Napoleon who was, in contrast to Snowball, against its construction was likely to be defeated in a vote. At that moment Napoleon "uttered a high-pitched whimper. . . . At this there was a terrible baying sound . . . and nine enormous dogs wearing brass-studded collars came bounding into the barn" (pp. 52–53). These were the puppies that Napoleon had taken away from their mothers and reared privately. Snowball was expelled. The other animals were shocked, and some of them would have taken action but they did not find the right arguments against Napoleon's coup.

Furthermore, the big dogs made any rebellion unlikely. Squealer—a pig that was a gifted speaker—went out to justify Napoleon's regime. His major argument was that it was a sacrifice for Napoleon to take responsibility for the animal farm and that he was promoting the common good. Anyway, from that time on Napoleon made all decisions, together with some other pigs that he selected and who were at his service. The meetings on Sundays continued, but there were no debates anymore. Instead, the animals received orders for the week.

In the remainder of the novel Orwell describes the life under a dictatorship. There were several policy changes over time. One was that Napoleon and his crew increased the social distance to the other animals. That is, they moved to the farm house, Napoleon was no longer addressed simply as "Napoleon" but as "our Leader, Comrade Napoleon"—which one would call personality cult (pp. 93–95), and the achievements of the new regime were glorified. An unexpected and radical policy change was that Napoleon and his crew took up trade relationships with the neighboring farms, although this was strongly rejected before the takeover. Again, as always, Squealer was the one who justified those decisions and made them acceptable to the other animals.

What are the general underlying propositions that explain the origin and stability of Napoleon's authoritarian regime? First, there must be a group that wants to seize power. This condition was met—and is probably met in every society. To be successful this person or group must have at his or her disposal the resources (i.e., the big dogs Napoleon had drilled) that enable him or her to impose very high costs on dissenters. The resource in this case is a blunt threat of physical violence, which is certainly the simplest way to come to power. In real dictatorships the means are more subtle: a group tries to seize central positions endowed with power, such as leadership in the military. This may happen by violence, but it can be achieved in various other ways as well.

An illustration is the takeover of power by the Nazis in 1933 (enabling law): Chancellor Adolf Hitler pretended with this law to recover the misery of people and empire. The law provided the power to the Nazis to pass laws without the consent of the parliament ("Reichstag" and "Reichsrat") and without the signature (and, thus, consent) of the president of the "Reich" ("Reichspräsident"). Hitler guaranteed that his measures would remain in the democratic constraints of the constitution. Due to this tactical warrant Hitler got the required two-thirds majority for this law. This, then, was the starting point for a dictatorship with the consequence of World War II and the Holocaust. In this case, power was not seized by some violent act. Instead, the first step was a completely legal procedure to submit a law. Only then was a regime set up that resembled the dictatorship of the animals.

Another implicit assumption seems to be that in order to maintain authoritarian rule some support of the subjects is needed: Napoleon tries to "legitimize" his reign (i.e., he tries to provide arguments speaking in favor of his authoritarian rule). He further uses symbols like a flag, the skull of old Major, a song and an ideology (which reduces to a single slogan "four legs good, two legs bad"). Another strategy to gain support of the subjects is to create a scapegoat that could be blamed if something went wrong. This was Snowball. For example, when a storm destroyed the windmill it was clear that this was not due to faulty construction, but it was the work of Snowball: he came overnight and demolished the windmill, "in sheer malignity" to avenge himself for his expulsion (p. 70). The animals believed the various stories about Snowball's deleterious activities (p. 79). Still worse, Squealer made the animals believe: "Snowball was in league with Jones from the very start!" (p. 79) Orwell thus describes in a general way how the necessary support of the subjects can be achieved.

As was mentioned already, there were basic changes in policy and ideology: what was bad at one time became good at another time and vice versa. Orwell seems to suggest that there needs to be a particularly gifted person or group of persons who finds the acceptable justifications. This was Squealer (pp. 57–58), who could convince the animals that even the worst situation was better than Mr. Jones's regime (p. 113). Squealer reminds one of the propaganda ministers in authoritarian regimes like Joseph Göbbels under Adolf Hitler.

There is always opposition in a dictatorship. Although propaganda most of the time worked "there was something resembling a rebellion" for the first time since the expulsion of Jones when the hens protested because their eggs should be taken away. But the revolt was not successful. "Napoleon acted swiftly and ruthlessly" (p. 76). Orwell described other strategies to ensure conformity, such as eliciting wrong confessions (pp. 83–84) and afterwards killing the "deviants" (p. 84). We may assume that these are hypotheses about general tactics that dictators use to stay in power.

Another general assumption seems to be that dictators try to preserve their rule after their lifetime. At one time 31 pigs were born, and Napoleon was apparently the father (p. 113). These pigs were raised separately from the others and, one may assume, should succeed Napoleon and the old elite.

So far we have omitted one basic problem of the Animal Farm: Mr. Jones wanted to restore his rule. One condition for the stability of a dictatorship (and any other kind of regime) is that there is some coexistence with enemies, if there is not a chance to defeat them. A strategy to achieve coexistence is to form a coalition or to enter contracts with potential enemies. Indeed, the pigs had concluded peace with the farmers in the area.

Orwell's novel is actually about humans, which becomes particularly clear at the end of the novel when he describes a meeting of the pigs and the farmers that ended with a card game. There was suddenly a "violent quarrel" because Napoleon and one of the farmers had each played an ace of spades simultaneously. The other animals who observed this quarrel from outside "looked from pig to man, and from man to pig, and from pig to man again;

but already it was impossible to say which was which" (p. 141)—this is the last sentence of the novel.

There is thus no difference anymore in the behavior of the oppressors (the humans) and those who have a long time ago expelled the oppressors and liberated the animals. In general, Orwell might have wanted to express that dictators are all alike in their behavior—be the oppressors humans or animals. This suggests clearly that the novel is—or is only—about human behavior. Our procedure to look for hidden general propositions that can be applied to humans is thus useful.

## GENERAL CONCLUSION

This chapter is an attempt to reconstruct the general hypotheses about a political process that starts with the overthrow of a weak dictatorship (of Mr. Jones and his four collaborators), the setup of a democracy, and its transformation into a new and stable authoritarian regime. We have reconstructed the conditions for this process in a general way that seemed to be implicit in the novel. The resulting theoretical model is not meant as a *stage theory* in the sense that each revolution goes through each of the stages described. Instead, the model outlines conditions that must be met for each stage. If the conditions are not met, the next stage does not come into being.

Does this model provide new insights compared to the present state of the social sciences? I doubt that any of the single conditions described is new to scholars dealing with protest, rebellion, or revolutions. What seems to be new is the theoretical stage model: I have not found in the literature any general outline of a revolutionary process that suggests the detailed conditions for the sequence described before.[1] So what we can learn from our reconstruction of Orwell's novel is the outline of a theoretical model addressing a revolutionary process. A task would now be to elaborate this model and apply it to successful or failed revolutions.

It has been noted that Orwell's novel refers to the situation in the Soviet Union after the Russian Revolution. If this is correct then this revolution would be the "context of discovery" that was used to formulate the model. A new, expanded model should thus not be applied to this specific revolution but to new cases. It would be ideal if these are cases where there is first a dictatorship; then, a certain group of the oppressed helps to topple the dictators and sets up a democracy; this group then organizes an overthrow of the democracy and establishes a new authoritarian state with themselves as the rulers. The sequence that is in line with Orwell's model is thus:

$$\text{dictatorship} \rightarrow \text{democracy} \rightarrow \text{dictatorship.}$$

It is difficult to find cases that match exactly this process. It might particularly be rare that those who were subjects in the dictatorship fight for the democracy, then overthrow it and become themselves dictators. Maybe one case comes relatively close to this sequence: the time before the Weimar Republic was a constitutional monarchy that was installed in 1871; the Weimar Republic originated after the first World War in 1918.

The Nazi dictatorship followed the collapse of the Weimar Republic. After the defeat of the Nazis in 1945 the Federal Republic of Germany was founded. It may be problematic to compare the constitutional monarchy with a dictatorship, but it was certainly not a democracy like Germany today. Another problem is that the actors who set up the first democracy and then a dictatorship are not the same in the sequence. This is excluded already through the long time of the process from 1871 to 1945. The question is whether at least basic ideas of the model could be applied nonetheless. There are probably more cases with the following sequence:

$$\text{democracy} \rightarrow \text{dictatorship} \rightarrow \text{democracy.}$$

An example is *Spain*: the Second Republic lasted from 1931 to 1936. After a civil war a dictatorship with Francisco Franco as head was established in 1939 and lasted until 1975. Then the transition to democracy began. *Chile* with the sequence Allende to Pinochet to Democracy is another example. The question to be addressed is this: to what extent can Orwell's theoretical model explain these transitions?

Our reconstruction of Orwell's underlying theoretical model provides conditions for each transition from one form of government to another form, which could be a transition from democracy to authoritarian rule or vice versa. The model should thus contribute to explain any such transition, even if the whole process is not identical to the one described in *Animal Farm*. It would be interesting to further explore the fruitfulness of the model in applying it to these or other cases.

## NOTE

1. See, for example, the work cited by Cohan (1975), Goldstone (2001, 2002), and Salert (1976).

# CHAPTER 7

# Robert Musil: State, Nation, and Nationality

*Helmut Kuzmics*

Musil's unfinished *opus magnum*—Musil worked on it until his premature death in Swiss exile in 1942—has been judged to be many things: a comment on the moral crisis of modernity or of its technical civilization and a reflection about the apparent limits of rationality (cf. Mozetič 1991, Kuzmics and Mozetič 2003). Reviews written immediately after the publication of the first volume of the novel (1930) placed it among the corresponding works of Proust, Joyce, and Thomas Mann as diagnoses of their time (cf. Corino 2003).

However, it also contains a many-layered analysis of the failure of a multinational empire, and it gives some surprising and by all means sociological answers to the question for its causes. Since these include both external factors (military success in state-competition) and internal factors (struggle of nationalities), and because these factors also have emotional consequences in terms of loyalty or disloyalty towards the Habsburg double-state, a specific reading of the *Man without Qualities* pays off, the more so as Musil expressed himself in a very complex and careful way that matches the complexity of the various layers involved.

The superior skill of the auctorial narrator Musil[1] is first shown in passages that describe the historically particular of Austrian society in a conceptually grounded synopsis that aims at a more general understanding of processes of this kind. Second, he provides us also with descriptions of the typical behavior and convictions of persons and groups that express the concrete emotional dynamic behind abstract notions and ideas, as can be found, say, in German or other nationalism.

Put more simply, Musil deals with Austria-Hungary as an entity shaped by aristocracy and princes relying on the respective patriarchal loyalties. It finds itself in symbolic and affective competition with Prussia-Germany as a powerful new nation-state, threatened from within by the loss of allegiance of all nations that once constituted the Habsburg Empire, including the ruling German-speaking minority.

Musil's ingenious literary construction was the invention of the so-called "Parallel Campaign," meant to celebrate the idea of an Austrian state guided by Habsburg clemency and wisdom. In 1918 and since then, other multinational states have also broken down, leaving us with a mess of sometimes truly global extension. What is the sociological value of Musil's thinking on state-formation, in particular the transition from dynastic state to nation-state?

## STATE AND EMOTION

"Kakania," defined and invented by Musil, is a term apparently not only suited to characterize the vanished Habsburg Monarchy, but, slightly changed into "Ukania," also functions as a model to indicate the nearly equally difficult relationship between the British crown towards their Celtic and immigrant subjects.[2] In contrast with "rationalistic" definitions of the state as we encounter them in Hobsbawm (1990) and Gellner (1983), not only the nation-state but already the traditional princely state is also always a matter of feeling.

> All in all, how many amazing things might be said about this vanished Kakania! . . . On paper it was called the Austro-Hungarian Monarchy, but in conversation it was called Austria, a name solemnly abjured officially while stubbornly retained emotionally, just to show that feelings are quite as important as constitutional law and that regulations are one thing but real life is something else entirely. (Musil 1996:29)

There is, thus, an Austrian state-patriotism. The novel makes it visible in different ways: first and seemingly by pointing to Austria as a state that had previously been exemplary under many aspects and had not been offered much recognition for this; furthermore, in the positive evaluation of the Austrian "state-character" (modesty, caution, benevolence) the average Austrian citizen disposes of (alongside other characters, eight or nine, a professional, a national, a class, a geographic, a sexual, a conscious, an unconscious, a private and, finally, a fantasy character that can be filled with everything possible. Cf. p. 30); and finally, in the said "Parallel Campaign" and the emotions of their originators.

Its fictitious content is to match the 30-years jubilee of the accession to the German throne by William II, expected to take place in 1918, by the even more venerable 70-years jubilee of the Austrian "Emperor of Peace" Francis-Joseph, to be celebrated in this very same year. Count Leinsdorf, its *spiritus rector*, is moved by emotions that result from the sometimes tragic competition for leadership in Germany with the now so powerful former junior partner there.

## AUSTRIAN PATRIOTISM AGAINST GERMANY

The Austrian patriotism against Germany had, in 1866, a quite solid basis—Königgrätz/Sadowa was one of the bloodiest battles of the nineteenth century, and it was the result of a dynastic-state rivalry with Prussia that had endured for more than 100 years. This sentiment is also linked with a more ancient, patrimonial understanding of the state:

> And so His Grace Count Leinsdorf had said to himself before the conference: "We must not forget that His Majesty's noble and generous resolve to let the people take part in the conduct of their own affairs, up to a point, has not been in effect long enough to have produced everywhere the kind of political maturity in every respect worthy of the confidence so magnanimously placed in the people by His Majesty. (p. 181)

It is one of the central motifs of the novel that this Empire patriotism becomes less and less tangible the longer the great "parallel" effort progresses. Musil's ironic plot has it that the jubilee is planned to be celebrated in the year 1918, when, in reality, the war was lost and the Empire dissolved. But already in the fictitious year 1913, this patriotism is thinned out with the formula "the true Austria is the whole world," invented by Diotima, the august friend of Count Leinsdorf and a formidable queen of the Viennese salon.

In stark contrast to the declared aim of elevating the public to patriotic heights, many who were recruited as supporters of the campaign use it for quite worldly purposes and appear as shameless lobbyists of their own cause. By creating the contrasting figures of Hans Sepp, a mystical German-nationalist student, and the nebulous philosopher Meingast, Musil contrasts the state-patriotic feeling with the national one. He is far from denying the relevance of emotions in this sphere even and just while scrutinizing their rational justifiability.

## THE STATE THAT PERISHED FROM A LANGUAGE DEFECT

The Habsburg Dual Monarchy was such a fragile and ephemeral construction that it could be brought to disappear by wrong pronunciation alone. In the following quotation, Musil seems to outmatch the "constructivists" in their sociological treatment of the state by far:

> the Austrians, however, were, to begin with and primarily, nothing at all, and yet they were supposed by their leaders to feel Austro-Hungarian and be Austrian-Hungarians—they didn't even have a proper word for it. Nor was there an Austria. . . . So if you asked an Austrian where he was from, of course he couldn't say: I am a man from one of those nonexistent kingdoms and countries; . . . Imagine a squirrel that doesn't know whether it is a squirrel or a chipmunk, a creature with no concept of itself. . . . So this was the way Kakanians related to each other, with the panic of limbs so united as they stood that they hindered each other from being anything at all. Since the world began, no creature has as yet died of a language defect, and yet the Austrian and Hungarian Austro-Hungarian Dual Monarchy can nevertheless be said to have perished from its inexpressibility. (pp. 491–492)

To say that Austria has perished from a language defect corresponds seemingly to the extreme variety of constructivist thinking as it expresses itself in the idea of the most radical version of the labeling-model applied to the explanation of madness, illness, or criminality, or in the literal understanding of the idea that the nation was invented (Anderson 1983):

> The fact that nowadays we study national images and national stereotypes rather than national identities and national characters bespeaks an important epistemological shift, which has taken place over the last decades: the shift from essentialism to constructivism. . . . Nationality now counts, at least in the human sciences, as a modality of perception and reputation than as a matter of essence or substance. (Leerssen 1997:285)

But it would not be Musil and his sense of irony and paradox if he would not mingle in this seemingly radical nominalism also its immediate refutation—since the squirrel is struck by panic fear. For Kakania is weakened, above all, by the fact that the nations (or "nationalities") withdraw from the state as a whole (or the Dual State) exactly those resources it needs for its self-assertion.

If we want to understand sociologically why multiethnic dynastic empires give way to nation states, we must also know if nations really are able to mobilize more resources in order to assert themselves in state-competition and to inevitably produce more cohesion than the multiethnic state. A separate, but related question is whether this force also means, first, the weakening of the multinational state and, as a further step, its dissolution.

It is not by accident that General Stumm uses the notion of "unredeemed nationalities"; he does this by way of irony—as we can expect of Musil—by reconstructing the everyday terminology of redemption: In everyday life, no one will in earnest demand to be "redeemed." He treats the term as "one of those verbal inflations not yet classified by linguistic science" (p. 565). These words, his detailed analysis leads him to reason, have much to do with artificially exaggerated, exalted, and sublime emotions.

In that sense, the nations—or in the language of Austrian bureaucracy: nationalities—longing for a messiah cannot claim their superior rationality. In a way similar to the argumentation of A. D. Smith (1986), E. Gellner (1983), and E. Hobsbawm (1990), Musil considers the reconstruction of national histories as ex post teleology: the history in Kakania had been replaced by that of the nation (p. 561).

How the historical-political thinker proceeds here has been suggested by Musil, in the case of the legitimist standpoint:

> For him the present period follows upon the Battle of Mohacs or Lietzen as the roast the soup; he knows all the proceedings and has at every moment the sense of necessity arising out of lawful process. If he is, moreover, like Count Leinsdorf an aristocratic philosopher trained in political history, whose forebears, wielding sword or spindle, had personally played their parts in the preliminaries, he can survey the result as a smoothly ascending line. (p. 181)

Differing from some leading representatives of the sociological theory of modernization who, like Talcott Parsons (1971), attribute to medieval federations of knights the power to develop modern parliamentarism—in the case of the "Magna Carta" and the path leading to British Parliament—Musil knows how open historical situations are. There are usually many more options than can be effectively realized. Referring to the way that leads to the rise of the nation-state, this means a considerable skepticism regarding the logic of progress that is assumed to be part and parcel of the discourse about nations.

## KAKANIA, "UNREDEEMED NATIONS," AND THE NATIONALITIES

For the old conservative Count Leinsdorf, the "nationalities" are an inapprehensible annoyance that he traces back to the "virus" of agitation (p. 561). But Leinsdorf is not a big theoretician, according to Musil, and we must not take his theory of agitation too seriously. Images of the wanted or the unwanted are behind the national wishes and anxieties, as Musil shows, of all things, with the example of the hostility towards Germany, common to many Europeans and also to Austrians.

Musil explains the genesis of these strong affects by pointing to the often diffuse dissatisfaction with life, the discontent existing in modern societies, to the emotions linked to failure in competition, among others, but with consequences that become very tangible indeed. The thinking that is tied to that kind of emotions is, now, magical as it had always been and, thus, all but reasonable.

> People alternately kill each other or swear eternal brotherhood without quite knowing just how real any of it is, because they have projected part of themselves onto the outer world, and everything seems to be happening partly out there in reality and partly behind the scenes, so that we have an illusory fencing match between love and hate. (p. 560)

Musil is, thus, not a rationalist who would deny the importance of emotions; he is merely a rationalist who demonstrates the impurity of the thinking associated with these emotions, its longing for projections that serve all kinds of surfaces. The inner, emotional conflict can turn into an outer, societal—which it has been, indeed, already since its emergence. This conflict cries for redemption and for a "Messiah," even in the case of intellectuals.

Soon, the Kakanian "nationalities" see themselves filled with deep averseness to each other, define themselves and each other as Germans, Czechs, Hungarians and so on and damage the whole state enormously. Since the state sees itself under pressure to balance national interests and, thus, also to proceed against the German "nationality,"

> [it] began to regard itself as an oppressed nationality . . . there was nothing left in Kakania except oppressed nationalities, the oppressors being represented by a supreme circle of personages who saw themselves as being constantly baited and plagued by the oppressed. (p. 562)

This idea—all nations become suppressed nations—is sociologically remarkable even today. It says that there are social dynamics that emanate from individual action and thus produce consequences that incorporate a lawfulness of its own, until all actors turn into prisoners of a men-shaped situation receiving the character of nature.

The great Parallel Campaign, in Musil's construction, comes to be seen as particularly suspicious in the eyes of German-nationalist circles. This hateful resistance is embodied in the figure of Hans Sepp ("against the threat of Slavification," Musil p. 601; cf. Wolf 2009). His German-romantic attitude

("Germanic blood") is linked to a whole lot of other romanticisms—the yearning for a "Community of the Purely Selfless" (p. 605) and "the shedding of one's armor in which the ego was encased" (p. 606). It is also tied to a mystical, anti-authoritarian, anti-capitalist, and anti-Semitic enthusiasm for the child within man as a feeling component of the German youth movement striving for the replacement of the sensual ego by the transcendent one, the naturalistic by a Gothic one—whatever this should mean.

Ulrich, Musil's hero and the man without qualities, is "irritated by this superstitious claptrap" (p. 608), and it is easy to find here not only the principled readiness to accept violence as a political means so fateful in later German history but also elements of a violence that was regarded as legitimate by many followers of the 1968 movement. Friedrich Heer (1981) has pointed repeatedly to the surprising aspect of the commonalities between the rise of Protestantism in the sixteenth century, the ethnic nationalism of Young Serbs and Germans, and even the "völkische" nationalism of the Third Reich: all owe their existence to youth-movements.

Gavrilo Princip, the assassin of Francis Ferdinand, heir to the Habsburg throne, was 17 at the time of his deed; the path to modern "terror" and its philosophical justification is not very far indeed (see again Wolf 2009). Musil describes the pure philosophy of action in the thinking of the mystical philosopher Meingast (modeled after the "Lebensphilosoph" Ludwig Klages, cf. Corino 2003:1154). For Meingast, " 'true' and 'false' are the evasions of people who never want to arrive at a decision" (p. 996).

Musil's judgment can be put into a single sentence, uttered by Ulrich in passing: "This Meingast lives on our current confusion of intuition and faith" (p. 852). Hans Sepp and its circle do not even shy away from the "ruthless suppression of all alien races," according to the postulate of the "great racial theorist Bremshuber" (the sentence is uttered by Hans's Jewish girlfriend Gerda Fischel, paradoxically). Musil was aware of the full destructive potential of the nationalisms set free by the demise of the baroque Habsburg Dual Monarchy; the word can become flesh, indeed.

## MUSIL AS A SOCIOLOGIST OF STATE-FORMATION: CONCLUDING REMARKS

As I hope to have shown, Musil's great novel contains a quite remarkable sociological analysis of an important stage in the history of the European system of states: the transition from dynastic Empire to nation-state and the emotions that are linked to each stage. Among the leading sociologists of our time, Norbert Elias has probably paid more attention than any other to the emotional aspects of this process. For him, states are "survival units"

(Elias 1987), and that the nation-state can perform as such depends on the increasing entanglement of its whole population in conflicts with other mass-societies (Elias 1996). He locates this inter-state level as the main driving force for the rise of nationalism as a system of beliefs.

Elias, however, did not develop a model for the peculiar "Irredenta"-nationalism characteristic for the Habsburg Monarchy or other dynastic empires. On the other hand, authors like Anderson (1983), Hobsbawm (1990), and Gellner (1983) dealt with these ethnic nationalisms but were not able or interested in explaining the corresponding emotions. Musil can help us bridge the gap and form a synthesis. He, too, shows the artificial element both in Empire patriotism and ethnic nationalism, but he also develops an understanding of the power of the magical beliefs linked to these affects.

The nationalisms define each other reciprocally, and the "ruling elite" stays alone and feels cheated. The dissolution of the Empire is a possible outcome, although it probably needs the war to give the disintegration momentum. Musil's method of analysis was literary, but it bordered on science. He strived to achieve conceptual clarity and empirical precision both in his "theorizing" and his portraits of central figures and interactions.

In order to check the validity and plausibility of this interpretation of Musil's analysis and also to consider how close he came to a correct picture of the last days of the Habsburg Dual Monarchy, it is possible to draw on relevant biographical information and, thus, to "deconstruct" different layers of meanings. Given the central place he dedicated to the "Parallel Campaign," it might be interesting to know how this ingenious plot came to be developed.

It seems that Thomas Mann's *Magic Mountain* and its atmosphere of unreality might have influenced Musil (cf. Corino 2003:928). The all-pervasive sense of detached irony that dominates this narrative has to be taken into account, and not all should be attributed to a lack of Habsburg patriotism, which might be simply a product of style. Musil's own emotions with respect to state and nation can be partly reconstructed in their development; the war aroused patriotic fire in him. Not only was he a decorated officer fighting at the Southern Front, but he also functioned as editor of the *Soldaten-Zeitung* and made propaganda for the unity of the Empire (Corino 2003:560). In the year 1919, he argued publicly for the *Anschluß* to Germany, convinced of the superiority of German culture and disgusted by the Mini-Imperialisms of the Slavs (cf. Corino 2003:602). We can assume that his position was not wholly impartial. Besides, he placed his political hopes in the hands of the Social Democrats.

Finally, we have to be aware that some of his interpretations of the German-nationalist sentiment were written from hindsight—the late 1920s offered better orientation of the path to and from democracy than 1913 and 1914, the fictitious years of the novel's happenings (cf. Wolf 2009). Nevertheless, Musil's approximations to truth and reality are no less and no more debatable than those of the social sciences themselves. Both fiction and science must situate their claims in a sociology-of-knowledge perspective without getting lost in the labyrinth of relativism.

## NOTES

1. This is Jane Smiley's unsurpassed abbreviated account of the novel's central narrative: "Ulrich is an unmarried man in his early 30s who has recently returned to Vienna from several years abroad. He is ostensibly a mathematician, but although his mind still works like that of a scientist, he has ceased to be inspired by his vocation, and finds himself in the midst of an existential crisis. He is a habitual thinker whose most characteristic activity is to continually refine his analysis of himself and the people around him. He is not meditative or contemplative—that is, he seeks neither peace nor enlightenment. Earlier, once through love and the natural world, and later through mathematics, he had sought truth, but not long before the novel begins, he slacks off, no longer passionate enough about it to be disappointed. He finds and redecorates a house and then takes up the typical activities of a Viennese gentleman—he procures himself a mistress and falls in with bureaucratic projects. As an idle pastime, he gets to know the leading lights of the Austro-Hungarian empire, who, somewhat like their counterparts in the American south of the 1850s, have no idea they are passing into history" (Smiley 2006).

2. In Ascherson's words: "It may be a long novel for politicians with infernally little spare time, but it's no exaggeration to say that Musil's masterpiece really has been the rediscovery of the decade in Britain. Ukania's own fin de siècle, seen through the lens of the millennium preparations, is prefigured with horrifying accuracy in this comedy about how a failing multinational state sets up a Great & Good committee to study ways of celebrating its own anniversary. The only reason to celebrate the Chief Minister's (Donald Dewar, H. K.) resignation would be the chance it offered him to get stuck into the Man without Qualities and discover for himself how witty, how shockingly relevant it is in 21st-century Britain" (Ascherson 2000, p.8).

# CHAPTER 8

# August Strindberg: Forms of Interaction

*Christofer Edling*

In his widely diffused *Invitation to Sociology*, Peter Berger talks about the good sociologist as a professional Peeping Tom, someone who is taken over by curiosity "in front of a closed door behind which there are human voices. If he is a good sociologist, he will want to open that door, to understand these voices. Behind each closed door he will anticipate some new facet of human life not yet perceived and understood" (1963:19). The drive to find out the details of the life of others thus feeds not only celebrity gossip, but also the academic discipline of sociology. The same drive forms the motivation for theatre, whose suggestive power emerges from a similar experience of getting to see what is going on behind closed doors, where something that was previously private or hidden is now played out in front of our eyes, becoming open to our interpretation, comparison, and explanation.

One of sociology's most imaginative contributors would even take it as far as to suggest that the theatre is a metaphor for social life, in which we act our social life as on stage (Goffman 1959). My starting point is not that radical. Rather, I would like to suggest that "theatre as disclosure" can play the role of models, assisting us to abstract away the general from the particular. I think the Swedish author August Strindberg explicitly strived to achieve exactly this effect in a set of influential dramas from the late 1880s, which he wrote under great influence and partly in debate with Zola and other contemporary naturalists. This essay is focused on Strindberg's *Fröken Julie* (henceforth *Miss Julie*), which is one of three "naturalist dramas" written between 1887 and 1889.

The preface to the play is a burning manifesto for modern theatre, believed to have been written in retrospect, which makes evident that Strindberg clearly wanted to satisfy the Peeping Tom sociologist in all of us. "[W]e want to know how it happened. We want to see the strings, look at the machinery, examine the double-bottomed box, try the magic ring to find the seam, and examine the cards to discover how they are marked" (Strindberg 1998:64). This effect was achieved both in the text, by having the role figures acting under a complex of motivational forces, but also in the technical aspects of stage scenery and choreography.

Strindberg (1998:67) regrets that "to turn the stage into a room with the fourth wall removed and some of the furniture consequently facing away from the audience, would probably have a distracting effect." And although he would desire it, he didn't believe the time was ripe to have "the actor to play for the audience and not with it." Therefore, he does not dare to suggest "revolutions, simply some small modifications." *Miss Julie* is a play in one act, and it is meant to be played in about an hour and a half. Strindberg left out the act division in order to keep the spectator under "the suggestive influence of the dramatist-hypnotis" (p. 64), the role he saw for himself at that stage in his artistic career.

## *MISS JULIE*: A NATURALISTIC TRAGEDY

*Miss Julie* is one of Strindberg's most well-known dramas and most likely his most widely played drama.[1] It has been translated into more than 30 languages and is still played on stages around the world, regularly provoking heated feelings. The plot of this dense piece is easy to recapture: On a Midsummer's Night, Miss Julie, a young woman, the daughter of a count, and Jean, a servant, meet in the kitchen of the count's house.

Midsummer's Night, the longest day of the year, holds a particular significance in Scandinavia. It is a night of festivities, full of promises, which Strindberg alludes to on various occasions in the play, such as when Jean repeats a popular folklore: "If we sleep on nine Midsummer flowers tonight, Miss Julie, our dreams will come thrue" (p. 80). This evening Miss Julie is as excited as anyone else, if not even more so. This is Jean's voice, this time giving a characterization of Miss Julie's state at the very opening of the play:

> I went with the Count to the station and on my way back past the barn I just stopped for a dance. And who do I see but her ladyship with the gamekeeper, leading the dance? But as soon as she claps eyes on me, she comes rushing straight on over and invites me to join her in

the ladies' waltz. And how she waltzed!—I've never known the like. She's crazy! (p. 71)

The beginning of the play is set around a teasingly and erotically charged dialogue between Miss Julie and Jean in which their divergent backgrounds, experiences, and future expectations serve to spell out their substantial social differences. When they both take hiding in Jean's room (off stage) to avoid the mockery of the peasants, he seduces her. Miss Julie finds the dishonor unbearable and realizes that she cannot stay in the count's house.

Fueled by Jean's vivid mind and experience in the ways of the world, they construct a plan to jointly flee and start a new life in Southern Europe, but the fantasy is shred to pieces under the pressure of a social reality in which they are indeed exemplars of two radically different species. Supported by Jean, Miss Julie sees no other way out than suicide, and the play ends by suggesting Miss Julie slashing her wrists with Jean's razor.

Besides Miss Julie and Jean, the only other character on stage is Kristin, the cook and also Jean's fiancé. The Count himself is ghostly present only to materialize in the form of a pair of riding boots and very late in the act as the source of the ringing kitchen bell. I will suggest that, from a sociological perspective, both Kristin and the Count are actually very important to understand the interaction between Miss Julie and Jean.

## AUGUST STRINDBERG

August Strindberg was born in 1849, the son of a steamship agent and a waitress, and he grew up in a fairly well-off bourgeoisie home in Stockholm. (I rely chiefly on Lagercrantz 1984 and Ollén 1984 for this section.) Strindberg's own account of his childhood is his autobiography *The Serving Maid's Son* (1886). By most accounts, Strindberg appears to have been a difficult personality. He was and is still controversial; known among other things as an atheist, a socialist, an anti-Semite, an occultist, and a misogynist. *Miss Julie* is often put forward as an example of the latter.

Strindberg went through many phases in his life, however, and his biography is a dynamic story full of paradoxes and high temper. He spent many years in self-selected exile, in Denmark, France, Germany, and Switzerland, including the so-called Inferno Crisis (1894–1897), and he was a vagabond also at home, said to have lived in 24 different apartments in Stockholm alone. He was married (and divorced) three times and had five children.

Strindberg died in Stockholm in May 1912, from what appears to have been stomach cancer. By the time of his death, Strindberg had been elevated to something of a national poet, and for his last birthday he was honored with a torch-lit procession of some 10,000 people and a substantial popularly raised fund, at the time conceived of as an alternative Nobel Prize. The only other author who has enjoyed a similar popular status in Sweden is Astrid Lindgren, the children's book author.

For his national audience, Strindberg is known mostly for his novels. His debut, *The Red Room*, was published in 1879 and is considered the first modern Swedish novel. He is one of Sweden's most widely translated authors, internationally known primarily for his dramas. He wrote about 60 of them, many considered too controversial at the time and premiered outside of Sweden. This includes *Miss Julie*, first staged in Copenhagen in 1889. However, even there the play was censored and the premier actually took place in a private party.

Strindberg's passionate interest for the social, evident already in his debut and illustrated here in *Miss Julie*, led him to travel trough France in 1886 to report on the conditions of the French peasantry. The report was published in journal articles and later in the book *Among French Peasants* (1889, *Bland franska bönder*), which at least among sociologists is taken to be the first Swedish work of sociology.

It is interesting that Strindberg was to be accompanied on the trip through France by the young Gustaf Steffen, who was later to become Sweden's first academic sociologist, holding a professorship in economics and sociology at Gothenburg University. However, for unknown reasons, but probably largely due to Strindberg's choleric nature, the two fell out early on and Steffen never completed the journey. Along with his contemporary French naturalists, one can say that at this point in his career Strindberg impersonated sociology between literature and science (see Lepenies 1988:80–90).

## TAKE SOCIAL INTERACTION AND SOCIAL FORMS

Georg Simmel, one of sociology's founding fathers, argued that sociology should be concerned with the forms of social interaction rather than the content of interaction. Conflict, domination, and exchange are fundamental forms of interaction and obvious candidates for sociological analysis. By definition, "the social" can only arise with more than one party, and it is easy to see that there can be no conflict, domination, exchange, and so forth without at least two subjects. The starting point for any type of sociology, then, is the dyad; that is, the interaction between Ego and Alter, between me and you.

Both Miss Julie and Jean come on stage with a personal history that has formed their personality and their beliefs, and that will roughly define the set of actions from which they can act. However, the exact action that each one of them will take is contingent on the dynamics of the interaction between the two, so that each of Miss Julie's actions becomes both a response to a previous action by Jean and an invitation to Jean to act again, and vice versa.

Simmel's point is that this kind of "strategic interaction," to borrow another term from Goffman (1969), will take on different forms depending on what type of interaction we deal with. Exchange and conflict, for instance, are quite different types of interactions and consequently they will take on different forms. From a sociological point of view, another pressing insight is that there can be no ego without alter; in other words, our identity and our beliefs about the world are constantly moulded in social interaction with others.

In the preface to *Miss Julie*, Strindberg says he wants to stay "in tune with the times" by having his leading parts motivated by a "multiplicity of motives" (p. 58). Thus, he does not confine his explanations for their actions only to physiological or psychological mechanisms. Instead, it is clear that his idea of human interaction was indeed embedded in a complex mosaic of motivations: "Every event in life—and this is a fairly new discovery!—is usually the result of a whole series of more or less deep-seated motives, but the spectator usually selects the one that he most easily understands or that best flatters his powers of judgement" (p. 58). Thus, the play is of course open to many readings and the one presented here is surely not the only one, not even the only sociological one.

*Miss Julie* is no ideal-typical representation of only one specific type of interaction as it sweeps through, among other things, flirtation, dominance, deception, and subordination. Rather, we get to see social life as consisting of multiple forms of interaction that lead from one type to the other in what sometimes appears to be a very haphazard pattern. In a famous scene where Miss Julie relieves Jean of a speck of dust in his eye, we are facing an example of flirtation as a social form. This exchange follows just after Jean's line regarding our dreams coming through in Midsummer's Night:

**Miss Julie** Something in your eye? Let me see.

**Jean** It's nothing—only a speck of dust—it'll be alright.

**Miss Julie** My sleeve must have caught you; sit down and I'll help you. [She takes him by the arm and sits him down; takes his head and pushes it backwards; with the tip of her handkerchief she tries to remove the speck of dust]. Sit still now; absolutely still! [Slaps his hand]. There! Will you obey me!—I do believe you're trembling, a big strong fellow like you! [Feels his upper arm] With arms like that!

**Jean** Miss Julie!

**Miss Julie** Yes, Monsieur Jean?
**Jean** Attention! Je ne suis qu'un homme! (p. 80)

Miss Julie proceeds to lead on, with a combination of mockery and incitement, demanding that Jean kiss her hand. When he tries instead to embrace and kiss her she slaps him. But the flirtation continues. Jean now tells Miss Julie that when he first set eyes on her in the rose garden when they were both children, she became the unattainable focus of all his early desires: "There was no hope of winning you of course, but you stood for how hopeless it was ever to escape from the class in which I was born" (p. 83)—which by the way he is strongly intended to do as suggested by his comfort in dropping French phrases in Miss Julie's invitation (above).

He tells Miss Julie that despite his young age, in his misery he tried to kill himself because of her. Part of the erotic tension arises precisely from the difference in social status between the two. The fine daughter of the aristocracy is the ultimate prize for Jean, but this is reciprocal in Miss Julie's sexual attraction to the "brute" of the lower classes. It is generally understood that here Strindberg drew on experiences from his own mixed-class marriage to Siri von Essen.

It is evident that Miss Julie takes pleasure from the scene and that to her this is a social game: As Jean asks her if she is not aware that it is dangerous to "play with fire," she tells him that she is "insured" (p. 81). Even though he tries to restrain himself and suggests that they say goodnight, Jean is full of burning desire—"[w]hat a splendid creature, though! Quite magnificent! Oh! What shoulders and—etcetera!" (p. 73)—and his story is clearly told to awake her sympathy for him. The whole interaction sequence of this scene encompasses many of the aspects that Simmel discusses under the label coquetry: "The coquette brings her attractiveness to its climax by letting the man hang on the verge of getting what he wants without letting it become too serious for herself; her conduct swings between yes and no, without stopping at one or the other" (Simmel 1971a:135).

Eventually, however, there has to be either "yes" or "no." This half playful and half serious interaction come to mark the turning point of the play, as Jean and Miss Julie are disturbed by the approaching peasants, and they flee into Jean's room, and I am inclined to think that in this case the flirt ends in an unintended "yes," at least as far as Miss Julie is concerned.

When Jean and Miss Julie return on stage, the situation is completely redefined and their interaction takes on another form. If it was Miss Julie that somehow had the upper hand before, Jean is now in command. As Jean plots their escape and lays out his plan for them to start a hotel in Italy, Miss Julie begs for his love and affection, but his focus is elsewhere: "One folly's enough, don't commit any more. The Count may return at any moment and by then we've got to have this sorted. What do you think of my plans for the future? Do you approve?" (p. 88) Miss Julie is now completely overcome with the consequences of her action and is close to panic, while Jean grows even more composed:

**Miss Julie** Oh God in heaven, take my miserable life! Take me away from this filth into which I'm sinking. Save me! Save me!

**Jean** I can't deny I feel sorry for you. When I lay in the onion bed and saw you in the rose garden, then—I'll say it now—I had the same dirty thoughts that all boys have.

**Miss Julie** And you, who wanted to die for me!

**Jean** In the oat-bin? That was just talk.

**Miss Julie** A lie you mean!

**Jean** More or less! I read it in the paper once about a chimney-sweep who lay down in a wood-chest with some lilacs, because he'd had a paternity order brought against him—

**Miss Julie** So that's your type . . .

This is interaction in the form of domination, where one party has a clear upper hand and can freely exploit the weaknesses of the other party. From here on, Miss Julie and Jean remain trapped in a vicious spiral that will come to its climax as the drama closes in Miss Julie's suicide.

## AND ADD A LITTLE SOCIAL STRUCTURE

However—and this was one of Simmel's key points—as a model of social interaction, the dyad is really an exclusive case. In the dyad, social interaction is terminated as soon as one of them steps away from it, and they both have the power to do so. That one social actor has this drastic impact on interaction is exceptionally rare in social life, which to a large extend is characterized by the constraints it imposes on our individuality. Therefore, even if it might look like a small and incremental numerical step, going from two to three social actors, in other words from a dyadic to a triadic structure, is a huge qualitative step (Simmel 1992).

For instance, consider from an exchange perspective the difference in bargaining power that B has in the triad (chain) A-B-C as compared to A-B. In the first case B is on top of all exchange between A and C. In the second case, B is left to the discretion of A. Similarly, consider A's power potential in the two examples. The triad also offers a way to explain why Miss Julie simply did not walk away.

As already noted, Strindberg was proud to have the play's characters being driven by a "multitude of motives," some physiological, some psychological, and some social. Indeed, he said the theme of his play, that "of rising and falling on the social ladder, of higher or lower, better or worse, man or woman is, has been, and always will be of lasting interest" (p. 57).

It would come as no surprise then to find that the dynamic dyad of Miss Julie and Jean is embedded in at least two different triads, each of which define the opportunities and constraints that the social actors face. First is the triad Miss Julie, Jean, and Kristin; second is the triad Miss Julie, Jean, and the Count. However, both of these triads have a class dimension and a gender dimension, suggesting to us that social interaction is multiplex and hinting towards contemporary analyses of so-called intersectionality (e.g., McCall 2005).

If we take the class dimension of the first triad, Miss Julie is the most powerful by birth, and the other two are her servants. Miss Julie naturally makes use of this power imbalance in the first part of the play in her demands on Jean as well as on Kristin. However, much of the dynamics of the play arise from the fact that not only masters expect things from their servants; servants have expectations on their masters too. Such expectations arise from the form of the social interaction.

Kristin, the cook, is the moral guardian who insists on taking Jean to church on Midsummer's Day. She surely does not approve of Jean's conduct—whom she intends to marry—but she flat out resents Miss Julie's: "I've never sunk below my own station. You tell me when his Lordship's cook has been with the groom or the pig man!" (p. 106).

Thus, Miss Julie receives no support from Kristin. Rather, in the social class triad Kristin is the one who reminds Miss Julie about her inappropriate behavior, also when Jean is trying to uphold it—"Kindly speak with a little more respect; she's still your mistress. Understand!" (p. 106). But Kristin will not accept the way in which Miss Julie breaches the social form of inter-class interaction, and in this respect she is indeed the third wheel.

Kristin is similarly harsh on Miss Julie in the gender triad, where Jean is clearly the stronger part. "Such sluttishness is quite beyond me" (p. 104), Kristin comments on Miss Julie. Again, Kristin can accept Jean's side-step, while Miss Julie, a woman, comes out as a slut (and here one comes away with the strong impression that it is Strindberg himself speaking through Kristin). So while Jean's and Miss Julie's interaction is situated in a society stratified both across class and gender, and while this clearly structures their interaction, it is in the triad—through Kristin—that social expectations turn into inexorable pressure. Miss Julie could live encapsulated in the imagination that Jean could save her from "sinking," but only for as long as they were a dyad. It is in the triad that the social impossibility of it all is laid bare.

In a similar way Jean is reminded of his relative class inferiority by the distant but real presence of the count. Having just declared to Miss Julie that he would never take his own life because this is "the difference between a man and a woman" (p. 107), Jean is called upon by the count demanding his newly polished boots with "two shrill rings on the bell" (p. 108). Again, the dyad shifts into a triad and everything is changed. Jean is no longer his cocksure self: "I can't explain it properly—but—oh, it's this damned lackey sitting on my back!—I believe if his lordship came down now and ordered me to cut my throat, I'd do it on the spot" (p. 109). Indeed, Miss Julie grasps this occasion and suggests that Jean pretend he is the count and that she is Jean. In this new role, he can issue to Miss Julie the order that he had just imagined for himself.

*Miss Julie* is chock-full of Strindberg's dusky view on men and women. Will they ever be equal, he asks rhetorically (p. 60), and he answers: "*Never*! Neither with the help of equal education, equal voting rights, disarmament, or temperance—no more than two parallel lines can ever meet and cross." This can surely obstruct the reading of his text. However, as is so often the case in Strindberg's work, *Miss Julie* is multi-layered and holds an abundance of stimulating and bold ideas that point to his great sociological intuition. I hope to have suggested how they can ring true when encountered by sociological theory.

## NOTE

1. There are no definite sources to back this claim. Based on its collection of press clippings, The Strindberg Museum in Stockholm is confident that it is beyond doubt that *Miss Julie* is the most widely played of Strindberg's dramas. Because the play calls for very small production resources, this is probably also true internationally. One could perhaps argue that *A Dream Play* (1901) or possibly *The Dance of Death* (1900) are equally well-known drama titles.

# CHAPTER 9

# Henrik Ibsen: The Power of Charisma

*Fredrik Engelstad*

## CHARISMATIC POWER AS A GENERIC CONCEPT

'Charismatic authority' should be counted among the successes of social science concept formation. If the name of Max Weber was remembered for only one thing, chances are great that charisma will be that thing. At the same time, the concept is surrounded by confusion. In Weber's work it takes on a multiplicity of meanings. In the religious realm it denotes ecstatic leadership of ecstatic followers, but also ritualized handling of religious mysteries (Weber 1978:400; Riesbrodt 1999). In politics, in contrast, with its totally different modes of operation, it refers to personalized leadership by exceptional individuals, but may also refer to small-scale leadership with an emphasis on personal charm (Weber 1978:241, 1994:75; Krogstad and Storvik 2007:213).

In the introductory paragraphs of *Politics as Vocation* (1947 [1920]) Weber signals charismatic power as the prime focus of his lecture, whereas the concluding characterization of politics as a "strong and slow boring in hard boards" (1947:128) has little of charismatic enchantment to it. These contradictions do not make the concept useless, but they indicate that charisma should be treated as a generic concept rather than serving as the core of specific models.

Going into its development in Weber's thinking, it becomes relatively easy to see how this multiplicity of meanings emerged. A core problem raised by Weber is found in the final section of *The Protestant Ethic and the Spirit of Capitalism*, in his famous statement that rationality threatens to enclose the modern world into an iron cage (1930:181). As a response to this observation Weber developed his conception of charismatic power as a counterweight to rationality. Thereby, he was drawing on two very different sources: on the one hand the detailed study by church historian Rudolf Sohm on organizational forms in early Christianity (Weber 1978:216; Riesbrodt 1999:5–8), and on the other hand a more diffuse inspiration from Friedrich Nietzsche.

To a large extent Weber put into practice Nietzsche's call for replacing sociology by a theory of power. More specifically, a source of inspiration for the concept of charismatic authority is found in *The Genealogy of Morals* (1887), where Nietzsche discusses the power of the ascetic religious leader, side by side with his classical depiction of master morality. Nietzsche's image of the master is not a full-blown image of charismatic power, as the master does not appeal to a group of followers, but it has the aspect of charisma connected to the gift of immediate assertiveness, which is a precondition for charismatic influence.

Another figure standing behind Max Weber, however, is the playwright Henrik Ibsen, in a peculiar sense Nietzsche's evil spirit, in some ways his double, and ridiculed by Nietzsche whenever he found an opportunity.[1] Drawing a connection between Ibsen and Weber may seem peculiar, but it is not. One of the core themes in Ibsen's dramas is precisely charismatic power. During Weber's formative years Ibsen was a towering figure in German intellectual life.

Weber was certainly well acquainted with at least parts of Ibsen's work. His presence, even articulated in emotionally dramatic situations, is testified in Weber's letters and in Marianne Weber's diaries.[2] This, however, says nothing about the strength of Ibsen's possible influence on Weber's work; more important is the observation that there are clear parallels between the two men. Reading Weber through the lenses of Ibsen may bring forth some significant aspects of Weber's conception and highlight a family of models consonant with Weber's thinking, while at the same time specifying some aspects of the problematic that he was encircling.

Along with Shakespeare, Ibsen is one of the authors in the Western canon who shows the deepest insights into problems of power—not so much because power was his prime concern, because in many ways it was not. Ibsen's main topic was self realization and the duty of the individual to realize the creative powers in himself or herself. His preoccupation with social power was mainly negative, an impetus to show how individuals are impeded from fully realizing their personal potentialities. Thereby, the idea of Calling became a central theme in Ibsen's work, as it was in Weber's and Nietzsche's writing.

The plays by Ibsen specifically treating charismatic power are spread over most of his career as a writer, from *The Pretenders* of the early 1860s to *John Gabriel Borkmann* of the mid-1890s. The plays in between treating charisma most insistently are *Brand* (1865), *Emperor and Galilean* (1875), and *Rosmersholm* (1886). In this essay, I will touch upon four of these. Many writers have a tendency to tell the same story over and over again, with only small variations. In contrast, Ibsen had an uncommon ability to explore a few general themes from ever new angles, with the result that his total *oeuvre* may be regarded as analogous to a series of experiments, each with a different focus and different outcome.

## MASTER MORALITY AS CHARISMATIC NOBLESSE: *THE PRETENDERS*

A constant feature of Ibsen's work is his tendency to problematize whichever theme he came over. This is true for power in general, and not less for charismatic power. In *The Pretenders*, however, which is the gateway into Ibsen's treatment of charismatic power, the critical aspect is almost invisible. The drama depicts the struggle over the royal power in medieval Norway between the young king-elect Håkon Håkonssøn and his guardian Duke Skule, who also claims the throne. There is a striking contrast between Håkon, who emerges as a visionary leader, and Skule, who only wants power for its own sake. Håkon claims the throne in order to fulfill his Royal vision of national unity. He expresses this vision[3] in the following way:

**Håkon** Norway was a kingdom, Norwegians shall become a people. People from Trøndelag stood against those from Viken, from Agder against Hordaland, Hålogaland against Sogn. Everyone shall be united hereafter, and everyone shall know and understand that they are one. This is the duty God lay on my shoulders. (2, 71)

This Calling is the source of Håkon's strength, and it is the final reason why he wins through and gains power on a permanent basis. His success as a politician is above all due to his vocation, Håkon is depicted as a gifted man and a gifted leader, but not in any way a great strategist. Is he a man who is slowly boring in hard boards? Yes and no. Håkon's sense of purpose is overwhelming, and he follows his course with great endurance. However, it all comes to him with a striking lightness; he is never troubled by doubts, as is his opponent Skule, and he gathers his men around him due to his natural appearance.

In one sense he has an aspect of ecstasy, but outwardly ecstasy in a temperate version, if that may at all make sense, along the same lines that Weber points out in his description of charisma as the extraordinary powers in religious leaders performing magical acts. "Where this appellation is fully merited, charisma is a gift that inheres in an object or person simply by virtue of natural endowment" (Weber 1978:400). Ibsen makes one of Håkon's enemies, Bishop Nicolas, describe a similar phenomenon, albeit in different words:

**Bishop Nicolas** Who is the greatest man? . . . The happiest man is the greatest man. The happiest is the one who makes the greatest action, . . . walking the road he does not know where leads, but that he *must* go, until he hears the people cry in joy and he looks around with his eyes wide open and realizes that he has made a great work . . . it is what the Romans called *ingenium*, my Latin is not too good, by the way, but it is called *ingenium*. (2, 32)

In one sense this description lies very close to the Nietzschean ideal of master morality. Håkon takes his right, and he succeeds because he lives up to his own vision, thereby making credible his own claims to the throne. At the same time he is very "un-Nietzschean" in that his sense of calling is based on religious ideals as well as visions of national unity. A consistent Nietzschean narrative would have been the story of a struggle between the master Håkon and the clergy representing the church and its slave morality.

Such a struggle actually lies at the root of the play, as Håkon's grandfather King Sverre stood up in a rebellion against papal power and was excommunicated for this reason. If Sverre was as a Nietzschean blonde beast, however, his grandson grew up as what Nietzsche despised; he was tamed, became mild and wise. Nevertheless, his wisdom also bears marks of master morality, as his vision is that of forcing the regional kinship groups into a national collective subject. Nothing succeeds like success; Håkon's birthright is the sign of his charismatic gift, and he is invincible as long as he preserves the unity of political goals and a religiously based vocation.

Ibsen would not have been Ibsen without an ironic twist to the ending. At the end of the play there is a small sign of Håkon's God-given power starting to crumble. When his defeated antagonist Skule is killed, it does not happen in a way worthy of a nobleman. Instead Skule dies by being hit by a soldier's sword in his face. For the first time the enchantment is broken. At the apex of Håkon's power as the head of an expanding Norwegian state, this marks the beginning of a long development toward the demise of a sovereign Norwegian kingdom.

## RELIGIOUS PASSION AND HUBRIS: *BRAND*

In his next drama, *Brand*, Ibsen begins a long process of direct exploration of problems of charisma. The main character of the play is the devout and forceful minister Brand, a man who despises any form of compromise and empty form of humanism and insists on the obligation of every human being to follow in the footsteps of Jesus. "All or nothing at all" he shouts out. Brand is a towering figure of Nietzschean dimensions, albeit conceived long before Nietzsche entered his career as a writer. Brand is the minister of a small mountain congregation, where he has earned the deepest respect of his followers. Their deference is based not only on his evidently strong personality, but as much on his personal courage and willingness to sacrifice. When he arrives in the small community for the first time, a storm blows up, while at the same time a message is brought that an old man lies dying at the other side of the fjord, and thus is in need of the last sacraments. Brand insists on crossing the fjord in the storm, but nobody dares risk their own life by accompanying him in the boat:

**Brand** Unmoor a boat and row me over.
**A Man** In this storm? No one would dare.
**Brand** Unmoor a boat!
**Second Man** Impossible! Look! The wind's blowing from the mountain! The fjord is seething!
**Brand** The soul of a dying sinner does not wait for wind or weather (1986:40)

Despite all warnings, Brand sails over the fjord and reaches the man in the moment he is dying. By showing himself willing to sacrifice his life for a higher cause, Brand lays the ground for his position as the spiritual leader of the community. If "charisma" implies a special gift of grace, Brand's gift is the willingness to sacrifice. However, his preoccupation with sacrifice grows more and more demanding, on himself and on the people around him.

Brand sacrifices his son by refusing to move out of the mountain community with its cold climate in order to save the life of the sickly boy. He sacrifices his wife by driving her into madness by his absolutist demands on her. And he ends up in a sort of delusion when he sets out to sacrifice the whole community by leading it away from their homes in order to settle in the Ice Church up in the inhospitable mountain area. In the end his congregation leaves him, going back to their farms and their everyday business. Brand dies alone, buried under an avalanche.

## CHARISMA WITHOUT MEANS FOR ITS REALIZATION: *ROSMERSHOLM*

If *Brand* is about limitless charisma, *Emperor and Galilean* is about its absence. After *Emperor and Galilean*, however, Ibsen's plays developed in a completely new direction, leaving behind the relationship between religion and politics in various forms of pre-modern societies. In the late 1870s he began working on his long row of dramas from the modern world, shaped by capitalism, political conflict, and the emerging professions. In these dramas religion may be a deep problem, but its presence is nevertheless precarious in a way that is specific for modernity.

*Rosmersholm* is about the battle between traditionalism and modernity, both in the political and the religious realm, in a small Norwegian community that is still in many ways dominated by the old estate of Rosmersholm. The master at Rosmersholm is the reverend Johannes Rosmer, no longer active as minister. The young woman Rebecca West finds her way into the estate, first as a companion to Beate Rosmer, the lady of Rosmersholm. However, Rebecca is a young radical who wants to be at the head of the modernizing forces. She enters into a spiritual community with Rosmer, stimulating his religious doubts and leading him into apostasy.

In Weber's words, they develop a calling for politics (1947:127). Simultaneously Rebecca drives Beate into suicide, in the expectation that she herself may take over as the leading lady of Rosmersholm, making the estate into a stronghold for the radical movement. When close to fulfillment, however, her project falls apart. Rebecca loses her momentum and her self-confidence due to her feelings of guilt over her part in Beate's suicide, but also because she realizes that her plans are unfeasible.

Rebecca is young, beautiful, and enchanting. She has a clear political vision that she wants to live up to. Her charismatic gifts are beyond doubt, her personality is magnetic, seducing both Beate and Johannes Rosmer; even her antagonist, the conservative headmaster Kroll, is touched by her. "Whom could you not bewitch when you set your mind to it?" he exclaims (1958:90). Rebecca's basic problem is that she wants to be politically active in a society where women have no political rights.[4] Hence, she is bound to act through a man in order to fulfill her political goals, and this is obviously what she is aiming at. She has singled out the weak Johannes Rosmer for this task, but this project is bound to fail. A man who is weak enough to act as her instrument is also too weak to be the head of any political campaign.

The political visions of Rosmer and Rebecca are in one sense very clear. They are freethinkers who want to liberate the population from the yoke of tradition, liberate the oppressed lives, and spread light and happiness in the world. At the same time Rosmer's ideas of what it takes to maneuver in a landscape of political conflict are helplessly naïve. He envisages himself spreading the word, much in the same way as evangelical preachers do. In Rebecca's words:

**Rebecca** You meant to take hold of real life—the real life of today—as you said. You were to go from home to home, like a guest who brought freedom. . . . To make men noble all around you—in wider and wider circles. (p. 76.)

Rosmer fills in:

**Rosmer** Oh what a joy it would be then to live! No more embittered strife. Only friendly rivalry. Every eye fixed on the same goal. All wills, all minds reaching forward—upward—each in the same way his own nature prompts. Happiness for all—created through all. (p. 86)

Evangelical preachers undoubtedly may be efficient in getting their message through, but that is dependent on their ability to evoke ecstasy. The spiritual power of the apostate pastor Rosmer in no way would suffice to enlighten the population. In the end Rosmer and Rebecca's reciprocal disillusionment with their political project turns inward and leads them into a process of *suicide à deux* in the roaring waterfall of the Mill Race close to Rosmersholm.

## CHARISMA WITHOUT ORGANIZATIONAL POWER: *JOHN GABRIEL BORKMAN*

John Gabriel Borkman was a successful banker with enormous ambitions. He set as his goal to organize an enormous set of financial transactions that would revolutionize society. In order to do so, he illegally took possession of the securities deposited in the bank. He did not succeed, however, and a large number of people lost their fortunes and Borkman himself was sentenced to eight years in jail.

The play starts several years after he is released. He is living alone on the second floor in his house, whereas his wife Gunhild, who hates and despises him, is living on the first floor. Borkman had built his career not only on personal talents, but also by building a social reputation. He appeared as a charismatic personality if anyone did. Looking back on the early days, Gunhild complains bitterly:

**Mrs. Borkman** Yes, the excuse always was that we must 'keep up an appearance.' And he kept up an appearance all right—with a vengeance! Drove a four-in-hand—as if he were a king. Had people bowing to him—as if he were a king. And

> they called him by his Christian name too—all over the country—just as if he were the king himself. 'John Gabriel,' 'John Gabriel.' They all knew what a great man 'John Gabriel' was! (p. 291)

Borkman not only had great personal ambitions; he is also obsessed by his will to power. He also has a vocation, however, that of building and shaping society through large-scale business activity. A miner's son, he wanted to hear the song of the metal deep in the ground, make it "come up into the day and serve mankind" (p. 313). His work was to be an act of creativity, like the sculptor Rodin, who set out to liberate the sculptural form hidden in stone. Now, creative impulses are undoubtedly an asset for ambitious people. But his inflated ego makes him completely overlook the organizational challenges as well as the innumerable instances of collective action required for modernizing a whole society.

**Borkman** All the mines I should have controlled! New workings stretched out endlessly! Waterfalls! Quarries! Trade routes and shipping lines over the whole world! All this—I should have created it all, alone! (p. 319)

Obsessed by his will to power, Borkman becomes the victim of his own ambitions. There is a very clear parallel between the characters of Brand and Borkman. Both have grand visions, too grand for real life, and both have evident charismatic gifts. And both end their lives in the cold snow. The differences are just as striking. Brand is a preacher and a devout Christian, whereas Borkman is a businessman living in a world without God. Brand realizes his charismatic ambitions, but for Borkman they remain an empty shell, nothing but appearances. Like Brand, Borkman finds death in the cold winter, with the words later repeated by Max Weber: "It was a hand of ice that took hold of my heart." But then he corrects himself: "No. No ice hand. It was a metal hand" (p. 369). Borkman is the victim not of the cold, but of the forces that he set out to release.

## MODES OF CHARISMATIC POWER

These observations in many respects have a common theme pointing back to Weber. His reflections on the power of charisma were initially based on a felt need to counterbalance the enormous forces of bureaucratic machinery. In this imagery, charisma functions as a free-floating force, bringing an element of spirit into the machine. Due to its juxtaposition with traditional and rational-legal authority, it lies near at hand to regard charisma as an autonomous mode of power. As Weber underlines, however, charisma is an unstable force (Weber 1978:1114).

Power presupposes a large amount of organizing and handling of practical concerns, which makes the institutionalization of charisma a necessary result. The spiritual element in power has a tendency to be swallowed up by organizational forces, which is in many ways the story read out of Weber's writings.

Out of Ibsen's dramas emerges a different story, whether he intended it or not. It is not so much about reification as about the longing for charismatic power as a dominant force, be it realized in practice in religious communities or present as a fantasy without practical foundation. Longing for purely ideational power, that story goes, with or without relations to God, tends to turn into its opposite: social destruction.

## NOTES

1. A close reading of Ibsen in the light of a Nietzschean existentialism is given by Atle Kittang (2003).

2. See Radkau 2006:235 on the symbolic meaning of *A Doll's House* to the fate of the marriage of the Webers. In a letter to Marianne about his nervous breakdown, Max Weber refers directly to Ibsen when describing his emotional state: "Like John Gabriel Borkmann I could say 'An icy hand let go of me'" (Marianne Weber, 1988:236, Ibsen 1958:369). Commenting on Weber's personality in the light of Ibsen's *Brand*, Marianne Weber writes in her biography: "Its profound symbolism stirred them [Max and Marianne] deeply," and she continues: "At some time in his life Weber might have become a man of "All or nothing." But again and again he opened himself up to the full earthly lives of others with all their wealth and conflicts. . . . He measured himself by absolute standards, but he did not force these on anyone else" (Marianne Weber 1988:667).

3. This royal vision has no connection to the historical Håkon Håkonssøn, it is a nineteenth-century idea, evidently inspired by the Italian politician Massimo D'Azeglio's famous remark to Vittorio Emanuele II, during the process of unification of Italy: "We have made Italy, now we must make Italians" (Collier 2003:4).

4. If Rebecca actually had entered politics, she would have discovered that female charisma may be a difficult thing (Krogstad and Storvik 2007), but that remains irrelevant in the present context.

# CHAPTER 10

# Chinua Achebe: Colonial Anomie

*Wendy Griswold*

Nigerian novelist and essayist Chinua Achebe is Africa's most widely read author. Author of 20 books over his six-decades-and-counting career,[1] Achebe's preeminence was ratified by the 2007 Man Booker International Prize as well as by the appearance of his books on countless secondary school and university reading lists. Indeed, there is a substantial literature just on how to teach *Things Fall Apart*, generally regarded as his masterpiece. Although Achebe's countryman, the playwright Wole Soyinka, was the first African to carry off the Nobel Prize for Literature—to the astonishment of most Nigerians—there is no comparison in terms of the reach of their work.

Achebe's stature rests not only on his immense literary gifts but also upon his extraordinary sociological analysis. Like most Nigerian writers, Achebe sees his calling to be less the modernist expression of inner life and more the realist representation of social change, the novelist "bearing witness" to Africa's tumultuous twentieth century of colonialism, independence, and political upheavals.[2] Born in 1920, Achebe grew up under British colonialism and lived through the heady initial days of independence, the disastrous civil war of the late 1960s (during which he represented Biafra's cause to the outside world), and the economic and political upheavals of the decades that followed. Using fiction to tell the story of these dramatic changes, Achebe tells a sociological story as well, one of social disorganizaton and its human consequences. Thus he offers an African rendition of a general account given by Emile Durkheim.

Durkheim's bleak vision began with human beings tormented by their appetites. "Unlimited desires are insatiable by definition and insatiability is rightly considered a sign of morbidity" (Durkheim 1979:247). To avoid this miserable condition, people submit to an exterior authority to restrain their passions, and that authority is society, "the only moral power superior to the individual, the authority of which he accepts" (Durkheim 1979:249).

Under normal circumstances society exercises the controls—norms, regulations, institutions—that restrain and channel desire. A sudden shock, "when society is disturbed by some painful crisis or by beneficent but abrupt transitions," can prevent society from playing its regulating role. The result is *anomie*, the absence of regulation, which often increases the rate of disorientation, unrestrained ambition, and—Durkheim's evidence to clinch his argument—suicide. The old laws fail, passions run free, and in William Butler Yeats's words:

> Things fall apart. The center cannot hold.
> Mere anarchy is loosed upon the world.[3]

Colonialism is by any measure a "painful crisis" that ruptures traditional social constraints, both by force (i.e., military action, colonial government) and by cultural impact (i.e., missionaries, new circulation of ideas). It follows that the colonial condition gives rise to anomie always and anarchy often. Perhaps not surprisingly, literature rather than social science offers the sharpest analyses of colonial and post-colonial anomie.

No one has given as vivid a picture of colonial anomie as the Nigerian writer Chinua Achebe.[4] Indeed, the titles (both from Yeats) of Achebe's first two novels, *Things Fall Apart* and *No Longer at Ease*, constitute a pocket definition of Durkheiminan anomie and its consequences. Just as Durkheim saw anomie as a disease of modernity, Achebe saw it as intrinsic to the colonial condition.

In *Things Fall Apart*, published in 1958 at the tail end of the colonial era, Achebe starts with a pre-colonial West African society, that of his own Igbo tribe. Although village life in Igboland was more complex than Durkheim's mechanical solidarity—a hypothesized primordial society where everyone resembles everyone else, sharing "an essential social likeness" and participating in a common "totality of beliefs and sentiments" called the collective conscience—it came close in that everyone knew what the rules were, even if they were not always certain how they should be applied (Durkheim 1964a:106, 79).

At the outset of the novel, the protagonist Okonkwo kills Ikemefuna, a teenage boy who has lived with Okonkwo's family for several years as hostage from a neighboring village. Ikemefuna has become close friends with Okonkwo's son Nwoye, and the whole family loves the boy. When an oracle advises the elders of Umuofia to kill Ikemefuna, a revered old man warns Okonkwo, "That boy calls you father. Do not bear a hand in his death." Okonkwo ignores this advice and participates in Ikemefuna's slaughter, forever alienating his own son. Okonkwo's loyal friend Obierika suggests that going along with the others may indeed have been an offense against the Earth.

This opening episode, often ignored when one considers *Things Fall Apart* as simply a tragedy of colonialism, clearly demonstrates Achebe's more complex understanding that, while the men of traditional Igboland shared a collective conscience, that conscience did not speak in one clear voice; here the claims of oracular direction were contradicted by the claims of fictive kinship, and men could draw sharply different conclusions about how to act.

In the Durkheimian evolutionary model, such moral differentiation would develop over time, but colonialism provided the sudden shock that prevented any gradualism. At the outset of *Things Fall Apart* "white men with no toes" were only a rumor in Igboland, but as time passes in Okonkwo's life, including some years of exile for an accidental killing, the Christian missionaries, trade with the outside world, and the British colonial government under a District Officer enter the scene. Okonkwo is disgusted with the changes, but others in Umuofia are ambivalent, and many send their children to the new school. Inevitably, conflict escalates. Zealots among the Christian converts provoke the traditionalists, who retaliate by burning the church. The District Officer briefly arrests Okonkwo, a grave affront to his status.

During a town meeting to decide whether Umuofia should take up arms against the new regime, as Okonkwo advocates, a court messenger shows up and Okonkwo impulsively kills him. Soon the District Officer and his men come to arrest Okonkwo. Obierika shows them a hanging body; Okonkwo has killed himself, and, as a suicide, he has offended the Earth and cannot be buried by his clan. (Durkheim had traced the evolution of suicide from a private decision to a moral crime evoking social abhorrence.) The hero's actions defending tradition have alienated him from that tradition: things indeed have fallen apart. The District Officer finds all this to be fascinating material for the book he is writing on *The Pacification of the Primitive Tribes of the Lower Niger*.

Achebe suggests that anomie can persist over generations, perpetuated both by institutions and by collective memories. In this respect his view is similar to that of Jeffrey Alexander and Ron Eyerman in their analyses of "cultural trauma," which occurs "when members of a collectivity feel they have been subjected to a horrendous event that leaves indelible marks about their group consciousness, marking their memories forever and changing their future identity in fundamental and irrevocable ways" (Alexander et al. 2004:1).[5] Thus Achebe's fiction traces anomie through the colonial period (*Things Fall Apart*, *Arrow of God*), late colonial period (*No Longer at Ease*), the immediate post-colonial period (*A Man of the People*), and the independent African state decades later (*Anthills of the Savannah*).

In *No Longer at Ease*, after two generations have passed Nwoye's son Obi Okonkwo, a classic torn-between-two-worlds figure, faces the conflicting demands and rules of the old and the new. Obi has been educated in England through support from Umuofia and returns to Lagos to take a prestigious civil service position with the scholarship board. Convinced that scholarships should be awarded based on merit, not nepotism or cash, he turns away from bribery. Falling in love with Clara, a fellow Igbo, Obi looks forward to a good life and career. But problems mount. Clara is *osu*, a member of a caste tainted by slavery, and Obi's family back in Umuofia opposes the marriage. Neither the modern, Western rules about individual choice in marriage nor the traditional Igbo rules about avoiding marriage with an osu can prevail, and Obi's vacillation poisons the relationship.

At the same time Obi is beset with financial worries—he must pay back his debt to the Umuofia Progressive Union, assist his relatives, and maintain a lifestyle appropriate to a rising member of the urban elite—while at the office he faces the colonizers' contempt for educated Africans. Eventually he succumbs to monetary and sexual bribery. At his trial for corruption, Obi breaks down in tears when the judge says, "I cannot understand how a young man of your education and brilliant promise could have done this." The judge had apparently never heard of anomie.

Just as Durkheim searched for what might replicate the collective conscience formerly perpetuated through religious belief, so Achebe asks what might offset anomie. Ultimately he is more consistent in his answer than Durkheim was. Achebe suggests throughout his work that storytelling itself can provide the needed orientation.[6] Moreover he increasingly seems to conclude that it is women who will and must pass on the guiding stories.

In *Things Fall Apart* the hyper masculine Okonkwo despises the animal stories that mothers tell their children at night, and he makes a point of introducing Nwoye and Ikemefuna to some appropriately male stories of violence and war. Nwoye secretly prefers the women's stories about the tortoise and other canny animals that prevail through means other than their strength, and Ikemefuna delights everyone with his "endless stock of folk tales."

One way of seeing the anomie of *Things Fall Apart* and *No Longer at Ease* is that the existing stories—the accounts of war and heroism, the things the oracle says, about the relationships between villages, genders, generations, and castes, the animal and folk tales—no longer suit the changed circumstances, while the new stories—about meritocracy, Christianity, Western individualism—cannot maintain the traditional social relationships. In the bitter irony that ends *Things Fall Apart*, it is the District Officer who will tell the tale of Okonkwo. Perhaps not so bitter after all, however, because of course it is Achebe himself who tells and controls the story.

Achebe makes the potential for storytellers to guide a fallen-apart world even more explicit in his novel of independent Africa, *Anthills of the Savannah*. Here the male protagonists are professional communicators—Chris the Minister of Information under an increasingly despotic regime and Ikem the radical editor—whose stories are unable to stem the tide of disaster. Both end up dead, as does the head of state, but the women and children remain, bearing witness like the "anthills surviving to tell the new grass of the savannah about last year's brushfires" (p. 28).

Beatrice, the female protagonist who has regretted not knowing traditional African stories, survives at the center of a group of witnesses who will pass on their stories as both documentary and creation. The group itself, very mixed—a student radical, a taxi driver, a military officer, a servant—has gathered in Beatrice's home to name a baby, Ikem's child by his illiterate girlfriend. They give the little girl a male name that means, "May the path never close." Achebe seems to be suggesting a future where new and diverse social participants mingle their voices to provide the new stories, a never-closing path.

Both Durkhiem and Achebe have understood the devastation that anomie brings. Both have looked for new schemas, new guides, to act as the structural equivalent of the shared beliefs and traditions that Yeats, another storyteller, had called "the old dispensation" with which modern people were "no longer at ease." It is not surprising that an artist like Achebe would see the expression of social experience through stories as a solution to anomie. A social scientist like Durkheim was more inclined toward envisioning an organic solidarity produced by the advanced division of labor or, later, perhaps some sort of professional associations.

Both thinkers have sought what holds society together in those conditions of trauma and unpredictability that characterize the modern condition. The two shared a similar analysis of the problem, while offering different solutions. Achebe's achievement is to locate the classic problem of anomie in a continent that has been terribly neglected by sociologists and to put flesh—African flesh—on its contours and consequences. That is what storytellers do.

## NOTES

1. Achebe's first book was *Things Fall Apart* in 1958; his most recent is *The Education of a British-Protected Child* in 2009.

2. Nigerian novelists almost uniformly describe their work as "bearing witness." For a discussion of Nigerian novelists' sense of their social responsibilities, see Griswold (2000). The present article draws on this book.

3. William Butler Yeats, "The Second Coming."

4. Achebe's novels, the subject of this essay, are *Things Fall Apart* (1958), *No Longer at Ease* (1960), *Arrow of God* (1966), *A Man of the People* (1967), and *Anthills of the Savannah* (1987). A prolific writer, he has also published volumes of essays, poetry, and short stories, and he has written books for children.

5. See also Eyerman (2002).

6. Sociologists have recently been paying more attention to the role that storytelling plays in social cohesion and change. One of the best examples is Francesca Polletta's 2006 book, *It Was Like a Fever: Storytelling in Protest and Politics*.

# PART II

# Sociological Concepts

# CHAPTER 11

# Ernst Cassirer: Science, Symbols, and Logics

*John W. Mohr*

Ernst Cassirer (1874–1945) was a prominent German philosopher, intellectual historian, and one of the first modern, systematic theorists of cultural studies. Although he sometimes addressed political and sociological topics, his influence on contemporary sociological theory is largely indirect. Cassirer is mainly important to sociology because of the position he occupied in the German intellectual field at a critical historical juncture, the way he addressed the research problems at hand, and the influence he had on a subsequent generation of scholars who went on to create their own influential theoretical programs in the cultural and social sciences.

Three of Cassirer's ideas are particularly relevant to the concerns of sociologists: his distinction between substantialism and relationalism (as developed in his writings on science), his conceptualization of cultural analysis (as worked out within his various studies of cultural fields), and his approach to understanding institutional logics as the deep structures that order symbolic systems that are interlinked together into articulated wholes (as expressed in his efforts to construct a general philosophy of symbolic forms).[1]

## CASSIRER'S LIFE

Cassirer was born in 1874 into a prominent Jewish family in Breslau, Germany. As a student at the University of Berlin in 1893, he began attending Georg Simmel's lectures on Kant. Simmel, "still a young privatdozent who delivered his lectures before a small but very interested and attentive audience" (Cassirer 1943:222), encouraged Cassirer to read the work of Hermann Cohen, founder of the Marburg School of Neo-Kantianism and, not insignificantly, "the first Jewish intellectual to hold a professorship in Germany" (Friedman 2000:4). "Simmel emphasized how much he himself owed to the study of Cohen's books, but he immediately added that those books, in spite of their real sagacity and profundity, suffered from a very grave defect. They were written, he said, in such an obscure style that as yet there was probably no one who had succeeded in deciphering them" (p. 222).

Cassirer embraced this challenge and moved to Marburg to study with Cohen. Gawronsky (1949) reports that Cassirer was an extraordinary student—he read prodigiously, had a photographic memory, was a relentless workaholic, and possessed an unusual facility with languages. For his dissertation, Cassirer examined the relationship between the Kantian theory of knowledge and the modern natural sciences. In a style that would go on to characterize all of his future work, Cassirer approached the problem through the lens of intellectual history. His project had two parts. The first (on Descartes) he submitted for his doctorate in 1899, and the second (on Leibniz) Cassirer entered into the Berlin Academy competition in 1901 (which he won). The two parts were published (together) in 1902 as a general treatise on Leibniz's philosophy of science.

In spite of this acclaim and the obvious brilliance of his work, faculty employment was scarce, especially for Jewish scholars, and so Cassirer lived for many years as an independent intellectual in Berlin. During this period he too became a privatdozent at the University of Berlin in 1906, thanks to the personal intervention of Dilthey. He published a number of important texts that made him quite famous, and finally in 1919 he was offered a professorship from the newly founded University of Hamburg.

In the next phase of his career Cassirer flourished. He wrote all three volumes of his signature work, *The Philosophy of Symbolic Forms* (1923, 1925, 1928), and, along with Heidegger, he came to be regarded as one of "the two leading philosophers in Germany" (Friedman 2000:1). He was made rector of his university in 1929 ("the first Jew to hold such a position in Germany," [p. 4]), but when Hitler came to power in 1933, Cassirer quickly left Germany. He taught at Oxford and the University of Goeteborg, and in 1941 he came to the United States as visiting Professor at Yale, then Columbia. He died of a heart attack in New York City in 1945, three weeks before the allied victory in Europe.

## SUBSTANTIALISM OR RELATIONALISM? HOW TO THEORIZE A SCIENCE OF THE SOCIAL

Many sociologists will recognize Cassirer's name from the writings of Pierre Bourdieu, who cited him frequently, most often with reference to Cassirer's distinction between *substantialism* and *relationalism*. On the first page of *Practical Reason*, a late-career collection of essays geared to show "what I believe to be most essential in my work" (1998:vii), Bourdieu says that there are really just two fundamental qualities that define his approach, a specific philosophy of action (articulated in his inter-related suite of concepts—field, habitus, capital, etc.) and a particular philosophy of science "that one could call *relational* in that it accords primacy to relations" (p. vii).

Bourdieu explains, "I refer here . . . to the opposition suggested by Ernst Cassirer between 'substantial concepts' and 'functional or relational concepts' " (p. 3). Bourdieu describes relationalism as the philosophical style of the modern natural sciences and, also, as the grounding for his own (distinctive) research program. He says:

> this philosophy is only rarely brought into play in the social sciences, undoubtedly because it is very directly opposed to the conventions of ordinary (or semi-scholarly) thought about the social world, which is more readily devoted to substantial "realities" such as individuals and groups than to the *objective relations* which one cannot show, but which must be captured, constructed, and validated through scientific work. (1998:vii)

So, Bourdieu sees himself as following Cassirer, trying to create a relational science of the social which is necessary to penetrate beneath the surface appearance of things, to move to a deeper level of understanding, down to "*the objective relations*" that serve as "*the structuring structures*" of the social world. But what exactly is relationalism? Is it different than structuralism? And what does it gain us? Why does Bourdieu think that we need it? Here, it is useful to recall Cassirer.

In his classic text, *Substance and Function* (1910), Cassirer introduced the distinction between substantialism and relationalism as two different modes of scientific thinking. Substantialism is the more traditional of the two. It begins with Aristotle, but variations lived on in scientific theories for another 2,000 years. Over all that time, "the actual center of gravity of the system had not changed" (p. 4). Like Foucault, Cassirer does not focus on the *content* of specific theories so much as the logical *form*, according to which statements within those theories come to be perceived as rational.

For Cassirer there are deep levels of scientific discourse—he calls them logics—that shape how scientific concepts are assembled. These core logics remain stable, even as different theories come and go.[2]

Cassirer describes the logic of substantialism by noting that it presumes abstraction occurs in the sorting of things, according to common features, into taxonomic hierarchies, as species and genus. "Just as we form the concept of a tree by selecting from the totality of oaks, beaches and birch trees, the group of common properties, so, in exactly the same way, we form the concept of a plane rectangular figure by isolating the common properties which are found in the square, the right angle, rhomboid" (p. 5). As a logic for analysis, this appears to have merit since "[i]ts presuppositions are simple and clear; and they agree so largely with the . . . ordinary view of the world . . . that they seem to offer no foothold for criticism" (p. 4).

Yet, this logic is deeply flawed. First, there is the basic Kantian objection that one cannot make judgments of similarity and difference without preexisting (a priori) understanding of the (synthesizing) categories themselves. "Without a process of arranging in series . . . the consciousness of their generic connection . . . could never arise" (p. 15). Second, it is not just bad logic, it is also bad science. In what amounts to a major innovation in science studies, Cassirer describes how a core logic grips those who operate within it by creating specific styles of knowledge. In this case, substantialism generates frames of understanding that are essentialist, that take *things* as given in their immediate appearances, and produce commitments to science as the quest for the elemental substances from which the things of the world are fashioned.

Cassirer describes many philosophical problems with this logic, but he also points to the profound implication that other possible conceptualizations are thereby foreclosed. For example, "Quantity and quality, space and time determinations, do not exist in and for themselves, but merely as properties of absolute realities . . ." (p. 8).[3]

Building on his earlier scholarship in the history of science, Cassirer traces the multiple origins of an alternate logic, one modeled on mathematical abstraction itself, which he identifies as emerging among a few scientists, starting in the Renaissance, when they refuse conventional questions (generated by substantialist logic). "Galileo avoided the question as to the cause of weight" (p. 139). Robert Mayer, "the discoverer of the fundamental law of modern natural science . . . [declined] . . . [t]he question as to how heat arises from diminishing motion or how heat is again changed into motion . . ." (p. 139). In this new logic ". . . the world of sensible things . . . is not so much reproduced as transformed and supplanted by an order of another sort" (p. 14). First, that order is defined by mathematical functions: "Fixed properties are replaced by universal rules that permit us to survey a total series of possible determinations at a single glance" (pp. 22–23).

In the most modern of sciences, however, even standard mathematical functions are too constraining (too essentialist), and so a new logic emerges in science that is based on pure relationality. Here, Cassirer highlights the work of Cantor and others who laid the foundations for modern topology theory (a branch of mathematics concerned with the formal analysis of relational systems). He describes similar developments elsewhere, in Chemistry: "With Mendeleyev's discovery of the periodic table, the elements that had previously comprised a mere conjunction or heap suddenly become visible as an ordered series . . . with further advances in sub-atomic physics, it becomes possible intellectually to *construct* the elements out of yet more basic particles. The elements have now lost every trace of particularity; they are revealed to be nothing more than resting–points in a continuous process of transformation" (Skidelsky 2008:368). Even Einstein's "special theory of relativity is such that its advantage over other explanations, such as Lorentz's hypothesis of contraction, is based not so much on its empirical material as on its pure logical form, not so much on its physical as on its general systematic value" (Cassirer 1953:354).[4]

About the time that *Substance and Function* was first published (1910), Kurt Lewin was a graduate psychology student at the University of Berlin. He was another young, brilliant, soon-to-be underemployed Jewish intellectual. He began attending Cassirer's lectures on the philosophy of science, which left an indelible impression on him and strongly influenced his subsequent work. After being wounded in the war, Lewin completed his Ph.D. under Stumpf, and, like Cassirer, left Germany in 1933. Unlike Cassirer, however, Lewin went to the United States almost immediately, where he became a famous, iconoclastic leader in the field of American social psychology.

Lewin arrived just as quantitative styles of analysis were firmly taking root in American social sciences (Platt 1996). He was skeptical of much that he saw. Though he was fiercely committed to developing a scientific psychology, he was convinced that his own discipline was hopelessly locked into susbtantialist styles of thinking (Lewin 1935), measuring "thing-concepts," which, often as not, end up producing "a well polished container of nothing" (Lewin 1949:272).[5] Recalling Cassirer's discussion of the history of physics and chemistry, Lewin notes that "[s]ome of the present-day theoretical problems in psychology show great methodological similarities to these controversies although they are historically separated by centuries" (1951:30).

Citing Cassirer, Lewin declares: it is "necessary to free oneself from the scientific prejudices typical of a given developmental stage" (Lewin 1951:189) which explains why Lewin developed his own unique system for formalizing social psychology based on a purely relational logic. He borrowed Einstein's notion of "field space" (the "totality of coexisting facts, which are conceived of as mutually interdependent," p. 240), and mathematics from modern topology theory to create a measurement system he called "hodological space." Here "the person and the psychological environment as it exists for him" (p. 57) are measured such that each element is defined relationally vis-à-vis every other, without reference to metric extension or dimensional orientation, an approach that allowed Lewin to bring formal mathematics to bear on qualitative phenomena.

Lewin says "That correct qualitative analysis is a prerequisite for adequate quantitative treatment is well recognized in psychological statistics. What seems less clear is that the qualitative differences themselves can and should be approached mathematically" (p. 31). Again, Lewin references Cassirer as one who "points out again and again that mathematization is not identical with quantification. Mathematics handles quantity and quality" (pp. 30–31).

Still, Lewin's legacy ended up not unlike Cassirer's. Lewin's own project on *hodological* measurement space quickly disappeared after his death while his indirect influence was strong and widespread. Many of Lewin's students went on to become leaders in social science, including some, like Dorwin Cartwright, who worked to decouple Lewin's measurement ideas from the more complex *hodological* measurement system, and switched it over to a young branch of mathematics known as "graph theory," thus channeling Cassirer's formulation of relationalism into some of the first mathematically precise approaches to the analysis of social networks (Mohr, forthcoming).

And then there is Bourdieu (2007). Originally trained as a philosopher, his experiences during the Algerian War led him to shift to sociology. Like Lewin, Bourdieu was dismayed by what he found in the quantification practices of his newly adopted disciplinary home, and thus Lewin's work had a natural appeal to Bourdieu, especially his innovations in the use of formal methods to analyze qualitative phenomena, his conception of field theory, and his commitment to Cassirer's relationalism. All of these ideas found full expression in Bourdieu's own project—in his conceptualization of social fields, his theories of capital, even his use of formal methodologies (Breiger 2000). Yet in spite of these appreciations, Bourdieu was ultimately quite critical of Cassirer's work, especially his studies of culture.

## FROM "THE CRITIQUE OF PURE REASON" TO "THE PHILOSOPHY OF SYMBOLIC FORMS"

The work on science was just a beginning for Cassirer. By the time he had taken up his professorship at Hamburg, he had survived the World War I (reading foreign newspapers for the German government), and like many of his generation he saw old things in new ways. For Cassirer, this meant questioning longstanding tenets of "Enlightenment" philosophy, suggesting that modern society would increasingly progress as it came to more fully embrace scientific rationality and (as Kantian theory had emphasized) its corresponding system of rational moral principles.[6]

Instead, Cassirer came to see that there were other discursive systems (beyond science) that had profound impacts on the trajectories of the social world, that these alternative "symbolic forms" also had logics and that would also be amenable to the same style of "critical" philosophical investigation that he had applied successfully in his studies of science. Thus, Cassirer declares "[m]an lives in a symbolic universe. Language, math, art, and religion are parts of this universe. They are the varied threads which weave the symbolic net, the tangled web of human experience" (1944:25).[7] Verene explains that in Cassirer's later work, philosophy itself makes a turn and for the first time "the critique of reason becomes the critique of culture" (2000:vii).

Cassirer begins conducting a systematic interrogation of symbol systems that is interpretive, relational, and focused on unpacking the varied logics of symbolization. As such, his project "anticipates remarkably most of the insights and concerns of structuralism. The symbolic forms—language, math, religion, art, and science—represent for Cassirer the different modes in which human thought expresses the world to itself . . ." (Caws 1988:16). Or, as Ricoeur (1970) says, "Let us do justice to Cassirer: he was the first to have posed the problem of the reconstruction of language." Indeed, there are many indications that Cassirer's work was known to some of the early leaders in structuralist theory (Steiner 1984; Bakhtin1981; Merleu-Ponty 1998).

But this then raises a new question. Why has Cassirer been so little noticed in the history of structuralism? Noting Cassirer's preference for the term "symbol" rather than "sign," Caws suggests that "[h]ad it not been, in fact, for an unfortunate terminological choice, Ernst Cassirer would certainly now be recognized as the founder of philosophical structuralism" (1988:16). Of course, as Caws well understands, the matter is complex. Cassirer's formal study of symbols was not the same as Saussure's formal study of signs.

A key difference was that Saussure and the structural linguists who followed him were social scientists, working with data. Cassirer was a philosopher, working with concepts. Thus, even though he devoted the entire first volume of his

*Philosophy of Symbolic Forms* to the topic of language, his concerns lay more with the philosophy of language than with the systematic workings of its grammar. In contrast, one of the great advantages of the Saussureian project is its widespread enactment in social scientific practice and the corresponding development of various methodological tools and research traditions. As Bourdieu points out, this fills in what was missing in Cassirer, "Structural analysis constitutes the methodological instrument which enables the neo-Kantian ambition of grasping the specific logic of each of the 'symbolic forms' to be realized" (1991:164).

There are other complaints as well. Ricouer (1970) thinks that Cassirer made a critical error by adopting an overly inclusive definition of symbol, "as the general function of mediation by which the mind or consciousness constructs all its universes of perception and discourse" (p. 10). He contends that Cassirer thereby surrenders a key component of a proper hermeneutic analysis of symbolization, "the distinction between univocal and plurivocal expressions. It is this distinction that creates the hermeneutic problem" (p. 11). Beyond this is a more general complaint that all of these traditions, semiotics included, are of limited utility if they are not well grounded in an understanding of the material practices of agents negotiating everyday life. Thus, Bourdieu criticizes the "idealist illusion which consists in treating ideological productions as self-sufficient, self-created totalities amenable to a pure and purely internal analysis (semiology)" (1991:169).

Though Cassirer's analysis took him down a different path from mainstream structuralism, there are some unique advantages to Cassirer's approach. For one thing, precisely because he was thinking philosophically, there is a breadth and conceptual inclusiveness to Cassirer's studies that give them an extraordinarily broad utility. "Cassirer approaches each area of culture in the manner of Kantian critique, analyzing the form of each in terms of space, time, number, causality, object, and so on" (Verene 2000:viii). In Cassirer's schema, "each area of culture, whether it is a myth, language, or science, has its own inner form. Each has its own 'tonality' in an overall harmony of forms that make up human culture as a whole" (p. viii). Thus, one of the merits of Cassirer's work is that it was equally inspirational to Panofsky (1991 [1927]), who applied it to the history of architecture, as it was to Suzanne Langer (1957), who used it to analyze music and the arts.

Langer argued that the unique symbolic form of music enabled it to capture and express the "forms of feelings" that cannot be expressed linguistically. "The real power of music lies in the fact that it can be 'true' to the life of feeling in a way that language cannot; for its significant forms have that *ambivalence* of content which words cannot have" (Langer 1957:243). Langer writes, "It was Cassirer—though he never regarded himself as an aesthetician—who hewed the keystone of the structure, in his broad and disinterested study of symbolic forms; and I, for my part, would put that stone in place, to join and sustain what so far we have built" (1953:410).

## CONCLUSION: FORM, CONTENT, AND LOGIC

Cassirer's thought had a variety of impacts on sociology. First, as a philosopher of science Cassirer provided a valuable intellectual bridge between the natural and the social sciences. Relational thinking in the former was thus made relevant and accessible to social scientists like Lewin and Bourdieu. Second, as a theorist of culture, Cassirer developed a philosophical foundation for modern theories of structuralism that was ahead of its time. Other structuralisms superceded his, but Cassirer's own distinctive program of symbolic analysis has inspired a number of creative investigations (by Langer and others) who have produced what we might now describe as a varied phenomenology of cultural fields.

There is, of course, much more that could be said, including a fuller discussion of the relationship between Cassirer and contemporary research programs on cultural and institutional logics (Friedland 2009). Not only does Cassirer have much to say about how to analyze a cultural logic, he also explicitly focused on the problem of assessing the linkages that connect different symbolic forms together. "The task of the philosophy of culture, for Cassirer, is to understand and articulate a sense of the whole while preserving the integrity of each symbolic form. Cassirer understood this unity as functional so that all areas of culture, all 'symbolic forms,' stand in a dynamic relation to each other" (Verene 2000:viii).

In this the logical implications of modern mathematics meet up with the intellectual conundrums of Neo-Kantian philosophy. Like his mentors—from Simmel to Cohen, his colleagues in Gestalt psychology, and the intellectual lineages that he draws upon—from Hegel, to Kant, to Leibniz, and beyond, Cassirer becomes focused on the relations between parts, wholes, and the articulations that link them together. Cassirer says, "we first have true knowledge when we survey the total movement of the process as a purposively ordered whole. We must understand how one element demands another; how all the threads are mutually interwoven finally into one web, to form a single order of the phenomena of nature" (1953:133).[8]

## NOTES

1. I have relied extensively on the many excellent Cassirer commentaries and collections (especially): Schilpp (1949), Verene (1966, 2008), Krois (1987), Friedman (2000), Lofts (2000), Bayer (2001), Skidelsky (2008), and Barash (2008).

2. Compare with Foucault's (1970) description of an episteme as "the apparatus which permits . . . separating out from among all the statements which are possible those that will be acceptable within . . . a field of scientificity, and . . . (thus) . . . what may (or) may not be characterized as scientific" (1980:197). Whether Foucault (the classic post-modernist) was at all influenced by Cassirer (the last great neo-Kantian) is hard to tell. It is interesting though to recall that Foucault (2008) began his career as a Kant specialist.

3. There are many resonances here to Bachelard and Kuhn, for example, not to mention Simmel, Lukács, and Weber. These connections are beyond the scope of this essay.

4. Cassirer was probably unaware of Einstein's work (which would have just been published) when he was writing *Substance and Function*, but he did follow up with a small book on Einstein that was then included as a supplement to the 1923 (and subsequent) English editions.

5. Lewin (1935) applied Cassirer's ideas about the two styles of scientific logic (The Aristotelian and The Galoliean) to explain the state of social psychology.

6. Skidelsky (2008) explains the linkage between Kantian theories of moral reason (and inclusiveness), the political situations of the Jewish intellectuals who rallied behind Cohen's banner at the Marburg School, and the philosophical program that defined this branch of neo-Kantian thought.

7. In his last book, *The Myth of the State* (1946), Cassirer argues that fascism was an expression of the return to mythic forms of culture achieving dominance in the logic of the state.

8. Recent scholarship has served to highlight the ways in which Cassirer was more dialectical than Bourdieu's reading of him (as an unrepentant cognitivist) would suggest. In this respect it is worth noting that there is a whole new part of Cassirer's work that is beginning to come to light, as the posthumously published fourth volume of *The Philosophy of Symbolic Forms* (1996) has now begun to attract the attention of scholars (Bayer 2001; Verene 2008). Here the most interesting news is Cassirer's apparent turn in these last works toward developing a more elaborate theory of practice and to a heightened sense of the interconnections of mind and body, logic and institution.

# CHAPTER 12

# Cicero: Persons and Positions

*Lars Udehn*

Marcus Tullius Cicero (106–43 BC) is not known to posterity as a really great philosopher, at least not as an original one. He is known above all as a great Roman orator and statesman with an interest in social philosophy. His writings on this subject are, according to common opinion today, made up of summaries and commentaries on the philosophical systems most popular in his day: Platonism, Aristotelianism, Epicureanism, and Stoicism, all of them originating in Greece. Cicero helped introduce these philosophies to the Roman public and, in one case, to the world. Cicero is still a main source of knowledge about early stoicism.

It was not always like this. In the Renaissance and in the Enlightenment, in particular, Cicero was immensely popular, and it has been said that his work *On Duties* is "perhaps the most influential book in the Western tradition of political philosophy" (Nussbaum 2004:178). Among his admirers are Voltaire, Montesquieu, and Rousseau, but in particular Locke, Hume, Smith, and Burke. This says something about Cicero's ideological leanings, which might be described as a mix of "liberalism" and "conservatism" in more recent vocabulary.

In the eighteenth century we witness a fall from grace, and the "final blow to the prestige of Cicero" came from the German historian Theodor Mommsen (Wood 1988:7; Morford 2002:95) who, by the way, was a friend of Max Weber's family and his mentor in academia. A consequence of this development is that Cicero exerted little influence on sociology.

In their great work on the history of social thought Becker and Barnes (1978:202–211) dismiss Cicero as an eclectic compilator of the work of other philosophers. I believe that this is to belittle Cicero's contribution to social theory. Even if you find little that is entirely new in his writings, he did much to systematize, criticize, and improve upon earlier ideas. The problem is that Cicero was influenced by earlier philosophers, whose writings are lost, and we do not really know to what extent Cicero is merely repeating the ideas of those philosophers and to what extent he adds something of his own to these ideas. This makes it difficult to assess the contribution of Cicero to social thought (Sharples 2009). This problem is perhaps most acute in the case of *On Duties* (*De Office*), which is based on the teaching of the Stoic philosopher Panaetius.

Even so, it has also been suggested in more recent writings on ancient philosophy that Cicero had some important ideas entirely his own (Wood 1988:11–13; Long 2006:331f.). The influence of Cicero's ideas on Locke and Smith might lead the reader to suspect that Cicero's main contribution was to rational choice theories of the state and of the market, but this is not the case. As I intend to show in this chapter, Cicero's theories of individuals in society are sociological through and through.

## SELF-LOVE, SOCIALITY, AND RATIONALITY

In the philosophical writings of Cicero we find discussions about many of the basic issues in the history of social thought; about the nature of the human individual, of society, and of the relation between the two. Some of these issues have been hotly debated in recent social science, and especially in the confrontation between the economic and sociological approaches to life in society. In sociology the main positions in this controversy have recurred in the debate about rational choice. At the heart of the matter lie questions about the role of self-interest, social norms, and rationality in the explanation of cooperation and social order.

Cicero's view of individuals and society is based on the Stoic doctrine of natural law, which says that human beings must live according to nature, both their own human nature and the nature of society and universe. Cicero takes his point of departure in the Stoic assumption that human beings have an innate tendency to preserve and love their own selves and, by extension, the things they appropriate for their own needs (*Duties*, p. 6; *On Moral Ends*, pp. 69–72,125ff.). Cicero was a defender of private property, and Long (2006:332) sees him as providing an ideology for capitalism long before the emergence of this economic system. More important for my purposes is the fact that Cicero saw self-interest as an important part of human nature.

Equally important, however, is the sociality of human beings. To be human is to live in society (*On the Commonwealth*, p. 18). Cicero's argument is not, however, that we become human by living in society. It is the other way around: "Human nature is so constituted as to have an innately civic or social character—what the Greeks call *politikon*" (*Moral Ends*, p. 140). We are gregarious animals, endowed with something like a herding instinct. According to Cicero, "we are born to join together and to associate with one another and to join natural communities" (*Moral Ends*, p. 86).

The first manifestation of this inborn sociality is marriage and the love of human beings for their offspring (*Moral Ends*, p. 96; *Duties*, pp. 6, 23). Beyond that, feelings of community extend, first of all, to family and more distant kin. No less important, and stronger than family ties, is the community of feeling between friends (*Duties*, p. 22; *On Friendship*, p. 186ff.). Besides family and friends, there are spatially organized human fellowships, such as households, neighbourhoods, cities, countries, and, finally, humankind as a whole. "Beginning with the bonds of affection between family and friends, we are prompted to move gradually further out and associate ourselves firstly with our fellow citizens and then with every person on earth" (*Moral Ends*, p. 42; see also *Commonwealth*, p. 10, *On the Laws*, p. 116ff., 127, and *Duties*, p. 21f., 57, 110). This cosmopolitanism is one of the most well-known ideas that Cicero derived from the Stoics.

The picture Cicero is painting of human fellowships forming a pattern of ever widening, concentric circles around themselves has been reproduced many times in the history of social thought. A main concern of Cicero is the political commonwealth, and his objective is to argue that it is, or should be, a community rather than an association. This means that he is critical of the theory of the social contract defended in Antiquity by the Sophists and the Epicureans.

Even though he sometimes says that the commonwealth is the result of mutual agreement, he did not accept Epicurus's, and later Hobbes's, depiction of the state of nature as a war of each against all. The first cause of the commonwealth is sociality (*Commonwealth*, p. 18; *Duties*, p. 61). Nor did Cicero accept the social contract as an historical fact. The Roman commonwealth, at least, is the result of a long evolution, not of decision-making (*Government*, p. 33ff.). As such it is based on tradition rather than on contract (*Duties*, pp. 23f., 30f.). This is the conservative element in Cicero's thinking.

For Cicero, there is a potential, but not a necessary, conflict between self-love and sociality. One reason for this, I believe, is that Cicero conceives of utilities as interdependent. We share the happiness of family and friends. Cicero's term is "community of feeling" (see *Friendship*, p. 216, passim). Another reason is that there are "public goods" such that many individuals may enjoy the benefits without a loss to any one of them. Cicero did not use the term, of course, but he was familiar with the idea: "A man who kindly shows the path to someone who is lost lights another's light, so to speak, from his own. For his own shines no less because he has lit another's."[1] Cicero goes on:

"With this one instance, he advises us that if any assistance can be provided without detriment to oneself, it should be given even to strangers" (*Duties*, p. 22).

A third reason is that sociality, in the form of morality, is really compatible with interest. Cicero makes an implicit distinction between enlightened and narrow self-interest, and this is where rationality comes in. Reason tells us that what is moral, or "honorable," is always beneficial (*Duties*, Book III), but unfortunately reason is fallible. The source of all our problems is that people often succumb to their myopic passions for power, glory, and riches. The result is both individual unhappiness and social disorder. The first point is argued at length in *On Moral Ends*, and the second point is argued in *On Government* and *On Duties*.

Cicero's main target is the hedonism of Epicurus, which is depicted, right or wrong, as implying an assumption of narrow self-interest focused on sensual pleasure.[2] The clash with the economic approach is evident already in Cicero's definition of morality: "By 'moral', then, I mean that which can justly be esteemed on its own account, independently of any utility, and of any reward or profit that may accrue" (*Moral Ends*, p. 41).

It may be noticed that Cicero is perfectly familiar with the modern idea of lexicographic preferences (see Sen 1979). Good people do not compare what is honorable with what is beneficial and always choose the former before the latter (*Duties*, p. 106f.). Nor are they deterred from doing wrong by any fear of sanctions (*Moral Ends*, p. 50; *Laws*, p. 119ff.). Good people are unaffected by whether they are witnessed or not (*Moral Ends*, p. 43f.) and refrain from doing wrong even in the dark (*Duties*, p. 113f.).

Since Cicero's interest is in ethics, most of his arguments are normative, but they are often backed up by empirical observations. This is what you would expect by an argument from natural law. Among the examples Cicero gives of non-selfish behavior are the love and care parents give their children (*Duties*, p. 110), the gifts and kind services bestowed on our friends (*Moral Ends*, pp. 52ff., 87f.), and heroic acts where people risk their lives for higher ends (p. 11, 83): "do brave soldiers go into battle to spill blood for their country only when a hedonistic calculation is in its favour, or is it rather a passionate spirit that drives them on?" (p. 46) Cicero did not hesitate about the answer.

The main bulk of Cicero's philosophical writings is devoted to demonstrating the fundamental importance of sociality, as an ideal and as a fact. This does not mean that he was blind to the fact that people are also motivated by narrow self-interest. On the contrary, it was because he saw the widespread passion for power, glory, and riches as a threat to Roman society that he puts so much emphasis on sociality (cf. Long 2006:313–333). Cicero was clearly aware that narrow self-interest may give rise to a collective action problem.

> When it is necessary to make a choice among three possibilities, to do injury and not receive it, both to do it and receive it, or neither, the best is to act without penalty if you can, the second best is neither to do nor to receive injury, and far the worst is always to be fighting in the arena both giving and receiving injuries. Therefore those who can achieve the first. (*Commonwealth*, p. 66)

The situation described by Cicero has a clear game theoretic structure. One alternative is missing, however; that of the sucker: not to do, but to suffer injustice. Because of this missing element, we cannot tell for sure if the situation, described by Cicero, is a prisoner's dilemma or a game of chicken, but both games pose a threat to social order.

The main message of Cicero's philosophy was that law and morality is necessary for social order and that narrow self-interest destroys it (*Government*, p. 70; *On Friendship*, p. 195). Like Durkheim, Cicero conceived of society as a moral order, and also like Durkheim he maintained that the source of the malady is unlimited desires (*Duties*, p. 11), or anomie. It may be doubted, of course, whether the diagnosis is correct, or not, but it is nevertheless interesting to find so many ideas in modern social science anticipated in the first century BC. And there are more.

## EXCHANGE AND SOCIAL CAPITAL

Cicero did not pay much attention to economic exchange, but what he had to say about it is of some interest to sociologists because of the importance he attached to justice and trust. To maintain justice is the chief task of government, and an important part of that task is to protect private property (*Duties*, pp. 9, 77). To maintain trust is the task of all human beings.

Like Adam Smith, Cicero argues that the "exchange of services" contributes to the common good, but he also argues that it helps maintain faith and trust (p. 10). Trust is strongest between friends (*Friendship*, p. 210), but it is needed also in business and other transactions. Trust is necessary for the maintenance of social order, and without it society will break down. "For there is nothing that holds together a political community more powerfully than good faith; and that cannot exist unless the paying of debts is enforced" (p. 97; see also pp. 75, 108, 123ff.).

Like Durkheim (1964:200–219) Cicero clearly realized that there is a social element in all economic exchange, and that element spells not just law, but morality, or virtue. On the other hand, there seems to be an economic element in all social exchange. Cicero discusses two types of social exchange: between patron and client and between friends. Of these Cicero pays most attention to the latter.

Since the state apparatus was poorly developed in the Roman republic, people had to rely on their social networks. Rome was a network society. In politics, there were no parties in the modern sense, but networks and alliances engaged in an often fierce competition for power (Earl 1967: Ch. 1). The republic was run by a small elite of aristocrats, usually, if not always, with the support of common people. The relationship between the powerful and the less powerful was that between patron and client, engaged in an exchange of "kind" and "dutiful services" (*Duties*, p. 89ff.).

It has been suggested that Cicero's relative neglect of patronage is due to his lack of interest in the less fortunate (Griffin and Atkins 1991:xxiv). Another possible explanation is his fear that patronage might degenerate into populism and end in mob rule and/or tyranny. According to Cicero, this is what happened when Caesar seized power (*Duties*, pp. 19f., 33f., 70ff.; see also Long 2006:318–326).

Friendship is, for Cicero, the most precious thing and a favorite topic in his writings. What strikes a modern reader as somewhat odd, perhaps, is the importance he attaches to the elements of utility and exchange in relations between friends (*Friendship*, pp. 191ff., 203). The benefits from friendship are so great as to "defy description" (p. 188) and those benefits derive, at least in part, from the exchange of services. Cicero goes at great length, however, to deny that exchange between friends is motivated by mutual utility, a view he ascribes to Epicurus (*Moral Ends*, pp. 23–25; *Friendship*, p. 201). "But surely this giving and receiving constitutes merely one feature and consequence of friendship. As for its origins, do these not, rather, in something more primeval and noble, something emanating more directly from the actual process of nature?" Friendship is based on love, and is by definition free from any calculation of profit (*Moral Ends*, pp. 52–55; *Friendship*, pp. 191ff., 206, 216, 226). According to Cicero, exchange between friends is the exchange of gifts (cf. Mauss 1960) and it is subjected to a norm of reciprocity (see Gouldner 1960).

The basic motive behind exchange between friends is love, or altruism, but there is also an element of duty, or social norms, involved. According to Cicero, we have duties towards our friends (p. 141). It seems as if Cicero makes a distinction between altruism and duties (*Moral Ends*, pp. 125, 127). At least he makes a clear distinction between friendship and virtue (pp. 24, 54f.), and duties derive from virtues. Exchange of dutiful services is not limited to friends, however. "Important also are the common bonds that are created by kindnesses reciprocally given and received, which, provided that they are mutual and gratefully received, bind together those concerned in an unshakeable fellowship" (*Duties*, p. 23).

Cicero's ideas about economic and social exchange, then, have many similarities with the theories of Durkheim and Mauss, but they also have much in common with recent ideas about social capital. There are two main senses of this concept (cf. Portes 1997), and Cicero clearly recognizes both. First, there is social capital as a private good; a network of friends and acquaintances that individuals can use as a resource and a means to achieve their various ends. Second, there is social capital as a collective good; a normative order that generates trust and benefits all.

## PERSONS, POSITIONS, AND ROLES

In sociology it is common to make a distinction between persons and the positions they occupy. To these positions are attached a set of social norms telling people how to behave in the positions they occupy. These normative expectations are called social roles. Cicero had quite a lot to say about persons and the roles they play. The main point of this chapter, however, is that Cicero may have been first to make a clear and explicit distinction between persons and positions. It may be, of course, that Cicero is merely echoing Panaetius, but we do not know the exact views of the latter.

The modern concept of "person" derives from the Latin *persona*, which in Roman Antiquity was used to denote both human individuals and the social roles they play. The original meaning of the term, however, was character mask. More specifically, it denoted the masks actors used in Greek theatre. The Latin *persona*, in its turn, is the equivalent of the Greek word *Prosopon*, which means not only character mask, but the way people appear before one another more generally. This indicates that Erving Goffman's well-known discussion of social roles in *The Presentation of Self in Everyday Life* (1959) is etymologically correct.

It has been argued by Gill (1988:195f.) that Panaetius's theory, as represented by Cicero, anticipates the modern social psychology of George Herbert Mead and Erving Goffman among others. We find in Cicero a self that is constantly engaged in mirroring itself in others, monitoring its own conduct, and planning its own life—but not in a social vacuum. Cicero resembles modern writers "in viewing the person from a strongly social perspective, and in regarding inter-personal relationships as the enactment of a set of largely pre-determined roles." ( p. 95). It may be added that Cicero makes frequent use of the theatre metaphor when writing about social life (see, e.g., *Moral Ends*. p. 72; *Duties*, p. 44f.; *On Old Age*, p. 241).

In *On Duties* Cicero recognizes four different *personae*:[3] First, there is a distinction between our common role as human beings and our unique individuality (p. 42). In addition, there are two more *personae* that are tied to social positions rather than to individuals. The third *persona* is "imposed by some chance and circumstances" (*Duties*, p. 45). Cicero mentions kingdoms, military powers, nobility, political honors, wealth, and influence as well as their opposites. The fourth role is the result of our own decision, and it consists in the kind of career we adopt, such as philosophy, civil law, or oratory.

The first *persona* is based on our common human nature and imposes duties that we have towards all other human beings. It derives from stoic natural law and is the basis of Cicero's cosmopolitanism. Marcel Mauss long ago (1985 [1938]:83f.) drew our attention to the moral individualism of Stoicism, which saw the moral person as endowed with both self-consciousness and conscience. Mauss also recognized the influence of Roman law on the Stoic person. In Roman law the person was seen as a bearer of rights and responsibilities. A. A. Long (2006:335–340) takes his point of departure in Mauss's analysis and goes on to suggest that the Stoics were important forerunners of liberalism. They were first to suggest that human individuals are the owners both of their own beings (self-ownership) and of their property (private property).

The second *persona* is closer to the modern sense of "personality" and includes character traits, such as wit, cunning, dignity, seriousness, craftiness, and humor. It tells us to develop our particular talents and to be true to ourselves. Christopher Gill (1988:177) believes that it is both the most interesting and the most problematic of Cicero's four *personae*. It is most interesting because it deals with personality rather than with personhood (the first *persona*) which was, by far, the most common in ancient ethical theory (p. 170).

The second *persona*, then, would be a forerunner of the modern individualist quest for authenticity. The problem Gill finds in Cicero's treatment, however, is that even individuality becomes too social. It boils down to little more "than that of the individual's actual or potential location in a social grid or class-structure" (p. 171). To develop our talents and be true to ourselves is to participate in social competition and become distinguished members of society (p. 181).

The third *persona* is the social positions individuals occupy and the roles they play in society. There are many such roles, such as husband, father, citizen, and master, but of all roles Cicero pays most attention to the role of public official, and none is more important (see *Duties*, p. 23, 68). As it happens, this was also the role played by Cicero himself. The focus on public life and on public officials was not exactly new. You find it also in Greek philosophy and in the traditional values of Roman society, or its ideology (Earl 1967; Long 2006:307ff.).

The fourth *persona* is "something that proceeds from our own will" (*Duties*, p. 45). As such it implies an autonomous individual making choices between different life courses. More specifically, the fourth *persona* chooses a career among the different positions in the third type of *persona*. This element of voluntarism is common with the second *persona*.

The fourth *persona* is a social position, but it presupposes an individual that chooses this position. Cicero's account of this *persona* and of the second is interesting for a contemporary sociologist since it casts doubts upon one of the most cherished ideas in recent sociology. I have in mind the thesis that late modernity is characterized by a new and more radical form of individualization.

According to Anthony Giddens (1991), the self has become a reflexive project in late modernity. People are supposed to plan their lives, including choice of lifestyle and intimate relations. I do not deny that you may find these phenomena in late modernity. My point is rather that you find it also in Antiquity, as is evident from the writings of Cicero:

> First of all . . . we must decide who and what we wish to be, and what kind of life we want. That deliberation is the most difficult thing of all; for it is as adulthood is approaching, just when his counsel is at its very weakest, that each person decides that the way of leading a life that he most admires should be his own. The result is that he becomes engaged upon a fixed manner and course of life before he is able to judge what might be best. (*Duties*, p. 46)

It might be added that no late modern person could be more reflexive about her or his self than was Cicero, constantly preoccupied as he was by writing his own biography and presenting himself in the most favorable light. It may also be added that Rome was a status society and that Cicero was extremely conscious of this fact. It may be that his social climbing had made him insecure about his status.

My last and most important point is that Cicero may have been first to make a clear and explicit distinction between individuals and the positions they occupy in social structure. I owe this point to Neal Wood, who suggests that "Cicero seems to differentiate between the person and office of magistrate" and goes on to argue that "Once offices of state are thought to be independent of the individuals holding office, a notion of government as the totality of offices arises" (1988:132f.).

The significance of this theoretical innovation is that it becomes possible, for the first time in history of social thought, to conceive of social structures as independent of the particular individuals who fill the positions in these structures and play the roles expected of individuals in those positions.

The main evidence for this view is of course the distinction he makes between the four *personae*, and especially between the third and the other three. In particular Cicero distinguishes the duties of public office holders, or magistrates, from those of private citizens and private individuals (*Commonwealth*, p. 29, 47).

> It is, then, the particular function of a magistrate to realize that he assumes the role of the city and ought to sustain its standing and its seemliness, to preserve the laws, to administer justice, and to be mindful of the things that have been entrusted to his good faith. (*Duties*, p. 48)

The implication of this quotation is that the office is one thing, the person holding the office another. It suggests to me that Cicero may have been first to make the important distinction between persons and the positions they occupy in society. This distinction is constitutive of most varieties of structuralism and essential to sociological analysis—or so I believe.

## NOTES

1. It may be noticed that the paradigm of a public good in contemporary economic textbooks is a lighthouse.
2. It has been argued by Sharples (2009:436–440) that Cicero sometimes used his considerable rhetorical skills to give tendentious presentations of the views of those he criticized.
3. See Hollis's article "Of Masks and Men" (1985) for a discussion of this distinction.

# CHAPTER 13

# Charles Darwin: Selfishness and Altruism

*Wendelin Reich*

## DARWIN'S PUZZLE

What do a parliamentary debate, a speed dating session, a family dinner, and a chess tournament have in common? To a considerable extent, they are all cooperative forms of social interaction. Cooperation occurs when an individual's actions succeed because of a voluntary contribution to his/her actions from another individual. If both gain from their combined effort, as in dancing or teamwork, it is fairly easy to explain scientifically why they would want to engage in the interaction in the first place (see Axelrod 1984).

More complex and difficult to explain, however, is the high frequency of *costly* cooperation in all human societies. Such cooperation occurs when one collaboration partner does not receive a direct benefit from the interaction—in other words, when his or her behavior is altruistic. Social-psychological research over the last 20 years has established that people routinely count on the altruism and prosociality of their fellow humans, that they experience much of their own social behavior as unselfish, and that their psychological well-being increases if they are able to act cooperatively in regular and meaningful ways (Thoits and Hewitt 2001). Such behavior is by no means confined to kin and close friends; instead, experiments involving members of many different cultures have shown that most adults are routinely kind and helpful towards strangers (Fehr and Fischbacher 2003).

Costly cooperation can be found in various species throughout the animal kingdom, which has led biologists to seek to explain it in evolutionary terms. These efforts can be traced back all the way to Charles Darwin, the person associated most closely with the biological theory of evolution. Darwin had spent the years between 1831 and 1836 on board the HMS *Beagle* as a private researcher, and he had collected evidence of natural selection and of species gradually adapting to environmental conditions.

Back in England, he worked for more than 20 years, until 1859, organizing and writing up his thoughts into his major book, *On the Origin of Species*. During this period he corresponded with dozens of scientists and naturalists, constantly on the lookout for facts that might confirm or contradict the nascent theory of evolution. One discovery that distressed Darwin particularly was the occurrence of extreme forms of costly cooperation, including self-sacrificial behavior, in bees, in ants—and, of course, also in humans (Darwin 1859: Ch. VII).

This discovery was unsettling because Darwin realized that purely altruistic forms of behavior constituted a problem for a theory of evolution by natural selection. The core of his predicament can be summarized in a few words. Natural selection, according to Darwin, acts on individual organisms. Those members of a species who are "favored" by an advantageous mutation produce more offspring, thereby outcompeting their adversaries.

Purely altruistic behavior does not fit into this framework, as it handicaps the altruistic individual while benefiting competitors. Natural selection, Darwin reasoned, should weed out pure altruism in the long run, yet the ultra-cooperative aspects of humans, ants, and bees are so painfully obvious that they must be explained within the framework—otherwise, natural selection as an explanatory principle has failed (Dugatkin 2006).

I will show in this chapter that the eventual resolution of Darwin's puzzle contains an important lesson for social scientists. It took more than 100 years for biologists to find the solution, but once they had it they were able to gain a radically deeper understanding of the many forms of costly cooperative behavior that occur throughout the animal kingdom. Most contemporary social scientists believe in the theory of evolution and realize, at least in a diffuse sense, that human nature has a biological side. However, they tend to downplay the importance of biology to human behavior and to assume that humans act altruistically—as neighbors, stepparents, members of social movements, and so on—for reasons that social science can ignore (van den Berghe 1990; Pinker 2002).

The contemporary biological solution to Darwin's puzzle, which I will discuss briefly in the next section, does not deny the existence of prosocial behavior as a behavioral (or surface) phenomenon, but it unmasks most instances of prosocial behavior as selfish in an underlying, deeper sense that I will specify. Understanding this understructure may help sociological research in several ways, as it leads to the discovery of new sociological phenomena, to deeper explanations of existing phenomena, and even to some revisions and new hypotheses. I will provide two such examples in the last two sections of this chapter, one illustrating a revision of a sociological theory and the other offering a deeper explanation of a known social phenomenon.

## FROM PURE TO SELFISH ALTRUISM

The modern solution to Darwin's puzzle is surprisingly simple. Part of its elegance is due to its reliance on the theory of genetic inheritance, which offers some important insights that Darwin did not know about. The theory of genetic inheritance explains variations in the physiology and behavior of individuals within the same species in terms of variations in their genes. It is these genes that natural selection ultimately acts upon (as opposed to the developed organisms, which are merely "vehicles" for the genes; Dawkins 2006).

Genes that lead organisms to produce more offspring crowd out alternative genes. Genes thus compete directly with alternative genes for the same spot of DNA, and "cooperation" among them is essentially impossible. Richard Dawkins intended to capture this harsh logic when he coined the metaphor of the "selfish gene." As long as we do not forget that it is just a metaphor and that genes do not have minds, it makes perfect sense and facilitates scientific thinking (Pinker 2002).

Importantly, selfish genes do not automatically translate into selfish organisms. There are two ways in which an unselfish organism can increase the reproductive success of a selfish gene, thus constituting recognized solutions to Darwin's puzzle (West et al. 2007). The first method concerns *kinship*. Genes "want" to maximize the number of copies of themselves in the next generation, but this number increases not only if their own vehicle organism manages to have a lot of offspring that reach reproductive age. It also increases if relatives—siblings, cousins, and so forth—have a lot of surviving offspring because relatives often share identical copies of a gene. Many animal species thus display altruism towards close relatives.

"Altruism" here means, more narrowly and technically, that individual organisms behave in ways that negatively affect the number of their own surviving offspring, but which lead to a significant increase in the number of offspring of their beneficiaries. Human societies abound with examples of kin-based cooperation, and in institutions such as marriage, custody laws, or guardianship, they even enjoy legal recognition.

The second method concerns *reciprocity*. A selfish gene may well code for behavior through which its vehicle organism provides costly benefits to non-kin individuals—but only if it can count on acts of reciprocation that compensate the organism for its costs. The basic "you scratch my back, I scratch yours" logic turns out to be highly flexible. On one hand, compensation does not have to be provided right away. If it comes reliably at a later point in time, biologists speak of *delayed reciprocity* (Trivers 1971).

On the other hand, compensation can also come from third parties. Such instances of *indirect reciprocity* (Panchanathan and Boyd 2004) are rare among other animals but are extremely frequent in all human societies. Indirect reciprocity explains social mechanisms, such as reputation and status, through which members of a human group can become preferred (or disfavored) cooperators. Research shows that human group members who are perceived as modest, agreeable, and "good" are more likely to receive unsolicited benefits from others. The old adage of kindness and meanness each leading to more of the same holds true, at least in a statistical sense (which is all that matters to selfish genes).

I mentioned earlier that most humans subjectively experience many of their own and their fellow humans' actions as essentially "good." Political and religious commentators therefore tend to find it offensive to think that two simple mechanisms—kinship and (direct/indirect/delayed) reciprocity—suffice in order to explain away human kindness (Pinker 2002). From a strictly scientific point of view, however, there is no contradiction between the subjective experience of goodness and the harsh objective logic of the selfish gene. They coexist side-by-side on two distinct levels of biological organization.

An emotion such as love can be a *proximate* cause of behavior, for instance, by motivating a father to sacrifice his health in order to protect his children. At the same time, the *ultimate* cause of his behavior lies in the evolutionary processes, operating over thousands and millions of years, which favored a genetic makeup that induces its vehicle organism to protect its offspring. The distinction between proximate and ultimate causes lies at the foundation of modern behavioral biology, and viewed from its angle, "selfish altruism" is no oxymoron.

Some biologists have argued that a third way exists that can better explain altruistic behavior in humans. They call it group selection, and the idea is that humans may act purely altruistically as long as it is for the good of their own in-group (e.g., their tribe). A large number of theoretical and empirical studies have shown that group selection, at least in this naïve sense, does not work (West et al. 2008).

Human groups are never isolated entities; throughout history, individuals have migrated between them. Selfish migrants would thus profit from selfless group members without paying the cost. In fact, Darwin himself guessed that group selection is a chimera (Darwin 1859:102). Using modern terminology, we can say that sacrificing oneself for the good of the group is not an *evolutionarily stable strategy*.

Together with the argument for group selection, the idea of pure altruism finally collapses. Whatever humans do in order to help others must, at a minimum, be *the kind of behavior which tends, on average, to benefit their selfish genes.* I will now turn to two examples that show how useful it can be for sociologists to search for ultimate (gene-level) selfishness behind proximately altruistic behavior. The point of this search is not to unmask an alleged "dark side" of human nature—which would amount to a drastic misapprehension of Darwin's puzzle—but to revise a few sociological theories (Example 1) as well as to get a deeper grasp of certain social phenomena (Example 2).

## EXAMPLE 1: EMBARRASSMENT AS A COOPERATIVE EMOTION

When people interact with each other face to face they rely on facial expressions, among other factors, to determine the emotional state of their counterparts. Erving Goffman was among the first to discover the sociological relevance of emotions and their facial expression. In a classical paper titled *Embarrassment and Social Organization* (Goffman 1956), he suggests that the emotional display of embarrassment serves not only the obvious function of communicating the psychological state of the embarrassed person. Instead, Goffman argues, it serves a wider societal purpose.

He notes that many social settings impose contradictory norms of conduct on their participants. A company cafeteria, for instance, demands that its patrons recognize both equality (i.e., no one is allowed to jump the queue) as well as hierarchy (i.e., managers are to be treated more deferentially than employees).

Goffman asserts that it is in such situations that displays of embarrassment become relevant (e.g., a janitor may act embarrassed when he chances upon the CEO at the counter), upholding the two conflicting sets of norms at the expense of the individual: "Social structure gains elasticity; the individual merely loses composure" (1956:271).

The embarrassed participant, according to Goffman, is a docile cooperator, ready to suffer for the good of society. However, the discussion of the preceding section hopefully put every reader on the alert: is suffering for the greater good really an evolutionarily stable strategy? The social psychologist Dacher Keltner answers this question in the negative.

Taking his cue from Darwin, who studied shame and blushing in his book titled *Expression of the Emotions in Man and Animals* (Darwin 1872: Ch. XIII), Keltner searches for a social explanation of embarrassment that is compatible with the selfishness of genes (Keltner 1995; Keltner and Anderson 2000). He begins by investigating precisely how embarrassment is displayed in social interaction. Across cultures, the following sequence of behaviors is recognized as such a display: the person turns her head away; eyes are downcast; she smiles in a tightly controlled, decidedly unhappy manner; she touches her face with one hand (illustrated in Keltner 1995:449).

A Darwinian approach to emotions, following Keltner, must thus ask in what way the universally recognizable display of embarrassment contributes to the survival and the reproductive fitness of the vehicle organism. Why do selfish genes not block the display and the accompanying feeling of unease (Keltner and Anderson 2000)? After all, embarrassment is unpleasant, and people who are embarrassed often worry that others ridicule them or think less highly of them.

However, experimental studies reveal that the display of embarrassment is actually socially advantageous for a person who has just violated a social norm or lost control of herself in the presence of others. In such situations, experimental subjects who display embarrassment are more easily forgiven, and liked more, than subjects who display indifference.

Embarrassment is thus only *proximately* a form of subordination to the laws of society (as discussed by Goffman), but *ultimately* a selfish mechanism for soliciting cooperation in the form of understanding, forgiveness, face-saving behavior, and sympathy. The cooperative co-interactants, in turn, also promote ultimate goals because their show of kindness obliges the embarrassed individual to be available as a future cooperation partner.

Following Keltner's approach, similar results have since been obtained for other social emotions, such as joy and contempt. Therefore, it is unlikely that they function in a top-down manner à la Goffman, putting society before the individual. Social emotions do support moral order in sociologically interesting and relevant ways, but they achieve this in a bottom-up Darwinian fashion, ensuring all the while that each participant in a cooperative interaction behaves in a way which tends (on averaget) to be ultimately compatible with the 'selfishness' of his or her genetic makeup.

## EXAMPLE 2: SOCIAL SCOREKEEPING

Cooperation often relies on a division of labor—you do X, I do Y. This can be a win-win situation for both of us, but it can also mean that you end up contributing more than I do, or vice versa. Such asymmetries occur very often in human societies. The most common way of reconciling them with the principle of selfish altruism is delayed reciprocity (see above). A person who contributes too much thus gets compensated at a later point.

However, in a typical social group with dozens of members (e.g., a tribe, a clique of friends, an extended family) this creates a new problem. There are so many dyadic relationships between group members that it is hard, and cognitively demanding, to keep track of all the asymmetric contributions that

**Figure 13.1**
**Excerpt from an interview with a romantic couple; both participants are 20 to 25 years old (video-recorded in 2004 in a midsized Swedish city).**

| | |
|---|---|
| 1. Interviewer: | Which of you cleaned [*the shared apartment*] most recently? |
| 2. Anna: | [*in a very decided manner*] I did. |
| 3. Bert: | [*turns his head down and displays a classical expression of embarrassment; laughs quietly; Anna briefly joins in the laughter after 2 seconds; 4 more seconds pass*] |
| 4. Anna: | And the time before that, and before that, and before that. [*Anna and Bert look at each other; he laughs embarrassedly but louder this time; she smiles coldly (without eye-involvement) and looks intermittently at him and the interviewer*] |
| 5. Bert: | Yes, well that's the way it was. |
| 6. Anna: | Yes. |

must be reciprocated later. In addition, people may be forgetful or even dishonest, so the group members cannot just privately remember the various asymmetries but instead must talk about and negotiate them.

This evolutionary logic explains an interesting phenomenon that occurs frequently in conversations among people: social scorekeeping (Orbuch 1997). Let us take a look at an excerpt from an interview with a young Swedish couple (see Figure 13.1). In the minutes before the excerpt, the interview had addressed a topic that is regarded as highly sensitive in gender-equal Sweden: the distribution of household labor (Nordenmark and Nyman 2003).

The key phrase here occurs in turn 4 (marked with an arrow). In a reproachful manner, Anna makes clear that she is most often the one who cleans the shared apartment. Her statement comes right after Bert avowed, through his embarrassed behavior in turn 3, that Anna indeed cleaned the apartment most recently. His continuing embarrassment after turn 4 confirms the general asymmetry in their relationship, as well as his realization that this situation is problematic.

The modern solution to Darwin's puzzle can, of course, explain why humans generally do not want to be taken advantage of by cooperation partners. But it can also explain why a person like Anna would use a public and reproachful manner for making her complaint. The method she uses turns the lopsided distribution of household chores in her relationship into a public (through the presence of the interviewer) and *ratified fact* (through Bert's behavior; Pinker 2007). It therefore allows her to *keep score* of her contributions to her relationship with Bert. In their next domestic argument, Anna will be able to refer to the socially ratified fact ("but you admitted yourself that . . .") and ask Bert to reciprocate—he might have to cook dinner or fix her computer.

Of course, we do not know if this is what actually happened after the interview in question, but this need not bother us. What we do know, through a wealth of social-psychological and anthropological research, is that people *tend to keep score* of their contributions to the various cooperative relationships they have with others.

Evolutionary social psychologists have even discovered specialized cognitive mechanisms that allow people to keep track of the cooperative contributions of others and to detect "cheaters"—that is, people who routinely contribute less than they gain (Cosmides and Tooby 2005). It is findings like these that show us that social behavior, altruistic and costly as it often may seem, is tightly connected to the selfishness of genes.

## CONCLUSION

When Darwin turned costly cooperation in bees, ants, and humans from a mere curiosity into an evolutionary puzzle, he did not yet have the scientific tools necessary to resolve it in a fully satisfactory manner. Sometimes, however, *asking the right questions* is the crucial step that is necessary to start a broad line of inquiry that now keeps thousands of researchers busy (in new fields such as behavioral economics, evolutionary anthropology, or evolutionary psychology).

I have tried to show that Darwin's puzzle, and the theoretical insights that were gained when biologists finally resolved it, can be of service to sociologists. His quandaries rendered a phenomenon problematic that sociologists all too often take for granted—the ultra-cooperative, seemingly altruistic behaviors that humans routinely display toward fellow human beings.

My two brief examples were meant to illustrate that Darwinian thinking can both revise (Example 1) and deepen (Example 2) sociological accounts. Beyond that, I believe that it can also be a valuable resource for generating new hypotheses or for discovering new patterns of order in the vast landscapes of our modern, complex society.

# CHAPTER 14

# François Rabelais: Materiality and Culture

*Emily Erikson*

"Indefatigable boozers, and you, thrice precious martyrs to the pox, while you are at leisure and I have nothing more important on hand, let me pose you a serious question" (Rabelais 1955:601): what does a musty old monk reaching out his cadaverous hands from the depths of the sixteenth century have to do with the rigorous pursuit of a science of social interaction?

In one sense, everything. Rabelais's contribution has been on two levels, the material and the ideal. His work comes well before academic disciplines had settled into distinct fields and the conceptual apparatus of sociology had developed into a set of key words—but without him our idea of culture would not be the same. In this way, he has been very important in drawing attention to the ideal world people live in and, remarkably, he has done so through work that is overwhelmingly and basely material. This has been his second great contribution, to draw attention to the muck of appetites, desires, jokes, hypocrisy, petty cruelties, mistakes, gluttony, and fun that make up most of our lives.

Readers of Rabelais like to imagine his life as a series of hilarious escapades punctuated by drunken revelry, hearty meals, and a good shag here or there—much like his narrative alter-ego Alcofribas. The reality was probably somewhat different, although of course there is no way of knowing for sure.

Rabelais was born in the countryside, near the town of Chinon in Touraine, around 1494. In his youth he left home to join the Franciscan Order, although he probably had little choice in the matter. As a monk he seems to have become familiar with and enamored of the work of the great Christian humanist Desiderius Erasmus. For several years he immersed himself in scholarly work, translating Greek to Latin, composing poetry, and building up considerable expertise in the fields of religion, law, and medicine.

However, it did not take too long for him to run afoul of the authorities—a problem that was to plague him throughout his life. Greek authors were becoming unpopular with the increasingly strict Faculties of Theology at the Sorbonne. Rabelais was censured for his translations, and his books were confiscated. He fled to a more permissive Benedictine monastery, retrieved his books, and then fled the church entirely.

Although it cannot be determined for certain, it appears that Rabelais's move was motivated, at least in part, by a desire to do something more immediately useful for society than merely annotate and translate texts. He became a doctor, enrolling in the Faculty of Medicine of Montepellier in 1530 and appointed to the Hôtel-Dieu de Notra-Dame-de-Pitié du Pont-du-Rhône in Lyons in 1532.

In the same year as his appointment he began a third career, finally entering the profession for which he was to become so widely celebrated (author!) with the publication of *Pantagruel.* From this auspicious beginning he went on to publish *Gargantua* in 1534, then returned to the story of Pantagruel with the *Third Book* in 1546 and the *Fourth Book* in 1552. The *Fifth Book* was published posthumously with some continuing contention over the book's true authorship.

These books are his masterwork and have secured his place as one of the greatest authors of all time—and also turned him into a kind of patron saint of overindulgence in liquor, wine, food, and whatever kind of crazy tomfoolery can be gotten up. The volumes chronicle the merry, fantastic, and often ridiculous lives of the fictional characters Gargantua and Pantagruel. Both are literally larger than life: giants.

While traveling, Gargantua suffered from the profuse attention of some curious city dwellers. "The people so pestered him, in fact, he was compelled to take a rest of the towers of Notre-Dame . . . then, with a smile, he undid his magnificent codpiece and, bringing out his john-thomas, pissed on them so fiercely that he drowned two hundred and sixty thousand, four hundred and eighteen persons, not counting the women and small children" (Rabelais 1955:74). Realizing that Gargantua had done this good naturedly and in jest, the people saw that they had been drenched for a laugh, i.e., *parris*—and that is how Paris got its name. Soon after, he accidentally ate six pilgrims in a salad, mistaking their staffs for snail antlers. They managed to survive by hiding behind his teeth until he flossed them out.

Gargantua's son, Pantagruel, was also built of mythic proportions. When an attacking army shivers under a sudden downpour, Pantagruel takes pity on them and sticks his tongue out to cover them from the rain. The author

(Rabelais's alter-ego Alcofribas) runs to join them—wanting to escape a drenching as well. He gets sidetracked along the way and ends up climbing over six miles of tongue into Pantagruel's mouth. After touring around the mouth for some time, he finally exits, sliding down the beard of Pantagruel to appear before him.

> "Where have you come from, Alcofribas?" "From your throat, my lord," I replied. "And since when were you there?" said he. "Since the time when you went against the Almyrods," said I. "That's more than six months ago," said he. "And what did you live on? What did you drink?" "My lord," I replied, "the same fare as you. I took toll of the tastiest morsels that went down your throat." "Indeed," said he, "and where did you shit?" "In your throat, my lord," said I. "Ha, ha. You're a fine fellow." (Rabelais 1955:275)

Both books follow their subjects through birth and early education. Gargantua travels the countryside and defends his kingdom from the attacks of the misled and misfortunate King Picrochole and establishes the Abbey of Thélème. Pantagruel receives a fine education in Paris and meets his thenceforth dearest and most constant companion, Panurge. Panurge animates the remaining books with cheating, lechery, folly, cowardice, cursing, and even some malicious cruelties.

After a memorable debate with an English scholar, Panurge decides to take a wife, but first consults an oracle to foresee whether the match will be good or disastrous. All signs point to disaster. Despite these clear warnings, Panurge perseveres, discarding received advice and leading Pantagruel and his entourage in a search for new oracles of wisdom to bless his forthcoming nuptials. The search culminates in a long adventure overseas to consult the most revered oracle of all—the divine bottle.

Now, if it is not immediately obvious why this story would have sent someone into fits of laughter, you are not alone. This opacity is part of how Rabelais came to contribute so much to our conception of history and culture. Mikhail Bakhtin, the most influential scholar of Rabelais to date, felt similarly. He wrote "Rabelais is the most difficult classical author of world literature. To be understood he requires an essential reconstruction of our entire artistic and ideological perception, the renunciation of many deeply rooted demands of literary taste and the revision of many concepts" (Bakhtin 1965:3). Really, all this for a couple of poop jokes?

First of all, as Lucian Febvre has shown, there is more than just poop jokes to Rabelais. Secondly, as Mikhail Bakhtin demonstrated, there is more to those poop jokes than just poop. And thirdly, those poop jokes really reveal something, if not profound, inescapable about human life.

My first problem then is to summarize what other than ribaldry and feces populate the pages of *Gargantual* and *Pantagruel.* Another element is irreverence. Priests, monks, and theologians are mocked, parodied, and plain insulted. Biblical passages are lampooned. In short, nothing is sacred. This irreverence led Abel Lefranc, another great scholar of his day, to argue that Rabelais was an atheist and *Gargantua* and *Pantagruel* were satirical attacks on Christianity (Lefranc 1905). This assertion did not sit well with Lucian Febvre.

Lucian Febvre was a French historian born in 1878. In 1929, he, along with Marc Bloch, founded the tremendously influential journal, *Annales d'Histoire Economique and Sociale*. Together, through the journal and their research, Febvre and Bloch were instrumental in reshaping the field of history. In their hands, history was no longer conceived as a series of events, but instead more like a foreign land, with its own customs and culture that needed to be deciphered and placed in context in order to be fully appreciated. They had little concern for great men and preferred to focus on the habits of everyday life and how these practices give shape and structure to society. Perhaps the most famous example of this approach is the book of Lucian Febvre's student, Fernand Braudel: *The Mediterranean* (Braudel 1995).

Febvre strongly disagreed with Lefranc's assessment. He used key moments in the text, Gargantua's plan for a utopic Abbey (the Abbey of Thélème), a letter of fatherly advice from Gargantua to Pantagruel, and an account of hell given by the character of Epistemon, to show that Rabelais was a good Christian—in fact a Christian humanist in the mold of Erasmus. Rabelais's jests and pranks poked fun at passages of scripture (or used passages of scripture to poke fun at others), but they were not truly rebellious.

Instead, they belonged to a tradition of clerical jests, or monk's jokes, located well within the Catholic tradition. These jokes did not signal disbelief; instead they were a product of deep familiarity. Clerics lived and breathed the scriptures. It was simply second nature to use them for all types of expression. In fact, the very learned puns and distortions, which betray nothing so much as a deep and thorough knowledge of the texts, were only possible in a world in which principled disbelief was itself not yet a possibility.

This insight became the basis for Febvre's book *The Problem of Unbelief in the Sixteenth Century: The Religion of Rabelais* (Febvre 1982). By using the strange ring of Rabelais's laughter in the ears of the twentieth century, he made a more fundamental argument about historicity. To understand Rabelais, we had to understand the world he lived in. It was a world before the Enlightenment, before the Scientific Revolution, and before—though on the verge of—the Protestant Reformation.

This world was fundamentally different because the church was not an optional part of people's lives; it was part of their basic world view. As a consequence something as important as disbelief meant something entirely different in the sixteenth century than in the twentieth, and actions and their consequences could not be properly understood without knowledge of the cultural context in which they occurred. Febvre showed that though Rabelais was a genius, he was also very much of a piece with the scholarly and well-educated circles of his time, giving us a glimpse of the culture of the sixteenth century in the process.

Bakhtin really did Febvre one better—he used Rabelais as a prism to show us the culture not just of elite circles of the sixteenth century, but of the popular masses. In this project, Rabelais was more than just a resource from which Bakhtin was able to extract information. Part of what makes Gargantua and Pantagruel so extraordinary and wonderful is the melding of high and low art, and part of Rabelais's genius was to see that low art—the gestures and doggerel jokes and pranks of the street—was worth writing about.

In the first place, Rabelais made the somewhat unorthodox decision to publish in French at a time when most educated individuals read and wrote in Latin. Using French allowed him to incorporate popular sayings, idioms, oaths, curses, and come-ons that might not have retained their "robust flavor" after translation into Latin (if you know what I mean).

Both of the characters Gargantua and Pantagruel are drawn from the existing folklore of the sixteenth century. Less than a year before he wrote and published *Pantagruel*, a small volume was published anonymously in France, *Great and Inestimable Chronicles of the Great and Enormous Giant Gargantua* (Powys 1948:47). In it Merlin conjured up the giant Gargantua to defend King Arthur and the Knights of the Round Table. It was a very different book than Rabelais's *Gargantua*—but it was immensely popular, funny, and seems to have been the inspiration for his work. Pantagruel was widely known to be a demon imp that poured salt down the throats of drunkards, causing great thirst everywhere he went.

Rabelais is funny now—honestly, I do think he is funny even if it takes a read or two—but he must have been even funnier to his contemporaries because he mixed and matched high and low cultural forms in ways that were instantly recognizable to people of the time. For example, the account of the Parisians being drowned in piss is laughable as it descends into the strict accounting of men drowned (260,418). It is even funnier if you are familiar (as I am not) with the biblical passage it references, the miracle of the five loaves and two fishes (Bakhtin 1965:92). What could be a modern equivalent? Maybe a picture of Anna Wintour saying "I can haz cheezburgerz?"

Bakhtin's book is organized around the popular forms and culture that Rabelais drew from and preserved in his text. We have the "Language of the Marketplace" (oaths, curses, and profanities), "Popular-Festive Forms" (the carnival), and popular imagery of the banquet, the grotesque, and the scatological. By incorporating all of these elements, Rabelais has given us an irreplaceable picture of the cultural lives of the overwhelming majority of people in the Feudal Era. It is almost unique in giving us insight into that fascinating and rich world.

Bakhtin was also able to weave a larger image out of these separate strands. Like Febvre, he believed that Rabelais's laughter and mockery were misunderstood. For Febvre, mockery of the church meant something entirely different before and after the modern period. For Bakhtin, laughter itself was something entirely different. We now divide the world into the serious and the light. Comedy is light, whimsical, and largely superficial, in contrast to the meaningful and important realm of the serious.

For Rabelais, however, laughter was profoundly serious—if never heavy. Laughter triumphed over death and supernatural awe by dispelling fear and thereby allowing the people to see clearly—without terror and superstition clouding their vision. It did so precisely by embracing the bodily, the scatological, and above all the material plane of existence.

Blood, feces, and urine are all signs of our corporeality, and therefore reminders of mortality and death. But as anyone with a child knows, the process of birth is also a profoundly messy event loaded with blood and urine and all sorts of strange bodily fluids. Poop in the sixteenth century was therefore not just poop. "Through its participation in the whole, each of these images is deeply ambivalent, being intimately related to life-death-birth. That is why such images are devoid of cynicism and coarseness in our sense of the words" (Bakhtin 1965:149).

In Bakhtin's telling, modern culture drained excrement of its life-fulfilling positive aspects and consigned it to the merely dirty, just as modern humor was drained of its seriousness and positive aspects and made into simple folly or purely negative satire. Again, the unique genius of Rabelais allowed us to see the extreme differences between modern and medieval cultures of Europe. Even the materials of our own body have changed meaning over time.

Bakhtin's work on Rabelais encouraged a new kind of reading that could penetrate the veils separating modern students from the mysteries of peasant cosmologies in the medieval period. In this way, Rabelais indirectly encouraged a new form of archival detective work practiced by Natalie Zemon Davis and Carlo Ginzburg. Their influence has spilled over into comparative-historical sociology and not least given us a new historical research method. Perhaps more importantly the concept of the carnivalesque, charivari, and topsy-turvy have given cultural sociologists a new lens with which to interpret many cultural forms.

But the deeper insight in both Bakhtin and Febvre's work is that actions and words depend very much on a cultural context that changes over time. What modern readers interpreted as an all out assault, Bakhtin and Febvre have shown were very much the opposite: mockery that laughingly but often lovingly embraced the contradictions and complexities of its age.

Finally, I believe there is a lesson in Rabelais that has to do not with distance from medieval culture, but instead its proximity. The subject of Rabelais's work is distanced from modern scholars in two ways. We are removed in time and also removed by culture. The academy is, essentially by definition, high culture and operates as the polar opposite of Rabelais's lively street life.

Part of what makes *Gargantua* and *Pantagruel* so wonderful is the way that Rabelais unites these two opposite poles into one fun-filled, if fictional, universe. I think the last insight Rabelais has for us as sociologists is not to get lost in the clouds of airy ideas and intentions, and instead always keep in mind the messy mechanics of everyday life. People are just as likely to act for the love of a sausage as to follow a rational plan.

# CHAPTER 15

# Émile Zola: Seductions and Emancipations of Consumption

*Helena Flam*

To many Émile Zola is known as the author of "J'accuse," an exemplary protest letter in which he took on the French political and military elite as well as its corrupt institutions in order to defend Dreyfus, a court-martialed and then long-imprisoned army officer whose only real crime—as the final investigation and court case showed—was his Jewish ancestry.

A colleague once offered a course in political science dealing with the great texts and their contexts in the past century. Zola's "J'accuse" opened it. Another colleague teaches sociology students about the working class and class conflicts relying on Zola's *Germinal*—his perhaps most famous novel in which he depicts the wretched working and living conditions of the coalminers and their devastating strike.

In my own teaching, short excerpts from Zola's *The Ladies Paradise*—a name given by its English translator to the true protagonist in this novel, a grand magasin—have provided a valuable alternative for as long as research on the first department stores and the early patterns of middle-class consumption remained sparse. Even now, however, Zola helps to make a few points not found in this burgeoning literature.

## ZOLA'S METHODS

In preparation for his book that appeared in 1882, Zola engaged in systematic research. He interviewed one of the first architects to build a grand magasin, and also department directors, managers, technicians, cooks, employees, and suppliers (Lehnert 2002:558). Today we call these "expert interviews." Although the original Bon Marché—that developed from 1852 into what became the first and largest department store prior to 1914—was his main model, Zola also visited grands magasins of his time to observe their workings, making detailed notes about their architecture, departmental divisions, working routines, displays, and sales strategies. Today we call this nonparticipant observation.

Finally, he systematically collected statistics, various documents, and press articles about the grands magasins to subject these to closer analysis—very much as sociologists do today. So far no researcher has questioned the accuracy of his information on the capital invested in the department stores, its turnover, the salaries paid, the numbers of various types of personnel, their employment, or their living and layoff conditions. Virtually every text on department stores and/or consumption refers to Émile Zola's book at least once, if not for some other reason than to dispute one of its many theses.

## ZOLA ON GRANDS MAGASINS

In *The Ladies' Paradise* Zola intended to depart from his usual gloom (Nelson 1998:ix). The book was to be a hymn to the nineteenth century—the power and gaiety that come from creativity. Grands magasins—along with grands hotels, monumental railroad stations, and impressive factory buildings—were new, imposing, and self-assured, urban phenomena (Geisthövel and Knoch 2005).

Zola picked the department store as his subject probably because it allowed him to best address not only the new temptations and satisfactions of consumption, but also the reorganization of production that it stimulated as well as the imperial appropriation, transportation, architectural encasing and, finally, incessant work involved in the sale of goods. Here I will limit myself to a few themes relevant to the sociology of consumption.

Grands magasins impressed by their monumental size and their novel iron and sheet-glass optics. They benefited from and reinforced the advances made at the time in architecture and engineering, featuring long glass galleries, a lacework of iron pillars, bridges and staircases, and an entire array of the most recent inventions ranging from gas heating through electric lamps to lifts:

> A sheet of fire was going through the great central gallery, making the staircases, the suspension bridges, and the hanging iron lacework stand out against a background of flames. The mosaics and the ceramics of the friezes were sparkling, the greens and reds of the paintwork were

> lit up by the fires from the gold so lavishly applied. It was as if the displays . . . were now burning in live embers. The mirrors were resplendent. In the distance . . . dazzling departments, teeming with a mob gilded by the sunshine. (Zola 1998:265)

Grands magasins hypnotized and enchanted at once, encasing and highlighting a hitherto unheard of quantity of mesmerizing goods. Zola gives us the first impression of a grand magasin through the eyes of the heroine, who just arrived to Paris from the province:

> this shop [that] had suddenly appeared before her, this building which seemed so enormous . . . held her rooted to the spot, excited, fascinated, oblivious to everything else. . . . Denise stood transfixed before the display at the main door. . . . It all cascaded down. . . . It was a giant display, as if the shop were bursting and throwing its surplus stock into the street. (Zola 1998:3–5)[1]

Grands magasins seduced and enticed by their advertisement campaigns raising expectations by their sales pitch, the artful and irresistible arrangements of goods, and the spectacles organized for the sole pleasure of the consumer.

The sales started at the entry to the store. The entrance itself should serve as a giant advertisement, just like a display of less expensive goods that adorned it and—like a magnet—attracted the passersby (Zola 1998:235, 240, 247, 392). Inside even more spectacular events and displays were to awaken desire to own the goods on display.

## RATIONALITY AND UNHINGED DESIRES

Zola expressed in many different ways the ambivalence felt about the grands magasins and their sales policies at the time. In his understanding, they combined the opposites of an indifferent, at times brutal, always disciplining, administrative logic of money-making with a passionate managerial vision meant to unhinge consumer desire. With his aim to juxtapose contrasting aspects of capitalism, albeit on its consumption side, Zola anticipated Max Weber's ambition to pinpoint the spiritual sources of the soulless modern, legal-bureaucratic capitalism.

He differed from Weber in showing that neither the rationalizing bureaucracy nor modern capitalism per se brought about the disenchantment of the world. Quite on the contrary, he demonstrated that rationality in the administration of and profit-making from consumption called for inventing ever new forms of enchantment to create consumer desire and induce a prospective consumer to buy.

Like Marx or Simmel, Zola saw (through) the fetishism of commodities. Unlike either of these two thinkers, however, who seemed to attribute it to the very essence of the production-divorced commodities themselves, Zola spared no effort to demonstrate how the ascending group of sales entrepreneurs innovatively invested in new and risky advertising as well as display and sales strategies to convert each commodity into a fetish to create the spectacular enchantments of consumption. He showed that that fetish, far from being sacred, was eroticized (Nelson 1998:xx).

Closer to Sombart than to Weber, Zola believed that capitalist production was driven forward by the pursuit of luxus by the upper classes, in particular by the desire of middle-class women for luxury, modern comforts, fashion, and beauty. In his novel this desire fills the brass cashiers of the grand magasin with money, allowing its owner(s) to open ever new departments, order and sell ever more goods and employ ever more people, stimulating production in the process.

Everybody in the novel refers to its true protagonist as "the machine"—a word meant to convey awe, fear, and helpless, frustrated disdain for the amazing power and the rational, incessant, efficient, unperturbed working of this money-making, desire-unleashing gigantic tool (Zola 1998:28, 49, 334, 339, 355). Not only its enemies—small businesspeople in its neighborhood threatened and ultimately brought to ruin by its territorial expansion and sales competition—call it also "the monster" or "the bitch" (Zola 1998:21).

The monster's appetite for goods seems insatiable, moving its owner(s) to create ever new departments, bringing ever more and ever more distant and exotic goods under its control. One of its shortest descriptions presents the grand magasin as a machine continuously gorging itself up on and spitting out goods:

> In the mechanical working of the Ladies Paradise, the staircase in the Rue de la Michodière constantly disgorged the goods which had been swallowed up by the chute in the Rue Neuve-Saint-Augustin, after they had passed through the mechanism of the various departments upstairs. (Zola 1998:41)

Rational means that are employed to unhinge consumer desire multiply in this era—Zola devotes long pages both to the routine and to the fantastic, financial extravaganzas of advertising conceived of by its main owner—here just one spectacular advertising campaign:

> [at] the entrance . . . an interminable procession of women and children [formed], above whom there floated a cloud of red balloons. Fourty thousand balloons had been prepared; there were boys specially

> detailed to distribute them. To see the customers who were leaving, one would have thought that in the air above them there was a flight of enormous soap bubbles, on the end of invisible strings, reflecting the fire of the sunshades. The whole shop was lit up by them. (Zola 1998:242)

Although few of the routine sales principles employed by the grands magasins were completely their own invention (Walsh 1999), they innovated by bringing many such principles together, expanding their scale beyond the imaginable. Probably no actual department store used all of the sales principles Zola named in his novel, but his ideal typical grand magasin featured (i) bringing together a great variety of goods to be sold in great quantities by various departments, each directly responsible for their purchase and sale, (ii) "free entry" to the passersby with no obligation to buy, but a purposeful confusion of departments to increase chances of selling other compelling goods on the route to the initially desired item, (iii) the "fixed prices" on display relieving the customer from the obligation to ask and to bargain, (iv) the possibility of making a bargain through (a) a system of price reductions, that is, progressively lowered prices on unsold items and (b) occasional big sales, (v) conquering the mother through the child as a conscious sales strategy, (vi) free gifts to go along with purchase, (vii) home delivery to facilitate buying large or large numbers of goods, (viii) mail order purchase, (ix) the return-system, making possible to give back a commodity if one changed one's mind (Zola 1998:235, 266–267).

Administered with a cool logic, thanks to the genius, fantasy, and passion of its main owner, the grand magasin in the novel fairly routinely succeeds in driving consumers to a state of frenzy (Zola 1998:37, 239–241). Cold, calculating rationality stands behind the orchestrated orgies of consumption. A tiny taste of Zola on the traces left by one such (sales) orgy:

> the lace and underclothes unfolded, crumpled, thrown about everywhere, gave the impression that an army of women had undressed there haphazardly in a wave of desire. (Zola 1998:116–117)

## CLASS

Zola perhaps exaggerated the contrasts between small businesses and the grands magasins, but his description of the neighborhood which harbored small shops—the predecessors of department stores—helps to make vivid the stupendous change in the sense of space, color, light, air, smell that grands magasins brought with them:

> [Madame Baudu] sat motionless behind the cash-desk, watching over the silent, empty shop . . . dismal chill fell from the ceiling; hours passed without a customer coming to disturb the gloom, and the goods, which were no longer touched, were getting slowly covered with the saltpetre from the walls. (Zola 1998:360, 367, but see also 7, 9–10, 12–13, 15–16, 372, 385)

Zola portrays grands magasins as engaged in a deathly competitive battle against small businesses but also describes the emotions and beliefs that moved small business to hate, fear, and mobilize against grands magasins, demanding the legal intervention of the state to curtail their progress. Vividly he depicts the stagnation and conservatism of this group that, faced with the competition, lived in "the resigned despair, which even the lengths of cloth were exuding" (Zola 1998:362). In contrast to the department stores, their businesses were unable to stimulate production.

These small businessmen believed that "[t]he art was not to sell a lot, but to sell at a high price!" (Zola 1998:23). The very conservatism and moral sense forbade them to even imagine (a) "chasing after the customer," (b) creating demand by attractive displays or advertisement, (c) selling some goods at a loss, to sell others at a profit, (d) selling quickly, so that the same capital could be used to purchase a new batch of goods, over and over again, thus creating additional profits from the capital's turnover, and so forth. These businessmen also did not believe in quick and efficient training of the personnel, high salaries, commissions, or opening up career possibilities and stock shares to the employees (Zola 1998:32, 35–36, 39). Instead, generation after generation saw slow training of the apprentices, their domestication, and their marriage into the family as the pinnacle of a business existence (Zola 1998:14, 23).

## GENDER

### Consumption and Women: Their Desire, Domination, and Emancipation

Zola suggests that grands magasins were the first to create consumer desire rather than to satisfy already existing needs. His book overlays different discourses on women and consumption. The first asserts that far from serving and caring for women, grands magasins seduced women for profit. Not only Zola's grand magasin, but also its main owner is a womanizer, keen on capturing, seducing, and enslaving women, ready to discard them, when he can no longer enjoy their company/profits (see Nelson 1998:xvi–xx).

From this perspective the grand magasin is a perpetrator: a brutal "monster" only pretending to desire—to warm, bring out, caress, and adore their bodies. In fact, it lures women to expose both their innermost desires and their bodies only to decapitate, dismember, and devour them. From this viewpoint, the grand magasins are powerful, cruel, uncaring seducers, and women as consumers are innocent, duped victims:

> Mouret's sole passion was the conquest of Woman. He wanted her to be queen in his shop; he had built this temple for her in order to hold her at his mercy. His tactics were to intoxicate her with amorous attentions, to trade on her desires, and to exploit her excitement. (Zola 1998:234)

Zola also proposes a contrasting perspective, however. He portrays female customers as ferocious and destructive in their desire, comparing their movements to overpowering currents, raging hurricanes, conquering armies, invading hordes, covetous, brutal mob and—as in the citation that follows—ravenous locusts:

> But it was in the silk department that the customers had been at their most voracious. There they had made a clean sweep . . . the hall was bare, the whole colossal stock of Paris-Paradise had just been torn to pieces and carried away, as if by a swarm of ravenous locusts. (Zola 1998:117; see also 16, 240, 249–250, 265)

Yet another discourse sees women come not only to discover and satiate their bodily pleasures, feasting on free space, lights and colors, but also to enjoy the full attentions of the personnel instructed to fulfill their every whim:

> they felt constantly courted with flattery and showered with adoration which entranced even the most virtuous. The shop's enormous success came from the seductive way it paid court to them. (Zola 1998:325)

Female customers can browse and order the personnel to let them see, touch, or try on an unrestricted number of goods. They can enjoy the pleasures of exploration and domination without the disappointments of consummation if that is their wish. The magasin provides them with an opportunity to boss over others. In one scene stretched masterly over many pages to make sure the reader suffers along with the novel's heroine—a "simple" salesgirl—Zola depicts how an upper middle class female customer humiliates her by letting her wait for a long time, minute after long minute, before calling on her to enter and try to correct—while hearing putdowns and insults—the invented shortcomings of a purchased item that simply could have been returned at no cost whatsoever (Zola 1998: 307–321; see also 257, 311–312).

The fourth discourse in the novel envisions grands magasins as liberators of women. For the disciplined female members of the working and middle classes, they offered relatively well-paid job and career possibilities, and thus emancipation from the restricted choice between roles as the nun, housewife, factory or shop employee (cf. Lancaster 2000:177–178). For the impoverished women they provided an alternative to more or less veiled prostitution—a "plague" of the nineteenth-century urban life.

More, the grands magasins were also revolutionary in presenting women with what men since long had: a public space in which they could move and enjoy themselves freely (see Nelson 1998:xvi–xx). At this time women still could not move outside unattended. Violent crime, the "indecent" gazes and advances of men, the high chances of being taken for a prostitute—at that time the only "public woman"—and the male notions of family honor kept them in the confines of their own home and the church. While earlier on in the nineteenth century the arcades—a system of passages harboring shops, bookstores, barbers, baths, theaters, hotels, saloons and brothels, opened up to men—they remained closed to the unaccompanied women. A rare visit to the local shops, the theater, or a grand hotel could not compensate for the lack of public space where women could visit, rest, meet their friends (or lovers!), gossip, and amuse themselves.

This is what grands magasins offered, providing a mixture of private (dressing rooms, bathrooms) and public (sales departments, a café, a buffet with drinks and sweets free of charge, a reading and writing room, an exhibition room). Insofar as they encouraged women to act as sovereign consumers, grands magasins—finally—sharpened their decision-making capacities and so prepared them for their role as rational voters.[2]

## CONCLUSION

As great as Zola's "research novel" is as a source of information and inspiration, recent findings on magasins and early patterns of middle-class consumption question some of its main "theses." For example, Zola's book suggests that grands magasins served all classes, offering different quality goods at different prices: at the entrance were the cheap wares for the working class, and deeper in and higher up the more expensive goods for the middle class were put on display (Zola 1998:4, 235, 240, 249).

Crossick and Jaumain (1999:25) cite new research that indicates a greater range of possibilities: some magasins caring just for one, others for more classes, while yet others attending to more classes, but not under the same name or roof. One also has to keep in mind that these early grands magasins did not offer a mass product at democratizing prices made possible by the mass production of the early twentieth century.

Zola's rendition of the relationship between the grands magasins and the small business was rather one-sided (Crossick and Jaumain 1999). It is true that much anti-big business sentiment, in some countries fueled by anti-Semitism, and rabid political mobilization could be found, but also the opposite was the case. Some small businessmen welcomed grands magasins since they believed that their business would thrive thanks to their vicinity to the grands magasins that attracted customers from which smaller shops also profited. The book is silent about this group.

It might need factual corrections, but Emile Zola's *The Ladies' Paradise* challenges social science classics in many different ways. For example, Adorno and Horkheimer condemned all mass consumption as low-brow and called it the new opium for the masses. Zola made a case for the ambivalence of consumption—for both its highs and lows, its seductive aspects but also its ability to emancipate.

In Veblen's theory women as consumers play a passive role—their very leisure, fashionable dress, and accessories are mere symbols of their husbands' economic prowess. In contrast Zola's women are active—they desire to consume, to dominate, and to occupy new public space. *The Ladies' Paradise* highlights not only why the magasins could be seen as a possible ersatz for the church (Zola 1998:427) but perhaps also as a step toward political emancipation. Zola's vivid descriptions, finally, help visualize the new sales and advertisement methods that made the first department stores such a resounding success.

## NOTES

1. The two most encompassing descriptions of the grand magasin as compressed into the ideal typical Bonheur der Dame by Zola are found in the beginning and toward the end of the book, when Mouret—its master and major owner—makes his daily inspection tour (Zola 1998:40–45, 334–338, 360). For the sake of brevity I omitted the thousands of goods that Zola names and describes while writing about goods displays.

2. Zola offers a very differentiated view of women both as workers and consumers. See his ideal typical portrayal of the impulsive, bargain-making, highly selective, and thieving female customer on pp. 79, 243–269. Even before sociology emerged, he highlighted the hard working conditions and disastrous emotions accompanying/driving forward competition among the personnel and between the subordinates and superordinates (see Marchand 1980).

# CHAPTER 16

# Fyodor Dostoevsky: On Extreme Political Violence

*Eva M. Meyersson Milgrom and Joshua Thurston-Milgrom*

Nietzsche called Fyodor Dostoevsky "the only psychologist from whom I had anything to learn." His writings span the ethical world, including the diametrically opposed political and religious views his life encompassed. In his youth he was intimately involved with underground revolutionary politics and Russian "nihilism." After being sentenced to death for revolutionary activity, his sentence was commuted at the last minute to a prison term in Siberia.

Later, his own spiritual crisis and that of his beloved "new Russian man" led him to become passionately religious and politically reactionary, devoted to Tsar and Orthodoxy. His work draws on first-hand experience with an incredible variety of milieus, including political ideologues, violent revolutionaries, and hardened criminals. Dostoevsky is often, and rightly, credited for his depiction of the modern age's crisis of faith as well as for his powerful explorations of the psychology of crime and extreme action.

In the rush to recognize Dostoevsky as a master criminal psychologist and proto-existentialist religious philosopher, however, his penetrating social critique is often underemphasized. His psychological portraits are simultaneously social commentaries, reflecting the effects of social and political structures as much as they do each character's individual history. Even as Dostoevsky's own idea of Russia's road to salvation became increasingly reactionary, his insight continued to come not only from his own intellectual and spiritual struggle, but also from the discourse among the many psychological, social, and religious strands that constitute the fabric of his works.

To the end, he remained as much a cultural theorist as a religious philosopher. The student of sociology can find in Dostoevsky not only myriad penetrating insights into individual and social psychology, but also an understanding of the crucial assumptions of sociological inquiry and the fundamental questions that sociology asks.

*Demons* (or *The Possessed*; Dostoevsky 1994) is perhaps the author's magnum opus, and it is certainly his most exhaustive treatment of many of his most prominent themes, from the recesses of the human psyche to the liberation of the serfs, and from the mentality of underground revolutionaries to the farcical mannerisms of nineteenth-century Russian provincial life. It recounts two loosely intertwined stories: one relates the machinations and circumstances leading up to an act of political terrorism, and the other concerns the self-destruction of a young aristocrat whose inner spiritual crisis leaves him with no outlet for his boundless strength.

This formal structure reflects its origin as a fusion of the two fundamental themes of Dostoevsky's life and work. These themes are also those of sociological inquiry. One is the basic needs that drive people's actions in society. The other is the systems that allocate the social goods that fulfill these needs. Sociology knows these dominant themes as agency and structure (e.g., Coleman 1990).

Dostoevsky also shares with the sociologist important assumptions about these themes. An agent's behavior is driven not only by material economic incentives, but also by various social goods, such as meaning or fulfillment. Social structures, meanwhile, often work like economic systems, outside the realm of individual psychology, to allocate non-material social goods. This essay reads a sociological model out of Dostoevsky's novel, showing that his two "faces," and the way in which they come together, reflect the crucial components of a more complete depiction of social mechanisms, which can allow us to model social life and predict social outcomes.

Beyond merely analyzing structures, we wish to predict social behavior and to understand how social structures influence it. In *Demons*, Dostoevsky seeks to defend the spirit of his motherland especially against the European nihilism that, in Russia, became associated with anti-Tsar insurgency; he is concerned to understand both the basic conditions that drive individual dissatisfaction, and the group dynamics that allow "demonic" ideologies to become systemically established as social goods, driving individuals to participate even in self-destructive violence. Today, when it is impossible to be unaware of the untold casualties and costs that political terrorism inflicts on our world, this topic may well resonate with us, too.

Despite Dostoevsky's famous depictions of the criminal mind, his treatment of the psychology of extremism is even more concerned with the effects of ideology and social and political reform. His individualism was balanced by a concern for the state of his homeland, and modern Russia's "spiritual" and political crisis was for him a case study in the mutual influence of these two themes: how changing systems affect the way people fill their social needs and how these needs generate and shape systems. *Demons* is a novel about the dynamic interaction of agency and structure and it consequences for systemic change.

## AGENCY, SELF, AND COMPARISON

Though Dostoevsky's social critique has been underemphasized, its value is crucially underpinned by his more noted concerns with psychology, philosophy, and self-reflection. Like a sociologist, he ultimately concerns himself with the interaction of structure and agency, but the dichotomy is reflected in the inception of *Demons* as two separate novels (Pevear 1994). One was to be a "religious" novel of redemption entitled *The Life of a Great Sinner*, and the other one was to be a "novel-pamphlet" about a grisly political murder.

The self-destructive young aristocrat Nikolai Vselodovitch Stavrogin was to be the central character of the former, and remains the catalyst underlying all the events of *Demons*. Despite Dostoevsky's liberal intellectual heritage, he moved early beyond the trends of historical materialism and maintained a lifelong artistic, intellectual, and personal concern with rescuing the self from the abysmal soul of modern humankind. This early conviction persisted through personal spiritual upheavals and the radical revision of his beliefs, as well as his own perpetual poverty from gambling debts.

In the final version of *Demons*, redemption is denied to Stavrogin (though his name means "cross"), but attained in the end by Stepan Trofimovitch Verkhovensky. Stepan Trofimovitch is Stavrogin's childhood tutor, the father of the murderous revolutionary leader and the novel's symbolic representation of the liberal intellectual milieu that Dostoevsky blames for spawning Russian Nihilism. His redemption comes only in eventually rejecting his own liberal ideas in favor of religion:

> Far more than his own happiness, it is necessary for a man to know and believe every moment that there is somewhere a perfect and peaceable happiness, for everyone and for everything. . . . The whole law of human existence consists in nothing other than a man's always being able to bow before the immeasurably great. (p. 664)

The basic human drive for authentic meaning that Dostoevsky posits alongside material needs reflects the importance of the notion of agency. The science of sociology works to explain empirical observations and finds agency indispensable in explaining what it observes. Thus Georg Simmel (1971b) can speak of the "fundamental motive . . . at work [in human life], namely the resistance of the individual to being leveled, swallowed up in the social-technological mechanism," and Viktor Frankl (2000), a social psychologist studying human motivation, can suggest that "self-transcendence is the essence of human existence."

Stavrogin's spiritual crisis is a study in the difficulty of such self-transcendence in the absence of real meaning, where a crumbling, nihilistic social order prevents fulfillment even for a character that Dostoevsky paints as an *übermensch*. Generations have also been fascinated by Kirillov, the only character Stavrogin seems to treat as an equal.

Kirillov, whose ideas often read like a parody of Nietzsche, believes that entrapment in the fear of death is the basic human predicament, and he has reached the conclusion that dispassionate suicide is the only way to overcome it and "become God" (p. 615). His nihilistic rejection of societal values is so extreme that he allows his suicide to be utilized in the machinations of the revolutionary activity, although he neither participates in it nor condones it.

These two characters have the most abstract, spiritual, and perhaps "noble" motivations in the novel. Though both inadvertently catalyze the violence, neither is responsible for it, and both end with suicide, each driven by an existential or spiritual crisis, not by shame or insufficient fortitude. However, the profound lack of meaning and faith that causes their demise is the same lack that allows the members of the murderous revolutionary group to be controlled and turned to violence by their leader, as well as allowing the representatives of the older generations to become indulgent of "modern ideas," infatuated with liberal posturing, and blinded to the threat posed by their nihilistic progeny.

This "spiritual lack" is developed more concretely in recent work on the notion of *significance*. The work of Arie Kruglanski et al. (2007) draws on Frankl's human-motivation theories to explore how the biological need for physical survival is intimately linked to the quest for personal meaning and significance, and how the latter stems from the threat of personal insignificance caused by humans' awareness of their own mortality. It is ultimately "the nightmare of ending up as a speck of insignificant dust in an uncaring universe" that motivates people to become good members of society by doing well in culturally prescribed ways. The individual's need for socially determined significance indicates the interaction of agency and structure in social life.

Aside from the existential struggles of Stavrogin and Kirillov, the more prosaic aspects of the human need for meaning are also abundantly illustrated in *Demons*, not only in the petty posturing of provincials but also in the more worldly, but often equally ridiculous, characters of the aging scholar Stepan Trofimovitch Verkhovensky (bumbling father of the nihilistic generation) and his domineering patroness Varvara Petrovna Stavrogina (representative of the old aristocracy). Often, among these characters, Dostoevsky delivers a sort of novel of manners that paints a picture of contemporary provincial life, including a biting critique of people's constant comparisons of themselves to others—or to the way they perceive others.

The motivations of the characters in *Demons*, from bumbling comedians to savage criminals, point up fundamental aspects of human social life at the same time as they symbolize Russian history and culture. People value social instrumental goods like status, even when they do not correlate to more wealth, but all determinations of status are made precisely by comparing oneself to a reference group of others: one's status is one's rank in this comparison group.[1] An individual's status at a given time thus depends on the reference group relative to which it is determined. This is comically represented by Dostoevsky's provincial aristocrats, doting on their titular superiors while flaunting their nobility among commoners.

The way that status is determined by comparison and reference groups, however, invites consideration of the structures—social as well as economic and political—that determine and distribute these social goods to agents. Understanding these systems is as important for us as it was to Dostoevsky, for status comparisons do not always result in the comically superficial manners of "polite society." The same needs for meaning, significance, and status that drive the petty intriguing of the average townsfolk in *Demons* are exploited, in other characters, to draw them into political violence.

## STRUCTURE, GROUP MEMBERSHIP, AND AUTHORITY

The "novel-pamphlet," which Dostoevsky ultimately combined with his "religious novel," was motivated by his desire to tell the story of Sergei Nechaev, a Russian underground conspirator who was fond guilty in 1873 of the murder of I. I. Ivanov, a St. Petersburg student who had left Nechaev's group. This took place in a milieu Dostoevsky knew all too well, and he was driven to portray the "demons" infecting Russian society, especially those powerful enough to drive idealistic students to participate in misguided violence.

This "anatomy of a murder" contrasts with *Crime and Punishment*'s well-known account of the depths of a criminal psyche. In *Demons*, the political murder of Ivan Shatov (based on Ivanov) by Pyotr Stepanovich Verkhovensky (based on Nechaev) and his group is ultimately ascribable to demons in the system; that is, to the corruption of the structures that allocate the meaning and social value upon which humans rely.

Given the atrocities perpetrated by Pyotr and the members of his revolutionary circle, one might be tempted to assume that they are the novel's title characters. In fact, though, translators have disagreed on how to render the Russian title, *Besy*, and the novel has been published in English as *The Possessed*, *The Devils*, and, most recently, *Demons*. The first makes the title refer clearly to human characters, especially the members of the would-be revolutionary society.

As recent translators Richard Pevear and Larissa Volokhonsky have pointed out, though, the latter, more accurate translation shifts the focus from the possessed to the forces that "possess" them, making the title refer not to the agents, but to the ideas and social currents that influence their behavior (Pevear 1994). Pyotor Verhovenksy insidiously devalues agency as he defends the members of his "crew" to Stavrogin: "And why are they fools? They're not such fools; nowadays nobody's mind is his own" (Dostoevsky 1994:417).

The demons of the title are identified in Pevear's (1994:xvii) introduction as "ideas, that legion of isms that came to Russian from the West—idealism, rationalism, empiricism, materialism, utilitarianism, positivism, socialism, anarchism, nihilism, and underlying them all, atheism." These demons seem to have infected almost all the characters to some degree, and not only the revolutionaries; still, the political murder that lies at the center of the novel demonstrates a concern not only with the psychology of extreme, violent action, but also with the often-violent effects of sweeping social change.

*Demons* depicts a Russia where political and social turmoil have undermined traditional sources of significance and meaning, including those connected with the authority of Tsar, Church, and the old social order. Having failed to replace them, this turmoil leaves people desperate for sources of social value and thus susceptible to demonic influence. This is a concern Dostoevsky shares with policymakers today, who must try to counteract extremist political violence by understanding how structures and policies drive violent action.

Though no character is immune, the members of Pyotr Stepanovich's revolutionary circle are among the most infected. In their need for ideological "faith" and group membership, all prove equally susceptible to his glib assurances and his tactics of control. However, group membership comes at a cost: members must sacrifice a portion of selfhood, or agency. The recent work of Kruglanski and his colleagues on significance in extremist groups attempts to explore how terrorists' various motives—ideological, personal, and social, in the traditional tripartite classification—may functionally relate to each other.

It offers an approach to understanding the social value members receive by defining their identities through group membership (including obedience to its leader, Pyotr Stepanovich).

Significance is here envisioned as something that is lost, and must be regained, when an individual undergoes a security-undermining trauma such as losing a family member to violence, or experiences feelings of relative deprivation or frustrated expectations in situations of political, social, or economic inequality. Individuals may seek to regain significance by contributing to some communally (that is, structurally) defined *collective good* (see Kruglanski et al. 2007). Thus, the authority of a community's leadership lies precisely in its ability to define collective goods.

The motley crew of characters that begins as Stepan Trofimovitch's circle and eventually becomes Pyotr Stepanovich's circle of revolutionaries offers a sometimes-comical, sometimes-sinister portrait of the agent's need to define an identity through group membership, even at a significant cost to the agent's autonomy. Before Pyotr's arrival, "what we had was only the most innocent, nice, perfectly Russian, jolly liberal chatter" (p. 33), but already each of the characters among this motley crew is marked by a seeming lack of fulfillment or deficiency of social value.

Pyotr Stepanovich Verkhovensky himself, who finally murders Shatov with his own hands, has been abandoned and subsequently dispossessed by his father Stepan Trofimovitch, quasi-intellectual lapdog of the old aristocracy. This overtly symbolizes Dostoevsky's conviction that the generation of liberal idealist "Westerners" spawned the nihilistic generation of Necahaev. Similar frustrations drive the others to group membership, finally putting them under the influence of Pyotr Stepanovich's machinations. This theme contrasts especially with Shatov's and Kirillov's diametrically opposite existential struggles with the agency-focused problems of faith and belief, but the less "noble" needs motivating the members of the circle are equally non-economic.

The group is bound by its members' need for group membership, and Pyotr Stepanovich is so confident in the strength of this social arrangement that he feels no need to hide it from his cronies:

> so the main thing still depends on you yourselves and on your full conviction, which I hope will grow firm in you by tomorrow. And that, incidentally, is precisely why you united together into a separate organization of the free assembly of the like-minded, so as in the common cause to share your energy among you at a given moment and, if need be, to watch over and observe each other. Each of you owes a higher accounting. (p. 607)

The characters in the group are "like-minded" not in their convictions, but only in their need for significance through group membership. The atheistic, impish Liputin gossips about the higher ranks that will not receive him into their houses, while Shigalyov's obsessive anarchic social theorizing parodies an egalitarianism that would bring everything to the lowest common denominator. The Jew Lyamshin is an eternal outsider, while Tolkachenko and Erkel are in the grip of youthful idealism and in thrall to Pyotr Stepanovich.

Finally, the earnest Virginsky, who declares, "I will never, never, abandon these bright hopes," is a cuckolded, henpecked autodidact: "no wonder," says the narrator, "the poor 'family man' needed our company to ease his heart" (pp. 31–33). These pitiable would-be revolutionaries represent a range of frustrated expectations and of ongoing searches for meaning or significance. And this significance is defined socially—it depends on structure.[2]

Dostoevsky's "religious" novel interrogated the values that incentivize agents, while the "novel-pamphlet" was concerned with how extreme ideologies and violence are linked to structural changes associated with the demons of social and political upheaval—much as we too might be in these days of constant ideological violence.

## GROUP LEADERSHIP AND EXTREME ACTION

When a central state's economy and government are destabilized, its ability to define the common good is undermined, and the diminished power of the centralized mechanism for establishing and allocating social goods opens the way for the emergence of others, including the more extreme. These other structures can include anything from community-aid organizations to religious sects to violent extremist organizations, and some organizations are all three.

In a Russia pervaded by nihilism, Dostoevsky's characters turn to "false" sources of social and spiritual value, whether by joining Pyotr Stepanovich's "fivesome" or simply being blinded by liberal ideologies, philosophies, and "isms"—the "demons" Dostoevsky wanted exorcised from the Russian spirit in which he came to believe fervently.

The members of Pyotr Stepanovich's revolutionary circle are not these demons; they are rather the possessed, each infested by a recognizable one of the "isms" listed above. This group represents more than a collection of studies in motivation, also readily symbolizing the panorama of novel social and ideological structures competing for ascendancy in late nineteenth-century Russia, as the serfs were being freed, the old aristocracy was breaking down, and the Continental influence was permeating traditional culture.

This group of characters stands for a whole field of identity—and ideology—defining groups, standing at various distances from the mainstream, all competing to provide members with significance. Pyotr Stepanovich dominates this group, not in spite of his being the most extreme, but precisely *because* of it.

Groups necessarily compete to gain adherents, and they must offer benefits in exchange for the cost of membership. When the traditional state and value systems are perceived as weak and corrupt, extremist alternatives become more viable. The opportunity cost to extremism declines, extreme ideologies become more attractive, and extreme actions have increased power to grant significance through their value as signal commitments to a group (see Ianconne 1992).

Pyotr Stepanovich realizes this, and it is the basis of his control over the group. His extreme revolutionary program far exceeds the capabilities of his group and sounds like a caricature when vapidly recited by one of his cronies. Yet, it is hardly an exaggeration compared with the modern realities of extremism:

> [The group] has as its task, by a systematic denunciatory propaganda, ceaselessly to undermine the importance of the local powers, to produce bewilderment in communities, to engender cynicism and scandal, complete disbelief in anything whatsoever, a yearning for the better, and finally, acting by fires as the popular method par excellence, to plunge the country, at the prescribed moment, if need be, even into despair. (p. 547)

Such extreme collective goods can serve as control mechanisms that operate very much like demons, indeed allowing the leadership to de-individuate members using its authority to constantly redefine the collective good. Internalized cultures and socialized members are a success for the leadership, but also a threat to them, for a member capable of acting independently, even in the leader's interest, will have increased "self weight," diminishing the leader's control (see Friedkin 2004). When Pyotr Stepanovich accuses two of his cronies of political arson, they defend their commitment to the common cause: " 'Isn't this your program? What, then, can you accuse us of?' 'Of self-will!' Pyotr Stepanovich shouted furiously" (p. 548).

Community members are forced to give up some selfhood in order to gain significance, perhaps making them more ready to commit to extreme demands by the leadership. By the time Liputin has an ideological disagreement with Pyotr Stepanovich, for example, he suddenly finds his self-weight gone: "It flashed like lightening through Liputin's mind: 'I'll turn and go back; if I don't turn now, I'll never go back.' He thought thus for exactly ten steps . . . " (p. 555).

Similarly, leadership can establish "points of no return," strategically making members commit to actions and invest in skills that make a return to an alternative, "normal" life impossible. This, of course, is precisely Pyotr Stepanovich's tactic in forcing his circle into complicity in Shatov's murder: " . . . they're all bound by yesterday now. None of them will betray us. Who would face obvious ruin, unless he's lost his mind?" (p. 626)

Pyotr's atrocities include not only killing Shatov, but also responsibility for the suicide, death, or social downfall of most of the other characters. Pathological or "evil" though his actions may seem, they in fact portray the strategies and tactics typical of extremist organizations that recruit and operate successfully. Even Pyotr Stepanovich is not himself a demonic agent, but rather one of the possessed, embodying the ability of a pernicious structural cycle to "infect" agency.

## CONCLUSION

In *Demons*, Dostoevsky examines the individual's quest for meaning in the context of sweeping social change, and he characterizes the politics, society, and ideologies of his time in terms of a cold-blooded murder. He blames structural demons for corrupting human agents, without exonerating agents from guilt for being vessels for the demons.

Dostoevsky's prognosis for exorcising these demons may be unhelpful from a scientific or policy perspective: near the end of his life, he concluded that Orthodoxy and true faith were the only redemption from the sometimes-pernicious interaction of structure and agency that we call systems. Still, to the student of social thought reading such a keen observer of individuals and society is still instructive, a century and a half later.

Even Dostoevsky's own intimate concern with the internal psychology of extreme action did not diminish the comprehensiveness of his view, for he immersed himself in the inner world of agency without ever losing sight of its mutual influence with social structures, remembering that human nature does not dictate these structures any more than the structures dictate it. The value lies at the nexus of these concepts. We can draw a meaningful picture of society, and meaningfully predict systemic outcomes, by looking to the *interaction* of structure and agency—and reading Dostoevsky can help us remember this.

## NOTES

1. See Jasso (2002) for a comprehensive survey of comparison theories. A *reference group* is a sociological concept referring to the community group to which an individual or another group is compared and relative to which the individual is ranked according to some socially defined good.

2. For a more developed analysis, see Meyersson Milgrom (2009).

# CHAPTER 17

# Goethe: The Ambivalence of Modernity and the Faustian Ethos of Personality

*Hans-Peter Müller*

## THE PHENOMENOLOGY OF A GENIUS

Whoever tries to enter his world treads onto a minefield. Goethe, the man and his oeuvre, is a cosmos of its own. He is *the* German poet, comparable to Shakespeare who stands for English literature. He has given an epoch his name—the "Goethezeit"—and his name represents the most important cultural institution of Germany—the "Goethe-Institut." Of privileged origin—he was born into a well-to-do burgher-family of the free city of Frankfurt—he became an aristocrat in the service of Prince Carl August in the principality of Weimar at the age of 26. Apart from his two-year-long journey to Italy, he remained there for the rest of his life and helped Weimar become a center of "world-literature"—a concept he coined, and which was later adopted by Marx and Engels in the "Communist Manifesto."

Goethe gained the high status of a "Dichterfürst," or "poet-prince," in the eyes of his many admirers. He became a "Fürstenknecht," or the "prince's servant," in the eyes of his rampant critiques. From early on he had access to the most important people of his age: As a young boy he watched Mozart play in Frankfurt, and as a poet in his sixties he met Napoleon (who claimed to have read "Werther" seven times) in Erfurt: the famous encounter of the world-poet and the world-emperor. Napoleon's remark "voilà, un homme!" became a standard phrase in order to describe the character of Goethe's incommensurable fame.

Goethe was probably one of the last "uomo universale" who disposed over the full knowledge of his time. He was a beacon of activity playing multiple roles: he was a statesman, a poet, theatre director, university rector, a collector of art and stones, and a passionate naturalist ("Naturforscher"), to name but a few. One role though is missing: he certainly was not a sociologist *avant la lettre*. Had he encountered the rise of this new discipline, he would not have become one of its advocates.

Quite the opposite. In a way, he might be regarded as an *anti-sociologist*. His whole work is animated by a philosophy and epistemology of nature that stresses the unity of knowledge. His evolutionary view of the "metamorphosis" of phenomena was quite kindred to Darwin's view, who later acknowledged Goethe as a forerunner of his own theory. It deals with the emergence ("das Werden" or "becoming") of entities but always in search of the original type or the archetypal model of every phenomenon ("Urphänomen")—from the so-called "Urworte" or archetypal words to the "Urpflanze" or the archetypal plant.

He draws all kinds of analogies and parallels between the different "natures" of man, society, and culture. In his "Farbenlehre," for instance, he launched an arduous attack on Newton and his mechanistic world view. This critique, from an organic standpoint, is as untenable today as it was bold in his own time, but it was seen by him as one of his greatest scientific achievements. Goethe stressed the "great chain of being," the natural order of things, and the recurrent rise and decline of entities. The "godly" and the "true" coincide. The creator made nature, and nature mirrors the creation of the creator.

Reality is a natural reality, not a social reality. *Nature* not *society* is Goethe's basic concept. As such it is a result of natural evolution. People and things have evolved naturally, and therefore only a natural scientific view of the world provides the royal avenue for insights gained by "Anschauung, Betrachtung, Nachdenken," or "viewing, contemplation, reflection."

This complex and complicated concept of nature that Goethe never developed systematically but only in various intimations is at odds with the mainstream constructivist view of sociology that society is man-made and can be changed at will by social action and governance. Quite naturally, Goethe's conservative view puts a premium on the established order and careful, cautious change. He did not share the enthusiasm of his contemporaries on both sides of the Rhine for the French Revolution. He was also afraid of the Revolution of 1830, which would bring again turmoil, disorder, violence and war in its wake. Goethe equally disliked revolutions and wars. He was a pacifist and an advocate of diligent change by reforms that he had tried to realize in Weimar, even if he did so largely in vain. Evolution, not revolution, is what holds the world together.

If Goethe's thinking is so distant from sociological thought, what can be learned from him? There are three features in his approach that merit sociological attention: *epistemologically*, the method of "Anschauung," such as the careful, concentrated "seeing" ("das Sehen") of phenomena, *analytically* the dislike of "grand theory" in favor of modest theorizing, and *substantially* the conceptualization of man and society. Goethe is both a gifted painter of portraits of human beings or characters *and* a genial painter of societal constellations and projects.

Goethe lived long enough to see the *Ancien régime* going into decline in the eighteenth century and the rise of the new "modern" society in the nineteenth century. His curiosity of and for history (Cassirer 1995; Koselleck 1997), his wide-ranging knowledge, and his wisdom enabled him to read and understand the signs of the time (Borchmeyer 2005). Sceptical of historical progress he developed a certain degree of ambivalence toward the new age. "Alles veloziferisch"—"all is velociferical"—was his diagnosis (Osten 2003).

Modernity combines velocity (i.e., speed) and Lucipher (i.e., the devil) in a curious way. Due to the "facilities of communication" life becomes faster, but due to the devilish pressures upon man the result is a state of mediocrity. There is no time for quality, only regard for quantity. With respect to society and the individual he sees two parallel processes unleashing, which sociologists like Durkheim, Simmel, and Weber later described as "Vergesellschaftung," or societalization and individualization. Both processes go hand in hand but they form an uneasy coalition. Differentiation of society does not necessarily entail integration into society as Durkheim (1978) had hoped in the *Division of Labor*. Individualization necessitates modern man, but this uprooted individual lacks the means, resources, and "embeddedness" to lead a meaningful life.

The sovereignty of the modern individual does not translate so easily into chances and realizations of a methodical-rational conduct of life as Weber (1972, Müller 2007), Goethe, and Nietzsche observed. It is above all the late Goethe who begins to read Saint-Simon and discovers "la société industrielle" as well as socialism. Old Goethe met this challenge in the "Wilhelm Meister"-novels, above all the "Wanderjahre" and the drama of "Faust," particularly part two.

## THE SOCIOLOGY OF AN ANTI-SOCIOLOGIST

Modern society can be understood as the result of a triple revolution: the economic revolution and the rise of industrial capitalism; the political revolution and the emergence of republican democracy; and the cultural revolution and the advent of individualism. Even today, at least in the Western world, the economic game is capitalistic, the political game is democratic, and the cultural game is individualistic. From the outset, however, and for more than 250 years the smooth interplay and harmonious balance of the three institutions of market, state, and sovereign individual were seen as problematic and the equilibrium as endemically precarious.

The so-called problem of order that philosophy and sociology alike were preoccupied with ever since their foundation had taken a new, "modern" form. How is a dynamic and just social order compatible with personal freedom and the moral autonomy of the individual? How can these two dynamisms—society and the individual—be reconciled? How could a new synthesis of modern man and modern society look like?

To put the problem in this way is typical for sociology. This was not Goethe's way to address questions. Yet, he was a contemporary of the transition from "tradition" to "modernity." He lived through the Seven Years War, the French Revolution, the rise and fall of Napoleon, the decline of the Holy Roman Empire, the Restauration, and the Revolution of 1830. As a member of the elite, he was an eyewitness to what happened in Europe. He and his *alter ego* Faust accompanied all these transitions and "metamorphoses" in his parlance of revolution and restoration, of war and peace, of conflict and violence.

The genealogy of Goethe's Faust from 1773, the "Ur-Faust," to 1831, the completion of Faust II, mirrors social change and its poetic appropriation as well as digestion. "Mon oeuvre est celle d'un être collectif et elle porte le nom de Goethe" (Goethe 2003b:27) was his comment in a conversation with French guests in 1832. This is why Faust becomes a mirror of the times that are changing. Young Faust, a figure of "Sturm and Drang," resembles the young man in search of his self and himself. Faust I presents the estranged scholar and intellectual, and Faust II sets out on an odyssey to make and manage the modern times.

Faust is the archetypical modern man in restless, impatient, and violent search of himself and his self. He expresses the cultural ideal of self-development in a fluid societal environment where the real social movement toward economic and political development (Berman 1988) prevails. The tragedy of development consists of the simultaneity of founding the new man and the new society. Who am I and in what kind of society do I live in? Who do I want to become, and in which type of society would I like to live?

This seems to be the modern condition of a "tabula rasa," which the great revolution prompted and which incited the imagination and vision of the people living in an age of transition. This open horizon for man and society equals the "project of a second creation" (Jaeger 2004, 2008): At first it was God and/or nature who created a primitive and traditional society; this time it will be man and society who in a "creatio ex nihilo" and based on the mechanism of a "deus ex machina" produce the modern individual and his social environment: a challenge of Promethean scale and scope, but what a powerful and promising vision of "paradise on earth" with Adam and Eve not expelled by God for their vain curiosity.

Goethe, therefore, presents Faust in the first part of his tragedy as the "Übermensch" or "Super-man" who sees himself on an equal footing with God as a future potential chance. But in the meantime reality looks bleak. Instead of a god-like superiority he a feels worm-like inferiority sitting frustrated in his Gothic room, fed up with academe and students, with science and research. He has studied it all, yet could not figure out what the world holds together in its inner core—the problem of order unsolved. His titanic striving has lost its object, and he falls back on "magic" as a kind of "mind doping" to go on in his quest for the ultimate.

As known, Mephisto promises to help him fulfill his limitless search for the "God knows what" at the price of his soul. If Faust ever wants to relax and enjoy the beauty of the moment ("Werd' ich zum Augenblick sagen: Verweile doch! du bist so schön," 1699/1700), then he has lost the bet with the devil and has to yield his soul. Mephisto, the "evil" force of negation, is positive to win. Faust, the modern Prometheus, is unsure wether the powers of the underworld will really be able to deliver what he is striving for. He does not pursue the traditional goods of society like money, power, fame, glory, and sex. He wants more:

> I tell you, the mere pleasure's not the point!
> To dizzying, painful joy I dedicate
> Myself, to refreshing frustration, loving hate!
> I've purged the lust for knowledge from my soul;
> Now the full range of suffering it shall face,
> And in my inner self I will embrace
> The experience allotted to the whole
> Race of mankind; my mind shall grasp the heights
> And depths, my heart know all their sorrows and delights.
> Thus I'll expand myself, and their self I shall be,
> And perish in the end, like all humanity. (1765–1775)

Faust wants to conquer the world by means of the devil's magic. Goethe's tragedy does not follow the path of Puritan religion Max Weber (1972) characterized a century later in his "Protestant Ethic." He rather sets out on the way of irrational magic but to the same end: the rationalization of the world. The modern project is here and there world-domination. Only the means vary: magic versus religion.

Goethe takes us on a journey into wide open transcending time and space in order to gauge the adventures of self-creation. This modern odyssey includes several "makings" in order to fabricate the new society: The making of *love* in the tragedy of Gretchen; the making of *money* at the royal court, introducing "paper-money" (Binswanger 1985); the making of *leisure* and diversion by producing the famous Greek couple "Helena and Paris" as idols of beauty for courtly consumption; the making of *man* by creating "Homunculus" as the first artificial "homo sapiens"; the making of *war* with the help of a military magic based on superior technology; and the making of a new *society* by colonizing the world.

For the sake of brevity, let us look at one micro and one macro case respectively: love and society. After rejuvenation Faust sets out to discover the other sex. Mephisto, though, has manipulated him to see in every woman his beloved significant other. Gretchen, a small town girl, is Faust's victim. The conversation between the two is couched in the modern language of romantic passion. Faust pretends to love and Gretchen falls in love. The consequences are most "natural" if *modern love* (i.e., arbitrary and free choice) happens in a *traditional* small town setting. Gretchen is regarded as a prostitute by the public after Faust deserts her, having consummated their love. Finally her brother, mother, and her child die in the end, and she too is condemned to death.

Faust has faked love by the means of money and manipulation in order to have sex and instrumental control over the female body without taking responsibility for his actions. He wanted fast love but prompted the death of four people as an unintended consequence of his "rational choice." The first part of the tragedy ends with a Faust in despair but seemingly on his way to new adventures of modernity.

The final stage of the odyssey in "Faust II" sees Faust as a man of deed and activity at the peak of his career. He has become an entrepreneur who colonizes land from the sea by creating dams and canals. This new land should be the territory for new people, workers and their families, who are supposed to work and live together happily in this new type of society—a rational working and achievement society. Goethe uses the projects and plans of Saint-Simon and the Saint-Simonians (Durkheim 1971) for a new industrial, scientific, and socialist society.

This utopia of an "active society" (Etzioni 1968) rests upon specific features that Goethe authentically mirrors in Faust's project: *temporally* speaking, what is crucial is the future of mankind, not the present let alone the past; *substantially*, the progress of society rests upon restless activity based upon science and technology, industry, and diligent administration; and *socially*, all relationships are based upon achievement and the equal distribution of goods. In addition the social stratification of the people should be based upon perfect meritocracy (Young 1958). This Saint-Simonian project of Faust's seems to be the epitome of rational man in a rational society. The reconciliation of a dynamic and just social order with the personal freedom and moral autonomy of the modern individual seems to work. Mission accomplished?

Not quite. As all modernizers painfully experience, there are always pockets of tradition and resistance in processes of rapid social transition that hinder rational progress. What to do? Since progress is irresistible, they must be done away with—voluntarily or by force. The happiness of the majority cannot be undermined by the backwardness of minorities—this is the credo of modernization and development. In Faust's case, a small strip of land is still inhabited by Philomen and Baucis, reappearing from Ovid's "Metamorphoses," an old traditional couple living a friendly and contemplative life yet unwilling to yield to modernity.

In the end, Faust for the last time asks Mephisto and his development aid workers for help in removing the old couple. They do so as fast as possible by killing the couple and a wanderer who stayed with them, burning down the old house and chapel. Faust is furious because he opted for "exchange" not "violence," but then at last such victims are the unintended consequences of modern progress. Faust believes himself to be at the end of his road to glorious self-fulfilment:

> I see green fields, so fertile: man and beast
> At once shall settle that new pleasant earth,
> Bastioned by great embankments that will rise
> About them, by bold labour brought to birth.
> Here there shall be an inland paradise:
> Outside, the sea, as high as it can reach,
> May rage and gnaw; and yet a common will,
> Should it intrude, will act to close the breach.
> Yes! to this vision I am wedded still,
> And this as wisdom's final word I teach:
> Only that man earns freedom, merits life,
> Who must reconquer both in constant daily strife.
> In such a place, by danger still surrounded,
> Youth, manhood, age, their brave new world have founded.
> I long to see that multitude, and stand
> With a free people on free land! (11565–11580)

Being content at last Faust speaks the words ("Verweile doch, Du bist so schön!"), he enjoys the beauty of the moment, he wants to settle down, his eyes rest upon his oeuvre, and he is ready to consume what he has accumulated. But like the Puritans, as described by Weber, this is a deadly sin that undermines the dogma of restless activity. While thinking his workers continue to make the greave

("Graben"), he sinks into his grave ("Grab"). The accomplishment of development at last renders the developer at last obsolescent (Berman 1988:70)—a routine experience of today's project workers (Boltanski/Chiapello 1999).

## THE POSTULATION OF THE DAY ("DIE FORDERUNG DES TAGES")

Is this somber view of modernity—the quest for self-fulfilment and the establishment of a rational society as vain illusions—Goethe's last word in the shift from tradition to modernity? Not quite. On the contrary, he was fascinated by big canal projects and wanted to live until the Panama Canal, the Suez Canal and the Rhine-Danube-Canal were completed, which would have taken him well into the twentieth century.

His ambivalent attitude refers to the radicalism of modernity, the revolutionary claim to remodel man and society completely anew even if it means to destroy all traditions and institutions of the past. His counterworld to the "vita activa" that represents modernity is a "vita contemplativa" (Arendt 1958), which has a vivid eye for classical beauty. In fact, Goethe generously leads Faust into this classical Arcadia where he meets Helena, slows down peacefully, and develops an appreciation for eternal beauty. They even have a son together, Euphorion, modeled after Lord Byron, but whose activism destroys soon enough the idyllic life of this nuclear family.

Goethe's philosophy of the "kairos"—the proper timing—avoids "velociferity" in favor of a classical art of life schooled in Greek philosophy. According to this view, the good life starts once the lesson is learned that the fleetingness of the moment is a symbol of eternity (Hadot 2002). In Goethe's eyes, we have to stand and endure the ambivalence of an inexorable modernity, but as self-conscious individuals we should not begin to overreach our personality in order to incorporate the idiosyncrasies of the modern times as Werther and Faust did in their inimitable ways. Instead, we should try to find out by means of "Bildung" who we are, what the demon of our personality tells us to do as the fulfilment of our self-determination's fate, and try to reconcile our unique individuality in a human manner (Simmel 2003) with the challenges of modern society.

Needless to add, this task is easier stated in theory than realized in everyday life. But whoever held that individual emancipation would be a walk in the park? With such a world view, the modern individual should be able to cope with a globalized modernity that is stoically unbound and with the necessary distance with which we experience this new "velociferity" at the beginning of the twenty-first century.

# PART III

## Meta Sociology

# CHAPTER 18

# Pearl Sydenstricker Buck: At the Intersection of Sociocultural Worlds

*Karen A. Cerulo and Janet M. Ruane*

Pearl Sydenstricker Buck, Pulitzer Prize winner and the first female winner of the Nobel Prize in literature, guided Americans and Western Europeans through the intricate corridors of China's rich, complex culture. In novels, short stories, and activist essays, she identified values and practices that made China and America, in her view, drastically different yet curiously compatible. At its core, her work was a relentless search for the common threads of humanity worldwide. For this reason, "the social, historical, and cultural values of Buck's works exceed their aesthetic value" (Liao 1997:ix).

## HER LIFE

Born on June 26, 1892, Buck lived in an era of powerful historical transitions. She witnessed the passage from rural to industrial economies, from national to international systems, from peace to world war to cold war, and in China, from Imperial dynasties to Communism.

Buck also lived at the intersections of various sociocultural worlds. When she was three months old, her missionary parents, Absalom and Caroline Sydenstricker, brought Buck from West Virginia to China. First schooled by her mother and her Chinese *amah* (governess), she became fluent in both English and Chinese. By age seven, she was reading Confucius, Mencius, the important Chinese poets, as well as Dickens, Tennyson, Browning, and the Bible.

She learned too about ordinary life in China, keenly observing the street worlds of Chinkiang, a city in which she lived for nearly 20 years. She often ate meals with the family's servants, honing her taste for local culture and cuisine (Conn 1996:25–26). Except for her college days at Randolph Macon College, Buck spent nearly all of her first 42 years in China. This experience placed her firmly at the intersection of Western and Eastern culture, making her, in her own words, "culturally bi-focal" (Conn 1996:xiv).

Religion and politics proved another important intersection in Buck's life. In contrast to the fundamentalist dogma that dominated the Presbyterian church of her era, Buck advocated a kinder, more pragmatic form of Christianity—one that easily interfaced with her support of gender and racial equality, improved living conditions for the poor, and a reexamination of Christian missionary activity.

In "Easter 1933" she decried strict Christian dogma and proclaimed Christ's historical nature irrelevant. She compared Christ to Buddha, elevating message over godhead, and argued that Christianity's truth should be found in "the essence of men's highest dreams" (Buck 1933:170). These positions ultimately resulted in calls for her resignation from Presbyterian missionary work. She complied on May 1, 1933 (Conn 1996; Loetscher 1954).

Buck's experiences placed her at the intersection of tradition and modernity as well. She championed feminism, denounced racism, and fought against poverty, relentlessly foregrounding these issues in her books and essays. At the same time, her writings on China eloquently described—even defended—the traditions and conventions in which gender bias, racism, and poverty were rooted:

> In some of Pearl Buck's works, we find sympathy for rather than criticism of some traditional conventions in the East. The arranged marriage . . . could be cooperative, constructive, stable, and enduring. . . . concubinage was shown as a reasonable convention, which provided poor women with a way of life much better than prostitution and gave rich men an outlet of lust somewhat better than adultery, wife-raping, or visiting the brothel. (Liao 1997:7)

She took a similar position on traditional servitude, writing "I know and hate the poverty that makes human labor cheap. And yet the servants in our Chinese home enjoyed their life, and they respected themselves and their work for us" (Buck 1954:56).

Buck's literary legacy presents one last interesting intersection. Her work inhabits the meeting place of elite and popular culture. Literary critics considered her a serious writer, and she was decorated with the most prestigious of literary prizes. At the same time, she was one of the most popular authors of the twentieth century. (Fifteen of her books became popular "book of the month" entries.) Because of her popular presence, she remains largely ignored by the academic community as too "common" for scholarly study.

## BUCK AS SOCIOLOGIST

We note Buck's position at sociocultural intersections because those so located are often best positioned to explain social worlds. In a community, but not of it, these figures stand somewhat removed—observing and spotlighting things that others background as everyday and routine.

Coser (1963) tells us that such observations are especially valuable in the hands of gifted writers. Literature can capture the context required for truly "understanding" social action. Buck proves Coser's point. While not a sociologist, she was able to "see" with a sociological eye and to render those visions in compelling language. Her work is replete with vivid, thick descriptions—the kind that place readers in social situations and allow them to adopt an appreciative stance. This quality is frequently missing in sociological writings. For in our efforts to advance the sociological eye, we often fall prey to jargon and technical language—a strategy that can lose potential "converts" to the sociological perspective. Perhaps appropriately then, the daughter of missionaries offers a literary path that invites those students back into the sociological "fold."

In a very basic sense, Buck promotes what C. Wright Mills called the sociological imagination—seeing the intersections of social, biographical, and historical realms. Buck's personal biography, the historical period in which she lived, and her position vis-à-vis two powerful sociocultural domains, equipped her to understand the complexity and nuances of the ordinary, and enabled her to see the social in the personal.

To demonstrate the sociological value of Buck's work, we use two thematic frames: her problematization of social deviance and her observations on social change.

## PROBLEMATIZING DEVIANCE

Buck writes of several Chinese practices that many Westerners view as essentially deviant: concubinage, female infanticide and slavery, and arranged marriage. Her treatment of these issues reveals a sociological eye at work.

## Concubinage

Concubines are women (or in some cultures, boys) who enter matrimonial relationships with high-status men. Concubines do not enjoy the legal rights of primary spouses. Unlike mistresses or short-term lovers, however, concubines have legal standing and limited rights of financial support, rights that extend to children fathered by the concubine's husband. The practice is referenced in the Bible and ancient Roman and Chinese documents, but eventually most modern Western cultures outlawed concubinage.

Concubines were a feature of Buck's China. And her writing on the topic provides a powerful example of Buck's desire to educate readers about cultural practices, explaining their roots and sustained support rather than judging or condemning them.

Buck's concubines take many forms. In *Imperial Woman*, for example, we meet Tzu His, the last ruling Empress of China. We follow her ascent to the thrown from the role of a low-ranking concubine in Emperor Hsien-feng's court—one of many girls prepared from birth for this "service." In *Pavillion of Women*, it is Yi Ding, a concubine Madam Wu chooses for her husband when she decides to "retire" from married life, and in *The Good Earth*, the concubine Lotus signifies the growing status of the novel's protagonist Wang Lung. Using such varied characters, Buck unfolds the logic and functions of something that is seemingly deviant in the Western mind.

To be sure, Buck acknowledges the problems concubinage presents, writing explicitly about the jealousy and misery the practice could inject in households. Yet, she also writes of specific benefits concubinage could provide. Note, for example, Madame Wu's comfort with the knowledge that another will take her place in the marital bed:

> How strange and how pleasant it would be to lie down at night and know that she could sleep until morning, or if she were wakeful to know that she could be wakeful and not fear waking another! Her body was given back to her. (p. 35)

When Madam Wu's "modern" daughter-in-law, Rulan, campaigns for a momogamous system of marriage, calling concubinage wicked and old fashioned, Madame Wu replies:

> Child . . . I think Heaven is kind to women, after all. One could not keep bearing children forever. So Heaven, in its mercy says when a woman is forty, "Now poor soul and body, the rest of your life you shall have for yourself. You have divided yourself again and again, and now take what is left and make yourself whole again, not only for what you give but for what you get."

In such exchanges, we find the voices that live in transecting cultural spheres—the opinions of those who see difference and mistake it for inferiority. Buck's work strives to return difference to its rightful status.

## Female Infanticide and Slavery

Practices such as female infanticide and slavery remind us just how wide cultural disparities can be. In Buck's time, the phenomena fueled images of China as bizarre, inhumane, and evil. Yet in Buck's hands, these practices were presented with the balanced eye of a seasoned social scientist. She urged readers to see the practices not as barbaric rituals, but rather as considered responses to harsh social structural arrangements.

Buck shows that traditional Chinese culture placed a high premium on males. Sons were essential for "satisfying" wives' obligations to their husbands; they were also considered signs of good luck or godly favor. Daughters were problematic, however, and class further complicated the issue. Daughters of wealth with desirable traits and training (i.e., delicate features and "gentlewoman" skills) could prove useful for arranging marriages of valued sons, but daughters of poor families were liabilities—a drain on already strained resources. In stable periods, poor families might be able to sell daughters to wealthier families—families that would use them as concubines or household servants. Under dire conditions (i.e., droughts and famine), however, these options disappeared. At such times, keeping and raising daughters became irrational.

Buck readers who bring Western values to these circumstances might further "normalize" the untoward practices of selling and killing female daughters. In the name of parental love, poor parents could rationalize selling their daughters to spare them a life of abject poverty. Similarly, female infanticide could spare newborn daughters the shame of both poverty and slavery. So it was for O-lan and Wang Lung, the protagonists of *The Good Earth* as they kill their fourth child—a daughter—before she drew a second breath.

> "Where is the child," he asked. She made a slight movement of her hand ... and he saw upon the floor the child's body. "Dead!" he exclaimed. "Dead," she whispered.... "But I heard it crying—alive—" and then he looked at the woman's face. Her eyes were closed and the color of her flesh was the color of ashes and her bones stuck up under the skin—a poor silent face that lay there, having endured to the utmost ... during these months he had only his own body to drag about. What agony of starvation this woman had endured, with the starved creature gnawing at her from within, desperate for its own life! ... he took the dead child

> into the other room ... upon the neck, he saw two dark, bruised spots, but he finished what he had to do. (p. 82)

This scene beckons understanding, perhaps even compassion. In the hands of Buck, "foreign" practices are placed in context.

## Arranged Marriage

Romantic love dominates modern western conceptions of marriage. Most Westerners view arranged marriages as cold, calculated unions based strictly on issues of lineage or finance. Buck hoped, in writing of Chinese marital traditions, to encourage in Westerners a broader perspective. Westerners "perhaps don't realize," she said, "that that ecstasy of first love is not the only form of love, nor even the most interesting."[1] Buck presented the differences between arranged and romantic marriages, without ridiculing or judging either form.

Buck's characters commit to a collective orientation, placing marriage above individual needs or desires. Thus, when Jade, the *Dragon Seed*'s protagonist is asked to choose among two competing suitors, she tells her father, "If they both have two legs, two arms, and all of their fingers and toes, and if they are not cross-eyed and scabby-headed, what is the difference between them?" (p. 17). Jade speaks not from indifference or resignation, but from duty.

Buck carefully notes that arranged marriages are not necessarily loveless or miserable. Romance and passion may not ignite these unions; indeed these qualities may never develop. But in their place can come common purpose, shared challenge, and commitment to family and country—all of which can breed a rich and enduring marital love. In writing of Jade, and her husband Lao Er, Buck describes the bond: "So close they were, these two, that in weariness and danger and in all the evil of the present world still they could give themselves up to the love there was between them, and return to it, and it was always there" (p. 268). Liao reflects on Buck's message:

> Individualism or collectivism, romantic love or arranged marriage, one can hardly say yet which is better. . . . Monogamy has certainly saved a good deal of "knocking against each other" in a polygamous household. Yet it has its own problems. Many people have fallen in love with two men or two women simultaneously and wish the social institution would tolerate their love ... is it better now for women to drive one another out and to take one another's place in turn in the name of monogamy? Is it better for men to fight and even kill one another for the romantic love of a beautiful lady? ... Human nature is imperfect

> and so are our institutions. . . . The important thing is to understand each other rather than judge. (Liao 1997:109)

Concubinage, female infanticide and slavery, and arranged marriage: in writing of these actions—problematizing their definitions—Buck's own words best illustrate her mission. "There is only truth as people see it, and truth, even in fact, may be kaleidoscopic in its variety. . . . I could never belong entirely to only one side of any question. I straddled the globe too young" (Buck 1954:56).

## SOCIAL CHANGE

Social change is a constant, dynamic feature of society. As such, it can easily escape our full consideration and understanding. Like day-to-day aging that goes unnoticed in our mirrors, social change may only be fully appreciated in retrospect. Buck's sociological imagination helps us overcome this "blindness." She placed her readers in the biographies of her characters, the uniqueness of the historical moment, and the sociocultural patterns of place. As such, she is able to tell the story of change in a way that accentuates its inevitability and its complexity.

Buck's tutorial on social change emphasized China's common people (a fact that drew criticism from a few of her early reviewers). Yet, there was a certain genius to her strategy. Writing of commoners allowed Buck to address change as a rather "ordinary" phenomenon occurring at the hands of simple people, often without their explicit awareness. Consider, for instance, *The Good Earth*'s protagonist Wang Lung. This character embodies the revolutionary change of his times. The reader meets Wang Lung as a young man, a humble farmer scratching out a meager, precarious existence. His fate is tied to the land . . . to the whims of nature—good weather and harvests, floods, droughts and locusts.

Despite many setbacks throughout his life, Wang Lung experiences remarkable upward mobility. Indeed, he becomes a major landowner who rents out his lands for others to work. Buck might have told Wang Lung's story in terms of personal change and triumph. Instead, she chose a more sociological path—one that attributed his transformation to broader social forces.

In route to his new station in life, Wang Lung benefits from the "redistribution" of wealth made possible by a disturbing yet predictable event. During a prolonged famine, desperate peasants loot a home deemed "too rich." While Wang Lung does not participate in the looting, his wife O-lan does. She finds a stash of jewels that will forever alter Wang Lung's future.

(Ironically, O-lan knows where to find the jewels because of her own years as a slave in a wealthy home; experience told her where precious goods were hidden.)

The stolen jewels become the means by which Wang Lung purchases more and more land, systematically increasing his wealth and station in life. When his home life is threatened by nefarious members of his extended family, he uses his new wealth to takes advantage of a common cultural practice and renders his relatives complacent with opium. Wang Lung's wealth, in turn, fuels another major engine of social change: education. His money allows him to send his sons to school, thus "sparing" them from the land. With educated sons, he is able to further protect and advance his socioeconomic interests.

In the end, Wang Lung becomes part of the landed gentry—someone who others might now judge to be "too rich." Yet, while he defined his life in terms of the land, his wealth ultimately separates him from the land; his wealth plants the seeds for further social change. Ironically, the man who loved his land dies an anguished soul knowing that his educated sons will never work the land, but rather, sell it. In Wang Lung's story, the reader is left appreciating anew the intricate and inescapable path of social change.

Buck provides the same "on the ground" view of social change in *Dragon Seed*, a book that documents the Japanese occupation of China during the 1930s and 1940s. Through the eyes of Ling Tan and his family, we learn of the ways in which social events can move ordinary people to extraordinary action. Further, we see how such responses set the stage for subsequent social movements.

The peasants of *Dragon Seed* have never before seen tanks (what they call strange huge shapes) or airplanes (called flying ships or silver creatures that, at first, were mistaken for geese). They are baffled by the bombs or "silver fragments" that drop from these creatures. In trying to make sense of the consequences of bombs, one peasant says:

> "I have wanted a pond on my land for ten years and never had time to dig it and here it is," he said joyfully, and they decided together that such was the purpose of these machines, to dig ponds, and wells and waterways when they were wanted (p. 68).

For Buck's commoners, the Japanese occupation proves foreign as much by its tools as by its perpetrators. Most peasants' initial response to occupation is acceptance. "When fire comes down from heaven," they say, "let it come down and bear it" (p. 84). Indeed, the peasants even organize a welcoming committee for the Japanese soldiers who invade their village:

> "Surely they will see that we are a defenseless village," Ling Tan said, "and even an enemy will not fall upon those who have made themselves willing for their coming. . . . Let us therefore think how to meet our conquerors courteously." (p. 118)

Almost immediately, however, the peasants witness the destruction of Nanking, which, to this day, is considered one of the most brutal attacks of the modern era. Most of the city was burned to the ground, over 200,000 civilians were murdered, and over 20,000 Chinese women were brutally raped (Weinberg 1993). Readers see this brutality through the eyes Ling Tan, who witnesses the rape and murder of an elderly neighbor, his daughter-in-law Orchid, and eventually his youngest son, Lao San:

> He saw them lay hold upon his youngest son, who had always been too beautiful for his own good. . . . (They) bound the father and his eldest son together . . . and they bound them so that they must face the thing they did, and prodded them when they closed their eyes, and so the thing was done, and the beautiful boy lay like dead on the ground (p. 164).

The story of Ling Tan represents thousands of stories that changed the peasantry from accepting to defiant. To be sure, this historical moment was fueled by the decades of suffering, as Chinese peasants endured the Opium wars, European imperialism, and the Boxer rebellions. However, the Japanese occupation created a "tipping point," uniting Chinese nationalists and communists behind the determination of peasant masses fighting to salvage their survival through the land. Thus, *Dragon Seed* does much more than tell the history of a single family. The book uses that family's trials to help us understand how the peasantry becomes such an important factor in China's political landscape.

## CONCLUSION

These themes, as well as others addressed by Buck—class conflict, gender bias, racial inequality, ethnocentrism—keep readers focused on social context as much as fictional characters. This tactic helps readers assume the appreciative stance essential for understanding social worlds.

Moreover, this strategy helps Buck forward a sociological agenda—to observe and understand rather than to rank and moralize. As her character Madame Wu remarks, "two equals are nevertheless not the same two things. They are equal in importance, equally necessary to life, but not the same" pp. 46–47. For Buck, difference is laudable and rich with knowledge. It must be nurtured and explored, and that exploration must not be done as a literary exercise, but rather as witness to the complex sociocultural world in which characters exist.

## NOTE

1. Quoted from a CBS television interview aired on February 8, 1958, accessed June 11, 2009: http://solstice.ischool.utexas.edu/tmwi/index.php/Pearl_Buck.

# CHAPTER 19

# Dante Alighieri: The Afterworlds Are Hell for Sociologists

*Peter Bearman*

## INTRODUCTION

Dante was born in 1265 and died in 1321. Like many of the most important sociologists his greatest work was composed when he was an outsider. This work was ethnographic, initiated at middle age, though the final volume was not finished for two decades. Great ethnographers use their encounters with the denizens of the worlds they enter as levers to reveal the essential qualities of the worlds inhabited by their readers. Dante is no exception. Learning how a field setting is structured, how those who live within it spend their time, and how they understand and speak about their situation allows the ethnographer to reflect back on to the world of the readers.

Many ethnographers visit settings that few of their readers will ever explore, even if they pass through them frequently—street corners where men pass the day (Leibow 1967), the aisles of department stores where kids snitch goodies (Katz 1988), small supper clubs where jazz musicians share what they know (Becker and Faulkner 2009), and city sidewalks where the homeless work and sleep (Duneier 1999).

Consistent with the experience of other great ethnographers, Dante rarely interviews his subjects. He has no questionnaires prepared. For the most part, he does not need them, for as he passes through their worlds his subjects come to him and tell him their life story; seemingly damned to talk they are such overly responsive respondents that Dante frequently has to wrest himself from their verbal grasp.[1] They are determined to learn if and how they are remembered, and they are determined to explain themselves to him, to describe not their experiences (these are revealed directly) but their nature.

If other ethnographers have similar experiences, their field sites are surely different. To my knowledge Dante is the only ethnographer to go places that everyone will eventually spend (under some theories) a great deal of time—or more precisely, an eternity. More specifically, if many people have—over the years—gone to hell, Dante is the first ethnographer to have done so (surely many will follow). And from observations and conversations with the residents there, he describes the world he finds. This essay considers what we can learn from Dante's trip to the worlds of the afterlife, with special reference to hell.

## AN OVERVIEW OF THE AFTERWORLD(S)

There are five worlds. The first is ours. The third to fifth worlds—hell, purgatory, and heaven—are the manifest concern of Dante in the *Divine Comedy*. People come and go in purgatory; as for the other worlds—they simply arrive. Once there, they stay for eternity. The second world is a densely crowded border region, where people who "lived" lives without reason, passion, desire, virtue, or sin are consigned. We will return to them later, but briefly—having never *acted* they never lived. They are ceaselessly blown around in circles, harassed by mosquitoes and black flies. They cry and moan. They are the mass, and both hell and heaven are too good for them.

Hell is ordered from top to bottom by degrees of sin; purgatory from bottom to top by degrees of purification, and heaven from bottom to top in terms of capacity to experience blessedness. Because virtue is not the opposite of sin the three hierarchies are not isomorphic. Even if there is hierarchy everyone is in precisely the right place. No one wishes to be anywhere else. Those in hell do not wish to be in heaven. They are in hell because they are unrepentant. Those in heaven in "lower" circles do not wish to be in "higher" circles. They are as blessed as they can be (Cogan 1999:156–159). One thing we learn is that sin must be more complex than virtue because hell is more complex than heaven.

First about these worlds a few words: there is no census and we do not have a sense of their demography, but they can never be full. The dynamics within them are consequently not driven by competition over scarce resources, or by the pursuit of advantage. The denizens of each of these other worlds know exactly who they are and why they are there. With the exception of purgatory, their action is not motivated by the desire to achieve ends.

We cannot therefore impute motive to their behaviors either from identity or interest. In fact, they do not act in a meaningful sense; their agency is the agency of mercury in a thermometer, driven entirely by exogenous factors

(Burke 1945). Consequently, many of the familiar sociological springs for action are missing. Finally, and most bizarrely, in contrast to our world, the actors who live within them do not shape the afterworld(s). The observed macro structure does not arise from micro-behaviors. It does not matter if positions in these worlds are occupied or not—whether empty or full hell, purgatory, and heaven would have the same structure.

David Byrne remarks somewhere that "heaven is a place where nothing ever happens" (Byrne 1979). That is true, but hell is also a place where nothing ever happens—endlessly. In the afterworld there are no mechanisms. There is no time. There is only a structure of positions filled (or not) by persons without agency. The worlds Dante visits are just pure structural platforms for the representation of the consequences of agency in our world.

The afterworlds are hell for sociologists.

## THE STRUCTURE (OF HELL)

Hell is organized in circles, one on top of another. With one exception, the rule is always the same and it is *just* (Auerbach 2007). The further down we go—circle by circle—the worse the sin. As we move deeper into hell the more the sin being punished arises from a failure of the exercise of reason. Whatever the punishment is, it is revelatory of the sin: punishments in hell are isomorphic to the sins committed in life.

The heads of fortune-tellers are twisted around so they can only see behind them (they pretend to see the future in life, they are condemned to only see the past); small flakes of burning snow fall on to and burn the bodies of usurers, like the small sums of money they scrape from their unfortunate debtors; schismatic's carry amputated body parts around with them (their bodies represent the whole that they have in life fractured); murderers bob in a boiling river of blood; gluttons are stuck in filth; the lustful are blown about helter-skelter by winds; the bodies of thieves are in a constant state of transformation; hoarders push giant weights rocks around and hurl insults at spendthrifts who do the same.

It makes sense that punishments are not allocated at random, one moment and location to the next as this would induce time, which arises from differentiation—if punishments varied, one could look forward to something. Since identity and action and the possibility for agency arise from frictions that necessarily occur in everyday life, whatever we may say in our colloquial discourse, life is *not hell and hell is not other people*. Hell is pure repetition.

In the first circle of hell—limbo—dwell men and women who lived lives well but were born too soon. They stroll around verdant fields talking quietly. They are condemned to hell for the original sin committed by others and passed down across generations. Having no opportunity to choose God, these men and women could nevertheless—and did—choose to lead virtuous lives; they controlled their passions, and opened their minds to philosophy and ethics.

It could be worse—and it fact it will be worse. In upper hell proper, the first sins we encounter are sins reflecting the absence of control. Luster's are consigned to circle 2, gluttons to circle 3, hoarders and spendthrifts to circle 4, and in the border region between upper hell, those with uncontrollable anger, both wrathful (toward others) and sullen (toward the world) are assigned to circle 5. Circles 4 and 5 are composed of opposites whose relationship to objects (money in circle 4) and emotions (anger in circle 5) are out of control.

The improper relationship to money (hoarding or spending) is more abstract than the improper relationship to love or food (Cogan 1999:47–48). As a consequence, it requires more "thought" and hence it is closer to the sins of the mind—deeper in hell—than the sins of the body (in circles 1 and 2). It is proper to be angry with cause, just as bad experiences can and ought to make one (temporarily) depressed. But those with wrath are those who enjoy being angry, just as those who are always sullen want to be sullen. The motive for one's actions matter in one's ultimate disposition because consignment to one or another circle of hell is not the consequence of a "one off decision" later regretted (Cogan 1999:57).

Recall that hell is where those who have not repented for their sins go. Sinners who repent—for whom the sin is not a pure reflection of who they are—go to purgatory. So the persons punished in hell are those whose *essential nature* is one of anger, or sullenness, or greed, slothfulness and so on. But this essential nature is not assigned—it is not already written, there is no predestination—rather it is an achieved nature; it is a nature that is inculcated through practice.

The river Styx marks the boundary between upper and lower hell. Above the river those with emotion management problems reside. Lower hell is for those whose sins are sins of reason, of agency, rather than of passion, or incontinence. In circle 6 are heretics, in circle 7—from "best" to "worst" are first those who commit violence to others (murderers), second themselves (suicides and squanderers), and third God directly (blasphemers), and indirectly by violating the nature of things (sodomites), and the fruits of human labor that contribute to the glory of God on earth (usurers).

Here we observe that sins that invoke a reversal of the natural order are worse than those that work with (however out of control) the natural order. Sex, which is fertile, is made infertile by sodomy; money, which is infertile, is made fertile by usury (Pequigney 1991). The sins of circle 7 are comparable to the sins in circle 2 (lust and sodomy), circle 5 (anger and murder), and circle 4 (spendthrifts and squanderers). What makes them different is their motive (thought directed toward the achievement of some end) that abstracts them from their natural habitat.

Spendthrifts spend money because they cannot not spend money—spending is out of their control; those who are in hell for squandering their patrimony are those who *set out* to destroy themselves and their family. They are not shopaholics who cannot resist new clothes; they are people determined to systematically bring themselves down. Those who kill with motive, as a means to an exogenous end are consigned to circle 7 rather than circle 5, which is reserved for those who kill because they cannot control their anger. In hell, serial killers are above (i.e., less bad than) thieves who lie in wait. In circle 8 are those who commit sins of fraud and therefore break the natural trust that flows between persons: counterfeiters, sorcerers, tricksters, grifters, corrupters, and hypocrites along with thieves, schismatics, and flatterers (Ferrante 1984).

Those who live from the transgression of norms of reciprocity and trust—grifters and confidence men—rely on them, and hence understand them. Their violation of those norms is thus an act purely of the will. Finally, in circle 9, are the traitors: first those who betray those who love them, second those who betray their friends, and finally, those who betray their benefactors. At the center is Judas, eternally gnawed on by Satan. (Cannibalism is in direct opposition to both Gods' and brotherly love.)

These assignments sound familiar because they are familiar. Hundreds of examples could be marshaled—the death penalty in the United States is reserved for murderers who couple their murder in the context of another felony, not who kill from mislaid passion; it was widely reported that there would be a special place in hell for Bernie Madoff, who systematically betrayed his friends, family, and benefactors; and so on (Kolker 2009).

The structure of the afterworlds reveals the underlying theory of the structuring of the world from which the residents came. Most people fail to act: they are the mass and they are revolting, too low for either hell or heaven. Those who desire and cannot control their desires are assigned to the upper reaches of hell: they are condemned to strive but never achieve what they seek. Those who will—and can control their will—can pursue virtue or evil; it is a choice, and because it is a choice it is a choice that can be repeated until it becomes a habit, until it reflects the essential quality of the actor—just what she or he is.

Here actors—those who act with reason—pursue callings. Because the action of the calling reflects the essential quality of the actor, the punishment and the pleasure that follows in the afterlife is exquisitely matched to their nature. This is why for the residents of upper hell, their arrival does not mark a break; it is simply a new context in which to be. They could never get enough, and in hell they can never get any. They were always what they are. Their life story is the story of their essential quality; it is not a narrative of how they became what they became because the theory of becoming that they have, and which Dante reports, is a theory of fate.[2]

However, this is not the case for those further below. They could and did choose their own habits. Because they had motive for their action, they could choose otherwise (Cogan 1999:69–72). The importance of choice is most clearly seen by those who failed to exercise it. Those who lived without living are consigned to the crowded border region where they mill about in circles like cows in an enclosed pen waiting endlessly for the slaughterhouse, besotted by biting flies above, filth and worms below.[3] Only those who acted—for good or for evil—are good enough for heaven or hell.

The self that is made is thus constructed through action, what we call social action; or action oriented toward others in its course. Social actors may be slaves to reason or desire, to passion, to uncontrolled urges and longings, even to slothfulness. Their desires can be pedestrian or refined, but they are still desires—passions for something; sex, drugs, food, drink, status. Animals live controlled lives because they have not emotions or reasons to control. In the end it is far better to live as a victim of ones' desires than to have no desires.

Humans have the possibility of projects, but they must act on them. Without a project people have no chance of going to hell, not to mention heaven. Best of course is a projectivity that is reasoned—to exercise will in order to actively and purposefully pursue virtue or true evil. In a simple way, this is also why the residents of the afterworld come to talk; for if dead, their projects remain.

## REFLECTIONS

In hell and heaven the subjects are morally exceptional, to use Jack Katz's phrasing (Katz 1997). Katz notes that in dealing with these people, ethnographers often swerve toward (and crash into) the shoals of two characteristic mistakes—stressing distinctiveness over framing (and losing framing) or stressing framing over distinctiveness (and losing distinctiveness).

There are many strategies for navigation. Dante makes effective use of the narrative warrant described by Katz as "deeply, even existentially underwritten"—involving understanding that becomes matters of habit long before we could focus self-consciously on social interactions" (Katz 1997:414). Or perhaps better put, this is what his subjects make use of as they encounter their own exceptionality.

The whole system is a giant fun house mirror. Is the real world reflected in the afterworld or is the afterworld reflected in the real? The fact that positions exist in the afterworld and await being filled suggests that the possibilities for virtue and evil were already exhausted in the fourteenth century. Just as the ethnographic context reveals simultaneously what is distinctive and general about humans, the relationship between the field site and the larger world of human interactions in which it is embedded is always complex.

There is nothing quite like observing the full range of humanity in ones' field site to be reminded that however exotic, there is an essential human quality to all contexts. And that is what Dante achieves—which is probably why he is considered by those alive in cultures far different than his and ours—to be a universal figure.

Still, if we wonder why Dante did not encounter in his travels, especially in hell, people who had yet to live (the twentieth century surely invented evil not seen in the fourteenth century) the answer can only be that the afterworld reflects what is possible in the world, and not the other way around. This suggests that it may be time for another field trip.

## ACKNOWLEDGMENTS

Alessandra Nicifero provided most of the good ideas that made this brief essay possible. Beatrice Renault helped move the program along. I am grateful for the patience of the editors who allowed me time to finish. The errors of attribution and understanding are my responsibility alone.

## NOTES

1. The serpents were my friends; for around his neck one of them rolling twisted, as it said, "Be silent, tongue" (Canto xxv:4–6).

2. For one example, of many: "Love, that releases no beloved from loving took hold of me so strongly through his beauty that, as you see, it has not left me yet. Love led the two of us unto death" (V:100–106).

3. There is no need for ethnography here, for the dialogical project: "Looking again, I saw a banner that ran so fast, whirling about, that it seemed it might never rest, and behind it came so long a train of people that I should never have believed death had undone so many. After I had recognized some among them, I saw and knew the shade of him who from cowardice made the great refusal. Straightaway I understood and knew for certain that this was the sorry sect of those who are displeasing to God and to his enemies. These wretches, who were never alive . . ." (Dante, Canto 3:52–81, in Singleton).

# CHAPTER 20

# Galileo Galilei: Which Road to Scientific Innovation?

*Roberto Franzosi*

## "STRANGE SPOTTEDNESSE"

In 1608, the news spread across Europe like wildfire. A Duchtman had invented an instrument (spyglass or telescope) that made far away things look as if they were close by (Van Helden 1977:5).[1] By the end of the year, such an instrument could be seen and bought at fairs in major European cities, from London to Paris. In Italy, as well, spyglasses had been circulating in early 1609 in Milan, Rome, Naples, and even Padua (Van Helden 1983:151).

It is a 6X telescope of this kind that Thomas Harriot, English astronomer, mathematician, and traveler, pointed to the heavens in the summer of 1609. We have an extant drawing Harriot made from his telescopic observations of the moon, dated July 26, 1609, reputed to be the first drawing of the moon as seen through a telescope. This priority aside, the drawing shows that "Harriot had no clear understanding of the phenomena that he was transcribing onto paper . . . no commentary accompanies the drawing to suggest that Harriot recognized the shading as a manifestation of lunar craters and mountains" (Bloom 1978:117).

In June 1609, while in Venice, Galileo heard the news about the spyglass. From what Galileo tells us in the *Sidereus Nuncius* (Starry Messenger) and *Il saggiatore* (Asseyer), he did not get to see an actual telescope (Galileo 1610:60, Vol. III Parte Prima; 1623:257–258, Vol. VI).[2] Instead, "Upon hearing this news, I returned to Padua, where I then resided, and set myself to thinking about the problem. The first night after my return, I solved it, and the following day I constructed the instrument . . . " When he pointed his new instrument to the moon, he saw that "the moon is not robed in a smooth and polished surface but is in fact rough and uneven, covered everywhere, just like the earth's surface, with huge prominences, deep valleys, and chasms." The beautiful drawings he made of the surface of the moon clearly show his understanding of what he saw. As William Lower, one of Harriot's closest scientific associates put it to Harriot after the publication of Galileo's *Sidereus Nuncius*: "in the moone I had formerlie observed a *strange spottednesse* al over, but had no conceite that anie parte thereof mighte be shadowes" (in Bloom 1978:117; emphasis added).

*Questions*: what did allow Galileo to interpret correctly as craters and mountains the "spottednesse" of Harriot's scientific circle? Did they possess different instruments? Did they have different scientific backgrounds as frameworks of interpretation? Put it differently, what role did method and theory play? Or was it sheer luck or . . . something else altogether? What then? It is the answer to these questions I wish to pursue here as they have a bearing on sociological debates.

## GRIND YOUR LENSES (METHOD)

The telescopes circulating in Europe in 1608 and 1609 were simple devices, 2-to-4 in magnification. The one Harriot used in 1609 to draw the first map of the moon was probably a 6X telescope, no different from the one Galileo would point to the moon a few months later.[3] By the end of August 1609, Galileo had built a telescope powerful enough to impress the senators of the Republic of Venice and get a permanent position at Padua and a much higher salary of 10,000 fiorini a year out of them. By early 1610, Galileo was already working with a 30X telescope. (In July Harriot was still working with a 10X upgraded to a 20X in August.)

Galileo's advantage was that he ground his own lenses. Not even Venice, a major glass-making center in Europe, could supply lenses with the required specifications for astronomical work. An extant "shopping list" written by Galileo on the side of a letter addressed to him by Ottavio Brenzoni on November 23, 1609 attests to that. Along with white garbanzo beans, farro, sugar, pepper, clove, cinnamon, spices, jam, listed also are the ingredients necessary to set up a small optical laboratory: lead organ pipe, German polished glasses, mirrors, cannon balls (to grind lenses), and more. With the ingredients of his "shopping list" (or at least some of them), Galileo built the 20X telescope that in January would allow him to gaze beyond the moon and see Jupiter's satellites, the strange appearance of Saturn and Venus's behavior.[4] These discoveries would deal a fatal blow to the reigning Aristotelian world view of geocentrism and perfect and incorruptible heavenly bodies.

## ARTIFACTS

On April 3, 1610, shortly after the March publication of the *Sidereus Nuncius* (Starry Messenger), in which Galileo had announced his astronomical discoveries to the world, Ottavio Brenzoni wrote to his friend Galileo in Padua warning him of the rumors being spread about his discoveries: "They say that the telescope is the cause of those appearances on the moon and of those stars and planets . . . " (doc. 286). Indeed, at the end of that month, on April 27, Martin Horky, "doctor, mathematician, and astronomer" thus described to Kepler the results of a two-day visit by Galileo to Giovanni Antonio Magini, fellow astronomer and mathematician at the University of Bologna:

> Galileo Galilei, the mathematician of Padua, came to us in Bologna and he brought with him that spyglass through which he sees four fictitious planets. On the twenty-fourth and twenty-fifth of April I never slept, day and night, but tested in thousands ways Galileo's instrument, in these lower as well as the higher realms. On Earth, it works wonders; in the heavens, it deceives, because other fixed stars appear double. Thus, the following night, I observed with Galileo's spyglass the little star that is seen above the middle one of the three in the tail of the Great Bear, and I saw four very little stars nearby, just as Galileo observed about Jupiter. I have, as witnesses, excellent men and noble doctors, Antonio Roffeni, a most learned mathematician of the University of Bologna, and many others, who with me in the house observed the heavens on the same night of 25 April, with Galileo himself present. But all acknowledged that the instrument deceived. And Galileo became silent, and on the twenty-sixth, a Monday, very early in the morning, dejected, he took his leave from the illustrious Mr. Magini. And he gave no thanks for the favors and the infinite thoughts, because, full of himself, he had peddled a lie. Mr. Magini provided Galileo with distinguished company, both splendid and delightful. Thus, the wretched Galileo left Bologna with his spyglass on the twenty-sixth. (In Galileo Vol. X.315, pp. 358–359)

## OF PAPER WORLDS

Other arguments, less familiar today although typical at the time, were also being voiced against Galileo. In his book *Dianoia Astronomica, Optica, Physica*, Florentine astronomer Fancesco Sizi argues that:

> There are seven windows in animals' heads . . . two nostrils, two ears, two eyes and one mouth; so, in the heavens, God created and placed

> two favorable stars [Venus and Jupiter], two unpropitious ones [Mars and Saturn], two luminaries [Sun and Moon], and Mercury alone undecided and indifferent. From this and many other similar phenomena of nature, which would be long and tedious to enumerate, we gather that the number of planets is necessarily seven. . . . Besides, the Jews and other ancient nations, as well as modern Europeans, have adopted the division of the week into seven days, and have named them from the seven planets: now if we increase the number of planets, this whole system falls apart. (Sizi 1611:214, lines 13–26 passim)

Sizi goes over traditional arguments about the relationship between macrocosm and microcosm, linking presumed properties of planets (Saturn's coldness, Mars's dryness, Jupiter's warmth, and Venus's humidity) to types of human characters—phlegmatic, melancholic, sanguine, and choleric—and to features of plants and animals (p. 215). He goes on to argue that Jupiter's planets cannot exist because the planets influence the earth depending upon their color and light and Galileo's planets have neither light nor color (p. 217, lines 1–16).

The fact that such arguments would make us laugh today gives us a clear sense of the distance traveled in the last few centuries. It was, indeed, Galileo's lasting legacy on the insistence on the principle of experimental science, that empirical evidence should provide a fundamental criterion of theory evaluation. As he put it repeatedly in his *Dialogue Concerning the Two Chief Systems of the World—Ptolemaic and Copernican* (1632:57, 71, 80, 139, Vol. VII): "Empirical evidence [*sensate esperienze*] must be put before any argument fabricated by the human mind . . . empirical evidence must come before . . . anything put forward by human argument . . . what experience and sense demonstrate must be put before any argument, however sound this may seem . . . welcome are reasons and demonstrations, yours or Aristotle's, and not the texts and naked authorities, because our arguments ought to be around the empirical world, and not a paper world." Yet, data alone are not sufficient for science. Mathematics is required in order to go beyond the mass of data. As Galileo put it in *Il Saggiatore* (The Asseyer) (1632:232, Vol. VI):

> Philosophy [natural philosophy, i.e., physics] is written in that vast book which stands forever open before our eyes (I mean the Universe); but it cannot be understood until one has learned to understand the language and to know the characters in which it is written. It is written in mathematical language, and the letters are triangles, circles, and other geometrical figures, without which means it is humanly impossible to comprehend a single word; without which we are wandering in vain through a dark labyrinth.

Mathematics allows one to go beyond the immediate data, to abstract beyond the particular, as Galileo put it in the *Discourses and Mathematical Demonstrations Concerning Two New Sciences* (1638:296, Vol. VIII): "The knowledge of a single fact acquired through a discovery of its causes prepares the mind to understand and ascertain other facts without need of recourse to experiment."

## COULD IT HAVE BEEN LUCK? (SERENDIPITY)

The word "luck" was not part of Galileo's vocabulary when it came to *his* role in the invention. As for "the Hollander who was first to invent the telescope," *he* was lucky (Galileo 1623:212–213). After all, "the Hollander . . . was a simple maker of ordinary spectacles who in casually handling pieces of glass of various sorts happened to look through two at once, one convex and the other concave, and placed at different distances from the eye. . . . But I . . . discovered the same by means of reasoning . . . "

## "BY MEANS OF REASONING" (THEORY)

What were these "means of reasoning" that Galileo boosts as having been behind his development of the telescope? Galileo himself tells us that story in private letters to various people and in the *Sidereus Nuncius*. There, he writes that, having heard about this invention, he decided

> to apply myself wholeheartedly to inquire into the means by which I might arrive at the invention of a similar instrument. This I did shortly afterwards, *my basis being the theory of refraction* [doctrinae de refractionibus innixus]. First . . . Then . . . Next. . . . Finally, sparing neither labor nor expense, I succeeded in constructing for myself so excellent an instrument that objects seen by means of it appeared nearly one thousand times larger and over thirty times closer than when regarded with our natural vision. (Galileo 1610:60, Vol. III Parte Prima; emphasis added)

Several years later, he tells that same story in the *Saggiatore* (Assayer 1623:212–213).

## THE TELESCOPE AND THE MICROSCOPE

On September 3, 1624, Galileo sent another invention to his friend and fellow Lynx-eyed academician Federico Cesi: a microscope (*occhialino*). In the accompanying letter, he wrote:

> I send to your Excellency an *occhialino* to see from close by minute things, of which I hope you will be able to get not small entertainment and joy, as happens to me. . . . [With this occhialino] I contemplated numerous small animals with infinite admiration: among which the flea is very horrible, the mosquito and the tick are beautiful; with great joy I saw how flies and other tiny animals can walk vertically on mirrors, and even upside down. (Galileo Vol. XIII.1665, pp. 208–209)

This was quite a different letter from the ones he had written some 15 years earlier at the beginning of 1610 announcing to various people the atronomical discoveries he had made with his telescope. All Galileo gets out of his new invention (and the microscope is truly *his* invention, contrary to the telescope) is only "not small entertainment and joy" rather than scientific discoveries. We have to wait for Cesi himself or van Leeuwenhoek or Hooke to put the microscope to a very different use. Science, rather than play, requires fitting "vague perceptions into a theoretical framework" (Bloom 1978:121). Certainly, Galileo lacked the "theoretical framework" required to interpret his microscopic evidence.

## *IMPARA L'ARTE E METTILA DA PARTE*

And yet . . . was it method, theory, or something else altogether that gave Galileo an edge over his competitors in the race of atronomical discoveries? After all, both Harriot and Galileo used similar methods to look at the moon (6X telescope); they could both rely on similar mathematical and astronomical theoretical backgrounds. (Harriot has left behind a great deal of scientific work, notably in mathematics, although mostly published posthumously.) What accounts for the fact that one's "strange spottednesse" was craters and mountains for the other? It was Galileo's training in drawing, art historian Edgerton (1984) would answer.

Galileo grew up in the humanistic and artistic culture of Renaissance Florence where Giorgio Vasari had set up the Accademia del Disegno in 1562. The Accademia trained the young artists not just in drawing, painting, and sculpture, but also in mathematics. After all, the principles of perspective were based on mathematics. Renaissance painter Piero della Francesca has left behind three treatises that "deservedly acquired for him the name of the best geometrician of his time," as put by Giorgio Vasari in his *Lives of the Artists* (1550): *Trattato d'Abaco* (Abacus Treatise), *Libellus de Quinque Corporibus Regularibus* (Short Book on the Five Regular Solids), and *De Prospectiva Pingendi* (On Perspective for Painting). The subjects covered in these treatises include arithmetic, algebra, geometry, and innovative work in both solid geometry and perspective. Much of Piero's work was later absorbed into the writing of others, notably in mathematician Luca Pacioli's *De Divina Proportione*, a work illustrated by Leonardo da Vinci.

Starting in 1584, after dropping out of the University of Pisa where he had enrolled in medicine, Galileo was tutored in mathematics by Ostilio Ricci. Through Ricci, in 1588, Galileo met another mathematician Guidobaldo del Monte (who later played a crucial role in getting Galileo a position in Padua). Both Ricci and Guidobaldo published treatises on perspective, where they show how differently shaped bodies cast light and shades on a plane. No doubt, Galileo knew how to interpret *chiaroscuro*, how in a drawing darker areas are deeper and lighter ones are higher (the craters and mountains he saw on the surface of the moon).

At Ricci's, Galileo met another student who was being tutored in mathematics: Ludovico Cigoli, later to become "the most important Florentine painter of his time" in the evaluation of art historian Panofsky (1956:3). In a letter to Galileo of 1611, Cigoli wrote, "a mathematician without disegno is not only a mediocre mathematician, but also a man without eyes." Indeed, Galileo's own skills as a draftsman were famed (Edgerton 1984:230), as attested by the high quality of the extant drawings of the moon he made for the publication of his *Sidereus Nuncius*.

Galileo and Cigoli became lifelong friends, helping each other out, Galileo helping Cigoli with "theoretical reasoning" behind chiaroscuro and perspective, Cigoli providing drawings of the sunspots to Galileo and even painting a moon as Galileo saw it through his telescope right in the papal Pauline Chapel of Santa Maria Maggiore in Rome (Panofsky 1956:3–4; Booth and Van Helden 2000).

And yet, that same art that allowed Galileo to interpret correctly what he saw through his telescope would later limit his ability to interpret correctly the motion of celestial bodies. In his classical view of the world, there was no room for the elliptical orbits embraced by Kepler (Panofsky 1956:13). He took these beliefs to his tomb.

## SIX LESSONS ABOUT SCIENTIFIC INNOVATION

Galileo's story allows us to draw some general points of interest to social scientists about scientific innovation.

*Point 1:* Many social scientists will recognize in Galileo's involvement in grinding lenses artisanal practices of their own (e.g., programming software for new techniques). Innovation, no doubt, requires expertise (often of a practical kind, "art") outside one's field.

*Point 2:* In Horky's arguments about Galileo's artifacts, we will also recognize similar familiar arguments about social scientific results as the product of the statistical techniques used, as measurement artifacts. Such were the arguments about polynomial distributed lags and the econometric estimates of the relationship between strikes and wages (Franzosi 1995). Such are the arguments about the biasing effect of outliers in regression estimates that have generated controversies in many social science subfields (e.g., Franzosi 1994; Treiman and Yip 1989; Muller and Karle 1993).

*Point 3:* Galileo ushers in a new world of science based on empirical observations interpreted in mathematical form. It is that world we still inhabit today, even in the social sciences, as made clear even by the layout of the functional parts of our journal articles: introduction, theory, data and methods, empirical results, conclusions.

*Point 4:* Theory, by his own account, allowed Galileo to develop his tool of discovery (his method) "far ahead of his nearest competitors" (Van Helden 1983:155). And by winning "the instrument race, Galileo was able to monopolize the celestial discoveries" (Van Helden 1983:155). Theory helped Galileo both to develop his method (theory of refraction) and to interpret correctly the data that his new method delivered (astronomical theory).

*Point 5:* By Galileo's account luck certainly played no role in his discoveries. Sociologist Robert Merton (with Elinor Barber) left behind a beautiful book on serendipity (or "accidental (luck) discoveries") (Merton and Barber 2004). There are, of course, those stories (from Roentgen's X-rays to Fleming's penicillin or Becquerel's radioactivity) but: "the discovery was bound to be made" or, in the words of science historian Sarton, "it was in the air" (cited in Merton and Barber 2004:215, 43) In addition, lucky "accidents never happen to common men" in the words of nineteenth-century science historian Whewell; "the inventor must be in some way prepared to take advantage of an accident" (cited in Merton and Barber 2004:44, 45). Both points are clearly illustrated by Galileo's discovery.

*Point 6:* For sure, with no method and no theory there would be no scientific discoveries. But in this case, with no art, perhaps no discoveries either. *Impara l'arte e mettila da parte.* Learn the art and set it aside. But which art? You never know beforehand what may come handy. Luck, in the end, does play a role!

## NOTES

1. The Dutch spectacle maker, Hans Lipperhey, in 1608 applied the States-General of the Dutch Republic for a patent on a spyglass. The word "telescope" (from the Greek *tele-* "far" + *-skopos* "seeing") was proposed to Galileo in 1611 by his good friend Federico Cesi, founder of the Accademia dei Lincei in Rome.

2. References to Galileo's work are from the 20-volume national edition edited by Antonio Favaro (Florence 1890–1909) and now digitized by the Florence Institute and Museum of the History of Science and made available on the Internet at http://pinakes.imss.fi.it:8080/pinakestext/home.jsf.

3. On the size of Harriot's telescope, see Bloom (1978), Van Helden (1977:27).

4. Still 40 years later, if you wanted to be an astronomer, you had better first become a lense grinder, as Hevelius tells the reader in his *Selenographia* of 1647: "I had to act as an artisan before an observer of the heavens" (cited in Van Helden 1994:16).

# CHAPTER 21

# Jorge Luis Borges: Reduction of Social Complexity

*Filippo Barbera*

## INTRODUCTION

Jorge Luis Borges was born in Buenos Aires on August 24, 1899 and died in Geneva on June 14, 1986.[1] His father, Guglielmo, an attorney who taught psychology at a special school, had a great influence on the development of his intellectual ability. Guglielmo delighted in writing stories and cultivated a great love for philosophy and poetry. Due to a hereditary condition, he passed both his literary passion and his blindness on to his son. Borges became short-sighted and was physically weak as a boy, so he was not able to join the army like so many of his ancestors had done. He longed to take up a literary career that his father had molded him for.

Borges loved books even when he was a child, and he wrote his first story when he was seven; he translated *The Happy Prince* by Oscar Wilde into Spanish when he was nine. His education and the fact that he moved from one country to another had a great influence on developing his intellectual ability. He grew up in a polyglot environment, where he learned English and Spanish when he was very young. Moreover, he did not attend a state school until he was nine. (His father was a "philosophical anarchist" who did not trust institutions.) When he did attend one (from age 9 to 14) dressed in starched clothes that were generally worn at English boarding schools, his schoolmates grimaced and punched him.

In 1914 his father took his family to Europe, but Borges had to remain in Switzerland for several years[2] as World War I broke out. The ensuing years had a great effect on shaping his intellectual abilities. He studied Latin,

French, and German at a boarding school founded by Calvino and came into contact with Western literature and thought. Borges believed Walt Whitman was a noble and "unique" poet. He drew closer to the works of Heine, Meyrin, Richter, Carlyle, and De Quincey. He met Schopenhauer and absolutely loved his works, which expressed the "enigma of the universe," the world as a projection of thought and the negation of time.

Borges read the original texts of other German philosophers, such as Stirner and Nietzsche. Two writers had a great influence on him, Rafael Cansinos Assens, whom he met in Madrid, and Macedonio Fernandez, whom he met in Buenos Aires. When Borges was in their company he discovered the pleasure of a daily life based on intellectual pleasure.[3] Borges had already launched his career as a writer when the whole family returned to Buenos Aires in 1921. He wrote seven books in 10 years (1920 to 1930) as well as four essays and three poems, and he started to become well-known as a "Public Poet." From 1929 to 1960 he spent most of his time writing prose.

*Ficciones* and *The Aleph* came out in the 1940s, and he firmly believed they were the best books he had ever written. His aesthetical stamp can be found in those works, and thanks to them literature from Argentina became, for the first time, concurrent with Western literature: metaphors, parables, a number of powerful symbols (labyrinths, libraries, circular lines, states of decay, mirrors, tigers, and so forth) all encircled by scholarly quotations, floods of metaphysics, and a hallucinatory but not supernatural earmark.

The spatial and temporal infinity are the recurring aesthetical themes of his works. Borges reaffirms that the problem of time is fundamental and if men were able to solve this problem they would be able to solve *everything*. Essays such as these make the reader feel uncertain and ambiguous in a world dominated by chaos. For Borges, however, when we come up against such problems we cannot shirk away from them: we need to find a meaning in a universe that is "chaotically well ordered."

## THE THEME

The theme of this essay is a paradox on the subject of "senseless completeness," or rather, a greater amount of *information* does not always provide better *knowledge*. Borges mentions this topic in many of his works and, to examine the theme and the consequences that sociologists may come up against, some essays have been selected from his most well-known works.

Before providing details we have to assert an overall supposition found in his oeuvre. Borges's world is a chaotic one, and consequently it is not possible to discover laws or overall principles governing it. However, when we do attempt to do so (Brown 2004) as in *Tlön, Uqbar, Orbis Tertius* (1962:18), we inevitably become absurd and ridiculous: "For one of those gnostics, the visible universe was an illusion or, more precisely, a sophism. Mirrors and fatherhood are abominable because they multiply it and extended it." He made fun of taxonomic classifications as well: " . . . animals are divided into: (a) belonging to the Emperor, (b) embalmed, (c), trained, (d) piglets, (e) sirens, (f) fabulous, (g) stray dogs, (h) included in this classification, (i) trembling like crazy, (j) innumerables, (k) drawn with a very fine camel-hair brush, (l) et cetera, (m) just broke the vase, (n) from a distance look like flies." In this way, any expectation of a unified cognitive field is frustrated: there is no "neutral space" in which "natural kinds" are simply classified and enumerated. Instead, we get a feeling of that space as a *contingent* and *precarious* achievement (Lynch 1991:13).

Yet, Borges did not give in to the chaotic reality and he was able to demonstrate how one could trace order within a chaotic world. He greatly admired, from an intellectual point of view, Poe's detective stories that had an *analytical style* (Bennet 1983).[4] We can locate Borges relevance for sociology precisely in this tension between on the one hand, the idea that complete knowledge is unattainable and on the other hand, a liking for knowledge that is effective even though incomplete. The idea relating to "senseless completeness" will thus be examined, and two issues that are of major importance to the sociologist will be discussed: description and interpretation.

## DESCRIPTION: HOW TO REMOVE EXCESS DETAILS?

Description is often looked upon as a "service" activity in social science, helping high-quality research that is geared toward explanation. This opinion implies that description is an easy accomplishment, purely observatory as well, that simply "puts facts in order" (see Sen 1980 for a critique). If this were the case, greater completeness would not be a major problem: the paradox referring to "senseless completeness" would not have come up. However, Borges informs us this is not the case.

Fanatical descriptive precision and the process of reproducing minute details may obstruct knowledge. For example, Ireneo Funes ("Funes, the Memorious," in *Ficciones*, 1962) fell off a horse and became paralyzed, but his ability to remember was still amazing. He could recall a whole day showing great attention to every detail, but this took all day! Ireneo was able to remember every leaf on a tree and every mountain, and even each time he had perceived them. However, he had so many details in his head that he was not able to think:

> Locke, in the seventeenth century, postulated (and rejected) an impossible idiom in which each individual object, each stone, each bird and

> branch had an individual name; Funes had once projected an analogous idiom, but he had renounced it as being too general, too ambiguous. . . . Two considerations dissuaded him: the thought that the task was interminable and the thought that it was useless. He knew that at the hour of his death he would scarcely have finished classifying even all the memories of his childhood. (1962:113–114)

Too many particulars hinder imagination/conceptualization and thus Ireneo:

> was, let us not forget, almost incapable of general, platonic ideas. It was not only difficult for him to understand that the generic term dog embraced so many unlike specimens of differing sizes and different forms; he was disturbed by the fact that a dog at three-fourteen (seen in profile) should have the same name as the dog at three-fifteen (seen from the front). (1962:115)

The same occurrence arises in *On Rigor in Science* (1998),[5] where Borges disclosed a project that was both ridiculous and useless: "a perfect cartography" showing only one province took over a whole city, whereas a map drawn up by the Emperor showing the whole empire was exactly the same in size and it corresponded exactly to the empire:

> In that Empire, the craft of Cartography attained such Perfection that the Map of a Single province covered the space of an entire City, and the Map of the Empire itself an entire Province. In the course of Time, these Extensive maps were found somehow wanting, and so the College of Cartographers evolved a Map of the Empire that was of the same Scale as the Empire and that coincided with it point for point. Less attentive to the Study of Cartography, succeeding Generations came to judge a map of such Magnitude cumbersome, and, not without Irreverence, they abandoned it to the Rigours of sun and Rain. (1998:325)

Borges thus places us up against a clear idea: description always entails selection based on a *relevance criteria*, namely selecting details that are most appropriate to the topic in hand. In this way description becomes a subset of a set of propositions that may be true (Sen 1980). As Borges shows, however, the relevance principle does not exhaust itself in *completeness*, and truth or accuracy are not enough to guarantee the good quality of the description.

In this respect, we may argue that Borges's insights are taking us into a core sociological problem: excessive details are virtually paralyzing for understanding society since they hinder abstraction and reduce the sociologist to a mnemonist who lives in a world of unique particulars. Nevertheless, Borges does not offer a solution to this matter. What is the sociological answer to Borges's dilemma? Actually, sociologists' opinions differ a great deal on what makes a good reconstruction of contexts and therefore which details should be removed (Abbott 1997, footnote 10).

Two well-known positions come to the surface here, put forward by John Goldthorpe (2000) and Andrew Abbott (1997) respectively. Goldthorpe believes that quantitative data analysis permits us to identify macro-regularity independent of the specific historical circumstances. The English sociologist takes into consideration a few examples that help to clarify his viewpoint. Thanks to the application of log-linear models, similar inter-generational mobility rates in different space-temporal contexts were found. Applying logit modeling to survey data has pointed to steady uniformity in the relationship between class inequality and educational attainment, even at times when the educational offer was growing.

Event-history analysis has permitted us to separate two different kinds of effects (Blossfeld and Rohwer 1995): an effect connected to the fact of being born in the same cohort, which therefore sums up the impact of the specific historical variables, and an effect caused by the life course events, which therefore does not concern the historical time. All these acquisitions allow for the construction of macro-regularity to supply phenomena of great sociological interest: social mobility rates, school choices, transition to adulthood, for example. These findings, according to Goldthorpe, make up pure *descriptive* sociological *explananda* that are detached from the historical and geographical contexts and are not self-evident for social actors during their daily life.

Abbott upholds a different viewpoint. Contrary to Goldthorpe, for Abbott good descriptions may only be obtained by contextualizing social phenomena within the space-temporal circumstances. By means of different degrees of contextuality in space and/or over time, clear descriptions of phenomena are obtained (1997:1154, 1166–1168). In this way, we have "natural stories" where the events are deeply rooted in distinct and quite predictable temporal sequences, such as patterns of social revolutions but also institutional change such as "The history of Welfare States." By increasing the degree of contextuality, careers are found, such as in the case of the dynamics in the growth of criminal groups. Lastly, in some cases it may be necessary to contextualize the phenomena in a set of spatial and temporal patterns, as in the urban sociological works in the Chicago School.

All in all, Borges's ideas about "senseless completeness in description" point to one of the—still unsolved—topical problems of sociology: the relationship between history and sociology and the role of the space-temporal circumstances in constructing contexts and good descriptions alike. History may serve its purpose as a residual category for sociology and mark out the point where sociologists constrain their vocation to generalize and define space-temporal details as a limit to their own analysis (Goldthorpe 2000: ch. 2).

The opposite view states that good descriptions of social phenomena need to be placed in the very space-temporal conditions. Therefore, whatever detail is eliminable within a conception becomes an ineluctable factor so as to have a *good description* in the other one.

## INTERPRETATION: HOW SHOULD WE RECONSTRUCT THE MEANING OF AN ACTION?

In *The House of Asterion* (1964), Borges provides the reader with the Minotaur's point of view on his life. Therefore, we have to face up to a unique but lonely creature who is closed up in a house that does not have any door: "I know they accuse me of arrogance, and perhaps misanthropy, and perhaps of madness. Such accusations (for which I shall exact punishment in due time) are derisory. It is true that I never leave my house, but it is also true that its doors (whose numbers are infinite) are open day and night to men and to animals as well" (p. 138).

He plays with his shadow and kills the nine people who every nine years "come and visit him":

> "I crouch in the shadow of a pool or around a corner and pretend I am being followed. There are roofs from which I let myself fall until I am bloody. At any time I can pretend to be asleep, with my eyes closed and my breathing heavy" . . . Every nine years nine men enter the house so that I may deliver them from evil. I hear their steps or their voices in the depths of the stone galleries and I run joyfully to find them. The ceremony lasts a few minutes. They fall one after another without my having to bloody my hands. They remain where they fell and their bodies help distinguish one gallery from another. I do not know who they are, but I know that one of them prophesied, at the moment of his death, that some day my redeemer would come. (pp. 138–139)

Borges skillfully allows us to get into Minotaur's mind. However, the reader only fully understands who the main character is and his sad condition when Theseus comes into the scene and confides with Ariadne by saying, "Would you believe it, Ariadne? The Minotaur scarcely defended himself" (Borges 1964:142). Asterion's endless psychological details and his kaleidoscopic of different interior experiences do not allow one to grasp the meaning of his actions: here the "senseless completeness" so as to the interpretation of social action. The meaning emerges when we come out of the main character's mind and reconstruct the "reception" that the action received within a particular context (demonstrated by Theseus in this particular case).

Without reception in a "circle of recognition," human action is hardly understandable from an external observer. For instance, in *The Writing of God* (1998) a man called Tzinacàn, the wizard of the pyramid of Qaholom, has been put in jail: there he lies down, and an external observer could easily think he is waiting for his death. That is not the meaning of Tzinacàn's action, however, for he is just dreaming the "writing of god." In the skin of the tiger god wrote 14 secret words, who can transform a man into a god. As soon as Tzinacàn works out the secret and became himself a god, however, he no longer wishes to escape from the jail, even if he could easily do it. Now he is a god and he does not even remember who the man called Tzinacàn is and what his needs and wishes are.

In this way Borges helps us to differentiate between an "inside the skin" way of clarify meaning and an "outside the skin" approach on the other hand. Regarding the first one, the meaning of the action may be found in the actor's mind (Elster 1998), whereas in the second the meaning depends upon the "circles of recognition" that evaluate the action (Pizzorno 1986, 1991, 2007). In this way, Borges places us up against the paradox of "senseless completeness": completeness of psychological and mental details in full may not be helpful when reconstructing the meaning of an action. Therefore, Borges seems to suggest a detachment between meaning and intentionality, a position also endorsed in some parts of sociological theory (Pizzorno, ibid.).

In actual fact, intentionality needs to be introduced also if the meaning depends on the action's reception within the "circles of recognition." First of all, Merton and Goffman have taught us that the "circles of recognition" do not always give rise to a *well-ordered reality* but produce non-coherent and contingent aggregations that do not have any well-defined edges, and we may therefore have "excessive recognition." Here the actor should *control* a cacophony that arises from the contrast among the different sources, as where the circles bring about uncorrelated values.

Bearing in mind Harrison White's (2008) standpoint, we may look upon control as a set of attempts and means that helps actors deal with uncertainty, confusion, and circumstances as well as the numerous and frequent contradictory stimuli coming from the recognition circles. In this case, the actor should deliberately keep well under control his/her own sources of recognition: *select* and *choose* who they want to be influenced by and also differentiate between the many possible sources of recognition. Second, the actor's intentional strategies come back due to the fact that the instability of the recognition criterion is endogenous as far as choices are concerned and does not depend only on external shock.

A typical example of *external shock* is a revolutionary change, such as the state brought about by capturing the Bastille on July 14, 1789 (Sewell 1996). As a result, complicated and implicit negotiations started up. However, they were not simple linguistic exchanges but declarations, debates, exchanges of opinion, and symbolic behavior. The turn in the symbolic definitions was accompanied by changes in people's attitude and the alignment of the different groups and parties (Pizzorno 2007:261–262). However, changes in the recognition criterion are often *endogenous* to the choices taken. For example, the value of an action is often subject to a threshold effect: when $N + 1$ actors carry out that choice, the values given to the reference criterion change a great deal.

This is the case of Hirsh's positional goods or the concept of social differentiation by means of consumption celebrated by Bourdieu: some choices are advantageous if only a few people are involved. Therefore, if the value given to the action by the circle of recognition depends on external shock as well as the action itself, then the *strategies* aimed at the construction of symbolic and material barriers when new actors come in are key. As a result, in this case as well, the active controlling strategies carry out an important role *even* if we are ready to accept that the meaning of the social action derives from someone else's recognition.

## CONCLUSION

What was Borges's solution to the tension that subsisted between radical skepticism that maintained complete knowledge was unattainable and a liking for incomplete but effective knowledge? His answer was a *style of writing* that has become known as "magic realism":

> According to the Magic Realism Weltanschauung, the world and reality have a dream-like quality about them which is captured by the presentation of improbable juxtapositions in a style that is highly objective, precise, and deceptively simple. The Magic Realist painting or short story or novel is predominantly realistic and deals with the objects of our daily life, but contains an unexpected or improbable element that creates a strange effect leaving the viewer or reader somewhat bewildered or amazed. (Menton 1982:412)

Likewise, even when sociologists have to face up to a world that is chaotic and complex they may bring reality's most counterintuitive aspects to the surface in a similar way by resorting, first and foremost, to a *style of writing* that is precise and simple. Precision matters when small and seemingly insignificant events can make a huge difference to the processes we are trying to explain (Hedström 2005). Thus, the style of writing is not only a formal matter, but it is also closely linked to the *content of writing*—a state of affairs very close to Borges's credo.

## NOTES

1. The information about Borges was taken from the introduction written in Italian of the complete work edited by Domenico Porzio (Borges 2008).

2. Four years in Geneva and one year in Lugana: He spent a couple of years in Spain before returning to Argentina in 1921.

3. In this regard, another well known South American writer, Jorge Amado, compared knowledge found in books with knowledge come upon over a lifetime and believed that knowledge discovered over a lifetime was the better of the two.

4. "Critics have noted in passing that Borges is the single most prominent perpetuator of literary forms pioneered by Poe. The detective story and the short tale that turns narrative action into philosophical speculation rank among the notable literary exercises of both writers" (Bennet 1983:263).

5. *El Hacedor* (1960), collection of short essays and poems.

# CHAPTER 22

# Isaac Asimov: Impacting and Predicting Sociocultural Change

*Kathleen M. Carley*

## ASIMOV

Isaac Asimov is widely recognized as one of the greatest and most prolific science fiction writers, producing the landmark *Foundation* series.[1] He was born in Petrovichi in Russia, and his family immigrated to the United States when he was three years old. He was raised in Brooklyn, became a professor of biochemistry at Boston University, and worked with U.S. military research in World War II. An avid mystery buff and Sherlock Holmes aficionado, Asimov also wrote mysteries, popular science books, and books about the Bible and Shakespeare. He is the only author to have published in all 10 categories of the Dewey Decimal System. He served as the president of the American Humanist Association and felt that people should be judged by the totality of their works, not their words. His life and ideas are chronicled in multiple biographies and autobiographies (e.g., Asimov 1994).

Along with Frank Herbert, Robert Heinlein, Arthur C. Clarke, Ray Bradbury, and Frederick Pohl he literally defined science fiction for a generation as the in-depth exploration of alternative sociocultural systems. A lover of history and mysteries, Asimov wove into his books profound explorations of what it meant to be a social human as his protagonists solved crimes in his alternate histories and social futures. And in doing so, Asimov affected our society. A subtle and positive indication of this is the fact that he introduced three terms into the English language: positronics,[2] psychohistory.[3] and robotics.[4] His work, particularly the foundation series and that on robots, contains many fundamental social insights and ideas that have inspired many scientists.

## FOUNDATION SERIES

Asimov is best known for the Foundation series, winner of the Hugo Award for Best All Time Series in 1966 (see Asimov 1951, 1952, 1953, 1982, 1986, 1988, 1993). In this series, he builds an alternate universe and describes hundreds of years of its history. The keys to this series are Hari Seldon and R. Daneel Olivaw. Seldon is a mathematics professor and the creator of psychohistory. Using computational and mathematical sociology he develops a model that is used to predict social change and identify potential courses of action that alter the fate of the universe, reduce barbarism, and enable the emergence of a new empire. R. Daneel Olivaw is a sentient robot who imagines the science of psychohistory and encourages Seldon to develop the practical application. He does this because he realizes that the three laws of robotics are limited and so he needs to create a social world where a zeroeth law of robotics can hold sway. Social prediction becomes a necessary prelude to creating an integrated approach to social adaptation and socially transformative technologies.

## ROBOTS

A key element of Asimov's writing is the exploration of how the incorporation of robots will change society's norms and culture. He postulated the existence of a range of robots, including ones who are sentient and have a conscience. On the one hand, the basic socio-technical principle is that restrictions on the technology will govern its ultimate forms of interaction with humans. Thus, the three laws of robotics define the space of interaction possibilities between human and robot. These laws, introduced by Asimov in *Runaround* (1942), state that:

1) A robot may not injure a human being or, through inaction, allow a human being to come to harm.
2) A robot must obey any orders given to it by human beings, except where such orders would conflict with the First Law.
3) A robot must protect its own existence as long as such protection does not conflict with the First or Second Law.

These laws constrain behavior and are dependent on each other, which leads to a "predictive" structure that is thought to eliminate unforeseen consequences of introducing robots and to make all adaptations by humans to the new technologies predictable. It just takes knowing the right model of human social behavior, which humans, unassisted by computers, cannot fully comprehend.

As a host of science fiction books demonstrate, even laws as well formulated as these, since they are written in "English" and not code, have elements of uncertainty. Consider, for example, the ambiguity in the word "harm." As any computational modeler will tell you, any verbal theory, no matter how seemingly complete, needs to be augmented when converted to its computational form.

Asimov is concerned not with human-computer interaction but with technology in a social context. As such, the robots must grapple with the issue of whether not harming a human is harming humanity. Asimov resolves this by the robotic construction of the zeroeth law: 0) A robot may not harm humanity, or through inaction, allow humanity to come to harm. And an amendment to the first law "except where such behavior would conflict with the zeroeth law." In *I, Robot: The Evitable Conflict* (Asimov 1950) the robots resolve all inconsistencies by taking control of humanity.

On the one hand, this is an argument for a science of group-technology interaction. Such a science would provide a detailed understanding of the limits of interaction. On the other hand, this is an argument that cultural advance, the reduction of barbarism, and the evolution of mankind require a focus on the group, not on the individual, as the actor of prime importance.

In the *Wrath of Khan* (1982), Gene Roddenberry has Spock, who is dying of radiation poisoning; tell Kirk that "the needs of the many outweigh the needs of the few." Asimov's argument is more than this social philosophy, however; it is a core rule in a rule-based model that can be used to direct the evolution of humanity. Indeed, Asimov is arguing that social scientists can and should create predictive models and use them to identify courses of action that humanity should take. Psychohistory lies at the heart of such modeling.

## PSYCHOHISTORY

While the sociological insights surrounding robotics are quite interesting, it is in the development of psychohistory that Asimov as sociological thinker is most visible. As he wrote in the opening to Ch. 4 in *Foundation* (1951), psychohistory is "that branch of mathematics that deals with the reactions of human conglomerates to fixed social and economic stimuli. . . . Implicit in all these definitions is the assumption that the human conglomerate being dealt with is sufficiently large for valid statistical treatment." Asimov further posits that "a further necessary assumption is that the human conglomerate be itself unaware of psychohistoric analysis in order that its reactions be truly random." This enables psychohistory to avoid the quagmire of game theoretic issues that arise when people know they are being analyzed.

The basic idea is that the behavior of groups, not individuals, can be predicted. The mode of prediction is statistical. Like modern machine learning, these statistical models are "derived" from data; that is, the entire Galactic History. Unlike machine learning models, however, they are also composed of rules inferred from basic cognitive and social principles.

The composite model is the result of both induction and deduction. Then the entire model is instantiated with information on the current population, the entire Galactic Population, at that point in time. This instantiation enables predictions to be based on the latest and most accurate information. The current situation, cognitive principles, and statistical regularities are needed to understand and predict social behavior.

Asimov's psychohistorical model is not a set of simple equations reflecting historical correlations, but a complex dynamic model of the process by which change occurs. In other words, he is arguing that to understand social phenomena you have to understand the processes. Moreover, these processes are complex. There are non-linear effects, discontinuities, and vast numbers of interacting components. The type of modeling envisioned by Asimov exists in the social sciences. Component models that point in this direction include the econometric models used to predict GNP and the system dynamics models originally envisioned by the Club of Rome in which sets of difference equations and statistical distributions characterize macro processes.

At its core, however, Asimov's vision had a stronger cognitive and social basis. Like White (2008), Asimov is arguing that social structure and culture emerge from the concatenation of individual lives. That is, his psychohistory was an emergent phenomena from understanding the basic way in which individuals respond to stimuli. His macro sociocultural predictions resulted from understanding the trends in detailed individual behavior. Thus, his vision was more consistent with modern agent-based models like Construct, where individual actors and groups are modeled and instantiated with actual census data (Carley 1990, 1991; Carley et al. 2009).

Asimov argued that the model, however complex, is still a reduced representation of reality. He used his understanding of social behavior to suggest how to make simplifying assumptions. He argued that, in essence, the social world had a core-periphery structure. The imperial capitol world Trantor and its attendant planets were the core. The activity and behavior of Trantor, therefore, needed to be modeled in detail. Anything in the periphery was less critical. Interventions would show direct effects on Trantor and second order effects in the periphery.

For Asimov, the model is never complete nor correct. After all, "finished products are for decadent minds" (Asimov 1953:78). However, the model is useful. Over time, the modelers continue to add refinements, which make it both more accurate and alter its predictions. In *Second Foundation* (1953) Asimov points out that the laws in the model are relative. As such the prediction, or as he calls it "the plan," is never finished. It is just the best that can be done with the data at that point in time. This is science as the quest for better answers, not perfect answers. Further, it highlights the role of human intellect and suggests that at the frontier, science is in part art.

The model generates not single-point predictions, but probabilities that different events will occur and large-scale trends in behavior. In other words, the model describes a space of possibilities. What Asimov is suggesting is that you cannot validate a model by forcing it to completely describe the events of the past. Today, we call that over-fitting. Instead, he argued that the way to use complex sociocultural models is to support intervention and to focus on future possibilities.

Social and economic stimuli lie at the center of the computational models of galactic change. The fall of Trantor and the collapse of the galaxy are predicted using basic socioeconomic principles. One such principle is that if a planet can provide for the basic needs (food and water) of the population, then the population will grow, curiosity and innovation will exist, and social mobility will be possible. Another principle is that as planetary land mass is covered in buildings, food needs to be brought in from outside the planet, thus reducing social stability on the planet. A third principle is that an increase in social instability leads to an increase in crime, which leads to an increase in instability. This is a classic example of a positive feedback loop.

Other principles include the following: increasing bureaucracy stifles innovation; rigidification of power and the development of a class system reduces social mobility; and destabilization of a social system's core leads to the eminent collapse of the entire system. Each of these principles can be represented by mathematical equations. Asimov puts these principles together in what is essentially a systems dynamics model of state stability predicated around a Maslowian hierarchy of needs. The end result is a computational system that can predict the fall of Trantor.

In addition, this computational model also predicts the descent of the galaxy into barbarism and the growth of the foundation as second order effects. Finally, it generates a large number of higher-order predictions at varying levels of fidelity, such as predicting that the dying empire could not wage a successful war against the fledgling foundation.

The overall Seldon model is not a single model; rather, it is an interoperable set of models. There are models of key individuals and models that enable reasoning about key events such as the likelihood that Seldon will be arrested or assassinated. These are the agent-based models. The agents are modeled using basic cognitive principles and statistical patterns of behavior in response to stimuli. The critical agents are embedded in an overarching model in which general patterns and the activities of key individuals are modeled. These key individuals are connected in networks of influence enabling reaction and response.

One of the ironies of Asimov's writings concerns the implicit role of social networks. The key actors in the books, such as Seldon and Daneel, use their social networks to acquire and gain information and consciously manipulate those networks to achieve their ends. In the psychohistory model, however, it appears that social networks are balance mechanisms dictating the level of influence and control that can be exerted before the system ruptures into imbalance and instability.

## COMPUTATIONAL SOCIAL SCIENCE

For Asimov, computational social science is characterized by being, an applied social science, a team effort, grounded in vast quantities of empirical data, cumulative, and enabled by computers. Yet, as was mentioned earlier, the science of psychohistory is capable of prediction only at the group level.

Asimov's social science is fundamentally computational and applied. Indeed, he envisions the type of computational technology needed to do practical social *science*—The Prime Radiant in the *Foundation* series. The Prime Radiant is a computational environment that enables the observation of mathematics, associated papers, talks, and images, and it enables changes to be made in the model and the results observed on multidimensional displays using simple color-coding schemes for ease of interpretation. Critically, in this environment all information is linked, and there is the ability to seamlessly move from source to prediction, from qualitative to quantitative analysis, from conceptual model to formula.

The Prime Radiant is also a central repository with external "mini" radiants able to access the main computational environment in real time. Robots could potentially be mini radiants. However, access to the Prime Radiant through mini-radiants is restricted to an elite modeling class—"The Speakers." Without the Prime Radiant, Seldon could not have created the basic model.

Asimov is basically envisioning an applied science. The social scientists are active participants in human evolution. Right from the start, Seldon uses the model to identify those courses of action that can alter the general trends. The model predicts that with no intervention the galaxy is headed toward 30,000 years of Dark Ages. Seldon and colleagues identify a series of action, setting up the foundation and second foundation, moving off Trantor, and so on, that will reduce the Dark Age to a mere millennium. Asimov is suggesting that scientists can and will be active in changing the course of history. The Speakers, for example, can alter The Mule, mentally, to render him harmless.

Asimov is arguing that there is a cycle in which a comprehensive model can be used to direct social change. The cycle has four parts: model development, model-based prediction, model-driven intervention, and model-based assessment. In the assessment phase one compares whether the course of change after the intervention is closer to and less deviant from that predicted by the model. If so, the model is validated; if not, the model is retuned with new data. This is an approach practiced today for large computational models.

For Asimov, modeling and theory building is a team activity, built over a dozen generations. The model is continually refined by researchers, the Speakers, who through deduction, induction, or observation identify new rules, assess deviations, run experiments with the model, and so on. The model is also being refined by other models, the robots, in particular R. Daneel Olivaw. Today, the best models of complex sociocultural systems are indeed built, assessed, and validated by teams. Auto-adaptive models and models that modify models are currently being built, though they are still primitive.

Psychohistory and the overarching model requires as input the entire Galactic History and information on the complete current Galactic Population. Indeed, one entire planet was devoted to the accumulation, storage, and processing of this information—Terminus. Similarly, the powerful computer in *I, Robot: The Evitable Conflict* (Asimov 1950) required Earth's real-time input as well as historical records.

According to Asimov, for a model to be predictive it had to be instantiated with real data. Without historical data, the computer of *The Evitable Conflict* was unable to predict meaningful conclusions, thus indicating that computational social science required both current state and context in order to make useful predictions. Indeed, the entire foundation enterprise nearly failed because the data available, particularly that from newspapers, was incomplete and often wrong. This same problem hinders real computational social science today.

In the *Foundation* series, Seldon's model is not a model, but a set of interoperable models. The level of detail, the level of validation, and the level of effort in development were all higher for submodels that described elements in the core of the Galactic empire. The model of Trantor itself, and that of the power behind the emperor, Chen, were more detailed yet linked into the other models. As is now argued by computational scientists, the purpose of the model drove the level of investment, validation, and veridicality needed.

Science, and the models developed, are essentially cumulative. Indeed, over time, through a process of build test extend, the model grows ever more accurate.

## AGENCY

Asimov argues that prediction is possible at the group level and that society can be directed using interventions designed to move the group in the desired direction. This might be seen as an argument that there is no individualism—that humans are in essence a collective. In fact, that is not the case.

Asimov's argument is more subtle. He is suggesting that human response to stimuli is part of the genetic makeup and so does not change over time. To be sure there are individual differences. However, there is a species norm. It can be discovered statistically, but it requires vast amounts of data to accurately map the distribution. This distribution can then be used in the model to identify first- and second-order effects of interventions.

It is always an individual who causes the greatest deviation in society from that predicted by the model; e.g., "The Mule" (Asimov 1952, 1953). It is always an individual who identifies the needed changes in the model to enable improved prediction. It is always an individual who is the intervention that brings the galaxy back into alignment with the predictions. However, the social intuition is that while the collective is predictable, it is the individual who directs and initiates change.

Key individuals have identities that are created by being in the right place at the right time with the right background (physiological, social, and cultural) and a sufficient social network that enables them to enact change. These individual are unique because of the low probability that two individuals would have identical backgrounds and social networks and be in the same place at the same time. Much in the same way as argued by White in *Identity and Control* (2008), for Asimov the individuals are not goal directed but use goals to explain the history of their actions.

Asimov, like White, argues that unique individuals, like The Mule, emerge as new identities from the patterns of relationships that make up the society. Exceptional individuals can shape history, but the opportunity to do so is created by macroscopic trends.

However, the individual cannot always change the course of history. Asimov also argues that in some cases, individuals are powerless. In *Foundation and Empire*, general Bel Riose, described as arguably the greatest strategist and tactician in Imperial history, equipped with a fleet that the Foundation has no expectation of being able to defeat in battle and having achieved an unassailable strategic position, is nonetheless unable to defeat the Foundation due to the imperial system itself.

Asimov, like Giddens, is arguing for structuration. Social structures constrain the actions of individuals. The actions of individuals, as a collective, in mass, reproduce the structure. Actions and structure co-evolve. But Asimov, unlike Giddens, enables change through key actors and possibly, mutation.

For Asimov, the actor is the social agent. The basis of the social agent is the ability to interact, have a conscience, and process and create information. Agents are about agency. Agents can be humans or sentient others, such as robots. In all cases, though, the agent's behavior is defined by a set of rules or "laws."

These laws are knowable and serve as the basic principles of psychohistory and so the overall model. These laws are inherently cognitive. Asimov's work is an argument that not only are people not rational, they are not even boundedly rational. Rather, much of the social agent is derivable from the further limitations that cognitive processing (or technically positronic processing for robots) puts on activity.

For Asimov, like White, socialness requires being embedded in society and having sociocultural knowledge. For Asimov, socialness also requires being a limited cognitive actor. The actor is limited in the Carley and Newell (1994) sense in that the omniscient actor has more capability cognitively than the rational actor, which has more capability than the boundedly rational actor, which has more capability than the cognitive actors, as each category is constrained by additional information-processing restrictions. Thus, Asimov's model social agent, used in Seldon's overarching model, is embedded in social networks and is both cognitively limited and imbued with a rich detail of sociocultural information.

What this means is that the entire enterprise of psychohistory rests on a less known assumption. To wit, psychohistory only works as long as humans are the only sentient race. Since robots are created by humans, they are basically viewed as humanesque in their sentience. That is, sentient technologies inherit the sentience of their makers. If there were another sentient race, whose cognition was encapsulated by fundamentally different rules than humans, the model would not work.

Whether mutation could lead to alternative sentience is a question left somewhat unanswered by Asimov. The Mule is a genetic abnormality and certainly operated at the very limits of the statistical distribution; however, he is sterile. As such, The Mule's mutation does not enter the gene pool and Asimov avoids the Genghis Khan effect where .5 percent of the male population are thought to be descendents of the great conqueror.[5]

Seldon's model did not predict "The Mule," but, as we later learn, there were elements of the model that predicted the likelihood of someone like The Mule if that analysis had ever been run. As the later books suggest, even with the presence of an anomalous event such as the Mule, the system can recover over a number of years since the fundamental laws are still unchanged.

This sentience assumption of psychohistory is in fact one of the basic principles of sociocultural modeling. If you change the nature of the agents, you change the model. The core scope or precondition of any sociocultural model is that it does not apply to the types of actors that obey different fundamental precepts. It is precisely because humans and their environment are bounded that we can model them; thus, if either changes, the probability landscape alters and the model must be changed.

## IMPACTING AND PREDICTING SOCIOCULTURAL CHANGE

Inspiration for science can come from anywhere. Asimov inspired countless scientists in many areas. Indeed, his work inspired myself and the center for Computational Analysis of Social and Organizational Systems. I found that his insights about the process of science were as important as those about computational modeling. We have found that computational models of complex sociocultural systems can open the window on understanding the space of future possibilities and the impact of the action of key individuals.

## NOTES

1. Many thanks to the CASOS group, and particularly Neal Altman, George Davis, Matt de Reno, Brian Hirshman, and Eric Malloy.

2. Positronic is an entirely fictional term referring to the type of brain that robots have, supposedly fueled by positrons.

3. Psychohistory, as defined by Asimov, is the mathematics of social human behavior. However, in history, it is the study of the psychological motivations of historical events.

4. Robotics refers to the engineering science of robots. The term was introduced by Asimov in 1941 in the short story *Liar*. The term robot, of course, was first used in 1921 by Karel Capek in his play *R.U.R.* (Rossum's Universal Robot) (Capek 2001).

5. http://news.nationalgeographic.com/news/2003/02/0214_030214_genghis.html.

# CHAPTER 23

# Alfred North Whitehead: From Universal Algebra to Universal Sociology

*Thomas J. Fararo*

Most people know of Alfred North Whitehead (1861–1947) mainly through quotations from his writings. *A clash of doctrines is not a disaster—it is an opportunity. Seek simplicity, and distrust it. The art of progress is to preserve order amid change, and to preserve change amid order. The deepest definition of youth is life as yet untouched by tragedy.* And so forth. In his various philosophical writings, he commented on topics of interest in economic sociology and in cultural sociology, and he strongly emphasized the role of emotions in human life.

A number of influential sociological theorists have been influenced by Whitehead's philosophical ideas, and one of the most original and indeed daring features of his greatest work is its social view of the entire universe. But just who was Whitehead, and how did he come to his views on the nature of things? We shall discover a devotion to utmost abstraction . . . and decisive concreteness, and in his "final interpretation" we will encounter an awesome and perhaps incredible climactic vision.

## THE STARTING POINT: UNIVERSAL ALGEBRA

Whitehead was a mathematician before he was anything else as far as his intellectual biography is concerned. At Cambridge, England, he studied mathematics and then was appointed to the mathematics faculty. His very first book already indicated in its title a certain disposition toward generality of formulation that would characterize his later writings. *Universal Algebra* (1898) is a lengthy and dense mathematical treatise. The bulk of the book deals with the exposition, comparison, and extension of prior work in the areas of pure mathematics that today are known as abstract algebra and algebraic geometry. There is a chapter, for instance, on Boolean algebra. In these studies, familiar operations such as addition and multiplication are generalized to have non-numerical application, while there is some retention of the abstract conditions that they satisfy (e.g., $x + y = y + x$, a commutative law).

Mathematical theories deal with abstract entities that satisfy certain abstractly stated conditions. Numerical algebra is only a particular instance of universal or abstract algebraic concepts. For Whitehead, this became a lifelong strategy of concept formation that I will call *conceptual generalization*, by which I mean that a concept in use with limited scope of intended application is generalized to have a far wider scope that captures the original usage as a special case.

This first book carries the subtitle "Volume I," but the planned second volume did not appear. Whitehead's former student Bertrand Russell had become deeply interested in the philosophy of mathematics and was excited by the idea of showing that all of mathematics could be derived from a small set of axioms of logic. The similarity of the projects of the two men led to a collaboration that resulted in the pioneering multi-volume treatise *Principia Mathematica* (1910–1913).

## TRANSITION TO THE PHILOSOPHY OF ORGANISM

Despite this in-depth immersion in pure mathematics and formal logic, Whitehead also maintained a strong interest in applications of mathematics in physical science. In 1914 he left Cambridge to become Professor of Applied Mathematics at the Imperial College of Science in London, a position that he held until 1924. During this period he published several books that established his reputation for original philosophical analysis dealing with what he called the theory of nature, notably *Principles of Natural Knowledge* (*PNK*; 1925).

One key notion in this work is a conceptual distinction between event and object. An event is an unrepeatable occurrence, while an object is a character of an event and as such has the potential for recurrence in other events. Events both extend over and are extended over by other events, smaller and larger, respectively, but there is no final or largest event, so that in this concrete sense events are implicated in the "becomingness" of nature. As Whitehead puts it, there is a "creative advance" of nature.

At the age of 63, in 1924, Whitehead accepted an offer of a professorship in philosophy at Harvard. Thereafter, he produced a substantial body of philosophical writings, two of which are the most important in terms of their influence on sociology, namely *Science and the Modern World* (*SMW*; 1926b) and his 1929 magnum opus *Process and Reality* (*P&R*; 1978).

*SMW* contains a critical analysis of the materialistic philosophy arising out of the advances in science since the seventeenth century in which the success of the abstractions of physics had led to a "fallacy of misplaced concreteness" in which an aspect of an entity is mistaken for its concrete reality. For Whitehead, the most recent advances in physics, especially Maxwell's beautiful electromagnetism, Einstein's breakthrough relativity theory, and the revolutionary quantum theory, were leading to a fundamental transformation in the presuppositions of science.

The world consists of *organized* actualities. The organic character of natural things is what he believes should be built into the philosophical presuppositions of science. With this in mind, he calls his approach "the philosophy of organism." Thus, in addition to its critique, the book sets out a difficult partial articulation of an emerging metaphysical perspective, especially in its daunting chapters on abstraction and concretion.

## IMPACT ON SOCIOLOGICAL THEORY

Two mid-twentieth century sociological theorists, Talcott Parsons and George Homans, interacted with Whitehead during their formative years at Harvard in the 1930s. They regarded *SMW* as a key source for ideas about science that could be applied to sociology, notably the idea that general scientific theories are based upon fundamental conceptual schemes. Parsons's *The Structure of Social Action* (1937) sets out an argument for the existence of a convergence in social theory (in particular in the writings of Weber, Durkheim, Marshall, and Pareto) on a common conceptual scheme that he called the action frame of reference. It was to be the starting point for the creation of general sociological theory. Such a theory was to be analytical, meaning that it would be based upon a conceptual scheme with a small number of analytical elements (analogous to mass and velocity in the theory of motion) that would be interrelated to constitute a set of analytical laws.

Drawing upon Whitehead's discussion in *SMW*, he called the philosophical foundation of this approach *analytical realism* and argued that if the distinction between analytical theory and concrete reality is overlooked—thereby equating the abstract with the concrete—an improper claim of the scope of the theory would occur, instantiating the fallacy of misplaced concreteness.

George Homans, in his influential book *The Human Group* (1950), adopts the same analytical approach (citing Whitehead in his preface) and formulates a distinction among three entities: events, customs, and analytical hypotheses. The recurrence of customs in social events is a distinction grounded in Whitehead's distinction between an occurrence (event) and an object (potential for recurrence). The empirical verification of analytical hypotheses would yield the analytical laws of the analytical theory. Although proceeding in a more inductive mode, Homans essentially agreed with Parsons's conceptual formulation of analytical realism, a Whiteheadian philosophy of science. For an extended discussion of this intellectual nexus of Whitehead, Parsons, and Homans, see Fararo (2001: Ch. 3).

As a contribution to the philosophical tradition, *P&R* is widely regarded as the greatest work of process philosophy in the twentieth century, with indications of increasing interest among social scientists in it.[1] Whitehead's magnum opus also provided part of the philosophical background of the general systems movement that was initiated in the 1950s and that continues to reverberate in sociological theory, such as in the writings of Luhmann (1995).

As systematically presented in *P&R*, Whitehead's process worldview is notable for its daunting complexity—in part due to the strategy of conceptual generalization—creating a barrier to understanding that has led to numerous interpretive studies and philosophical debates, many of them published in the journal *Process Studies*. Sherburne (1966) has responded to the problem with a very useful "key" to the book that rearranges its content and also provides a glossary. The remainder of this essay draws upon, but does not attempt to explicate, Whitehead's process philosophy in order to focus on the aspect of it that I am calling his universal sociology.

## UNIVERSAL SOCIOLOGY

The key concepts from *P&R* that we require are *actual entity* and *nexus*. With one exception to be noted below, an actual entity is also called an actual occasion. It is a process of becoming concrete—in Whitehead's terms, a *concrescence*. A nexus is a grouping—a field or network or complex—of actual occasions. Each actual occasion arises in an *actual world*, which is an instance of the notion of a nexus. In fact, the occasion is an emergent synthesis of *prehensions*—generalized perceptions—of items in that world.

Whitehead's concepts include two that are key terms in social theory: "social order" and "society." We can approximate their Whiteheadian meaning without quoting the more elaborate formal definitions. In *SMW*,

Whitehead had noted in his critique of scientific materialism that it tended to think of things in term of their separateness whereas in his own *organic mechanism* approach things must be seen in their *togetherness* aspect. Actual entities are not free-standing substances. They are social and they are processes.

Chapter 3 of *P&R*, called "The Order of Nature," sets out a series of definitions of various types of societies that characterize our cosmic epoch using the general notion that a *society is a nexus with social order*. In the togetherness of actual entities comprising some nexus, if some common element of form exists that is derived from earlier members of the nexus, then that nexus has social order (with respect to that form). The common element of form is called the *defining characteristic* of the society. A form, also termed an "eternal object," may be objective or subjective, and one can readily instantiate this idea to human culture in terms of institutional practices and internalized normative orientations.

So in this context Whitehead is suggesting what amounts to a generalized sociology of the known universe, interpreted as a cosmic epoch with its emergent social structure. For instance, the widest society in the universe is the extensive continuum with its space-time structuration ("Extended Society"), and embedded in this environment is "Geometric Society" within which there is "Electromagnetic Society." The members of the latter are electromagnetic occasions.

A multitude of other societies are embedded in what he refers to as this "social environment," such as stars, planets, and living and non-living things on Earth. It might be thought that in adopting this generalized concept of society that Whitehead is doing no more than framing an analogy, but his own view is stated in a little book (Whitehead 1927:64) in which he informally discusses the nature and functions of symbolism:

> In order to appreciate the necessary function of symbolism in the life of any society of human beings we must form some estimate of the binding and disruptive forces at work. There are many varieties of human society . . . we will fix attention on nations occupying definite countries. Thus geographical unity is at once presupposed. Communities with geographical unity constitute the primary type of communities we find in the world. Indeed the lower we go in the scale of being, the more necessary is geographical unity for that close interaction of individuals which constitute society. Societies of the higher animals, of insects, of molecules, all possess geographical unity. A rock is nothing else than a society of molecules, indulging in every species of activity open to molecules. I draw attention to this lowly form of society in order to

> dispel the notion that social life is a peculiarity of the higher organisms. The contrary is the case . . .

Returning to *P&R*'s formal treatment of societies, Whitehead treats the embedding of societies within societies quite explicitly. *Structured societies* have subordinate societies as their components in a pattern of interrelations (e.g., the above-mentioned rocks in which molecules are subordinate structured societies). Some societies are single-stranded in the sense of forming a series in which each actual entity inherits the defining form from its antecedents in the series. These are called *enduring objects*. A society that is analyzable into strands of enduring objects is said to be *corpuscular*.

Using these concepts, Whitehead treats a biological organism as a type of structured society, reversing Herbert Spencer's analogy. Namely, through an extended conceptual analysis he is able to specify a general definition of life that leads to the compact proposition that *a biological organism is a living society*. The general systems theorist James G. Miller, influenced by Whitehead in the 1930s, later constructed an elaborate theory of what he called "living systems" (1978) that is attuned to the variable empirical features of life on planet Earth in contrast to Whitehead's universality. Miller returns to the "ordinary" or restricted usage of the term society and uses "system" for the universal term.

However, is a Whiteheadian society no more than a "system" in the sense of a set of elements or parts in specified relationships? It would appear this is not the case without the conceptually required common element of form that is inherited or derived from earlier members of the nexus. So a "system" is a nexus but not necessarily a society in Whitehead's sense. Luhmann (1995), employing later developments in general systems thinking, did incorporate something like this Whiteheadian feature in his "systems theory" by emphasizing autopoiesis. Perhaps Parsons in his later work was closer to the mark with his notion of a societal pattern maintenance imperative in terms of cultural traditions that are "handed down" to new members through formal and informal modes of socialization.

Whitehead's treatment of generalized societies is not confined to concept formation. In addition to structural analysis, for example, he addresses the problem of stability and suggests some propositions about conditions favoring it, emphasizing the importance of the environment (*P&R*, Ch. III). In his later book *Adventures of Ideas* (*AI*) the same notions are applied to the human case, although also framed in such a way as to have a more generalized scope in terms of the concept of a *civilized society*, such as one that may exist on some other planet in this cosmic epoch.

In discussing the nature of any civilized society he specifies five elements defined in all abstract generality—using the strategy of conceptual generalization again: truth, beauty, adventure, art, and peace. A society is civilized to the extent that these values are realized in it. Of course, these elements do vary in their extent of realization in empirical human societies. In treating these value concepts, Whitehead is more analytical than normative in his approach—which is true in general of his philosophical approach to societal functioning.

A helpful way to grasp one aspect of Whitehead's social vision of the world is to think of a model object in which the actual world is a matrix of relationships among actual entities and such that the extensive continuum is analogous to a structuration of the world discovered through a network model yielding positions or standpoints that are potentials for occupancy by actual entities. However, in Whitehead's system an actual occasion is a transient entity that inherits from its past and passes on aspects of itself to arising occasions.

It is this continuous entity—an enduring object—that corresponds to a person or other familiar sociological actor in such a model. In a short interval of time, each transient occasion of such a person prehends its immediate predecessor with particular richness of reception of its content while anticipating an immediate future "self" for which its purposes will exercise a control function (in the cybernetic sense). In a short enough time interval, the spatial aspect of the standpoint may be the same while the temporal aspect is advanced somewhat as the generative process moves on to "update" the state of that node, including prehensive syntheses of influences of others in the network.

The emphasis on process in Whitehead should not be misinterpreted in the application of his ideas to human societies. As mentioned earlier, he recognizes the importance of stability analysis in treating intrinsically dynamic systems. In one discussion, for instance, he notes that it is a "fundamental sociological truth" that routine is "the god of every social system. . . . Unless society is permeated, through and through, with routine, civilization vanishes" (*AI*, 90). A routine is a system of acts with a certain *form* such that this form can and does recur through realization in analogous systems of acts by the same or other actors in the given social system.

## THE UNIQUE ELEMENT IN UNIVERSAL SOCIOLOGY

One aspect of Whitehead's universal sociology has no instantiation within academic sociology. We might want to dismiss it as a trace of nineteenth-century idealist metaphysics that Whitehead had encountered in his years at Cambridge in frequent philosophical discussions with British idealists (Lowe 1985). However, it is a fascinating aspect of his general framework, worthy of intellectual appreciation (and critique). As noted earlier, "actual entity" is synonymous with "actual occasion" but with one exception.

The logic of this exception can be grasped with a return to the key feature of Whitehead's first work, *Universal Algebra*, recalling that it deals with abstract algebra. The axioms that define a particular abstract algebra with a (generalized) multiplication of elements may include an axiom that says that there exists an identity element, often denoted 1, satisfying $1 \times x = x$, for any element $x$. Conceptually, although 1 is an element, it is "exceptional" in how it acts in relation to other elements. Thus, in one sense it is just another element satisfying the axioms while in another sense it is unique.

The point is that in *P&R* there is a unique actual entity in this sense of satisfying the postulates but being distinctive. Let us call it G. There is a metaphysical requirement for G, argues Whitehead. The argument is not easy to comprehend, especially without a complete grasp of the entire philosophical system. In brief: The already actual occasions in the actual world of any novel occasion never exhaust all possibilities, and Whitehead assumes that an unrealized form must be "somewhere," where this means within some actual entity, so as to be available for "conceptual" prehension.

As contrasted with physical prehensions of the past actual occasions, a conceptual prehension directs the concrescent process toward realization of the form prehended. Whitehead postulates an actual entity that I am denoting G that arises as a prehension of the entire realm of forms, of possibilities—the eternal objects. This is the Platonic element in Whitehead's philosophy. However, he differs from Plato in that the eternal objects are not restricted to perfect forms that are only imperfectly copied in the actual world. Jaggedness, as in the fractal character of a coastline, is an eternal object as well as a perfect straight line.

Note that G, as an actual entity, is also an instance of concrescence—but one that is "everlasting," i.e., non-terminating, since it functions in *every* actual occasion to make hitherto unrealized possibilities relevant to the actualization process. In turn, because G is an actual entity satisfying the general postulates of the system, we must conclude that it prehends each actual occasion of the world and that is does so with some subjective form of reception.

Whitehead's term for what I have called G is *God*. The conclusion is that in Whitehead's universal sociology we find an ultimate form of social interaction—between God and the world. The unique actual entity that is God is the everlasting macroscopic process of concrescence—growing together—accomplished through G's integrative prehension of the incessant microscopic processes, the actual occasions. This micro-macro interaction is the *togetherness* of these actual entities in an ultimate social bond in which, to use Whitehead's metaphor, G's prehensions "save" the world.

Whitehead's masterpiece closes with this "final interpretation" of his cosmological scheme, an enthralling burst of deductive reasoning and lyrical interpretation that can be admired by secular readers but that also can be employed to entertain and possibly support certain religious beliefs. Contemporary "process theology" is inclined in that direction, albeit featuring extensive debates about the religious significance of Whitehead's cosmological concept. The previously mentioned journal *Process Studies*, devoted largely to Whitehead studies, includes many papers in this process-theological mode. However, to some extent this development is not quite aligned to Whitehead's own secular viewpoint. He writes:

> The secularization of the concept of God's functions in the world is at least as urgent a requisite of thought as is the secularization of other elements in experience. The concept of God is certainly one essential element in religious feeling. But the converse is not true; the concept of religious feeling is not an essential element in the concept of God's function in the universe. In this respect religious literature has been sadly misleading to philosophic theory, partly by attraction and partly by repulsion. (*P&R*, 207)

Whitehead's treatment of religion is discussed briefly in the following section.

## FROM UNIVERSAL SOCIOLOGY TO EMPIRICAL SOCIOLOGY

Let us return to Whitehead's own instantiation of his universal sociology to a more scope-restricted system of ideas that also can be related to empirical research. One can find something of this sort in *Adventures of Ideas* (*AI*) as indicated in the discussion above of "civilized society." The research implication would be the study of ultimate social values in relation to social structures, a direction for sociology we find strongly advocated by Parsons (1937).

In the sociological section of *AI* we also find an extended commentary on political economy, including criticisms of approaches that are defective in terms of lacking a comprehensive sociological vision. Whitehead's critique of the economic approach to human society anticipates contemporary economic sociology in regard to the embeddedness of economy in society.

The transition from universal sociology to empirical sociology in its more scope-restricted sense relating to human societies, or more generally animal societies, can take other routes. Here is a brief sketch of one such route. An animal group is a highly structured society in Whitehead's sense. Each animal organism includes a strand of controlling actual occasions whereby the rich inheritance of inputs from various parts of its body are integrated to both perceive the acts of others and to generate acts toward them. Much of such animal interaction is ritualized. Such interactions generate changes both in the individual animals and in their relational nexus, and in the human case also in their symbolic representations and emotional feelings concerning that nexus.

This puts the instantiated Whitehead system in direct contact with the heritage of Durkheim and Goffman found in ritual interaction theory (Collins 2004). Indeed, Whitehead anticipated this theory in his treatment of religion. In *Religion in the Making* (1926a) he sets out what amounts to a theoretical and historical sociology of religion. He specifies four sociological elements—ritual, emotion, belief, and rationalization—and then argues that the origins of religion lie in *ritual* with successive elaborations over time that brought in the other elements.

Whitehead puts forth a theoretical argument that the combination of rituals with accompanying shared emotion generates social integration—as in Durkheim's functionalist theory of religion. Implicitly agreeing with critics of Durkheim, however, he adds the qualification that religion is not necessarily good since the history of religion is also one of brutality and horror. In both its theoretical structure and in its critical qualification, the argument converges with contemporary interaction ritual theory. This is but one small example of a transition from universal sociology to empirically-oriented theoretical sociology.

## NOTES

There is no lack of papers dealing with topics in *P&R* (especially in *Process Studies*), and there are many book-length interpretive treatments of Whitehead's philosophy, including an extended critique of *P&R* by Pols (1967). The contemporary philosopher Nicholas Rescher (2000) surveys basic issues in process philosophy. There has not been space in this essay to compare and contrast the sociological relevance of Whitehead's process worldview with that of other process-oriented philosophers such as Peirce, James, Nietzsche, Bergson, Dewey, Hartshorne, and, of course, George Herbert Mead. An anthology edited by Browning and Myers (1998) contains excerpts from these writers as well as a section on Whitehead that includes an outstanding introduction to his thought by his biographer Victor Lowe.

1. See, for instance, Halewood (2008) and the accompanying articles in a special section of the journal *Theory, Culture & Society* as well as the Web site of the French sociologist Bruno Latour.

# CHAPTER 24

# Kurt Vonnegut: From Semicolons to Apocalypses

*Barry Markovsky*

Kurt Vonnegut (1922–2007) was an American novelist and writer of short stories whose influence and popularity spanned much of the latter part of the twentieth century. The reference to semicolons in the above title borrows from a 2005 speech in which he advised, "Here is a lesson in creative writing. First rule: Do not use semicolons. They are transvestite hermaphrodites representing absolutely nothing. All they do is show you've been to college." He cultivated this curmudgeonly persona, perhaps as a way to demonstrate that he remained in touch with life's minutia even while taking on some of the grandest issues the human condition has to offer.

Vonnegut's body of work ranged from the whimsical to the bleak, using devices as wide-ranging as war, science, art, time travel, primitive sketches, global catastrophe, and punctuation marks to air his points of view on American society and its people. He was adept at walking his readers through world-altering phenomena at ground level, striking balances between the unfathomable complexities of big events and the experiences of individual human beings awash in their wakes.

Step back a little and you hear the voice of a cynical and pessimistic thinker, perhaps too intelligent, too liberal, and too atheistic for his own good. Step closer, however, and you can hear a softer voice expressing love, pain, compassion, and hope. I doubt that anyone really knows whether the smaller voice was the True Vonnegut, or whether it was merely his cynical concession to what he surely regarded as the demons of mass-marketing. Whichever it was, the stories were better for it.

Along with many other baby-boomer sociologists, most of my exposure to Vonnegut's writings occurred in my pre-professional years during high school and college. Revisiting his work now through a sociologist's lens, I am particularly struck by a theme that seems to recur in many of his stories: The narratives frequently play out simultaneously at multiple human scales—multiple *levels of analysis*, to use our technical jargon. This was a perfect recipe for young students whose eyes were just opening up to the world. Vonnegut provided a literary bridge that spanned the monumental social phenomena of the era—the space race, the cold war, women's liberation, Vietnam, the civil rights movement, the sexual revolution, the Watergate scandal—to the egocentric impulses of adolescence.

To illustrate briefly what I mean, consider the novel *Slapstick*. In this story, a heavily medicated U.S. president manages to legislate a scheme for establishing artificial extended families via computer-generated middle names and numbers. All "Daffodil's" instantly become members of a large extended family; all Daffodil-11's join a smaller, closer-knit family, and so on. "Lonesome no more!" was the president's successful campaign slogan, striking affiliative chords in the hearts of the citizens of that story's post-apocalyptic nation. This cautionary tale was an elegant jab at the political quick-fixes promised in every presidential campaign, here playing out the implications of one man's odd vision of a public policy solution for an entrenched national dreariness.

A very different approach was taken in *Deer in the Works*, a short story employing one of Vonnegut's recurring themes: big corporations squeezing the life out of the common man, even while providing his livelihood. The twist here was the juxtaposition of two parallel and, ultimately, intersecting stories of individuals from two different species. One was a newly hired employee trying to adjust to life in the fictional Ilium Works, the country's second-largest industrial operation. The other was a deer that wandered onto company grounds, became confused, and panicked. As the drama unfolded within that cold and cut-throat environment, it appeared that both central characters were doomed to be crushed under the corporate thumb. Much to the reader's pleasure, both were freed in the end.

## MICRO-MACRO LINKS

If not already evident from the introduction, I believe that Vonnegut's greatest sociological insight concerned the dynamic interpenetration of micro and macro social processes. This is not to say that his works directly imparted sociological knowledge, but rather they made a contribution via their meta-theoretical orientation. At least this was true for me.

Over the years my research has been infused with this orientation; that is, that it is feasible, relevant, and important to understand micro-macro linkages; that sometimes the small and seemingly insignificant event can play out on a vast scale; that the thoughts and behaviors of individuals can be largely determined by social conditions. It is conceivable that Vonnegut's major novels may have helped to inspire a generation of sociologists to investigate the interrelationship of micro and macro social processes.

In the early 1980s, there really was nothing called "multilevel theory" in sociology, despite the existence of well-developed statistical and mathematical methods for multilevel modeling. To be sure, some of sociology's founding fathers—along with many of their sons, daughters, and further descendants—have been concerned about processes that operate at multiple levels of social aggregation. Rarely if ever were linkages between levels articulated explicitly, however. Over the decades we have borrowed and coined a variety of terms to help us conceptualize objects and phenomena at different levels of analysis: *mind, actor, value, social tie, dyad, role structure, network, stratification system, market, institution, state* and *world system*, and many more.

Furthermore, collectively we have devised a number of theoretical arguments—mostly of the "loose" variety—to help explain how one or another of these entities comes to manifest its unique set of characteristics, and how, when, and why events at one level affect what happens at other levels. Interest in multilevel theorizing *per se*, at least among American sociologists, accelerated during the 1980s and early 1990s, spurred by the publication of collections such as *The Micro-Macro Link* (Alexander et al. 1987) and *Macro-Micro Linkages in Sociology* (Huber 1991). The Annual Meetings of the American Sociological Association even had "Macro/Micro Sociology" as its conference theme in 1989. Still, while micro-macro linkages are seamlessly integrated in the theories of other sciences—cosmology, economics, biology, physics, cognitive science—sociologists still grapple with the question of how best to construct such theories (Turner and Markovsky 2006).

Great artistic expressions, whether communicated through painting, literature, music, theater, or other forms, often seem to involve multiple levels (Hofstadter 1979). Micro-level objects and events that are relatively small in scale, short-lived, and/or fast-changing, but still recognizable and beautiful in their own right—e.g., brush strokes, phrases, notes, and the spoken word—are shaped into macro objects that are relatively large in scale and enduring, such as allegories, themes, movements, and productions.

Classic examples abound, but to select just a few: one family's struggle to survive against the backdrop of depression-induced poverty in John Steinbeck's *The Grapes of Wrath*; one man's sensory experience of a great city expressed through the interplay of individual instruments and powerful orchestral passages in George Gershwin's *An American in Paris;* an artist's psychological torments and sense of despair made visible through the dynamic skyscape of Vincent van Gogh's *The Starry Night.*

In writing about micro-macro linkages, Huber (1991:11) argued that "The basic problem is to explain how persons affect collectivities and how collectivities affect persons *over time.*" It is one thing to assert that phenomenon *x* at one level affects phenomenon *y* at another level in some particular way. It is quite another to imagine the process unfolding as in time-lapse photography.

Vonnegut's narratives are like this, zooming in and out between multiple levels of social aggregation, unpacking little stories inside big stories, and establishing critical points of connection between them. By transcending a single-level focus in his stories, Vonnegut not only adds interest and complexity, but also provides greater insights into the mutual impacts and interactions of society's micro and macro components.

## MULTILEVEL THEORIES AND PHENOMENA

Elsewhere (e.g., Markovsky 1997) I have offered formal criteria for building and evaluating multilevel theories. Summarizing these informally, a theory consists of a set of abstract, general, logically related conditional statements. Let us call these *propositions* that express how one thing is presumed to lead to another. In order for a theory to be multilevel, propositions must satisfy two conditions with respect to the linkages they use to span different levels of analysis. First, the *containment* condition requires that each higher-level unit contains multiple units at lower levels. For instance, a network contains nodes, and a cult contains followers. Second, there must be either a *propositional bridge* or else a *definitional bridge* that fleshes out the linkage.

In the first case, the level of the antecedent condition in a proposition differs from the level of its consequent. For instance, "If political sentiments are skewed toward the liberal end of the spectrum, then the Democratic Party candidate will be President." This establishes the macro-to-micro (or micro-to-macro) bridge simply by assuming it to be so. In the second case, a definitional bridge, the subject of a higher-level proposition is (elsewhere) defined in terms of a lower-level subject. For example, in "A class system exists if and only if socioeconomic strata form a transitive hierarchy" the macro-level "system" is defined in terms of its multiple micro-level strata.

Propositions are the heart of a theory, and through them express the abstract and general conditions and dynamics that account for the concrete and specific social phenomena it seeks to explain. Just as the structures of propositions and theories are not limited to any particular subject matter, so are multilevel theoretical methods unconstrained as to their substance.

Vonnegut's fictional social dynamics illustrate multilevel processes through a wide array of concrete story lines. Typically the micro objects, macro objects, and linkages are more than apparent as we observe macro-level machinations trickling down on the common person, or conditions arising wherein the individual suddenly impacts the entire society or world. More than this, he shows in exquisite detail *how* these things can happen and that, when they do, it is very, very interesting indeed.

## *CAT'S CRADLE*

This novel, assigned in my eighth grade English class, was my entrée to Vonnegut. I had never heard of the author and, in retrospect, it is surprising that my relatively straight-laced teacher would have required a group of impressionable 14-year-olds to read it. The story has a wild plot that defies brief summarization. At a most general level it is about the diffusion throughout an entire culture of one person's false story disguised as truth.

The cat's cradle metaphor refers to one of the figures that is formed in the children's game involving the looping of strings between left and right fingers and hands to create different crossing patterns. A character in the story recalls being shown the game as a child, staring and staring at the zigzagging strings, but seeing "No damn cat, and no damn cradle."

Life is portrayed as deeply cruel and unjust, rife with unnecessary hardship and pain, sometimes inflicted person to person, but usually attributable to the military-industrial complex. Enter the cat's cradle of Bokononism, a religion offering a hopeful world view for the individual, an opiate for the masses, all concocted from "happy lies" rather than chemical compounds.

Chemical compounds actually do play a central role, but not in the form of recreational drugs. The plot involves a dangerous substance known as "ice-nine," a variant of water that freezes at temperatures below 45.8 degrees Celsius (114.4° F). In the story, Bokononism is used by one of the unscrupulous protagonists to control and exploit the population of an economically depressed island nation.

Narrative lines interweave the religion, some ice-nine seeds, and several other elements, with all story threads ultimately ending badly. In a plot twist that pre-dates the Jonestown and Heaven's Gate tragedies, the thousands of Bokonon followers are instructed by their spiritual leader to commit suicide. So, too, do things end badly for nearly all of the citizens of planet Earth.

In one of his most memorable passages, Vonnegut constructs a scene that begins with micro-events and ends with their world-changing macro-consequences. A dictator near death with access to a vial of ice-nine decides to end his pain by ingesting an ice-nine crystal. He freezes solid. His personal physician touches the body and he, too, freezes. A plane crashes into the nearby hills and triggers a rockslide that eventually sends the dictator's frozen body into the ocean below. The ocean freezes, and since the planet's waters and population are all interconnected, practically everything else freezes solid—including virtually the entire human population of Earth.

Neither the plot nor the message about religion in this mostly sad and cynical tale could ever be construed as subtle. Against the social injustices wrought by scientific, corporate, and state powers beyond our control, it is made to seem that the only recourse for the common person is a fourth institution: religion. Yet at the places where devout individuals and organized religion meet, we again see almost nothing but more institutionalized cynicism and unscrupulousness.

The message is that religion at least *pretends* to care about the heart and soul of the individual in ways that the other institutions do not, as if this were really a good thing. In the end, however, the house of cards built from the accumulated lies of Bokononism collapses upon itself, in perfect synchrony with the collapse of life as we know it.

Throughout the awful events conveyed in *Cat's Cradle*, the tone of Vonnegut's narrative remains so lighthearted and ironic that the reader cannot help but smile rather than weep when setting down the book upon completion. The injustices and deceptions at the core of a corrupt religion may be horrible and sad, but at least in the end they are exposed and eliminated. For Vonnegut, even the fact that the planet and most of its people have been destroyed collaterally is not enough to render the ending an unhappy one.

## *SLAUGHTERHOUSE FIVE*

Vonnegut's best-known work, *Slaughterhouse Five*, offers up the strange account of a meek fellow named Billy Pilgrim who becomes "unstuck in time" and so flits uncontrollably among the various people, places, and ages of his life. The most powerful and memorable components of the book have a strong anti-war bent, but it was a different kind of anti-war story for its time.

In non-chronological sequence, the narrative of Billy's life spans his awkward early years, his military service in World War II, his stellar career as an optometrist upon returning from the war, his marriage and suburban life, his survival of a plane crash, the bizarre accidental death of his portly wife, and his experiences as a sort of zoo animal following his abduction by aliens and confinement on the planet Tralfamadore. Only Billy experiences his life out of sequence, and so he has no evidence with which to convince others of the sheer weirdness of his existence.

Billy Pilgrim appears to be a pawn in some cosmic game, and neither he nor the reader ever is privy to the rules. As are we all, Billy is pushed and pulled by what could be regarded as the book's predominant macro-character: "The System." It consists of the broader social, political, and economic forces that shape American society, but in his case there is an added time-bending force that sometimes takes the pushing and pulling to extremes.

What keeps the novel from falling off the edge of absurdity are its recurring visits to the sub-plot of Billy's experiences as a soldier and prisoner of war. For these episodes Vonnegut drew from his own service and imprisonment experiences. Although it has been more than 35 year since I first read this book, I can still recall the emotional impact stirred by the vivid descriptions of the bombing of Dresden, Germany.

This atrocity is set up by rich descriptions of the city's beauty as Billy and his fellow prisoners are marched through town on their way to an internment camp. Soon comes the allied bombing and the reduction of the city to cinders and charred corpses, a scene into which the dumbstruck prisoners and guards emerge from their underground bomb shelter.

Much has been written about *Slaughterhouse Five*, and many kinds of interpretations have been offered. The relevance of the story for the purposes of this essay is quite simple, however. Vonnegut centered his story around basic injustices at micro and macro scales: the pointless deaths of innocent people, the nonsensical destruction of a picturesque city, and the mutual vilification of, and efforts to destroy, competing ideologies.

The reader is witness to atrocities perpetrated by both sides, upon everyone from lovable individual characters to faceless masses. The System carries out its functions, indifferent to the injustices perpetrated by, and upon, its countless victims. The Tralfamadorian episodes afforded Vonnegut the opportunity to insert an omniscient perspective about the human condition, confirming both the inevitability of war and the rationality of Billy's unwavering passivity in the face of cataclysms large and small. The novel ends horrifically, but for a reminder that somewhere springtime is occurring.

## CONCLUSION

Multilevel social phenomena are not always easy to grasp or to communicate. Often there is a sense of mystery attached to multilevel phenomena, as when we ponder how miniscule properties of genetic material give rise to biodiversity; or how air molecules organize themselves into city-flattening cyclones; or how if conditions are right, social traps draw otherwise peace-loving couples, groups, or nations inexorably into conflict. Multilevel theories are designed to help disentangle, simplify, and clarify these processes by identifying and defining the crucial objects involved and, more importantly, by providing explanations for how phenomena at different levels produce and affect one another.

It does not help that we are so embedded within our socially constructed world, and sometimes it is good to have this pointed out to us. In spite of our professional training, and in much the same way as some of Vonnegut's hapless characters, we may have trouble seeing forests for trees. For at least some of us in sociology, however, Vonnegut helped stir an interest in understanding the ways that social phenomena are vertically integrated. He did so by devising edgy, entertaining, and sociologically insightful stories that alternated in their focus between the lives of his characters and the social environments within which they operated.

Vonnegut's stories can be rip-roaring fun, but to think of them as mere entertainment would miss the point. These are not sweet candy treats to be consumed and forgotten. Every tale has multiple textures and layers, with all manner of riveting apocalypses and metaphorical semicolons. In reading Vonnegut's stories we feel that we have become part of something bigger than ourselves. While my recreational reading interests may have moved on, my interest in multilevel theories has only become deeper and broader.

# CHAPTER 25

# Jonathan Swift: Political Satire and the Public Sphere

*Gary Alan Fine*

Jonathan Swift is the first English-language prose writer of the public sphere whose literary output is of lasting significance. For this reason alone his oeuvre warrants sociological attention. Public writers—whether we define them as political journalists or as artist-journalists (Mahanta 1983; Orwell 1946)—take the responsibility of writing "occasioned pieces" to shape ongoing public dialogue (Said 1984:55) through the prism of literature. Ultimately the task of the public writer is to shape the imminent, debated, and *hot* concerns of the public weal. Jonathan Swift in his literary career as a satirist and as a partisan wrote both for contemplation and for action.

Swift established himself as a public writer at a moment of Anglo-Irish history (the reign of Queen Anne and the Hanoverian succession) that witnessed the development of a literary component to public discourse. To appreciate Swift's potency as a political commentator (and as a social theorist given his famously dyspeptic view of human nature) is to appreciate the eighteenth-century belief that writing can inspire political action: the coffeehouse and the salon were linked to magazines and pamphlets that provided the basis for talk.

Writers addressed the events of the moment from a recognizable standpoint in the political field. To appreciate Swift's significance as a public writer is to recognize the webs of political affiliations in defining his persona. Swift wrote first as a Whig, and then he shifted sharply to become a Tory propagandist after the Tories gained control of the government.

Later, housed in Dublin, Swift wrote on behalf of Irish interests while holding fast to his role as a partisan for the dominance of the Anglican Church against perceived threats from Catholics and Protestant dissenters in his office as Dean of St. Patrick's Cathedral. Swift's affiliations are crucial to treating his writings as sociological documents. Swift addressed politics, human nature, war, and inequality, stripping away what he perceived as unjust, misguided, and oppressive practices and policies.

In Swift's most lasting works—the creations by which Swift entered the literary canon—he wrote as a particular kind of public writer, a satirist. As in all examinations of humor (Fry 1963), a core question is how a text is framed in order for its audience to interpret it as the writer desires. More than most forms of discourse, humor presumes a self-conscious framing by the author. More than most forms of humor, however, satire presumes an authorial stance that differs from that of the text's narrator, often presuming a hostility to that which is being depicted (described as "militant irony").

In satire, the voice that claims to be animating the text is rarely the author's own. This is a general problem in discourse (Goffman 1974: Ch. 13), but in satire the issue is particularly germane. Satire often involves a claim that appears absurd or meretricious, but it becomes moral when the reader can separate what the author means from what the text announces (Elliott 1960). The ambiguity inherent in the structure of satire—the gap between the speaker and the author—provides a challenge in that satire may easily be misunderstood.

For instance, many audience members missed the satiric themes of the 1970s American television situation comedy, "All in the Family." Some viewers felt that the show endorsed the bigoted claims of the central character, Archie Bunker, instead of challenging and ridiculing them (Vidmar and Rokeach 1974). The same is true for the contemporary satiric show, the Colbert Report (LaMarre, Landreville, and Beam 2009) in which the progressive Stephen Colbert mocks a bloviating right-wing commentator. Swift, too, had this problem with some contemporaries and with later critics. Because of the difficulty of establishing the self of the satirist, Edward Said (1984:54) commented that it is easier to define "Swiftian" than it is to find "Swift" within.

## JONATHAN SWIFT (1667–1745)

Who was Jonathan Swift, often considered the finest English prose satirist (Quintana 1958:vii)? Several biographies provide the details of Dean Swift's life. Most respected and detailed is a trilogy by Irwin Ehrenpreis (1962, 1967, 1983; see Quintana 1936; Murry 1955). Born in Dublin to an English mother and Irish father, Swift was a widely known writer of political pamphlets and poems. Educated at Dublin University (Trinity College, Dublin), he left for England during the political turmoil surrounding the Glorious Revolution in 1688, when he received a position as the secretary and personal assistant to William Temple, an influential English diplomat and memoirist.

Swift began his own career penning pamphlets and essays for the Whigs and was one of the group of wits associated with Addison and Steele, eventually writing for the *Tatler*. By 1710, however, he had switched his allegiance to the Tories under the leadership of Robert Harley, Lord Oxford, then in power during the reign of Queen Anne, editing and writing for the Tory sheet, *The Examiner*, and organizing the Scriblerus club along with Pope, Gay, and Arbuthnot in 1712. Although he hoped for an Anglican position in England, Swift allegedly was disliked by Queen Anne and in 1714 was awarded the Deanship of St. Patrick's Cathedral in Dublin where he remained, only twice returning to England.

As a writer Swift is now best known for his book-length satire *Gulliver's Travels* and his powerful satirical essay, *A Modest Proposal* ("*A Modest Proposal for Preventing the Children of Poor People in Ireland, from Being a Burden to Their Parents or Country; and for Making Them Beneficial to the Publick*"), a essay that proposed that Irish babies be sold to the wealthy English as gourmet delicacies. Other works that addressed important controversies of the late 1600s and early 1700s were widely read and discussed at the time, such as *A Tale of a Tub* or *The Battle of the Books* and later *The Drapier's Letters*. Swift died in 1745 at the age of 77 after a three-year illness coupled with mental instability, which led some critics to claim that his earlier, fierce satires resulted from an early onset of this mental illness.

## THE WRITER IN THE PUBLIC SPHERE

Jonathan Swift, along with a set of early eighteenth-century contemporaries, such as Joseph Addison, Richard Steele, Alexander Pope, and John Gay, established the role of public intellectual within the Anglo-Irish context. These writers stood outside of government, but they wrote for political actors and their engaged public (Oakleaf 2008:101).

Jürgen Habermas's (1989) analysis of the development of the public sphere emphasized the role of discourse within English coffeehouse society. As Fine and Harrington (2004) emphasize, the development of "tiny publics"—groups that engage in self-referential interaction—are necessary for civil society to flourish. The field of public writer with its institutional logic, linking author to party, permitted political debate to gain an audience beyond the reach of oral transmission.

Given the partisan divide in English politics in the early eighteenth century, those who wrote on politics were forced to choose sides, even if, like Swift, they could switch party affiliation. (Parties, too, were internally split.) The issues of the day—war and peace, government succession, the colonial treatment of Ireland—concerned the very survival of the state. Swift was central to each of these debates, as in his 1710 essay, "The Conduct of the Allies," which pointedly criticized the unwillingness of the Whigs to sign a peace treaty with France, supporting the Tory attempt to establish separate (and illegal) negotiations with France to end the War of Spanish Succession.

In the 1724–1725 *Drapier's Letters*, Swift attacked the English attempt to debase Irish currency. Yet, whether his topics were consequential or not, Swift self-consciously wrote for an engaged audience: not merely a set of isolated readers, but an active *public*. Such writing, never acquiring mass readership, gained a *following*, a tight-knit elite network that recognized common concerns and drew upon standards of discourse.

## FRAMING SATIRE

In many writing genres, meaning adheres to the surface, easily available for conscientious readers. What the writer says, when properly interpreted, is what the writer means. A close linkage exists between textural claims and authorial intentions. Although inadvertent slippage occurs, this slippage often reflects the misunderstandings of readers or the infelicities of writers. In contrast, the satirist has a different challenge.

As noted, in many satires, including those of Swift, the narrative voice is not the author's voice. The author proposes the narrative as a text to be critiqued, a text that demands role-distance to avoid stigma. An interpretive distance exists between the narrator and the author; they live in different moral universes (see Goffman 1974). Satire asserts one conclusion while *ostensibly* claiming another.

Part of the fierceness of Swiftian satire results from the chasm between his presentation of a cracked and base world as *proper* and the recognition of the world's iniquity. Audiences are directed to the error of their ways, but given that many are comfortably embedded in the status quo, they often miss the point. Satire does not simply proceed directly by making overt claims of injustice, but through forms of indirection.

The satiric genre is framed with different levels or laminations of meaning. In most texts, the audience is to identify with an (alleged) author. But in Swiftian satire this identification leads to unacceptable implications, a contradiction should provoke moral outrage. Perhaps audiences do not recognize these implications or mildly treat the text as an amusing jest, but the creation of moral discomfort is the aim.

To appreciate the framing of satire, consider the implications of the two great examples of Swift's later writings, *A Modest Proposal* (1729) and *Gulliver's Travels* (1726). The core of Swift's political concerns, as presented in his texts, constitute passionate critiques of colonialism and inequality (particularly the English treatment of the Irish, by which Swift became known as an Irish patriot) and militarism (particularly the English wars against France, in which Swift took a line consistent with that of the Tories in opposing the Whig wars against France [Oakleaf 2008:96]).

The challenge of how to read Swift's stance in light of local politics remains with us as present readings suggest that Swift might today be a pacifist or a fighter for a united Ireland (implausibly transforming Swift into a precursor of Mahatma Gandhi or William Butler Yeats [Oakleaf 2008:5–7]).

*A Modest Proposal* is structured as the advice of a "reasonable man"—the wise sociologist (or economist)—a man whose sole interest is to benefit his countrymen. The writer proposes, given the reality of *the world as we know it*, that the infants of the poor of Ireland should be raised for consumption by the wealthy in England. The narrator proceeds to justify this proposal—a modest one, not so different from the current circumstances, it is alleged—and then dismisses all possible objections.

Swift's narrator propounds: "I grant this Food will be somewhat dear, and therefore very *proper for Landlords*; who, as they have already devoured most of the Parents, seem to have the best Title to the Children" (Swift 1958:490). In these lines a double interpretation is required. Beyond the claim of the wholesome and nourishing quality of the food, the underlying argument suggests that eating the children of Ireland is figuratively identical to how Irish renters are treated. Economic subjugation becomes metaphorical cannibalism.

But what is to be done? The problem for the satirist generally—and for Swift in particular—is that satire says what it doesn't mean. It is a negative discourse. When readers can separate the author from the narrator, they comprehend what the satire opposes, yet satire typically lacks a positive program. This does not mean that there is none, but it is presented indirectly.

Swift, in seeming opposition, presents policies that implicitly he as author endorses, but that he as narrator considers impractical: "taxing our Absentees at five Shillings a Pound: Of using neither Cloathes, nor Household Furniture except what is of our own Growth and Manufacture . . . Of learning to love our Country . . . Of quitting our animosities and Factions . . . Of putting a Spirit of Honesty, Industry, and Skill into our Shop-keepers" (Swift 1958:494).

Given its ferocity, it is startling that *Gulliver's Travels* ("*Works Containing Travels into Several Remote Nations of the World*") is seen alternatively as a children's book, an early example of science fiction, an account of local politics, a condemnation of modern civilization and the power of elites, or a corrosive social and political diatribe against all humanity. Even at the time of publication, each reading proved possible, even though today the third has been long forgotten.

Again we ask how the text is to be framed. What was the illocutionary force of Swift's writing: what did he intend to do through his text? *Travels* is divided into four parts: voyages to Lilliput; to Brobdingnag; to Laputa, Balnibarbi, Luggnagg, Glubbdubdrib, and Japan; and to the country of the Houyhnhnms). Each has its own tone, ranging from amusing but largely gentle satire in the third book to the harsh, "inhumane," scatological savaging of the Yahoos in the fourth, a hatred so intense that Gulliver becomes, in effect, a hermit upon his return to England.

It is particularly through the fourth book—the depiction of the gentle horse-like (but controlling) Houyhnhnms and the odious and all-too-human Yahoos—that Swift acquired his reputation as a hater of humanity. The question becomes how much of this fierce critique did Swift mean? There is a soft reading and a hard reading: did he hope for human improvement or had he given up hope for a species whose sin was not only original but continual? Given the ambiguous stance of the writer either interpretation is possible.

The voyages are known through the reportage of Lemuel Gulliver, a ship's surgeon and later sea captain, who presents his memoir. The search then is to situate Gulliver, and to situate Swift in light of Gulliver. While there is an understandable tendency to reflect Swift in Gulliver, Swift sometimes attacks his "reasonable" narrator as naïve and misguided. The task of the reader at each moment is to determine the allegiance between author and narrator, unpacking the complex framing.

## THE REPUTATION OF THE SATIRIST

A third issue relevant to analyzing the *sociological* place of Jonathan Swift as a writer builds upon the other two (the public Swift and the satiric Swift), but it focuses on the responses of the audience. Given the challenges that a satirist has in framing issues for contemporaries, how are texts to be remembered by future generations? Writers—and satirists especially—might be relieved that they are happily deceased for all the attacks that are made upon them. This is surely the case for Swift, who gained vituperative critics from the decades after his death through the nineteenth century, including Samuel Richardson, Thomas Macaulay, and William Thackeray. For instance, Thackeray describes the morality of *Travels* as "horrible, shameful, unmanly, blasphemous," and the man himself fares little better.

The twentieth century has been kinder, although the view of such prominent critics as Edward Said and George Orwell are decidedly mixed, proclaiming Swift's fundamental conservatism while also noticing his radical strains. Orwell wrote that, "Swift's greatest contribution to political thought . . . is his attack . . . on what would now be called totalitarianism. He has an extraordinarily clear prevision of the spy-haunted 'police State,' with its endless heresy-hunts and treason trials, all really designed to neutralize popular discontent by changing it into war hysteria" (quoted in Oakleaf 2008:6).

Through the generations Swift has been vilified for his obscenity, his unflinching hostility to humanity, and for his reactionary politics. Only recently do the claims of seeing Swift as being fundamentally pacifist and opposed to the hegemonic colonial state outweigh his alleged nastiness, mental illness, reactionary outlook, and blind support for the Anglican Church. The satirist, writing with his own contemporary issues in mind and grounded in moral practices of the age, becomes judged by later standards. He is not a man of our time, even if he can be made so.

Swift's reputation is problematic in that he is very much tied to his historical moment through his sensitivity to immediate politics, but he continues to be discussed for his universal themes. Perhaps Swift is not so different from George Orwell, his admiring but sharp critic. The strain between the timeless Swift and the local Swift is central to reputational battles.

## SWIFT AND THE SPOILS

To capture a writer and transform him into a sociologist demands disciplinary hubris. What is "sociological thought" after all? Surely this is a topic that a satirist would put to merry use.

In this essay I addressed three fundamental themes that help to explain the position of Jonathan Swift as a writer whose work bears on the sociological project. First, Swift was a writer who was directly concerned with, and participated in, the development of a public sphere. His network helped transform English society into a place in which (educated) publics could and should speak to governing policies. As much as formal institutions, the institution of the public sphere helped lay the predicate for democracy.

Second, as a satirist Swift was challenged by the proper framing of his writing. This builds on the recognition that he was writing for a knowing contemporary public, addressing occasioned issues. He assumed that his audience would "get the joke." Even if a particular reader missed the point, a consensus could be established by participating in a world of discourse. Later generations of readers consume literature in isolation (or in the authority-based classroom with its academic dicta), but in the coffee shop culture, meanings emerged through interaction, whether they were precisely what the writer hoped. The key task for the reading public of Swift's era and for the reader of later generations is to separate the narrator from the author—and this separation in identities makes a writer like Swift particularly open to an analysis based on the framing choices of the reading community.

My third concern, building on the previous issues, is to examine Swift as a sociological object, pointing to perturbations in reputational politics over time. Swift is a writer who was concerned with persuasion, and yet as a satirist his stance was not always readily transparent. Was Swift a hater of humanity, was he a pacifist, and was he a precursor of the fight for Irish freedom? Enough material exists in his texts for the formulation of multiple Swifts. Jonathan Swift—and Swiftian satire—is an object constituted by the responses of audiences.

Jonathan Swift is not the only early modern writer whose texts still speak to us, but the continuing relevance of his texts stands in sharp contrast with the irrelevance of equally powerful texts that speak only to the moment. In this Swift is like all great writers, ready to have his work borrowed, refined, twisted, and stripped for purposes that he could never have imagined but which we now require.

# PART IV

## Sociological Foundations

# CHAPTER 26

# Baruch Spinoza: Monism and Complementarity

*Ronald L. Breiger*

As a sociologist who has been discovering for the past few years Spinoza's influence on the shaping of my discipline,[1] I have often felt the enchantment expressed in a different context by Friedrich Nietzsche in the summer of 1881 when he recognized in a flash of insight the kinship of his thought to Spinoza's and wrote breathlessly to a friend:

> I am utterly amazed, utterly enchanted. I have a *precursor*, and what a precursor! I hardly knew Spinoza: that I should have turned to him just *now* was inspired by "instinct." . . . Even though the divergencies are admittedly tremendous, they are due more to the differences in time, culture, and science. *In summa*: my solitude, which, as on very high mountains, often made it hard for me to breathe and made my blood rush out, is at least a dualitude.

The translator of this exclamation of Nietzsche's (Yovel 1989b:105) maintains a pun between the final word, *Zweisamkeit* (literally, "two-someness"), and *Einsamkeit* (translated by Yovel in the passage quoted above as "solitude"). In this essay I indicate some important ways in which Spinoza was a precursor for two sociologists who brought the discipline into the twentieth century—Durkheim and Simmel—and in particular for their methods of grappling with the alignment between singularity (at both the individual level and that of the total society) and the complementarity of opposing attributes and forces such as mind and body (Spinoza), forms and contents (Simmel), and the dualism of human nature (Durkheim). The purpose of this exercise is to provide one means of striving for clarity as to the path sociology has followed and, therefore, the possibilities for future twists and turns that we might choose to traverse.

## SPINOZA'S LIFE

Spinoza descended from a family of Portuguese or Spanish-origin Sephardic Jews. The family name may derive from the town of Espinoza in northwestern Spain. By the beginning of the fifteenth century Spain had become a flourishing center of Jewish life, first under Moslem and then under Christian rule. A few months before Columbus set sail, however, an official edict expelled Jews from Spain or forced them to convert to Christianity on pain of death, and a similar law was soon passed in Portugal.

Many Jews maintained their religious identity in secret. Yovel (1989a:28–38) provides a compelling account of how the "crypto-Jewish" life of these Marranos resulted in a number of features associated with Spinoza's mature thought, including a this-worldly disposition, a metaphysical skepticism, a quest for alternative salvation through methods that oppose official doctrine, dual life (living on two levels, enforcing an opposition between the inner and outer life, one concealed and one overt), and dual language (speaking to different audiences in different ways, masking one's true intention to some while disclosing it to others).

In the early seventeenth century some of the former Marranos began to emigrate to the more tolerant clime of Holland. Spinoza was born in Amsterdam in 1632. His parents named him in Portuguese Bento, or "Blessed," for which the Hebrew word is Baruch and a Latin version is Benedictus, as Spinoza came to be known subsequent to his expulsion from the Jewish community of Amsterdam. As a young man Spinoza knew the Bible by heart, found many contradictions in it, and was not shy about sharing his skepticism.

Spinoza maintained a conception of God as the embodiment of the eternal, the infinite, and the perfect. However, this deity was not in his view a unique and separate being or force existing above or outside the world or apart from the nature God created. God was rather the universe itself, insofar as it could be grasped as a single whole. *Deus sive Natura* (literally: God or Nature), as Spinoza was to write in his mature work: "God" is the name of the one and only substance, whose other name is "Nature" (MacIntyre 1967:533).

The distinction between God and the world, a contrast at the heart of both Judaism and Christianity, is obliterated in Spinoza's philosophical system. For this and other unconventional thinking, the Jewish community of Amsterdam took the rare action of excommunicating him in 1656, when he was 24 years old, for his "horrible heresies" (Yovel 1989a:3).

Spinoza stayed four lonely years longer in Amsterdam, moving in 1660 to Rijnsburg and then Voorburg, earning a living by grinding and polishing lenses while discussing philosophical problems with friends. (My source for this paragraph, except where another citation is given, is MacIntyre 1967:531.) He corresponded with and met Leibniz (Stewart 2006) and corresponded with Huygens. Spinoza refused the chair of philosophy at Heidelberg in 1673 because he thought it would have compromised his independence. He died of consumption, aggravated by the dust from lens grinding, in 1677, at the age of 45.

Spinoza published an account of Descartes' philosophy in 1663 and his major work *Tractatus Theologico-politicus* in 1670, the latter anonymously due to his notoriety. His *magnum opus*, the *Ethics*, was published in 1677 immediately following his death.

## SPINOZA RECEPTION BY DURKHEIM AND SIMMEL

Spinoza is largely ignored today by sociologists seeking to understand the history of our discipline and to shape its future. My goal is not to present Spinoza's thought directly or with philosophical adequacy (for this see Della Rocca 2008; Gatens and Lloyd 1999; MacIntyre 1967; among others). I focus instead on its refraction in the reception of Spinoza's thought as it informs and in important ways shapes the sociologies of Durkheim and Simmel.

## *DEUS SIVE NATURA*

René Descartes was a dualist, distinguishing between the mind and the body as two separate entities organized hierarchically. "I think therefore I am." The mind, or in Christian theology the soul, can transcend the body.

Spinoza, by contrast, was a monist. As already mentioned, he believed that there is only one thing that could truly be said to exist in its own right, a Being or "Substance" known equally as God or as Nature. This substance has properties but is itself not a property of anything else. The one Substance in fact has an infinity of attributes, examples of just two attributes being minds ("thought") and bodies in motion ("extension"). Spinoza explained that "By God I understand a being absolutely infinite, that is, a substance consisting of an infinity of attributes" (quoted by Della Rocca 2008:51).

Spinoza's radical monism, however, does not give us (so to speak) the whole picture of his thought. There are also disjunctive forms of "complementarity" (Yovel 1989a:159–161), the second concept stated in the title of this chapter. Spinoza's "apparently extreme version" of philosophical monism is tempered in that each totality (God and Nature), "precisely because each is a complete expression of Substance under one of its attributes," is causally insulated from the other (Gatens and Lloyd 1999:2–3). Let us continue with the example of thought and extension. For Spinoza, "body and mind are not causally related at all; they are identical, because thought and extension are two attributes under which one substance is conceived" (MacIntyre 1967:534).

Substance considered under the attribute of Thought leads us to minds, ideas, and decisions, whereas the same Substance under the attribute of Extension connotes physical bodies in motion (Stewart 2006:168). Spinoza did not see mental events as the effect of bodily causes, nor did he postulate reciprocal causality between body and mind. Body and mind are not causally related at all; they are identical because thought and extension are two attributes under which the one substance is conceived.

In this sense, Spinoza reminds us of no one more than our sociological forebear, Georg Simmel. For Simmel, the individual does not "cause" society, nor is the converse true. Individuals and societies are *the same* contents, merely two different categories. As Simmel puts it, "the two—social and individual—are only two different categories under which the same content is subsumed." Moreover, "the 'within' and the 'without' between individual and society are not two unrelated definitions but define together the fully homogeneous position of man as a social animal" (Simmel 1971a:17–18). In this sense, Simmel's sociology draws upon Spinoza, and Simmel acknowledges the influence in many places.

The fundamental distinction upon which Simmel founds his conception of sociology—that between form and content—is very much related to Spinoza's logic of complementary systems (to use the phrase of Yovel 1989a:159) distinguishing (while unifying) thought and extension, mind and body, and the order and connection of things and the order and connection of ideas.

Religion, for Simmel, is "a fundamental formal category" within which a wide variety of contents are subsumed (for example, the response of the pious soul to traditions and objects that the past has transmitted, and the response of a person of aesthetic disposition to that which is beautiful to look at; Simmel 1997:125). Simmel admits to the reader, "I am convinced that we will not understand religion in its strict and transcendent sense until we come to interpret it as the result of radicalizing, sublimating, and absolutizing these dispositions" (p. 126) which nonetheless constitute the formal category of religion. Concerning religiosity as a form and "the world views of reality" as contents:

> [t]hose categories are related to one another as are *cogito* and *extenso* in Spinoza's philosophy: each expresses in its own language everything that exists, and precisely for that reason, neither of the two can invade the other. If religiosity is one of these categories—if it really is, when viewed from a particular perspective, the totality of being—then indeed it is bound to reject not only any testing against the worldviews of reality, of volition, and so on, but also any internal and factual association or connection with them . . . (Simmel 1997:124)

Just as Spinoza's postulation of a complementarity between God and Nature "allows science and theology their own territories" (MacIntyre 1967:533), so Simmel's duality of form (religiosity) and content (world views of reality) means that "neither of the two can invade the other" (as in the quotation above). It is as if Simmel has learned from Spinoza a playful attitude toward the relation of monism to its opposite quality, which is diversity or (more radically, as we are about to see) relativism.

Indeed, in *The Philosophy of Money* Simmel portrays money, with incisive irony, in this distinctive way: money is the universal substance that relativizes value. Moreover, this formulation is allowed by Simmel's reading of Spinoza (recall the "infinity of attributes" comprising Spinoza's single substance):

> [O]nly through the continuous dissolution of any rigid separateness into interaction do we approach the functional unity of all elements in the universe, in which the significance of each element affects everything else. Consequently, relativism is closer than one is inclined to think to its extreme opposite—Spinoza's philosophy—with its all-embracing *substantia sive Deus*. . . . [A]ll the contents of the world view have become relativities in a monism such as Spinoza's. The all-embracing substance, the only absolute that remains, can now be disregarded without thereby affecting the content of reality—the expropriator will be expropriated, as Marx says of a process that is similar in form—and nothing remains but the relative dissolution of things into relations and processes. The interdependence of things, which relativism establishes as their essence, excludes the notion of infinity only on a superficial view, or if relativism is not conceived in a sufficiently radical way. (Simmel 1990:118)[2]

It is owing to the dual quality of money as both universal and relativizing that "the essential quality of money now becomes comprehensible. For the value of things, interpreted as their economic interaction, has its purest expression and embodiment in money" (p. 119).

## *SUB SPECIE AETERNITATIS*

Writing in a different context, Simmel noted that "Spinoza demanded of the philosopher that he view things *sub specie aeternitatis*, that is, purely according to their inner necessity and significance, detached from the arbitrariness of their here and now" (quoted by Frisby 1992:105). Literally "under the aspect of eternity," the phrase *sub specie aeternitatis* expresses Spinoza's insistence on the durability of the one universal substance.

Continuing my suggestion of Simmel's playful attitude (perhaps learned from Spinoza) toward monism, I mention (thanks to Frisby 1992:102–103) that Simmel authored seven contributions, between 1900 and 1903, to a German journal (*Jugend*) that promoted the *art nouveau* style of art and the applied arts (known in German as *Jugendstil*), these contributions appearing under the title "*Momentbilder sub specie aeternitatis*"—literally, snapshots viewed from the aspect of eternity.

Frisby explains that, in Simmel's terminology, "the snapshot of social reality may capture a transitory content but the sociologist should be concerned with the more enduring social forms within which that content is embodied," thus adeptly connecting Simmel's playful reading of Spinoza with the sociologist's central distinction between the forms and contents of social life.

A segue to Durkheim, Simmel's contemporary, is now overdue. Writing in 1914 on the dualism of human nature, Durkheim (1964b) opposes body and soul, sensory appetites (egoistic and individualistic) versus conceptual thought and moral activity (impersonal, disinterested, and social). There is in us a being that represents everything in relation to itself and from its own point of view. "There is another being in us, however, which knows things *sub specie aeternitatis*, as if it were participating in some thought other than its own . . . "

In brief, "we possess both a faculty for thinking as individuals and a faculty for thinking in universal and impersonal terms." Durkheim does not resolve this tension by the end of his essay; instead, "all evidence compels us to expect our effort in the struggle between the two beings within us to increase with the growth of civilization."

Donald Nielsen's (1999) book, to which I am indebted, elaborates an argument that Durkheim's sociology bears a striking resemblance to Spinoza's philosophy. He traces the Spinozan phrase *sub specie aeternitatis* to Durkheim's mature theory of religion, society, and the categories. Nielsen suggests that Durkheim's totalistic concept of "society" played a role for him analogous to that of the single eternal "substance" in Spinoza's system, and Nielsen observes that in 1933 a historian of modern philosophy (J. Benrubi) referred provocatively to Durkheim's work as a philosophy *sub specie societatis* (Nielsen 1999:33).

In the final footnote to the "Conclusion" of his last major work, Durkheim (1968) writes that totality, society, and deity are three different facets of one idea ("*Au fond, concept de totalité, concept de société, concept de divinité ne sont vraisemblablement que des aspects différents d'une seule et même notion*"). For Nielsen (1999:230), this one idea is "the notion of substance, perhaps more specifically, social substance" which in Durkheim's theory "can be nothing but social life itself in its true reality as power, force, energy, and concentration of human social life."

## CONCLUSION

Any discussion of Spinoza's thought necessarily omits an infinity of attributes. A more complete treatment would emphasize his purely relational approach to human reality and his rejection of the illusions of methodological individualism (Citton and Lordon 2008). It would review the origins of social network analysis and Heiderian's balance theory in Spinoza's propositions on the affects (Breiger 2003:19; Martin 2009:43; see also Bramsen 1999). It would recall Durkheim's application of "Spinoza's idea that things are good because we like them, rather than that we like them because they are good" to his theory of the social construction of crime ("we do not condemn it [an act that offends us] because it is a crime, but it is a crime because we condemn it"; Durkheim 1984:40).

A full treatment would give pride of place to Spinoza's concept of *conatus* in providing a new prism for viewing Bourdieu's sociology (Guillory 1997; Lordon 2006). A more adequate presentation would deconstruct the so-called Hobbesian problem of order from the point of view of his less well-known seventeenth-century contemporary rationalist philosopher, a project to which Simmel contributed by observing that "[m]odern competition is described as the fight of all against all, but at the same time it is the fight of all *for* all," simultaneously a fight "*against* a fellowman *for* a third one" based on the "possibilities of gaining favor and connection" (Simmel 1955:62–63). There is indeed a Spinozan approach to the construction of sociological theory that needs to be more fully recognized so that it may be extended.

## NOTES

1. Earlier expressions of this interest are my talk on "The Spinozan Problem of Order" at the Roger Gould Memorial Conference in New Haven, Connecticut, in October 2003, my keynote address on "Social Networks and the Spinozan Problem of Order," at the International Network of Social Network Analysts Annual

Conference, in Redondo Beach, California, February 2005, and my brief discussion of Spinoza and social network theory (Breiger 2003:19, 31). I am indebted to participants at these conferences, to Omar Lizardo for many stimulating discussions early on in my thinking about Spinoza, to Lynette Spillman for pointing me in Durkheim's direction, to Emmanuel Lazega for telling me of Lordon's work, and to Horst Helle for sharing his interest in Spinoza and Simmel.

2. Simmel's reference to Marx concerns the latter's theorization of the increasing universality of capitalism, leading necessarily to "the monopoly of capital becom [ing] a fetter upon the mode of production, which has sprung up and flourished along with it, and under it." The new contents—the socialization of labor and "the entanglement of all peoples in the net of the world-market"—can no longer be contained by the membrane ("integument") of the capitalist mode. "This integument is burst asunder. The knell of capitalist private property sounds. The expropriators are expropriated" (Marx 1906, Part VIII, Ch. XXXII, Sect. 2).

# CHAPTER 27

# Isaiah Berlin: On the Sociology of Freedom

*Margareta Bertilsson*

Freedom is just another word for nothing left to lose.

—Kris Kristofferson

As a sociologist interested in social theory widely, why at all relate to a thinker whom many sociologists would regard as an anti-sociologist? Isaiah Berlin is known as a liberal thinker par excellence and a stout defender of individual freedom. Such a position is difficult to defend from a sociological point of view on the ground that social life and its demands on cooperation are left out of consideration. But one could turn around and ask: Can sociology afford to discard the issue of freedom? And to what costs?

A concern with the issue of freedom is at the same time a concern with the overriding value of liberalism. Among the social sciences, sociology typically pronounces critical views of prevailing liberal societies. As Zygmunt Bauman has noted, sociology is a science of non-freedom rather than freedom (1988). We are, in the words of J. J. Rousseau, prone to look at the shackles of freedom rather than freedom. A concern with Isaiah Berlin, as a social thinker, can help in sharpening our view both on liberalism and on freedom among which the liberal kind is but one, albeit a prominent one.

Isaiah Berlin (1909–1997) was born in Riga, which at the time was part of the Russian Empire. His parents were well-to-do secular Jews who had built up a fortune from wood merchandising. In 1916 the family moved to Sankt Petersburg. In 1917 the young Berlin observed the early events of the Russian Revolution when a policeman was dragged away by an angry mob—an event that profoundly shaped his view on political violence. The family moved to London in 1921.

Berlin received his academic education at Oxford University, where he read philosophy and history. Oxford University did not harbor many Jewish students at the time, and Berlin apparently adjusted to its anti-Semitic environment by becoming "very British" (Ignatieff 2000). Apart from a few years service at British Foreign Offices in New York and Washington D.C. during World War II, Berlin stayed in Oxford all through his life. In 1958 he was appointed professor of social and political theory.

## ON NEGATIVE AND POSITIVE FREEDOM

Most well-known among Berlin's texts is undoubtedly his inaugural lecture on *Two Concepts of Liberty*, on negative and positive freedom (1979). Berlin defines *negative* freedom as follows: "I am normally said to be free to the degree to which no man or body of men interferes with my activity" (1979:169). This concept of freedom is often referred to as *non-interference* and is as such relating to a human being in sole contact with the environment.

It stands in a stark contrast to what Berlin calls *positive* freedom: freedom given to us through our membership in various collectives. Foremost among positive freedom-rights are those that the (welfare) state provides to its members, such as freedom to enter schools, treatment in hospital, parent privileges, and pensions rights. Another formulation in distinguishing among the two concepts of freedom is as follows: negative freedom is freedom *from*, while positive freedom is freedom *to*.

A sociologist can profitably look at the two forms of freedom as the difference between *assigned* versus *achieved*: in the first case, the individual is assigned a sacred quality, while in the latter case the individual achieves a set of (freedom) rights because of membership in socio-political communities. As a corollary, negative freedom is by definition vague and diffuse, while positive freedom is more specific. With reference to the legendary Swedish sociologist Johan Asplund, it seems suggestive to link the two concepts of freedom to that which Johan Asplund calls "social responsivity" and "abstract sociality" (1987).

As noted by both friends and foes of Berlin (Ringen 2008; Taylor 1979), it is especially his concept of negative freedom that has caused concerns and quarrels. Does it at all make sense to conceive of freedom as totally nonsocial, as a quality only of the individual qua individual? Commentators have been occupied with raising various absurd consequences of such a formulation: when I see a person stabbing another person to death, should I then refrain from intervening, as such an action from my side would interfere with the freedom of the stabber?

Examples easily multiply as to the absurdity of defining freedom as non-interference; what about the person en route to commit suicide or else step into dangerous territory with consequences for his or her health or perhaps even life. Is it not our duty to interfere to save a life? Or what about stopping for red traffic lights when passing a crossroad—is that an interference with individual freedom? Is it at all meaningful to view freedom as an individual rather than social quality?

## ON NEGATIVE FREEDOM—SOCIOLOGICAL CONSEQUENCES

Well aware of many absurd (social) implications of formulating freedom as non-interference, I shall nevertheless proceed with Berlin's own insistence of its intrinsic value. Non-interference, Berlin continues, does not necessarily entail a picture of man as a Robinson Crusoe, isolated from other human being. It refers rather to a social relation where we may conceive of intervention in the lives of other persons along a continuum: from the point where the coercive intervention of others in the life of an individual is almost complete, as in the case of parents intervening in the activities of their children for the reason that it is in the best interest of the child to be governed. Also, prisoners are to a great extent under surveillance from the outside, although they may have a little free space left to their own discretion in their respective cells.

Michel Foucault's famous picture of Panopticon reveals the control mechanisms in operation as the power of surveillance, as does his concern with "bio-politics"; how modern societies install both bodily and mental control of their members (1977). Indeed, it can be asked, as I will do later, if not Foucault's popular treatises reformulate the relation between the two kinds of freedom that Berlin labels respectively negative and positive!

The other extreme point along a social continuum is when two or more people interact in full recognition of one another's right to a "free space." Erving Goffman provides us with rich illustrations of how such mutual recognitions proceed without interference: when walking along a street, individual walkers occupy the same circumscribed space, but while seemingly ignoring one another they have to take care of one another's presence in order not to cause discomfort to one another. A lot of "recognition-work" is demanded in order to uphold the freedom rights of one another in such seemingly a-social situations (1963).

Goffman's many observations as to forms of silent "rule-following" profoundly qualifies Jean-Paul Sartre's classic dichotomy between social and non-social action: there is, in Sartre's view, a qualitative difference between a mute queue waiting for a bus (1976) and that of a debating Oxford society.[1] In the first instance social life is merely incidental and physical (we happen to be at the same place at the same time), while in the latter instance social life is "psychical," where people take account of one another and control their conduct, in "taking turns" as to who has the right to speak.

Goffman's brilliance in observing rule-following also in the seemingly non-social profoundly widens our consideration of an almost infinite social continuum in constant operation: how "sacred" individual territories arise and are upheld as a matter of routine and habit. From such a sociological point of view, it seems meaningful to view even routine social interaction as generated by a whole number of various spatial and temporal freedom recognitions: turn-taking in speech is clearly a case in point where we refrain from interfering until occasions arise. Avoiding stepping into the bodies of other people is another illustration of how we routinely seek to respect the freedom of others while at the same time we expect the same recognition from others.

To unduly intervene in the time-space matrix of another person is what Goffman calls degradation work; in special circumstances such work amounts to "ceremonies" undertaken by collectives (1961). Mobbing seems a case in point. On the more formal-juridical level, the treatment of refugees in today's Denmark can best be illustrated as the state's official degradation of expelled individuals: in order not to adapt to Danish society, these individuals, especially children, are not allowed to associate outside the camp. In the language of Berlin and Goffman, the refugees are stripped of their right to humanity; they are the "homo sacer" of modern liberalism; like in Antiquity they can as well be thrown to the beasts (Agamben 1998; Fallesen 2008).

Although sociologists tend to react instinctively against the notion of "negative freedom" as a construction of liberal ideology, having a "room of one's own" (alluding to Virginia Woolf) is, I believe, essential in upholding the dignity of human life. Artistic works of any kind—painting, writing, composing—are usually assumed to demand considerable free space on behalf of the creative artist. Also, the contemplation and execution of criminal acts assumes some "free space," although such action is deemed less beneficial for the social order. The point is, and here I follow in the footsteps of Berlin, the claim to freedom as "free space," however little, is an essential moral value to be granted all individuals, and not just the elected few.

The worth of freedom as non-interference cannot (and must not) be justified in terms of the social consequences that it may generate: it is a "sui generis." It is with regard to this "existential ethics" of a most essential freedom that Berlin takes issue with many of his fellow liberalists, especially the utilitarianism of John Stuart Mill.

## THE RADICALIZATION OF FREEDOM—AND ITS CONSEQUENCES

It is worthwhile to take a look at the wedge within the liberal tradition with regard to the issue of freedom. Mill's formulation of freedom especially irritates Berlin:

> civilisations cannot advance; the truth will not, for lack of a free market in ideas, come to lights; there will be no scope of spontaneity, originality, genius . . . (Mill as quoted in Berlin 1979:174)

Berlin's quarrel with Mill's formulation depends upon what he regards as three unhappy "facts":

a. that there would be a necessary link between the value of freedom and other valuable social values such as the pursuit of truth or the expression of genius and originality, or for that matter social progress. Such a relation, if it were to exist, is at best empirical, and thus historically contingent. Genius, the search for originality, and even the pursuit of truth can also be found in communities which we would not call "liberal." To use a more current illustration: to draw a dogmatic link between individual freedom and public efficiency is equally misplaced: public efficiency can be produced by large scale bureaucracies (stifling freedom): the curtailing of individual freedom in China now appears as an efficient social good promoting capitalist growth!
b. Berlin also takes issue with the Mill's position that the doctrine of freedom is concomitant with the rise of civilization and universal social progress. The Greeks and the Romans did not put much value on personal freedom, he notes. The modern expression of freedom as non-interference, he claims, is in fact quite recent; it traces its origin to the Renaissance and Reformation primarily: to find one's freedom in Jesus Christ is at the same time to distance oneself from Imperial Rule. As elaborated by Max Weber, the Puritan sects achieved their inner freedom by placing themselves in radical opposition, spiritually and materially, to the social orders of their time.

   As a primary value, Berlin notes, negative freedom is more of an exception than a rule in the history of mankind; and it will probably never be a popular banner of social mobilization. Its appeal among wide population strata is likely to be quite restricted for the reason that as an inner motivation and force, it is deeply individual. When called upon by the masses, the value of freedom is often mixed with other worthwhile social values as opposition against oppression and injustice.

c. Curious in Berlin's argument with Mill's position is also his quarreling with the alleged link between freedom and democracy as twin values. Like the value of justice and equality, the linkage between democracy and freedom is in Berlin's view empirical and contingent rather than intrinsic and necessary: Autocratic regimes, he says, can very well make possible the existence of private liberty for individuals—or for some of them, while democracy can have it curtailed (p. 178).

Berlin's standpoint is an expression of existential ethics, a position that is shared by such classic Russian writers such as Alexander Herzen and Lev Tolstoy (Ignatieff 2000). Max Weber's view on science and politics expresses the similar views; however important science and politics are in shaping collective life, the individual always stands alone with regard to the central question of the "meaning of life" (1946:143).

In "progressive" liberalism, freedom and democracy are twin pursuits; in its "tragic" version (as in Weber, Berlin, and Goffman!) the issue of freedom is a great deal more precious and can never be subsumed under any other (worthwhile) value.[2] Indeed, Berlin's radicalization of freedom as a non-negotiable moral value has affinities with the position of many radical social theorists such as Adorno, Foucault, and more recently Agamben, primarily known for their critique of modern liberalism!

Besides freedom, liberal rule in practice demands several other important social values. Berlin himself opens up for the necessity of curtailing "negative freedom" with other primary social values such as justice, happiness, culture, security, equality, or what a specific culture now may consider components of a good life. In time of crises as in war or, as now, in threatening climate change further restrictions as to the freedom rendered individuals may be urgently called for. The conduct of modern life and the intercourse with others, Berlin admits, demand that freedom of individuals be curtailed. "[I]t remains true that the freedom of some must at times be curtailed to secure the freedom of others. Upon what principle should this be done?" (p. 173).

Such frontiers, says Berlin, are always relative to circumstances and cannot be stipulated dogmatically: ". . . the need of an Oxford Don is different from that of an Egyptian peasant" (p. 171). Referring to Dostoevsky, Berlin admits that "there are situations in which boots are superior to Pushkin; individual freedom is not everyone's primary need" (p. 171).

> The Egyptian peasant needs clothes or medicine before, and more than, personal liberty, but the minimum freedom that he needs today, and the greater freedom that he may need tomorrow, is not some species of freedom peculiar to him, but identical with that of professors, artists and millionaires (p. 172).

In this quotation lies the radicalism, I will suggest, of Berlin's position. Western liberals, he says, have trouble grasping this sense of private freedom as they keep relating it to other important values such as justice and equality. To propose that the Egyptian peasant is in possession of a sense of freedom when lacking clothes and medicine strikes us as cynical and non-progressive.

Such a stance may lead us to abstain from advocating measures of social reform, but this is not, as I read the text, what Berlin proposes. He is not a conservative thinker. He merely warns us of mixing freedom with other worthwhile social values, and in such a way weakens its inherent qualities (p. 173). The concrete manifestation of freedom is certainly historical and contingent on social conditions: the freedom of an Oxford Don is different from that of an Egyptian peasant, but to dismiss the freedom claim of the peasant is also to dismiss him from humanity and thus from personhood!

The radical implication of Berlin's position is in my view the plea that all persons, independent on their stations in life, has a legitimate claim to be treated with respect as to their personhood and humanity. In this regard, Berlin's insistence on the value of negative freedom comes close to the "sacredness of the individual" inspiring Goffman's remarkable observations later on. The "sacred individual" was a theme already in Durkheim's sociology—and can in these "post-liberal" times be posited in starch opposition to antiquity's view on "homo sacer" (Agamben 1998). The ushering of refugees into outcasts in today's liberal democracies is a warning signal that liberalism is at war with itself: it curtails freedom for the sake of other (worthwhile) social values "in the best interest of the state."

## ON POSITIVE FREEDOM—ITS SOCIOLOGICAL END?

I will be brief in discussing the second concept of liberty in Berlin's exposition for the reason that it is much more legitimate and accepted in wide social science circles. Positive freedom, Berlin notes, derives "from the wish on the part of individual to be his own master. . . . I wish to be a subject, not an object" (p. 178)

The wish to master one's own life drives the wish to be a rational human being; and not be a slave of the passions—or of outside social forces. This (legislator) insight once led Rousseau (1762) to his formulation of the dual subject: I am a subject and an object at the same time; as Sovereignty I partake in formulating those laws which I am also obliged to obey.

The dual nature of self, so prevalent in the social sciences, is also generating various notions of our "higher" and "lower" self; the transcendental and the empirical self. The higher part of myself (i.e., my more rational self) typically corresponds with my collective being; that part of me that identifies with a greater entity: the nation, the class, the religion, the state, the globe. Real freedom only reigns in the transcendental realm of a collective principle, while my empirical—bodily—self enslaves and betrays my true self.

Isaiah Berlin is—this is well-known—profoundly skeptical of this positive notion of freedom for the reason that he sees it as a subtle form of coercion (p. 179). Especially risky are such formulations that allow some men to coerce others in "their own interests"; that is, what they would do if they had been cognizant of their own principled interests.

Clearly, sociologists together with many other state/welfare professions risk promoting such a subtle form of coercion that Foucault later popularized as the link between knowledge/power. The value of reading Berlin in parallel with Foucault, I will propose, is to broaden our view of what freedom is all about; that there are many shades of freedom at stake in modern society, and that these shades more often than not are in rampant conflict with one another.

The wide acceptance of Foucault among younger sociologists risks throwing them into a "cul-de-sac" with regard to the issue of freedom and liberal society. Liberal freedom is becoming concomitant with bio-politics, with surveillance and control. The adoption of Foucault's exclusive notion of freedom as "the ethic of self" is also the adoption of an anti-liberal view of an individual elevated over enslaved masses (1997). To throw out the issue of (negative) freedom as an ideological construct of liberal society, while at the same time being led to believe that positive freedom is but an expression of power is to end up in a thorny space: it is to throw out the baby with the bath water.

Without the notion of freedom, positive or negative, sociology risks losing its critical edge: as a liberal society not yet in place for the many, or else a liberal society curtailing freedom for some (or many) for the sake of "common interests." With Berlin, we learn how precious, and contextual, the line always is in drawing the frontiers between the collective and the individual and between positive and negative freedom.

## NOTES

1. This dichotomy is also the one pursued by Max Weber in his classic definition of social action (1978, I:4).

2. Alex Callinicos (1999:67–68) labels the tragic version of liberalism "agonistic," a position he also says was that of J. S. Mill in referring to a discussion pursued by Berlin's primary biographer, John Gray. I admit that a more complex elaboration as to immanent value-conflicts is called for, but can for reason of space not enter into such a discussion here.

# CHAPTER 28

# Bertrand Russell: Insights on Power

*David Willer*

Bertrand Arthur William Russell, who became the third Earl Russell, was born on May 18, 1872 and died on February 2, 1970. Over his 97 years, one stream of Russell's work—Bertie to his friends—ranged from the logic and philosophy of mathematics through the philosophy of science to the science of politics. There were other streams. Russell was very active in opposing the Great War and was imprisoned for it, writing and marching for women's rights, supporting birth control when that support was considered wicked, and opposing the Vietnam War as well as the displacement of the people of Palestine, to mention only a few of his causes.

For most of us, Russell is remembered more for his writings than his political activities. Wikipedia's selected bibliography of his books contains 66 entries, including as single entries the three volumes of his (and Whitehead's) *Principia Mathematica* and the three volumes of his *Autobiography*. In the face of his overwhelming body of work, this essay will be very selective indeed. It will be limited to the insights in Russell's *Power* (2003).

I will focus on what Russell wrote, not on the source of his ideas. Only in a few instances, as in the possible influence of Hobbes, will I relate Russell's thoughts to prior sources. My reasoning is this: it is my strong impression that Russell's *Power* owes very little to previous scholars. Two come to mind to whom Russell might have owed an intellectual debt: Marx and Weber. Though I am acquainted with the work of both, I was surprised to find nothing in Russell's *Power* owed to either. Of more contemporary social scientists, Russell quotes only Berle and Means (1968). In fact, he explicitly adopts their thinking on the primacy of corporate control over ownership, which they put forward in *The Modern Corporation and Private Property*.

Though *Power* owes little to the long tradition of social thought before it, three qualifications of its author recommend it to our attention. The first is his very wide-ranging, detailed knowledge of human history from classical antiquity to the events of his time. He wrote authoritatively on the religions of Greece and Rome, on the significance of the Peloponnesian war, the structure of the medieval Church, the rise of Islam up to the Umayyad Caliphate, elements of kingly power in Europe, modern corporate structure, including its impact on the state, and the strength of the Papacy in the eleventh and fourteenth centuries. To the delight of the reader this knowledge is put to good use in comparative analyses.

Russell does not suffer from the racism or sexism of his era. I found nothing in *Power* driven by aristocratic class interest. Yet he appears to know little of tribal societies, which he dismisses as being ruled by unreflective tradition, a mistake he shares with others too proud of their modern rationalism. Fortunately, he makes only a few offhand comments about "backward savages" (55).

Russell's second qualification is the aristocratic status position he inherited from birth. High inherited status may seem an odd qualification for an author, but remember, this is a book about power. Russell has the great advantage of seeing societies from the top down, a perspective that renders transparent the power relations that might well be viewed as opaque when seen from below.

How exactly do ruling classes rule? How do large and important policies come to be resolved? Being born into England's ruling class, for specifics on policy formation, he need only ask his brother, Frank Russell, the leader of the Labor Party in the House of Lords. Or he could turn to any number of other sources personally known to him.

Russell's third qualification is the one that most strongly recommends *Power* to the reader: his remarkable intellect. The reader beginning *Power* knows he is reading the insights of one of the most significant philosophers of the twentieth century. The writing is exquisitely clear such that the strength of Russell's intellect jumps off the page. Furthermore, this is a philosopher with considerable practical experience of the world stemming from the pursuit of his many causes.

In this essay I begin with the concept of power and then turn to the uses that Russell intends for it. Like Weber, Russell's discussions of power, its transformation, and exercise show great insight. Again like Weber, there is a disjunction between his definition of power and his analyses. Russell defines only individual power but discusses only social power. Still, as shown below, it is straightforward to extend his concept to social power. Then the discussion turns to Russell's claim that power is the fundamental concept of the social sciences and his subsequent focus on the transitions across forms of power. The essay concludes with an issue at the core of Russell's concerns, the taming of power.

## THE CONCEPT OF POWER

For Russell, "power may be defined as the production of intended effects" (2003:23). Since only individuals have intentions, his definition is for the power of an individual and, in that regard, is like one offered by Hobbes. For Hobbes, "the Power of a *Man* . . . is his present means to obtain some future apparent good" (1952:66). The two definitions point to the same phenomenon, but differ in one important regard. Russell defines power as an act, whereas Hobbes defines power as a potential to act. Because potentials may or may not be observable, whereas acts always are, Russell's definition is easier to employ.

Russell defines the power of individuals, but his subsequent discussions are not about the power of one or another individual. Instead, he discusses social power, the power exercised by one person over another, an idea he does not define. Still, he mentions three means to power over humans: physical coercion, as in imprisonment; rewards and punishments, as in giving and withholding employment; and influence, as in propaganda broadly conceived (24). The examples are helpful, but they cannot take the place of assigning a precise meaning to social power.

Should Russell have consulted Weber? Here is Weber's definition of social power:

> In general we understand by "power" the chance of a man or number of men to realize their own will in a social action even against the resistance of others participating in the action. (1978:926)

In Weber's definition, power occurs when a man realizes his "will" over another. But what is "will" and how it is to be observed? According to Ryle, a close associate of Russell's, will "is an artificial concept" (1949:62):

> No one ever says such things as that at 10 a.m. he was occupied in willing this or that, or that he performed five quick and easy volitions and two slow and difficult volitions between midday and lunch-time. (Ryle 1949:64)

Will, being artificial, has no sensible referent: it cannot be observed. Since will cannot be measured, it has no scientific value.

Instead of borrowing from Weber, Russell's individual power can be extended to social power by inserting a second person into the production of effects:

> *A person exercises power over a second when the second produces effects intended by the first.*

Social power is about control that occurs in a social relationship such as coercion or exchange. Referring to Russell's three means of power, in coercion, control occurs through force or threat, as in mugging or tax collecting. In exchange, control occurs through payoffs gained and the threat of payoffs lost, as in the loss of employment by laborers or professors. Alternatively, power can be exercised through influence, what Russell calls "propaganda broadly conceived."

## POWER AS A FUNDAMENTAL CONCEPT

Early in *Power*, Russell drops this bombshell:

> In the course of this book I shall be concerned to prove that the fundamental concept in social science is Power, in the same sense in which Energy is the fundamental concept in physics. (1938:4)

That power is fundamental is a very strong claim, and, while Russell goes some way toward making it plausible, no formal proof is forthcoming. Instead of proof, Russell offers example after example of power and its transformations from one form to another. While not formally proven, Russell's thesis, that power is social science's fundamental concept, strikes me as true and obviously so. Indeed, I am as convinced of its truth today as when I first read *Power* 40 years ago. Just as energy moves physical things, social power moves social things.

Russell offers three parallels between social power and physical energy that highlight power's importance. Taken together, the three parallels point to a program of research that just might transform the social sciences into sciences of considerable explanatory power:

1. Like energy, power has many forms, such as wealth, armaments, civil authority, influence, and opinion. No one of these can be regarded as subordinate to any other (p. 4).
2. The laws of social dynamics are laws that can be stated in terms of power, not in terms of this or that form of power (p. 4).
3. [P]ower, like energy, must be regarded as continually passing from any one of its forms into any other (p. 5).

Russell adds that "it should be the business of social science to seek the laws of such transformations" (p. 5). I will take up the three points in order.

Russell's first claim, that no form of power can be considered subordinate to any other, runs headlong into Marx's claim that economics is fundamental to all social change and dominant over all other parts of society. In this case,

I believe that Marx is wrong and Russell is right. While economic power is important, that importance is not more fundamental than, for example, political power. There is no economic power without property rights, and the economy does not produce property rights. The state does. Therefore, no state, no private property as we know it, and thus no economic power.

The economic power of the greatest American fortunes such as Rockefeller and du Pont or of the largest corporations such as Exxon-Mobil or Ford rivals that of all but the largest states. Without the U.S. government producing property rights every day, however, that economic power would not exist. Conversely, it is no accident that the particulars of the state's property rights are formed and formed again by economic power.

When property rights are reformed against the interests of great economic powers, that reform is an exception and is well known as such. For example, early in the twentieth century the attack on Standard Oil Trust by Ida Tarbell and other muckrakers led to public outcry and the Supreme Court decision to break the Trust into its component parts. Tellingly, it has taken almost a century for antitrust laws to be put aside and for the two largest parts of the Standard Oil Trust to recombine into Exxon-Mobil. That recombination claimed little media attention, triggered no public outcry, and instituted no disestablishing action by the Supreme Court.

Russell's second point, that the laws for social dynamics can be stated in terms of power, presumes we know those laws, which, as he admitted, we do not. In the more than 70 years since Russell's *Power*, nothing that I would count as a law of social dynamics has been offered in any social science. Certainly social theory has advanced since the 1930s, but measured against Russell's vision that advance has been small.

Russell's third point, the claim that power is continually passing from one form into another, is extensively documented throughout *Power*. There are many examples of economic power being transformed into military power and military power being transformed into economic power, of church power becoming secular and of secular power being legitimated by the Church. Russell's insights on those transformations are reviewed in the section to follow.

## RUSSELL'S INSIGHTS

Power is not a rigorously organized work. Instead, Russell rambles charmingly from topic to topic. But rambling is not a symptom of disorganization. The work makes a sensible whole held together by the wisdom of his insights. Following are some of the high points.

## Priestly Power

In antiquity, Greece and Rome were almost unique in being free from priestly power (p. 37), to Russell a highly desirable state. As an afterthought he adds that only in China has priestly power remained almost as weak (p. 39). Where religion is strong, as in the Middle Ages, the Papacy bested the Emperor because the former and not the latter was able to garb his cause in piety (p. 46).

Still, any organization with a reputation for superior virtue will, in the long run, prove its superiority only in ruthlessness (p. 53). He notes that, in the United States, reverence of the kind given to the Pope in the Middle Ages is given to the Supreme Court. How times have changed! Applying Russell's rule, the Supreme Court's reputation for superior virtue pre-staged its superior ruthlessness, the ruthlessness of its recent rulings on U.S. elections.

## Naked Power

"Power is naked when its subjects respect it solely because it is power and not for any other reason" (p. 75). When power is naked, justice is platonic, which is to say justice is the interest of the stronger. Renaissance Italy together with ancient Greece combined high civilization with low morality and thus naked power (p. 73). Nevertheless, Russell notes that periods of naked power tend to be brief. They end in one of three ways: foreign conquest, stable dictatorship, or the rise of a new religion (p. 74).

The "great abominations" in history are due to naked power and include slavery and the slave trade, judicial torture, the evils of early industrialization, and the treatment of political opponents in Russia and Germany in the 1930s. To those Russell might add, if still alive today, that the treatment of "alien combatants" in undeclared wars of the United States is power in its most naked form. In fact, war itself is the exercise of naked power, according to Russell (p. 81).

## Economic Power

Russell begins by noting that economic power is derivative of political power through property rights (see above). Nevertheless, either can be transformed into the other:

> The possession of economic power may lead to the possession of military or propaganda power, but the opposite process is just as apt to occur. Under primitive conditions, military power is usually the source of other kinds insofar as different countries are concerned. Alexander

> was not as rich as the Persians, and the Romans were not as rich as the Carthaginians; but by victory in war the conquerors, in each case, made themselves richer than their enemies. (p. 103)

He adds that military and economic power were never before as closely connected as in his day (p. 104)—a connection that continues to grow ever closer today and very likely will do so into the future.

## THE TAMING OF POWER

The problem of taming power, as Russell notes, is a very ancient one that has yet to be solved. Toward its solution Russell suggests the following.

> While, therefore, public ownership and control of all large-scale industry and finance is a *necessary* condition for the taming of power, it is far from being a *sufficient* condition. It needs to be supplemented by a democracy more thorough-going, more carefully safeguarded against official tyranny, and with more deliberate provision for freedom of propaganda, than any purely political democracy that has ever existed. (p. 238)

War as raw power is the most important promoter of despotism (p. 243). Therefore, for Russell, war "is an essential part of our problem," the problem of taming power (p. 243).

The motivation for Russell's advocacy of public ownership of the means of production is quite different from Marx's. For Marx, capital rightly belongs to the workers and should be restored to them to be used for their benefit. For Russell, the modern corporation, including finance capital, is out of control because it is beholden only to those who have usurped high positions in corporate bureaucracies. Only public control can bring the corporation under control.

In the closing pages of *Power*, Russell emphasizes the role of education in taming power. He is right to do so. If education today eschewed propaganda and focused instead on the tools of critical thinking, it would be far more difficult to exercise power over the people of contemporary societies.

Going only slightly beyond points made by Russell, I want to suggest that an education system that promotes an understanding of power would make a great contribution toward its taming. Are basic questions of social power difficult to understand? Are they so difficult, so very complex, that they cannot be taught to any but advanced scholars? I believe that Russell's answers to these questions would be "no," and "no" again. Something has been learned about power since Russell, but the answers to basic questions, as in Russell's *Power*, remain straightforward and simple. The next paragraph is an example.

Here is how power is centralized in human societies. Throughout human prehistory and history power has been centralized by one organizational means only, bureaucracy. Bureaucratic structures create officials and offices by separating people from owning the positions they occupy. Positions are arraigned in a pyramid, with each higher level having pay and perquisites enough larger than the one immediately below to motivate all officials to seek promotion. Obedience in all official acts is the necessary condition for promotion. A permanent record of official acts allows obedience to be reviewed by officials at all higher levels. Promotion is controlled from the top down. Therefore, power is centralized at the top and extends throughout the organization (Willer 1987, 1999).

Russell began the taming of power with his quite marvelous insights, insights that help us understand power in its many forms. It would be quite wonderful if today Russell's *Power* was part of everyone's general education. It would also be wonderful if what has been learned about power since Russell could also be part of that education.

Great events have happened since *Power* was written, but nothing invalidates Russell's understanding of power or his formula for taming it. On the one hand, we have seen tyrannical Communism rise and fall in Europe. When it prevailed, private ownership of industry was abolished, not in favor of the workers, but, as Russell explained, under elite control. On the other hand, we have seen democracy, particularly in the United States, increasingly transformed into a uniquely modern form of plutocracy. As Russell anticipated, in capitalism today power is held not only by owners of capital, but also by those who control the capitalist corporation.

# CHAPTER 29

# Immanuel Kant: An Analytic Grammar for the Relation between Cognition and Action

*John Levi Martin*

Immanuel Kant is undoubtedly the single most important thinker in modern Western philosophy.[1] He represents a fundamental turning point, after which vast areas of philosophical inquiry were nearly boarded up, or at least the few who still insisted on venturing in became romantics at best, hysterics at worst. His arguments were decisive for sociology, as both Weber and Durkheim were Kantians of one sort or another, and their theoretical frameworks fundamentally Kantian.[2]

Kant's own system, however, was richer and less one-sided than the versions seized upon by our sociological progenitors. If we are doomed to make use of some sort of Kantian theoretical vocabulary, we would do well to reincorporate the portions left out. The "practical turn" in the social sciences has done this to an extent, but we may find Kant's own writings to provide a rigorous basis for our development of a consistent vocabulary for social explanation.

This essay does not attempt to give an exegesis of Kant's main system nor to engage in the extensive secondary literature (for most philosophy in the nineteenth and twentieth centuries is in some ways part of this literature). Instead, I give a thumbnail sketch of Kant's basic system from his pivotal works and then discuss how these were adopted by Weber and Durkheim (leaving out the various middlemen).

I then propose that serious problems (now being addressed in sociological theory via the interest in practice and in pragmatism) came from Weber and Durkheim seizing on two of Kant's critiques and ignoring the third. Discussing some themes of Kant's work on judgment, I then argue that we have a way of revivifying our theoretical interest in the relationship between cognition and action.

As Burke (1945) has argued, social theories have "grammars" of action—different ways of dividing up the crucial moments that are fused in any act. My argument is that mainstream sociologists have adopted a partial grammar from Kant. I review Kant's well-known discussions of two aspects of our cognitive powers before concentrating on the one we neglect, namely judgment.

## THE TRUE, THE GOOD, AND THE BEAUTIFUL

We are familiar with the phrase "the true, the good, and the beautiful," often misattributing it to the ancient Greeks. In fact, the phrase seems instead to have solidified during the Enlightenment, in the circle of those *philosophes* working on the Encyclopaedia.

The influential theoretical work linking each of these to a faculty was almost certainly that of Immanuel Kant. Although he did not begin with this triad, his exploration of the limits of reason led him to a parsing of our cognitive powers that paralleled the trinity of the true, the good, and the beautiful and provided a coherent grammar of action.

### Kant's Trinity of Faculties

Kant proposed that we have the capacity to think in concepts (to understand the unity of appearances through rules) (the *understanding*), a capacity to determine what to do (to transform rules into principles) (*practical reasoning*) and a capacity to determine the relationship between these (*judgment*) (Kant 1987:17ff.; 2002:B359; 2006:93, 123).

This is an extremely reasonable parsing of functions. It can be, for one, tied to the proper division of state functions, and was by Kant himself. This same division emerged in the governmental structure of the United States of America, which divides public functions into the legislative (in which we choose what principles to put into effect), the executive (which pertains to the practice of such principles), and the judicial, in which we use judgment to determine the relation between these two.

This does not mean that this is the *only* way of dividing these governmental functions, but it does mean that a government that had the first two and not the third would be hampered. Sociology has been in that position: two of Kant's three portions have been built upon and the third nearly completely ignored; I briefly review the first two and give the third more consideration.

There are some changes to Kant's system as it evolved from the breakthrough of the *Critique of Pure Reason*, but in this overview of the first two critiques I blur such differences and draw promiscuously from the *Critique of Pure Reason*, the *Critique of Practical Reason*, the *Prolegomena to any Future Metaphysics that Will be Able to Present Itself as a Science*, and (predominantly) the *Groundwork for the Metaphysic of Morals*.

## THE THREE CRITIQUES

### Pure Reason

How do we produce knowledge? Some is inherent in the concepts we have before us and comes out upon analysis, but some requires something else. Such an "else" can come from our empirical engagement with the world, but it can also come from the nature of our reason itself. Thus there are *a prioris* to our knowledge and, in particular, to our sensory engagement with the world—we must sense objects "in" time and space, although we have no reason to be confident that the objects themselves are in time and space, for time and space are (so far as we know) aspects of our experience.

Put another way, when we sense objects, we sense not the things-in-themselves, but the things-as-they-appear-to-us, and we must rigorously maintain a recognition of this distinction. Similarly, there are *a prioris* of the understanding—that faculty which allows us to manipulate concepts. We cannot be sure that "causality" exists in the world; all we can say is that our way of engaging with the world is one that requires that we treat certain relations in causal terms.

Kant's key argument was to establish the limits of the understanding, and in so doing to uncover certain forms of metaphysical thought that were necessarily unstable. But sociology has drawn more from the general "apriorism" that asserts that there is something in our minds "from the start" that organizes experience. It is this epistemology that characterized the neo-Kantianism from which both Weber and Durkheim drew.

For Weber (1978), this reliance is seen in his theory of concept formation and especially the notion of ideal types. Confronted with the infinite multiplexity of the world, we find that we cannot engage with this world without first making some sort of conceptual organization. The good scientist is the one who makes this organization consciously for particular explanatory purposes.

In Durkheim, this is seen most obviously in his attempt to demonstrate the social ontogenesis of the categories of knowledge, in his remarkable (1995)

*Elementary Forms of Religious Life*. Durkheim, too, adopted a basically neo-Kantian understanding of concept formation, as formalized in his (1938) *Rules*. And it is a similar epistemology—that we must first define theoretical concepts by highlighting certain parts of the world or certain attributes of our cases—that we teach to each new generation of sociologists.

## Practical Reason

The First Critique demonstrates as a corollary that we cannot deny free will. All the laws of physics that indicate our complete determination are well and good, but they apply to us only as objects-of-experience. That fact that as objects-of-experience we are determined in no way demonstrates that as things-in-ourselves (as persons, as acting subjects) we do not have free will. Indeed, our moral nature (our activity) demands that we treat ourselves as if we did have such a will; that is, the capacity to determine how to act morally.

What does it mean to act morally? We categorize an act by the grounds of its action. Some grounds are forms of non-freedom in that they are subjective instincts or inclinations arising from natural causes. We certainly can behave thusly and are then no freer than one of the lower animals, basically an automaton. However, other grounds of actions are rational motives that we must understand as binding on all rational beings.

The moral status of our actions, then, comes from whether or not we are guided by such motivations, and we can determine whether any principle of our action falls into this category by carrying out the thought experiment, "can I and would I wish the maxim guiding my action to be a law for all rational beings?" When we act because our maxim meets this criterion—when we observe the moral law if only because it is a law, regardless of its anticipated results—then we do our duty.

This perspective on morality was key to the works of both Durkheim and Weber. We see it in Weber's (1978) distinction between the types of action that are rational (whether instrumentally rational or value rational) and those that must be understood sympathetically (affectual and habitual). This bifurcation is fundamentally Kant's, between free actions based on motives derived from reason and un-free action based on inclinations derived from nature. We see it in Durkheim's (1961) distinction between those impersonal actions that might be considered moral and those personal ones that we consider merely self-interested—here a typical sociologization (and a reversion to Rousseau) of Kant's answer.

Weber ignored one key part of Kant's work, namely the insistence that the two forms of reason (pure and practical) are fundamentally the same—the lawfulness uncovered by the understanding is that which allows free will, for it is that which allows us to act in accord with the nature of the universe; that is, it allows us to have the causality of our will unaffected by other causal laws and indeed in perfect harmony with all forms of lawfulness of the world.

Durkheim accepted this idea that our freedom can mean nothing other than willing the constraints of the natural world. Because Durkheim lacked Kant's faith in a single reason stemming from our created nature, however, this ends up sounding more like Comte's tiresome preaching of the virtue of enlightened submission to a sociological priesthood.

Thus classical sociology began by phrasing itself in terms largely taken from Kant's two critiques. The vision of the good was largely a sociologization of Kant's critique of practical reason, though adapted in various ways to conform to sociologists' need to treat their own pronouncements as binding on humans as actors—as things-in-themselves (Martin 1998).

The ethical project was then one of determining the sort of mature autonomy that would be consistent with the laws revealed by sociological investigations. The vision of the true was a sociologization of Kant's theory of knowledge in the critique of pure reason. What was missing was an understanding of judgment, and, correspondingly, a consideration of how beauty might be said to exist.

## THE ROLE OF JUDGMENT

According to traditional ideas of concept formation, we begin with discrete units with attributes (e.g., animals), and collect some together in a concept (e.g., birds) by stressing some attributes (e.g., feathers and bone type) and ignoring others (e.g., mode of locomotion). It is this act that we properly call "abstraction." Using concepts, we may predicate some particularity with a generality when we identify identity along some lines. Thus, we may say that a badger is a mammal because the badger satisfies the attributes used to define the concept mammal (live birth, hair, and nursing, say).

This is not only our theory of our own theories in sociology; it is generally our theory of others, and it leads to a flatness and a set of paradoxes when we cannot tell the difference between "badgers are mammals" and "we are badgers," the latter being some sort of metaphorical act of predication. Further, it makes the attachment of other sorts of generalities as predicates hard to defend: for example, "badgers are tenacious." But it is only because "badgers are tenacious" that we (in Madison, that is), might say "we are badgers."

If we call "judgment" the act (or the faculty) of determining that some specific case can be attached to a more general term, we see that the act of subsumption (e.g., badgers are mammals) is one type of judgment. The Durkheimian approach in particular, but also the Weberian, restricts judgment to this one form, and in effect banishes to the realm of poetry all predications that cannot be reduced to a subsumptive form.

The resulting model of cognition that results is one in which we only have a partial set of operations. For there can be other cases in which we merely begin with a particular and need to find the universal, which requires what Kant terms a *reflective* power. If this sort of judgment is used in social life (as argued by, for one, Simmel), then we cannot excise it from our understanding of human cognition. As reflective judgment is best seen in the realm of aesthetics, we can follow Kant in using the case of judging something to be *beautiful* as a way of exploring how we may make non-subsumptive but synthetic judgments.

## AESTHETICS AND COMMUNION

To say that beauty, purpose, or value is not simply in the eye of the particular beholder is to claim that there are "ends" (an inherent purposiveness as opposed to mere existence) in nature or in created objects and not just in our attitude toward them. However, what is notable about aesthetic perception is precisely its *independence* of intention.

Few would want the stained glass of medieval cathedrals restored to its original (intended?) garishness, because we find the meanings of the altered form more congenial (even though these "meanings" were never "meant" to be). The first task of an aesthetic is simply to determine how we may be able to attribute qualities to objects even when we cannot simply posit that they were "put there" by their creator.

We can begin with the question of what it means to consider something "beautiful," a paradigmatic case of aesthetic judgment. While beauty seems to be a characteristic of the objects themselves, we realize that this cannot technically be the case. "For a judgment of taste consists precisely in this, that it calls a thing beautiful only by virtue of that characteristic in which it adapts itself to the way we apprehend" (Kant 1987:145).

We believe that our judgment of beauty must be accepted as valid (as opposed to idiosyncratic), but as Hume (1985:84) emphasized, we know we cannot *prove* this to someone through concepts in the way that we can prove that a cat is a mammal. Indeed, we understand that to locate something under the banner "beautiful" means not (as with concepts) to *suppress* its particularity, but rather to *highlight* its particularity.

Accordingly, Kant (1987:19, 24ff., 65) argued that the possibility of such judgment implies the existence of trans-individual principles of regularity (otherwise beauty would merely be in the eye of the beholder), which we can consider laws. These laws, however, have the curious characteristic that they cannot be derived from concepts and hence are empirical (which might lead us to consider them contingent), but since they are laws they would seem to be necessary.

Kant concluded that these laws need to "be viewed in terms of such a unity as if they too had been given by an understanding (even though not ours) so as to assist our cognitive powers by making possible a system of experience in terms of particular natural laws."

In other words, if we are to assume the existence of such empirical principles of regularity (some things truly *are* beautiful), we must treat the world as if it was made *for* us to be able to judge beauty. Kant is at pains to emphasize that we do not need to posit the existence of such an understanding (that is, a creator with personhood), but we do need to treat the world *as if* it had so arisen. Hence, we can derive the "harmony of nature with our cognitive power" (which Bourdieu terms the "ontological complicity" of our faculties with the world).

One key aspect of our aesthetic perception is our ability to perceive *purposiveness* (*Zweckmäßigkeit*) in objects or other experiences. Thus, for the case of beauty, we get a sense of pleasure if some representation brings the imagination into harmony with the understanding—this being an aesthetic judgment of the object's purposiveness. The object's purposiveness does not necessarily imply that anything exists that has or had this purpose.

Thus, "a bird's song proclaims his joyfulness and contentment with his existence. At least that is how we interpret nature whether or not it has such an intention." We attribute the purposiveness to the nature of the bird and do not rely on evidence of a subjectively held purpose. On the other hand, in fine art, if the intention becomes visible, then the effect is ruined (we might say it is "strained" and "unnatural").

Thus we see, argued Kant, that aesthetic experience reaches toward a naturalization of what is subjectively experienced. While the beautiful appears purposive (as opposed to senseless or random, say), we do not need to *understand* the purpose of any existent being in order to understand beauty, for we *feel* a pleasure when we encounter beauty. Taste is then our ability to make judgments on the basis of such pleasure (Kant 1987:30f., 169, 174).

Let us call the set of *a priori* principles that justify our treating purposiveness as if it were in the world a "supersensible" realm, as it is inaccessible to our cognitive powers of empirical inquiry (Kant 1987:14, 140, 220). It is the postulating of such a supersensible that allows us to demand that all others (more on this below) agree with us as to our judgments of taste. This is not the case for other things that we find agreeable.

Thus, we may enjoy having our back scratched at some time but do not demand that all others find this equally agreeable. (Indeed, we may even recognize that we do not always find this one thing agreeable.) When we compare the experience of beauty to these other agreeable experiences, we can conclude that aesthetic judgments are peculiar in that we expect them to be communicable and to provoke assent, "and this without any mediation by concepts" (Kant 1987:159; cf. 157, 162, 156). It is sufficient to point and ask "is this not beautiful?"

## Beauty and Intersubjectivity

It is of the utmost importance that Kant does not ground this universal communicability in the objectivity of the judgment—instead, it is more closely related to our "sociability," our innate desire to interact with others (cf. Barnes 2000). Taste is what allows us to judge whether we can communicate our feelings, and the refined person is he who is "not satisfied with an object unless he can feel his liking for it in community with others" (Kant 1987:163f.; cf. 231).

Yet Kant (1987:58) acknowledges that we may find this desire for universal confirmation of our tastes to go unsatisfied. Since there can be no determinative or objective rule governing what is beautiful, "the broadest possible agreement among all ages and peoples regarding this feeling that accompanies the representation (*Vorstellung*) of certain objects is the empirical criteria for what is beautiful" (Kant 1987:79).

For practical purposes, then, the beautiful is generally what is generally taken to be beautiful: yet Kant does not here propose a democratic basis to beauty,[3] for he posits a distinction between cultivated and uncultivated taste; as some *persons* have cultivated tastes and others do not, this ties Kant's philosophy to seemingly exogenous social divisions of domination. It is the fact that Kant's approach to aesthetics *necessarily* involves a form of normativity that is linked to class-based opposition (refined/coarse, for example) that provokes Bourdieu's (1984) sociological critique.

## The Puzzle of Judgment for Sociological Theory

Bourdieu's work has often puzzled those who imagine that the *habitus* must involve subsumptive judgment, a mistake encouraged by Bourdieu's description of the *habitus* as if it were a grid imposed on the world. But the strength of his argument is that the *habitus* (an actual phenomenon of each person's "way" and not some fanciful idea coined by Bourdieu) is itself the faculty of judgment—and the production of actions suitable for reflective judgment. To make this argument clearer, and to tie it to specific cognitive processes, will almost certainly require a basis in Kant's adumbration of the nature of this sort of judgment.

Further, Kant's own thoughts here are sociologically plausible and significant. While Bourdieu emphasizes the divisive nature of the social substrate for the formation of these judgments, we see that Kant's more general approach that links judgment to intersubjectivity may point to other possible social forms in which our capacity for reflective judgment is less in need of a sociological critique and more in need of a sociological appreciation.

But sociology is still groping unsteadily toward an understanding of the social production of intersubjectively valid judgments. This is seen most clearly in the discussion of the relevance of Wittgenstein's (1958) argument regarding what it means to follow a rule. In a sense, the key issue goes back to Lewis Carroll's paradox (or even Zeno's); namely, that to convince someone that our act of subsumptive judgment is correct, we must appeal to some grounds of agreement, and if they insist on asking us to convince them of this, we are in for a very long night (see Kurzman 1988).

Bloor's (1997) ideas, derived through great pains from Wittgenstein, return us to Kant's fundamental notion that there are judgments that must be anchored in intersubjective concordance. Thus, not only is it the case that our theory of human cognition cannot do without Kant's third critique, but our theory of concept formation, if purged of reflective judgment, has been proven to be inherently unstable.

Further, there may be key areas in which the things we want to explore—paradigmatically predications of quality—defeat conceptual (subsumptive) thought. Weberian ideal types are of no use, nor are "definitions." ("For the purposes of this article, I define 'beautiful' paintings as. . . . ") Rather, these things refer to a social process of reaching-out toward (partial) intersubjective agreement—the harmonization of our orientations and reactions. Thus, we may begin with Kant as we try to provide a sociological analysis of qualitative experience. Although we need a sociological critique of this process, and must not confuse our *need* to make this attempt with a complacent belief in its success—or even possibility of success—we can study the empirical process whereby such judgments are made, and we can explore the social productions anchored in them.

## NOTES

1. I wish to thank Daniel Silver and Mario Small for their detailed and thoughtful criticism, and in grateful return I absolve them from any remaining errors.

2. An expanded version of this chapter will be published elsewhere, defending some intellectual-historical statements here that are made without support given space constraints.

3. The empirical agreement does not, it should be emphasized, *define* beauty; rather, it is *prima facie* evidence of a "deeply hidden" basis to the commonality of judgment. This basis, however, cannot be formalized by an objective rule.

# CHAPTER 30

# John Dewey: The Sociology of Action

*Christopher Muller and Christopher Winship*

## INTRODUCTION

There is a paradox in advocating that sociology become more pragmatic—one that Ian Hacking perhaps observed best: "One of the few domains in which I am a consistent pragmatist is pragmatism itself: use it when useful, but don't when it isn't" (Hacking 1998:93). The strengths of American pragmatism, like those of sociology, lie in its flexibility and pluralism. The same is true of the work of John Dewey, whose theory of action we defend here.

Our reason for recommending that Dewey join the sociological canon is twofold. First, Dewey advances a theory of action that combines the best insights of Hans Joas on the importance of creativity, Erving Goffman on the importance of context, and Pierre Bourdieu on the importance of habit. He demonstrates how action can be voluntary without being purposeful; habitual and contextual without being incidental. The use of such a theory has already been demonstrated in psychological research on decision-making and moral reasoning. We argue here that it ought to be taken up by sociology as well.[1]

Second, Dewey advances his theory within an overarching epistemology favoring fallibilism and theoretical pluralism. For Dewey, some theories work better than others, depending on the situation in which they are used. "In all inquiry," Dewey writes, "even the most completely scientific, what is proposed as a conclusion (the end-in-view in that inquiry) is evaluated as to its worth on the ground of its ability to resolve the *problem* presented by the conditions under investigation. There is no a priori standard for determining the value of a proposed solution in concrete cases" (Dewey 1988 [1939]:232).

Sociologists by now are used to the maxim that one should permit one's question to determine one's method. We argue that pragmatism likewise counsels that one should allow one's question to determine one's theory. This is neither to claim that all theories are equally valid, nor that questions themselves are pre-theoretical; only that one need not stake a paradigmatic claim on how the world *is* before beginning a scientific endeavor.[2] Some theories may be better suited to the task of prediction or explanation while others are better suited to description. The strength of Dewey's theory of action, therefore, should be measured against its ability to guide specific research programs within sociology and social science more generally.

## HISTORY

John Dewey was born in 1859 in Burlington, Vermont, and he died in 1952 in New York City. His life bookended the American Civil War and World War II. Dewey's longevity was matched only by his prolificacy. He published on topics spanning psychology, ethics, education, logic, politics, philosophy, and art, and the bibliography of his collected works runs more than 150 pages (Menand 2001; Bernstein 1967). Early in his life Dewey established himself as one of America's most important philosophers. By the end of his life he was one if its most prominent public intellectuals as well (Westbrook 1991).

Dewey studied as an undergraduate at the University of Vermont and pursued graduate studies at Johns Hopkins University, where he crossed paths with—but never took classes from—Charles Sanders Peirce and where he studied with experimental psychologist G. S. Hall and Hegelian philosopher G. S. Morris. Upon completion of his doctoral dissertation, he joined Morris at the University of Michigan. There he collaborated with philosopher and sociologist George Herbert Mead.

In 1894, Dewey was appointed chair of the Department of Philosophy, Psychology, and Education at the University of Chicago, where he remained until 1904. Mead moved with him. Many of the empirical projects that would influence his philosophy were born in Chicago—most notably his affiliation with Jane Addams's Hull House and his founding of the University's Laboratory School.

Dewey spent the remainder of his career at Columbia. During this period his reputation reached its highest level of national and international prominence. *The Journal of Philosophy* was founded as a vehicle for examining his work. Dewey traveled and lectured internationally and was a frequent contributor to *The New Republic*. Throughout his career he maintained a balance between scholarship and advocacy of social and political causes.

## DEWEY'S THEORY OF ACTION

Dewey's theory of action can be described in three simple theses. First, action is *experimental*. Second, it is *contextual*. Third, action is *habitual*. Each thesis has been advanced elsewhere, but Dewey's novelty is to demonstrate how the three fit together. He takes as his point of departure a critique of the theory of rational action.

### Action Is Experimental[3]

For Dewey, the problem with theories of rational action is not that they lack predictive or explanatory power, but that they presuppose a division of means from ends that fails to accord with the reported lived experience of many individuals. Broadly defined, rationality is difficult to quibble with. Jon Elster, for example, provides a definition so expansive that it easily accommodates facets of action usually thought to reside outside the bounds of rationality.[4]

Dewey objects not to the notion that people strive to do what is best, but instead to the notion that this act of striving is especially deliberate. Seldom, he holds, do we specify a particular goal, interest, or end, then select the appropriate means by which to achieve it. More often, we experiment with lines of action, stumbling on them, selecting them intuitively or in accordance with models provided by actors surrounding us, or pursuing them unreflectively.

In most situations, in other words, we "puzzle" rather than "deliberate" (Winship 2006). For Dewey, ends are rarely pre-given and sought; more often they emerge in the course of action and are retrospectively justified. The ability to separate ends from means, Dewey maintains, is an artifact of retrospection. "[T]he distinction between ends and means," he writes, "is temporal and relational" (Dewey 1988 [1939]:229). "The 'end,' is merely a series of acts viewed at a remote stage; and a means is merely the series viewed at an earlier one. The distinction of means and end arises in surveying the *course* of a proposed *line* of action, a connected series in time" (Dewey 1988 [1922]:27).[5]

Whether an object appears as an end or a mean depends upon one's temporal position vis-à-vis a course of action and social position vis-à-vis other individuals. Contemporary decision research in psychology has gone some way toward vindicating this claim (see especially Simon et al. 2007). Experiments have shown, for example, that individuals who initially view evidence in support of a decision as ambiguous rewrite the evidence to minimize ambiguity once a decision is made (Hastie 1994; Simon 2001, 2004; Simon et al. 2004). Moral reasoning, too, is often constructed *post hoc* (Haidt 2001).

Action, for Dewey, is more a method by which we recognize or discover our ends than it is a means by which we achieve them. "An individual within the limits of his personal experience," he writes, "revises his desires and purposes as he becomes aware of the consequences they have produced in the past" (Dewey 1988 [1939]:243). Here Dewey often relies on evidence from developmental psychology.

Barry Barnes supplies a helpful illustration: "Consider an ER [economically rational] baby, lying in its cot facing its new world of threat and opportunity. Will it consult its preference schedule and reflect: 'Well what should I do now? A restful nap perhaps, or a spot of healthy foot-kicking for muscle development. Or perhaps a cry for mother, to do a bit of language-learning' " (Barnes 1995; cited in Loury 202:43). Clearly not. The baby instead experiments with courses of action.

Barnes's point—one he shares with Dewey—is that experimentation persists over the life course. As babies mature into infants, adolescents, and adults, they continue to experiment, but they also improve their ability to read situational cues for clues about appropriate comportment. They come to rely not only on intuition but on context—the second facet of Dewey's theory of action.

## Action Is Contextual

"The confusions and mistakes in existing theories," Dewey claims, "arise very largely from taking desire and interest as original instead of in the contextual situations in which they arise" (Dewey 1988[1939]:240). If ends emerge in action, they result not simply from a gradual recognition of the individual consequences of a given line of action, but also from the way others respond to the action and provide alternative examples of action upon which to model our own. Ends, in other words, often are realized through mimicry or social influence (Richerson and Boyd 2005; Gambetta 2005; Iacoboni 2008).

Within sociology, Goffman (1963) scrupulously documented the ways situational cues give rise to varieties of action. Social psychologists have extensively theorized situational determinants of action (Katz and Allport 1931) and vindicated them experimentally (Prentice and Miller 1993;

Cialdini and Trost 1998). Recent network studies in sociology document peculiar associations between the actions of linked individuals to support a model of aggregate social influence (Christakis and Fowler 2009). As economist Glenn Loury puts it, often "one undertakes to see the world as others do—not because the benefit of doing so outweighs the cost, but because that is the way of being in the world with these people" (Loury 2002:44).

Although it was neither novel nor original, Dewey's early recognition of the contextual determinants of action anticipated rich research traditions in sociology and psychology alike. Coupled with his notion of action as experiment, Dewey's contextual theory provides a powerful rejoinder to the claim that ends must be given for action to occur. Still, our daily activity is governed not by trial-and-error or convention alone, Dewey claims. Instead, much of what we do is routine.

## Actions Tested Through Experiment and Contextual Cues Form Habits

Once actions have been tested experimentally and contextually, Dewey held, they crystallize into habits.[6] Actions originally borne of experimental verification or social sanction become unreflective rituals. Dewey's theory, like theories of habit in the work of Bourdieu (1977), aims to explain courses of action not preceded by deliberation.[7]

"When someone finds that his foot has been stepped on, he is likely to react with a push to get rid of the offending element. He does not stop to form a definite desire and set up an end to be reached. A man who has started walking may continue walking from force of an acquired habit without continually interrupting his course of action to inquire what object is to be obtained at the next step" (Dewey 1988 [1939]:221).

What sets Dewey's theory apart from other theories of habit is its insistence that habits result from experimentation and social sanction. Because, for Dewey, action is experimental as well as contextual and habitual, it can be voluntary without being purposive, as when one makes quick moral judgements but struggles to articulate reasons to defend them. Habits, rather than being dictated strictly by one's situation, are borne also of voluntary experimentation. Dewey's integration of the experimental, contextual, and habitual sources of action, therefore, is progressive.

Experimental actions are reinforced by their consequences for individuals and by contextual sanctions and rewards. "[A]s the baby matures," Dewey writes, "it becomes aware of the connection that exists between a certain cry, the activity evoked, and the consequences produced in response to it" (Dewey 1988 [1939]:198). "[I]n the history of individual persons and of the human race," he concludes, "there takes place a change from original, comparatively unreflective impulses and hard-and-fast habits to desires that incorporate the results of critical inquiry" (Dewey 1988 [1939]:218).

## CRITIQUES

Our call to fuse American pragmatism and sociology via Dewey's theory of action departs somewhat from previous attempts. The most noteworthy pragmatism-influenced subfield within sociology is symbolic interactionism, whose forefather is Dewey's once colleague and fellow pragmatist George Herbert Mead.

When Mead became too old to teach, sociologist Herbert Blumer took over his lecturing duties and eventually published in 1969 his interpretation of Mead in the key text on symbolic interactionism. Contemporary symbolic interactionists, therefore, might argue that our call for a pragmatist sociology comes 40 years too late.

In our view, however, the inspiration for symbolic interactionism derives solely from Dewey's and Mead's insights about the contextual determinants of action.[8] Symbolic interactionism has less to say about action's experimental and habitual roots. Reading Blumer today one is struck by how closely his theory of action hews to the very division of means from ends that Dewey abhorred. "In order to act," Blumer claims, "the individual has to identify what he wants, establish an objective or goal, map out a prospective line of behavior, and interpret the actions of others, size up his situation, check himself at this or that point, figure out what to do at other points, and frequently spur himself on in the fact of dragging dispositions or discouraging settings" (Blumer 1969:64).

Action so conceived, while attentive to context, is deliberate and ends-oriented. The symbolic interactionist's commitment to purposive action is further enshrined in Anselm Strauss's shibboleth that there is "no order without negotiation" and George McCall's argument that symbolic interactionists consider pragmatism "a philosophy taking seriously the practical consequences of ideas for intelligent, purposive action" (Strauss 1978; McCall 2006:5). The problem with purposive theories of action, as we have seen, is that they cannot explain ends. Ends must be pre-given for action to occur.

Other sociologists might object that all that is worthwhile in Dewey can be found in the work of Pierre Bourdieu. We argue that although the affinities between Bourdieu and Dewey are manifold, and that Bourdieu offers perhaps a more thoroughgoing description of the role habit plays in forming action, it is Dewey's emphasis on experimentation that has borne the greatest fruit in contemporary decision research.

That Bourdieu devoted less of his work to studying experimentation in social action is unsurprising since his aim, in most of his works, was to explain social reproduction, not change. Defenders of Bourdieu, however, would be correct to point out that Dewey says too little about the place of power in his theory of action.

Finally, others (Emirbayer and Maynard 2007) argue that Garfinkel (1967) effectively carried Dewey's torch within sociology. Although we agree that parallels between pragmatism and Garfinkel's program of ethnomethodology can be found, we disagree that Dewey would especially favor a return to "concrete experience" as a scientific method. Dewey's epistemology could just as easily support a reasoned defense of quantitative causal modeling.

While Dewey's theory of action springs from incongruities he locates between the means-ends distinction in theories of rational action and the lived experience individuals themselves report, the strength of his theory of action lies not in its ontological veracity. "The pragmatist," Dewey writes, "says that since every proposition is a hypothesis referring to an inquiry still to be undertaken (a proposal in short) its truth is a matter of its career, of its history: that it becomes or is *made* true (or false) in process of fulfilling or frustrating in use its own proposal" (Dewey 1998 [1911]:112). Deweyan ideas, accordingly, are valuable because they predict the results of recent research programs on social action in psychology and, to a lesser extent, sociology. Our wager is that by making these connections more explicit we might generate additional successful programs of research.

## SHORTCOMINGS

The strongest criticism of Dewey's philosophy can be leveled against his epistemology. If the truth of an idea is determined by its use, who determines what is useful or not? Falsehood and propaganda, after all, can be said to have uses. We argue that for pragmatism to be useful to sociology, the sociologist must define at the outset what she means by "use."

As we have argued here, the use of a Deweyan theory of action has been demonstrated in empirical work on the sociology of networks and in psychology investigating the experimental and contextual sources of action. If one defines use to mean hypothesis formation, Dewey's theory of action should have a long career within sociology generally. Theories of action as flexible as Dewey's do have deficits, however. As Bruce Western (2001) has demonstrated, the more complex the theory, the weaker the predictions it yields.

This is one reason to prefer theories of rational action, which tend to produce stronger predictions, especially regarding aggregate behavior. Using a model for predictive purposes, after all, does not require that the model be "true" in some ontological sense (Hacking 1983; King 1998).[9]

As Neil Gross points out, this insight has long motivated the work of Charles Tilly, who argues that "the secret is to sketch a model that brings out the salient features of its object, but never to confuse model with reality" (Tilly 1998:29). When use is defined to mean predictive capacity, Dewey's theory of action faces a formidable competitor in the elegant simplicity of rational choice theory.

Viewed from another angle, however, this weakness could be considered a strength. The merits of Dewey's epistemology stem from its ability to accommodate theoretical pluralism by tying the worth of a theory to its use in solving a specific problem. Theories, like methods, should be question-specific. To advocate for pragmatism generally, or for its theory of action in particular, then, means not to argue for its blanket superiority over other philosophical traditions. Theories of rational action can sit comfortably among experimental, contextual, and habitual theories once sociology apprehends the pragmatist insight that a theory is only as good as its use in solving a particular problem.[10]

## CONCLUSION

We have argued here that John Dewey offers a useful theory of action—one that integrates its experimental, contextual, and habitual facets. We have not recommended that this theory supplant others—theories that might better serve other purposes—for such would be to misapprehend the pragmatist enterprise. However, acknowledging the Deweyan spirit of contemporary programs of research in psychology and sociology leads us to conclude that revisiting Dewey is a social scientific exercise well worth undertaking.

## ACKNOWLEDGMENTS

We thank Mustafa Emirbayer, Neil Gross, and Hans Joas for helpful comments.

## NOTES

1. Neil Gross (2007, 2009), Josh Whitford (2002), and Hans Joas (1996) have argued the same point forcefully, although their reasons for doing so differ slightly from ours.

2. In this sense, Dewey's use of theory closely resembles Elster's (2009:2) defense of mechanisms. The goal of social science, Elster claims, is not to uncover general laws, but rather situation-specific mechanisms. For this reason we can invite contradictory mechanisms into a single argument: "As laws they could not both be true; as mechanisms they may both be applicable, albeit in different situations" (Elster 2009:2).

3. We take Dewey's claim about the experimental nature of human behavior to be the most important contribution of his theory of action. Joas (1996:148) prizes a pragmatist conception of action for two additional reasons—its analysis of "the specific corporeality and the primary sociality of all human capacity for action." Due to space constraints, we cannot take up these points here, except to note that what Joas calls "types of action that result from the pre-reflective intentionality of the body" we claim fall under the broader category of "habit" and what he calls action's "sociality" we claim can be subsumed under the label "context." Some would argue we have downplayed Dewey's interest in intelligent, purposive action. Our justification for doing so is twofold: first, we consider this the least interesting of the facets of action Dewey discussed. Most people, after all, *assume* that people are intelligent and purposive decision makers. Second, recent research has demonstrated that this type of action is less prevalent than social science traditionally has assumed (see especially Haidt 2001 and Pentland 2008).

4. "When faced with several courses of action, people usually do what they believe is likely to have the best overall outcome" (Elster 1989:22).

5. Dewey (1988[1922]:185) here draws upon the example of building a house: "We must not confuse the act of building with the house when built. The latter *is* a means, not a fulfillment. But it is such only because it enters into a new activity which is present not future. Life is continuous."

6. Greene (Forthcoming), defending a dual-process theory of cognition, uses the example of driving a car to make a similar point. For veteran drivers driving is largely habitual. Thankfully, the same cannot be said of new drivers.

7. Bourdieu acknowledged the affinities between his and Dewey's "notion of habit" (Bourdieu and Wacquant 1992:122).

8. Joas (1987) provides an historical account and more extensive critique of symbolic interactionism.

9. What social scientific dictum is more pragmatist than Box and Draper's (1987:424) claim that "all models are wrong, but some are useful"?

10. To cite just one example of parallels between pragmatism and rational choice theory, compare James's (1975[1906]:28–29) claim that "beliefs are really rules for action," to Elster's definition of rational choice, in which, "the aim of belief formation is not to arrive at the truth, but to guide action" (Elster 2009:31).

# CHAPTER 31

# Charles Sanders Peirce: On the Sociology of Thinking

*Richard Swedberg*

> [I intend] to make a philosophy like that of Aristotle, that is to say, to outline a theory so comprehensive that, for a long time to come, the entire work of human reason, in philosophy of every school and kind, in mathematics, in psychology, in physical science, in history, in *sociology*, and in whatever other departments there may be, shall appear as the filling up of its details.
>
> —Charles Peirce, 1887

Anyone who reads this quote and is not familiar with Peirce would think that he must have been something of a crackpot. When sociologists these days talk about Lester Ward as "the American Aristotle," it is with a snigger and not out of admiration. But Peirce is different—he was truly a genius and perhaps even in the class of Aristotle. He especially made contributions to logic, philosophy, and semiotics. To judge from the quote above, he also thought that his ideas were vast enough to one day also include "sociology."

## LIFE AND WORK

Charles Sanders Peirce (1839–1914) was in many ways a remarkable man with a remarkable life (see, especially, Brent 1993). He was born in Cambridge, Massachusetts; and his father, Benjamin Peirce, was a Professor at Harvard and one of the best mathematicians of his generation. Benjamin Peirce wanted his son to become a first-class scientist, and from early on he trained Charles in mathematics and the art of concentration ("I was forced to think hard and continuously"—Peirce 1953:37). It does not seem that Peirce had much of a normal childhood, and his education was in some ways similar to the one that John Stuart Mill received from his father.

At the age of 12 Peirce came across a textbook in logic and immediately fell in love with the topic. For the rest of his life, his main ambition was to be a logician and to develop a new system of logic. So even if Peirce had talents in a large number of scholarly areas, the red thread in all of his intellectual endeavors was always logic. Among the topics that Peirce practiced and excelled in during his career are mathematics, chemistry, physics, engineering, astronomy, geodesy, philology, psychology, cartography, astronomy, and spectroscopy—and a few others.

Peirce had a violent temper and a willful nature; he only followed his own ideas and he ignored social conventions. In 1862 he graduated from Harvard with a Master of Arts and looked forward to an academic career that matched his formidable talents. This, however, was not to be. Because of his willful and difficult nature he instead ended up working for some 30 years for a federal organization that had a scientific part, the U.S. Coastal Survey. He also held an untenured position at Johns Hopkins University for a few years, but that was as far as his academic career went.

At the age of 44 Peirce had to leave Johns Hopkins, and seven years later his employment at the Survey was terminated as well. The reason was that Peirce, because of his affairs with women and his general failure to behave like the average academic, had come to be seen as a deeply immoral person.

After his dismissal from the Survey, Peirce led an extremely difficult life. Sometimes he starved and was undernourished. His only income during the next 10 years or so came from gifts and the writing of an occasional article or book review. In 1907 his friends put together a fund that provided him with a very modest income. Peirce died at the age of 74 as a social outcast. His books and manuscripts were donated to Harvard University, where they still can be consulted.

Outside of circles of specialists in logic, Peirce is today mainly known as one of the founders of pragmatism and as the creator of semiotics. His collected works were first published by Harvard in the 1930s (1931–1935, 1958; 8 vols.). A new and more complete edition has been undertaken by Indiana University Press (1981–; a handful of volumes have appeared so far). All in all, Peirce produced one book (in science) and something like 75 papers and 150 book reviews. He also left behind about 80,000 pages of handwritten and unpublished material. The secondary literature on his work is enormous.

## PEIRCE AS A SOCIOLOGIST?

Peirce, as we know, wanted his system of philosophy to be so comprehensive that it could also house "sociology." But what did he mean by sociology? Peirce was mainly active during the late 1800s, and during this time sociology was more or less identical to the works of Auguste Comte and Herbert Spencer, both of whom viewed sociology as a kind of evolutionary doctrine of society, with strong philosophical and/or religious overtones.

We know that Peirce had read Comte and Spencer, but also that he did not care much for their works (e.g., Peirce 1867–1868, 1931:242ff., 2000). He had further studied John Stuart Mill's *System of Logic*, which contains a sociology among other things. And in his activity as a contributor to *The Nation*, Peirce at one point critically reviewed Franklin Giddings's book *Inductive Sociology* (Peirce 1979).

The closest that Peirce ever came to outline what he himself meant by "sociology" is, to my knowledge, to be found in his unfinished manuscript for a book on philosophy called *A Guess at the Riddle* (1887–1888). Following chapters on reasoning, metaphysics, psychology, physiology, and biology, there was to be a chapter on sociology that is described as follows:

> Chapter 8. The triad in sociology or shall I say pneumatology. That the consciousness is a sort of public spirit among the nerve-cells. Man as a community of cells; compound animals and composite plants; society; nature. Feeling implied in firstness. (Peirce 1991:187–188)

Nothing more than these few lines are known about the projected chapter on sociology.

Given Peirce's cryptic view of sociology, can his ideas be of any interest to modern sociologists? According to the small number of sociologists who have studied his work, the answer is yes—but they all point to other parts of Peirce's work than his project of sociology as a pneumatology. C. Wright Mills, for example, has drawn attention to Peirce's pragmatism (Mills 1964; cf. Lewis and Smith 1980).

Norbert Wiley has argued that Peirce's theory of sign is similar to the anthropological notion of culture and that he created the so-called dialogical self (Wiley 1994, 2009). Margareta Bertilsson has shown that some of Peirce's ideas can add to the sociology of science (Bertilsson 2009).

My own sense is that given the fertility of Peirce's thought, one may well want to explore a bit further his enigmatic statements about sociology as a kind of "pneumatology" (approximately, the study of spiritual beings or phenomena). This article, however, is not the place to do this; and here I will instead suggest that Peirce can be of help in developing the sociological analysis of thinking. The reason for choosing just the topic of thinking is that during the last few decades thinking is an area where cognitive psychology has made huge advances—but where sociologists have been slow to move in.

That the sociological approach can be an effective tool in analyzing certain aspects of thinking should not be a proposition that is very surprising since sociology has a long tradition of contributing to social psychology. (For a general introduction to the topic of the sociology of thinking, see Swedberg, forthcoming.)

Since Peirce's work is broad and sprawling as well as enormously difficult to interpret, I will only deal with his earliest writings in this article.[1] I have chosen to draw on his two famous articles on pragmatism, "The Fixation of Belief" (1877) and "How to Make Our Ideas Clear" (1878) (in Peirce 1955). Neither of these two articles explicitly refers to semiotics, and I will therefore also draw on some other early writings by Peirce (1991). I will begin by outlining the relevant parts of Peirce's early writings, and I will then show how these can contribute to a sociological analysis of thinking.

## THE PRAGMATIC THEORY OF THINKING

"The Fixation of Belief" contains, among other things, a theory of what makes thinking emerge as well as die away. Thinking starts with doubt, according to Peirce, or more precisely it starts with the irritation that doubt causes and which results in a struggle in the mind. Once we think, we also start to look for what we view as the truth or what Peirce calls belief. And once we have reached a belief, we stop thinking. We now enter "a calm and satisfactory state" (Peirce 1955:10). Belief, Peirce says, can also be understood as a habit.[2]

Our beliefs are linked to our desires, and we engage in actions that aim at satisfying our desires. The full chain of thinking starts with doubt, but it has to be "a real and living doubt" (Peirce 1955:11). This is then followed by a process that ends in a belief, which sets off actions that aim at satisfying the desires.

"How to Make Our Ideas Clear," published one year after the essay on belief, begins with a handsome argument directed at Descartes's confusion of what is clear with what is distinct. What is clear has to do with the overall identity of an idea and how it can help to produce new knowledge, Peirce claimed. What is distinct, in contrast, relates exclusively to the definition of something and can never lead to new knowledge. These two terms must be kept separate, according to Peirce.

As part of exploring what he means by the clarity of an idea, Peirce connects what he says to his earlier argument about doubt and belief as the two poles of thinking. What he now adds is, for one thing, an emphasis on belief being the same as a rule of action. What this means—and this constitutes a second addition—is that thinking is part of a circular and never-ending process. Doubt leads to thinking, which leads to belief or a rule of action; this, in its turn, leads to action, which always entails doubt and therefore new thinking.

Thought and action are, in brief, closely related, and Peirce suggests that what is at the heart of an idea is the action it produces. Thought always leads to action of some kind. "To develop its meaning, we have, therefore, simply to determine what habits it produces, for what a thing means is simply what habits it involves" (Peirce 1955:30).

"How to Make Our Ideas Clear" also contains the following famous definition of pragmatism:

> Consider what effects, that might conceivably have practical bearings, we conceive the object of our conception to have. Then, our conception of these effects is the whole of our conception of the object. (Peirce 1955:31)[3]

While this definition contains no reference to Peirce's doctrine of signs, it does point to an interesting quality of pragmatism that is often overlooked: its simultaneous emphasis on the individual and the community. By this I mean that the actor both creates something new with his idea and is influenced in doing so by what Peirce calls the community.

To see that this is the case, we need to take a closer look at Peirce's definition of pragmatism and try to unpack it. There are, on the one hand, the practical effects of some actor's ideas or thinking. Let us call these A. But there is also the actor's own conception of the effects of ideas, which we may call B. If the Actor is X, we realize that X is situated at exactly the point where A and B meet. The individual, in other words, is influenced by the practical effect of some earlier ideas (from the community), and he or she also encounters and understands existing ideas through their practical effects.

To this should be added that Peirce sees thinking as always producing something that is novel, and the model of pragmatism that has been presented so far does not show how this is possible. Peirce's solution is only hinted at in "How to Make Our Ideas Clear" and was not worked out in full detail until later. The individual, he suggests, creates something new by coming up with, and trying out, different hypotheses or guesses. This occurs in a process that Peirce has famously termed abduction. The success of these hypotheses depends on whether their results are accepted or rejected by the community.

Another element that is also missing from Peirce's early theory of thinking, as developed in his two famous articles from the 1870s on pragmatism, is his doctrine of semiotics (e.g., Peirce 1991:23–33, 54–84, 141–143). According to Peirce, the role of concepts is to reduce sensory impressions to unity. They accomplish this by becoming part of the sensory impressions, say the way that the sensory impressions of patches of red and green become "a rose" through the concept of rose.

A sign, according to Peirce, has three parts. There is the sign itself; what it relates to; and the effect that it produces in someone. "*A sign is an object which stands for another to some mind*," to cite an early and precise formulation (Peirce 1991:141, emphasis added). Signs are of different types, and from early on Peirce distinguished between three types of signs that he later would call icon, index, and symbol (Peirce 1867–1868, 1991). An icon shares some quality with its object; an index corresponds to its object in fact; and a symbol is by habit understood to represent it.

If we now return to the model of the individual standing where X and Y meet, we can now add that his or her relation to X and Y are always mediated through signs. One remarkable quality about signs is that they point in two opposite directions at the same time and, in doing so, to some extent span the subject-object split. A sign is always pointing to something, and its effects are felt by someone.

## TURNING THE PRAGMATIC THEORY OF THINKING INTO A SOCIOLOGY OF THINKING

How does one make sociology out of Peirce and why just a sociology of thinking? Many of Peirce's central terms are social in nature—such as habit, belief, and community—and this of course facilitates the process of turning his ideas into sociology. In many cases, such as with his semiotics, it is also easy to introduce his theories into a larger and overall sociological argument.

It is natural to look at Peirce's contribution to the sociological analysis of thinking since an important part of his work deals with this topic. Peirce, to recall, argues that thinking is set off by doubt, and then it proceeds until it ends in a belief. This belief, in its turn, results in action; and whenever there is action, there is doubt—and new thinking.

How, then, is thinking empirically related to doubt? In which cases does doubt quickly and directly result in thinking? And in which cases is there doubt and irritation, and perhaps also belief, but very little thinking? These kinds of questions can easily be translated into sociological hypotheses by relating them directly to, say, different kinds of work, organizational structures, and educational institutions. Besides contributing to the sociology of thinking, these questions could also help to create a sociology of doubt—which would seem useful in modern society.

All the other links in the chain of doubt-thinking-belief-action-new doubt can also be studied sociologically, and so can the whole chain itself (cf. Foucault 2001:74, with its discussion of what differentiates the history of ideas from the history of thought). Note also that thought and action are usually not seen as being organically linked; hence the Marxist project of "realizing philosophy" and the desire of social scientists to translate their ideas into social policy. Again, in other words, it would seem that social forces may reinforce Peirce's links—but also break them off.

I earlier argued that Peirce's famous definition of pragmatism invites a more complex model of analysis than simply that thought and action go together. Peirce views the individual not only as thinking forward, so to speak, but also as being linked backwards, to the past. To use a metaphor, we all have our back in the past while we face the future.

Being linked to the past also means being linked to society. To illustrate with an example of how Peirce includes the social dimension into his theory of thinking, take the following statement about doubt:

> We cannot begin with complete doubt [as Descartes]. We must begin with all the prejudices which we actually have when we enter upon the study of philosophy. These prejudices are not to be dispelled by a maxim, for they are things which it does not occur to us can be questioned. (Peirce 1955:228)

To include the social dimension into thinking represents, to my mind, the second most important contribution to the analysis of the human mind since Kant. Translated into modern terms, Kant discovered that the structuring of the human mind is crucial for an understanding of the knowledge that human beings can have. Peirce's Copernican Revolution, I would argue, consists of the argument that thinking is not only structured by the mind but also by society.

What allows Peirce to make the move to a social theory of thinking is his theory of signs. To show the power of his approach on this point, one may compare it to the approaches of middle-range sociology and networks analysis in modern sociology. Both of these are handy and useful approaches that help to conceptualize and explain various types of social structure. But what they lack is a theory of signs; and when they refer to the role of language, symbols and the like (which is rare), they do so without much sophistication.

This is where Peirce's ideas, to my mind, can be used by sociology. Peirce has a very powerful and little explored theory of semiotics, which introduces signs straight into his theory of action and community. Action is tied to doubt, and the community is both a producer of signs and something that can only be approached through signs. Sociologists, in brief, can use Peirce's ideas to address some very difficult types of social behavior in which meaning and action are closely interlinked (say creative and religious behavior that both draw on different types of signs, in different and shifting combinations).

## CONCLUSION

The pragmatists are not known for their contribution to the analysis of thinking, even if this topic stands at the very center of their concerns. Who today reads *How We Think* by John Dewey (1910), which is directly based on Peirce's ideas about doubt and belief? And who remembers that when William James referred to "the stream of consciousness," he did not mean the meanderings of the mind so much as "the stream of thought" (James 1950:239).

Most important of all, however, is the contribution to thinking that can be found in the work of Peirce. It is true that he produced some interesting ideas about the way that doubt and belief are linked to thinking. However, his most spectacular contribution is to be found in his attempt to introduce his ideas about signs into the theory of thinking. This resulted in the second Copernican Revolution, which was to show how thinking is organically linked to society. So far, this part of Peirce's work has not been explored very much. Given the profound nature of his writings, however, one has the right to be optimistic about the kind of insights that can be generated by working on this part of his vast work.

## NOTES

1. For a useful scholarly introduction to the core of Peirce's work, which is his theory of semiotics, see Max Fisch, "Peirce's General Theory of Signs" (Fisch 1986:321–355).

2. Peirce, like later G. H. Mead, Randall Collins, and others, conceptualized thinking as a dialogue of the self with the self—a view that goes back to Socrates (via Plato; see e.g., Fisch 1986:442).

3. The term pragmatism cannot be found in "How to Make Our Ideas Clear." This definition was however also later used by Peirce, word for word, in defining pragmatism (or "pragmaticism," the term that he later came to prefer to pragmatism, since it was ugly and harder to "kidnap"—Peirce 1955:290).

# CHAPTER 32

# Thomas Hobbes: On Generating Social Order

*Mohammed Cherkaoui*

## LIFE AND TIMES

Thomas Hobbes was born in 1588 at Westport near Malmesbury, the year the Invincible Armada was poised to attack England. He lived a long life, reaching the age of 91. Hobbes's father, a pastor in Malmesbury who was barely literate, abandoned his family after a quarrel. At the behest of his uncle, a wealthy merchant without family, Thomas was pushed to study. At the age of 14 he entered Magdalen Hall in Oxford. Five years later, he earned his bachelor's degree. Immediately after his studies, upon a recommendation by the principal of Magdalen Hall, he was hired as a tutor to the son of William Cavendish, Count of Devonshire.

For almost his entire life, he remained attached to the service of the Cavendish family either as a tutor or private secretary to his masters, to whom he was linked by genuine friendship. During trips to the continent when accompanying in succession his three pupils—one was the son of Gervase Clinton of Nottinghamshire—he became acquainted with Galileo, and in France with all the erudites and philosophers in the entourage of Father Mersenne, the unquestionable center of the largest European intellectual circles of the seventeenth century.

Amid the political and religious crisis that shook England in the seventeenth century, Hobbes supported royal authority by fighting for it with the quill and attempting to provide a strong foundation to the absolute power of the sovereign. He left England in 1640 at the outset of the Civil War when the conflict between Charles the First and the parliamentarians started to become disquieting. He set himself up in France for 11 years, where his principal frequentations were the Mersenne circle and the community of English immigrants revolving around the Prince of Wales who, after the execution of his father in 1649, was the pretendant to the English throne.

The spreading rumors about his lack of piety played a role in his decision to leave France. Did he not develop arguments in the *Leviathan* recently published in 1651 that smacked of heresy? Did he not support the principle according to which moral behavior must be founded on reason, thereby excluding any reference to God as the foundation of moral order? Besides, by attacking the Roman Catholic Church, his situation in Paris became untenable. In the winter of 1651 and 1652 he returned to England, where in conformity with his doctrine he accepted subjection to the new regime. However, his submission to Cromwell was no indecent adhesion.

Upon the Restoration in 1660 he was not hassled, and Charles II dealt with him sympathetically. In spite of his criticisms and the disquiet he may have entertained due to the religious doctrines as well as ethical and political thought, Hobbes was not a man on the run. His old age was peaceful and honored by certain masters of the day, in particular Charles II, who provided him with a pension, Louis XIV, and the grand duke of Tuscany, who admired him tremendously. He died in 1679 in the home of his employers at Hardwick Hall castle in Derbyshire.

It is highly significant that his first intellectual endeavor was the translation of *The Peloponnesian War* by Thucydides, from whom he gleaned at least two essential ideas. According to the first idea, of methodological order, any argumentation must be in connection with empirical proof and not remain at the level of pure thought and sterile dialectical approach used and abused by education in Oxford and elsewhere. As for Bacon, with whom he developed a friendship, he shared the taste for history and observation. As a matter of fact, he was his secretary and helped him translate his works in Latin. Actually, apart from the mutual rejection of scholastics, both English philosophers shared no philosophical ideas. The second idea is of political order; Hobbes states in his autobiography that the works of Thucydides are akin to a warning about the dangers of democracy.

## THE DEDUCTIVE-NOMOLOGICAL MODEL AND THE NEW SCIENCE OF SOCIETY

One can wonder where the idea came from about hypothetico-deductive methodology that plays a central role in his style of thought. It appears that it was in *The Elements* of Euclidides, which he discovered very late. He knew nothing of the very existence of such a science because in England mathematics was not yet part of the subjects taught in the curriculum.

Indeed, it was by chance that he stumbled onto a copy of *Elements* in a library. The great importance he attached to deductive thought brought him closer to Descartes and the physicians, primarily Galileo, whom he met in Italy and of whom as he says in the autograph of the book *De Corpore*, "he opened the first door to all of physics, in other words the nature of movement." It is reported that Galileo also called his attention to the possibility of ethics deductively, analogue to physics.

The philosophy of Hobbes matured for a long while in his mind and in the confidential exchange of ideas in the circle of thinkers that Father Mersenne led in Paris, of which Hobbes was also a member. "As soon as, says Hobbes in his autobiography, I made known to Mersenne my ideas that he also made known among the others, I in turn was among the philosophers. His circle was worth more than any school." It was also Mersenne who later sent to various thinkers, including Gassendi and Hobbes, the *Metaphysical Meditations* of Descartes and also sparked the most remarkable philosophical discussions of the seventeenth century. This was the origin of the dispute between Descartes and Hobbes.

If one treats separately the *Short Tract on First Principles*, so named by Ferdinand Tönnies, who discovered this as-yet-unpublished manuscript entitled *Elements of Law, Natural and Politic* published in 1650 but written in 1640 and early 1641, that constitutes the first major treatise where Hobbes broadly spells out the fundamental issue of an anthropology to which he was to devote his entire work. It was to be in part reexamined and deepened in *de Cive* (1642), and above all in the *Leviathan*, published in London in 1651, of which we present herein the axioms and the principal propositions of political theory.

These three works unquestionably constitute the major treatises of the founding father of modern political thought. Apart from *De Corpore, On the Body* (1655), and *De Homine, On Man* (1657) that are lesser known than the previous books, the other publications of Hobbes are philosophical, historical, scientific, or autobiographical contributions, as well as translations.

Upon the publication of *Elements of Law* (a title probably chosen in honor of Euclidides), Hobbes definitively adopted the deductive method. It was certainly no accident that the introduction to the *Leviathan* commences with the famous statement: "Let us make man." Hobbes, like a true demiurge, wants to produce man and society from a combination of a limited number of elements. He functions like Plato in *Timeus*, according to the methodology of what today we call "generating mechanisms."

He puts forward hypotheses in connection first with the biological and mechanical character of the body, then with the passions and interests to produce the individual. Actually, Hobbes says explicitly that this operation is artificial, in other words, in the meaning *stricto sensu* the result of an art, a new science of man and society of which he thought he was setting the foundations. Is it that what we now understand as simulation upon model?

The principles, the approach, and the spirit of such a science for him are unprecedented, as are those of the science model of his times founded by Galileo. Let us recall that it was during his encounters with the scientists belonging to Father Mersenne's circle and especially his long conversation in Florence with Galileo that he had to develop the premises of his future theory that he continuously proceeded to explain and develop his whole life. Therefore, it is not surprising that Hobbes took inspiration from mechanics—paradigmatic science for all others at that point in time—to construct his models of man and society from which he deduced, like the geometer, the most complex propositions from the simplest and most evident ones.

To be convinced thereof, all that is necessary is to read the introduction to the *Leviathan*, where Hobbes gives a foretaste of his method, and follow step by step the principles of the hypothetical deductive construction highlighting the originality this work represents from all standpoints. One will say that other theories or other philosophical works such as *Ethics* by Spinoza are held to be *more geometrico* developed. The links between their propositions to me actually appear to be merely rhetorical rather than deductive, as opposed to the *Leviathan*.

## ON THE ARTIFICIAL GENERATION OF MAN AND SOCIETY: SIMULATING COMPLEX PHENOMENA

God created nature according to the laws of physics. Hobbes feels he can generate the individual, the institutions, and the society in accordance with the same methodology. No philosopher, even Leibniz and his *mathesis universalis*, and no social scientist would ever have had the Hobbesian audacity to claim the ability to generate everything based on simple hypotheses on the individual, on laws, on mechanisms, or algorithms. It was not until the advent of contemporary specialists on complex systems, artificial societies, and simulation techniques that it was possible to direct social science research toward this objective.

In this respect, I would like to recall that certain founding fathers of sociology, for example Durkheim, explicitly rejected this method and thought that only observation and analysis of empirical data via suitable techniques would be able to enlighten us on individual and social behavior. While making use of the Durkheimian approach and codifying it by means of the multivariate analysis, Lazarsfeld and the Columbia school were only following along the lines of the author of *Suicide*.

Social scientists were unanimous on the advantages offered by this approach. Today, without denying the need for conventional statistical analysis, social science research is increasingly geared toward the experimental study of the behavior of individuals and societies thanks to simulation techniques, which *a posteriori* gives reason to Hobbes.

Hobbes would not have rejected this approach insofar as it admirably responds to the principles he put forth and those he barely dared to dream of: starting from the social atom that the individual is, designing hypotheses on the individual's genetic nature and his human nature essentially defined by rationality but also passions and interest, and deducing from the interaction of individuals several propositions on social behavior, thereby generating macro-phenomena such as norms and institutions. He deemed that only fiction, in other words what today we refer to as modeling, was in a position to help us understand the complexity of social phenomena.

One of the most eloquent examples that we will see further on is the state of nature that in fact is a modelization of the English society in the throes of civil war. Hobbes knew that this society was too complex to allow him to propose an explanation of the changes it was undergoing. However, it is thanks to artifice, in other words an abstract and simplified construction of a complex reality, that he was able to conduct thought experiments ("*Gedankenexperimente*").

Man is firstly a mechanism consisting of sensorial organs, muscles, nerves, imagination, memory, and reason, the movements of which constitute the effects of external stimuli. Like the principle of inertia developed independently of each other by Galileo and Descartes, Hobbes contends that humans have an impulse to keep on moving and in particular to shun death.

These efforts to continue "being" are either appetites or aversions. The most complex actions are explainable by this mechanical system as reflexes and also as voluntary actions resulting from a calculation relative to a person's desires and aversions. This constitutes the content of the first six chapters of the *Leviathan*. Chapters VII to XI deal with demonstrating how humans behave with respect to one another.

## THE RATIONAL FOUNDATIONS OF SOCIAL ORDER

There are three axioms in Hobbes's theory: interest, rationality, and equality, with the contract and transfer of powers being deduced. Furthermore, the following two elementary and obvious propositions constitute the basis of his system. According to the first one, the human being is influenced by his/her desires and aversions, which can differ from one person to another, partly in accordance with his/her biological heritage and partly according to culture. It follows that the desires of different people will be satisfied by different degrees of power, wealth, honors, and so forth.

The second fundamental proposition has to do with power, which is referred to as being all the resources the individual currently possesses in order to procure future benefits. Actually, the remainder of the definition of power leaves no doubt about the relational character, which therefore excludes any essentialist vision. Unlike those who see power as an individual's intrinsic feature, ready to use any time he/she deems it relevant, Hobbes states that power is a feature of the relations among the individuals.

Hobbes distinguishes natural power, which is the *preeminence* of the faculties of the body and mind, from the instrumental power expressing itself by economic power, prestige, or what we understand today as the social capital. Instrumental power is acquired thanks to the first element and is measured by the number of individuals whose power can be limited or that which one can command. Social relationships are all subject to the rule of the infinitude of the desire to accumulate power, resulting in a struggle by each against all.

The infinitude of desire is explainable by the fact that each individual must make sure that what he/she has acquired cannot occur without a continuous power increase. This characteristic, which recalls Durkheim's anomie, is the essence of each society characterized by the absence of law. Bentham also considered the infinitude of desire as the principle of his theory unlinked to capitalism, as some Marxist interpretations would have it.

Based on these basic assumptions about human nature, Hobbes deduces the need for sovereign power by using four abstract concepts consisting of the state of nature, the right of nature, the law of nature, and the social contract. In chapter XIII of the *Leviathan*, he introduces the hypothesis of the state of nature characterized by the absence of sovereign power capable of limiting the power of each individual. In this fictive society, no one is in a position to ensure his/her acquired property or even his/her own existence, and in which no industry or culture could eventually see the light of day.

Hobbes introduces the concepts of natural rights and laws by distinguishing between them. The first one is a right, in other words the liberty of each individual to use his/her power and all the means necessary to preserve his/her life. Because in such a state war by all against all others is the rule, each individual has the right, if possible, to do what he/she wants with the property and even the person of others. As for the right of nature, which is a series of rights discovered by reason alone, it is a duty according to which the reasonable person refrains from any action likely to destroy his/her life. The individual must of course seek to use peaceful means to live, but the possibility of war is always an open issue if he/she deems it necessary.

Within the state of nature—an artificial society not far removed from the English society in the civil war that is the subject of meditation by Hobbes—this endless war never keeps safe the benefits whatever the degree of power reached in this type of society, where law does not yet exist and where humans are rational and equal, each always in a position to destroy others either alone or in coalition with others. The sole means of ensuring the death and loss of property is the mutual transfer of a share of their power, in other words that of protecting one's self. Coercive laws not only ensure the security of life and property, but also define the contracts and make sure they are respected.

Of course, rational individuals are aware of the advantages they procure from this contract. If they remain faithful to the rules of contractual society and always comply therewith, they have no need for sovereign power to settle the inter relationships (Chapter XVII). However, an individual is never sure that he/she and others would not be tempted by short-term advantages, implying that a violation of the said rules would from time to time bring the emergence of free riding. He even realizes by experience that the rules are sometimes infringed upon. Only a common sovereign power established above the relevant parties, with a right and force large enough to impose the execution thereof, is capable of ensuring respect of the rules. In that way, no one could constantly suspect the probability that other individuals would violate the rights and act in unpredictable manners.

The transfer of certain individual powers to the sovereign, either a person or assembly of people, occurs according to the following principle: "I authorize and give up my right of governing my self, to this man, or to this assembly of men, on this condition, that thou give up thy right to him, and authorize all his actions in like manner" (Chapter XVII). Some thinkers deem that the said abandonment of rights is the first expression of the notion of alienation that Rousseau was to take up himself in the *Social Contract*. Other contemporary theorists likes Coleman (1990) consider this as the rational solution of the category of phenomenon such as panic, mob behavior, and the emergence of leadership.

The contract and transfer of powers are deduced concepts. Hobbes's model of the contract makes it possible to generate a supra-individual reality undisputed among each of the contracting parties (Chaper XVII). For Hobbes, the legitimacy of domination no longer resides in transcendental principles. It is founded on individual interest and rationality (Chapter XLVI). It is suitable to distinguish the contract as a transfer of control and the "trust" that is specific to the political theory of Locke.

We know that in the *Second treatise of government* Locke will substitute this notion for that of the contract to define the relationships between the governed and the governors, which for him are not contractual. Trust is a mission given by the people to the government to follow certain collective ends. It founds neither society nor the state and imposes obligations only on the government, with the people at all moments being able to get rid of the government or even overthrow a king.

This perspective is incompatible with what Hobbes thinks can be deduced from the legitimacy of the sovereign power. For him, this power is not only absolute and perennial but also likely to be inherited, which his followers and critics were subsequently to contest. If political bodies exist, it is essentially in the form of advisors to the sovereign who do not limit the latter's sphere of power.

The administration to which the sovereign delegates authority has the sole function of executing the tasks and achieving respect of the laws proclaimed by the sovereign to which he is not subject (Chapter XXVI). Then there is the Kingdom of God, which does not belong to this world, whose function of ecclesiastic power is solely limited to teaching human beings about the means necessary to reach it and not to settle their relationships on earth (Chapter XLII).

There is no shadow of doubt that Hobbes has strongly influenced all Western thought and theories on the foundations of social order. The issues he invoked, the solution he proposed, and the methodology he created turned him into a contemporary of ours; his writings remain an unlimited source of meditation.

# CHAPTER 33

# Jean Piaget: Sociology Beyond Holism and Individualism

*Omar Lizardo*

## INTRODUCTION

In an article that appeared in *The British Journal of Sociology* in 1991, Richard Kitchener (1991) proposed and convincingly defended the thesis that Jean Piaget is quite possibly the most important sociologist that no (Anglophone) sociologist has ever read seriously (or has ever seen characterized as a sociologist). Kitchener diagnosis remains as true today as when his article was published almost two decades ago.

Jean Piaget currently does not belong in (nor any attempts have been made to induct him into) the established (post-war) "canon" of traditional ("classical") figures of sociological theory or a presence in "contemporary" social thought. His work is not usually discussed as having any sociological implications, nor is he thought to have made any substantive contributions to social theory or the methodology of the social sciences more broadly conceived.

This absence is puzzling for the simple reason that Piaget's early reputation outside of Europe was developed as a sociologist (Hsueh 2004), and "sociological" issues were a constant theme in his thinking throughout his career. For example, it is not a secret (Piaget 1977:132) that Piaget taught sociology (however briefly) at the University of Geneva.

In addition, a collection of essays of his sociological writings—originally published in French in 1965 and reprinted in 1977—has already been translated into English (Piaget 1995). As Kitchener (1991:422) puts it, "[t]hese works . . . form the basis of his complete sociological theory, a rich and complex theory having fundamental similarities to exchange theory, to symbolic interactionism, to functionalism, to Habermas's theory of communicative competence, and to certain versions of structuralism."

Given this context, my job in this chapter is both easier and a bit harder than that of most of the other contributors to this volume. My job is easier because I do not have to engage in any sort of rhetorical acrobatics to establish the point that Piaget is a central figure in sociological thought. Both institutionally and intellectually Piaget was a sociologist (among other things).

In what follows I could have easily concentrated on the relevance of Piaget's thesis that knowledge is an active *construction* on the part of the child for studies of socialization and work at the intersection of the sociology of culture and cognition (Bourdieu 1990; Lizardo 2004; Toren 1999) or on Piaget's influential development of a brand of "generative structuralism" (Piaget 1970) in which the classical concept of social structure is recast in a dynamic, historical way so as to liberate it from its connotations with static analysis.

Instead, I will concentrate on Piaget's *meta-theoretical* writings, especially as they pertain to broad issues on the philosophy of social science. The reason is twofold. First, these are still the least well-known of Piaget's contributions to sociology. Second, they reach at the core of fundamental issues in social ontology and epistemology—relevant to the conduct of social science at least since Durkheim's programmatic formulations in *The Rules*—for example, structural explanation and the coherence of the notion of "social causes" as well as the relationship between the styles of explanation used in sociology and those prevalent in other cognate disciplines—issues that have yet to receive a thoroughly satisfactory treatment in the philosophy of social science (Turner 2007).

We will see that Piaget's treatment of these issues was not only capable of sidestepping some of the basic conceptual dilemmas that beset the thought of the classical theorists, but that his solutions converge with some of the most "cutting edge" work in contemporary theory.

## SOCIOLOGICAL EXPLANATION

Is there such a thing as a specifically "sociological" mode of explanation? According to Durkheim, sociologists should rely on a mode of explanation that is no different from that of other sciences (establishing patterns of "concomitant variation" across two or more properly characterized phenomena). Sorokin (1937) and more recently, Archer (1996) have argued that depending on the subject matter, explanation can take radically divergent forms, as follows:

1. Establishing covariation or "functional" relations of dependence between postulated causes and their corresponding effects (the Durkheimian view).

2. Establishing "logical" or "meaningful" linkages between cultural (or institutional) items. This "dualist" argument is required if sociologists are to make sense of such things as "culture," "knowledge," or "ideas."

Piaget appreciated the strength of the Durkheimian argument, but in many ways he sided with the dualist point of view. He saw this dualism between two forms of explanation (cause-effect versus logical or implicational linkages) as a key point of epistemological convergence between sociological and psychological explanation, since in both disciplines analysts resort to these two analytic frameworks in order to account for the coherence or patterning of phenomena.

On the one hand, there are analysts who resort primarily to the postulation of *causal* relations (or "functional" relations, in Sorokin's terms) between distinct aspects of overall phenomena (as this is understood in traditional Aristotelian philosophy). On the other hand, there are those analysts who dispense with a purely causal explanation and resort instead to the postulation of relations of logical (or socio-logical) implications, or "axiomatized analyses" in which different aspects of sociological phenomena are connected to one another by systems of relations that are less constraining than the asymmetric, non-reflexive strictures characteristic of the causal relation (see, for instance, Sorokin [1937] for an example of "implicational" analysis that dispenses with "causal" forms of analysis).

According to Piaget, relations of implication are in fact unique to those macro-level forms of cultural order that Durkheim referred to by the term "collective representation." Cultural explanations based on the causes of cultural forms (which may include the postulation of material or interactional causes) are thus analytically distinct from those based the autonomous implicational patterns exhibited by the elements of a given cultural Gestalt.

In both the sociological and psychological domains we can find analysts drawing on both implicational forms of explanation "alongside real or concrete explanations" based on concrete causes. In Piaget's view, this duality of implicational and causal analysis cannot be easily transcended by appealing to either one-dimensional causal or implicational explanatory schemes (as has currently been proposed by Alexander [2003] in the case of the latter).

Nevertheless, the "duality of implication inherent in collective representations and of causality raises a fundamental problem of explanation" in the social sciences. This problem has been a key axis of contention in classical social theory, especially in the work of Marx and Pareto. In classical Marxist theory, the duality of implication and causation took the form of the traditional problem of "infrastructure" and "superstructure."

This is a problem that has been addressed in different ways by analysts in the Marxian tradition, and which received a classical treatment (in the form of his theory of "residues") at the hands of Pareto. Piaget proposes that the seeds of explanatory progress—and transcendence of the base/superstructure problematic—are already implicit in the classical tradition. In order to solve this dilemma, sociologists must make the same theoretical turn that led to progress in psychological explanation: the enactive or *action-focused* turn (e.g., Varela et al. 1991).

It was precisely after psychological theorists realized that "the contents of consciousness alone explain nothing causally and that the only possible causal explanation must move back from consciousness to behavior" (Piaget 1995:35) that they were able to make progress on this front. It was only after psychologists turned from a preoccupation with the contents of consciousness and toward a systematic concern with *action patterns* that progress was made in psychological explanation.

Piaget recommends the same remedy to sociologists. These last, if they wish to propose causal forms of explanation, must reject explanations "based on ideology, in favor of explanations through action." In particular, actions related to what Marx called *praxis* (e.g., collective action "... carried out in common to preserve the life of the social group in a material environment") and what Mauss referred to as *bodily techniques* (e.g., "... concrete and technical actions that become perpetuated in collective representations"). Thus for Piaget, after we take an enactive perspective, it is easy to see that "[t]he problem of relations between infrastructure and superstructure is, therefore, closely linked to that of relations between the casuality of behavior patterns and the implications within representation" (Piaget 1995:35).

## THE LOCATION OF THE SOCIAL AND THE ISSUES OF "LEVELS"

Piaget's basic strategy, as can already be noted, is to draw abstract commonalities between the explanatory projects of sociology and psychology (and biology) with an eye toward establishing the ultimate "location" of specifically "sociological" processes and mechanisms in relation to those studied in the other two disciplines.

This issue is a contentious one since it gets at the core of the struggle to "differentiate" sociology from other disciplines and deals with the issue of whether there exists phenomena that are "purely" sociological (Durkheim 1982; Parsons 1937). Piaget takes a conciliatory stance in this debate, denying that there exist "sociological" phenomena *sui generis* while at the same time attempting to carve out a division of labor between the three disciplines, especially as it pertains to key distinctions in the *styles* of explanation that are routinely deployed in each field.

His main conclusion in this regard is that "[t]he mental . . . exists *between* the biological and the social" (Piaget 1995:33, italics added). This way of formulating the issue provides us with an opportunity to establish a preliminary distinction between psychological and sociological explanation. First, however, it is important to realize that the relationship between sociology, psychology, and biology cannot be readily conceived as comprising a series of hierarchical "levels" of inclusion (see Wiley [1986] for an example of this way of thinking about the issue), such that the biological is included in the psychological and this latter in the sociological (as suggested by the initial statement that the psychological lies between the sociological and biological). Instead, it is best to conceive of it as comprising " . . . a simultaneous link from biology to psychology and sociology together, these [last] two disciplines *having the same object*" (Piaget 1995:33, italics added).

In a surprising passage, especially for those who see Piaget primarily as a psychologist, Piaget notes that "human knowledge is *essentially collective, and social life constitutes an essential factor in the creation and growth of knowledge*" (Piaget 1995:30, italics added). This assertion stands in sharp contrast to the usual pictures of Piaget's conception of the knowing subject as an isolated individual interacting with a material world of objects in isolation from any form of collective or social influence (as in the naive textbook line of critique that invidiously contrasts Vygotsky's "sociological" approach to Piaget's "individualistic" approach to cognitive development). Instead, for Piaget all forms of knowledge, in particular the most scientifically rigorous and logical forms are—following Durkheim (1995)—collective products through and through. It is clear that if Piaget belongs in any recognizable tradition of social theory (Levine 1995), he is part of the French tradition of "collective epistemology" that begins with Comte and Saint Simon and continues with Durkheim, Lucien Levy-Bruhl (a thinker that Piaget insists has been widely misunderstood and unfairly dismissed), and Marcel Mauss.

Piaget's notion that psychology and sociology study the same set of phenomena but from alternative perspectives (mainly by giving different processes and mechanisms different *explanatory weights*) might sound controversial to some who prefer to draw a sharp boundary between the various disciplines, or those who think of sociology as an interpretative discipline and not a natural science. But this way of conceptualizing the issue is distinctive of the "French" tradition that Piaget belongs to, going at least all the way back to Durkheim (Schmaus 2004).

Thus, Piaget rejects as counterproductive the standard picture hat suggests that there are three aspects of the individual: the biological, the psychological, and the sociological. Instead, for Piaget "there is on the one hand the organism, determined by hereditary characteristics as well as by ontogenetic mechanisms" and on other hand there is human behavior and activity, which has both mental and social aspects. In this respect "[p]sychology and sociology are comparable, in their interdependence to two closely related biological sciences" (Piaget 1995:33).

In this respect, psychological and sociological explanation cannot be easily separated, and it has been the failure of most psychological and sociological theorists (including Durkheim) to have proposed shaky criteria with which to justify a hasty division between these two alternative forms of understanding and accounting for human activity. According to Piaget, all of the problems of psychological explanation "are therefore also found in sociological explanation, with virtually the sole difference that the 'I' is replaced by the 'we', and that actions and [cognitive] 'operations' become, when a collective dimension is added, interactions" (Piaget 1995:33). This is a bold thesis and a key to the understanding Piaget's approach to one of the most contentious issues in the history of the social sciences.

As has already be noted, Piaget's primary meta-theoretical move in this respect is to establish correspondences between the fundamental entities and activities (Machamer et al. 2000) that constitute the phenomena that psychology and sociology aim to explain. Thus, he draws a one-to-one correspondence between the primary activity that is postulated in psychological explanation—the notion of (mental) *operation*—with the primary activity that is postulated in sociological explanation: the notion of *interaction*.

Piaget defines interaction in a very particular manner as consisting of "behaviour patterns which are capable of *reciprocal* modification." This formulation—emphasizing the notion of reciprocal modification of activity on the part of two organisms—is reminiscent of that proposed by George Herber Mead (1913). The key point to keep in mind is that beyond these formal commonalities, all of the types of questions that figure prominently in sociological explanation have an "analogue" in psychology: " . . . [t]his is particularly true of the central notion by means of which Durkheimian sociologists have wished to sever all relations between sociology and psychology, and this is the notion of totality" (Piaget 1995:34).

## BEYOND HOLISM AND INDIVIDUALISM

To tackle the perennial issue of whether the individual should form part of sociological explanation (or whether the individual should be subsumed under some overarching construct), Piaget revisits Durkheim's seminal argument, most clearly laid out in the essay "Individual and Collective Representations" (Durkheim 1953), that the *sui generis* status of society has to be conceded if *sui generis* emergence is granted in other domains of inquiry (the biological, chemical, and mental).

Piaget notes that "[t]here is a very curious passage . . . in which Durkheim compares, by a sort of analogical proportion, the collective consciousness in relation to its individual elements with an individual state of consciousness . . . in relation to the organic elements in which it depends."

Piaget goes on to repeat Durkheim's conclusion that just as any individual mental representation, whether cognitive or perceptual, is not the result of a simple combination between its organic elements each considered in isolation—e.g. individual neuronal synapses—but is "rather an unity from the outset" (its identity lies in the pattern of neural firing and interconnectivity across regions of the brain), " . . . so collective representations are not reducible to the individual representations whose synthesis they constitute." Piaget notes that "[t]his comparison of Durkheim's is more far-reaching than he could have imagined in 1898" (Piaget 1995:34).

What are the (far-reaching) implications of Durkheim's "emergence" argument (Sawyer 2001) that Durkheim himself did not envision? According to Piaget, the notion of emergent totality constitutes in fact one of the primary linkages between sociological and psychological explanation because the phenomenon of *sui generis* emergence appears in both psychology and sociology. For Piaget, the prototypical example of emergent totality in psychology "corresponds closely to the notion of total form or 'Gestalt.' " Piaget notes that while the objections that have been leveled at the Durkheimian notion of emergent totality are equally applicable to the notion of Gestalt, "more *relativistic* conceptions of totality can be developed in both domains" (Piaget 1995:34, italics added).

It is precisely one of the goals of Piaget to develop a more "relativistic" notion of sociological totality (as he believed he did in psychology with the notion of "schema") that bypasses the problems that he will outline vis-a-vis Durkheim's notion. Piaget's conception of totality relies on the specification of relational mechanisms that account for emergence, and thus is closer to his own meta-theoretical position of *analytical interactionism.* From this point of view:

> [s]ociety itself . . . is a system of interactions beginning with relations between two individuals, extending to interactions among each of these and the set of others, and extending also to the actions of all previous individuals, i.e., of all interactions in history, upon existing individuals.

## CONCLUSION

As we have seen, Piaget provides a distinct point of view on some of the perennial issues that have bedeviled social theory. From this point of view, sociology is neither the "Queen" of the social sciences (as was dreamed by Comte) nor is it a residual field without a subject matter of its own. Instead, sociology emerges as a field endowed with a (partially) distinct set of empirical phenomena (those related to interaction and the reciprocal modification of individuals) but not endowed with a particularly "unique" mode of explanation. Instead, sociology relies on explanatory strategies that have clear analogues in fields that deal with issues of "structured composition" and "emergence" of levels of higher-order organization from lower-order interactions (such as biology, psychology, and has been discovered today in the field of "network science," even physics).

In the very same way, some of the subject matter that sociologists study end up being the same as those dealt with in other sciences. The only difference is that the sociologist always locates and contextualizes these phenomena (e.g., cognition, emotion, and development) within a larger field of reciprocal interactions (both spatially and chronologically) with a spatial care to *analytically* emphasize these interactional linkages. Piaget thus shows a way of thinking of the sociological enterprise as tightly integrated with the other social, cognitive, and historical sciences, even as he demonstrates that there is indeed a particularly distinctive approach that deserves the name of "sociological."

# Bibliography


Abbott, A. "Of Time and Space: The Contemporary Relevance of the Chicago School." *Social Forces*, Vol. 4 (1997): 1149–1182.

Abbott, A. "Against narrative: A preface to lyrical sociology." *Sociological Theory*, Vol. 25(1) (2007): 67–99.

Achebe, C. *Things Fall Apart*. London: Heinemann, 1958.

Achebe, C. *No Longer at Ease*. London: Heinemann, 1960.

Achebe, C. *Arrow of God*. London: Heinemann, 1966.

Achebe, C. *A Man of the People*. London: Heinemann, 1967.

Achebe, C. *Anthill of the Savannah*. London: Heinemann, 1987.

Achebe, C. *The Education of a British-Protected Child*. New York: Knopf, 2009.

Agamben, G. *Homo Sacer: Sovereign Power and Bare Life*. Stanford: Stanford University Press, 1998.

Alexander, J. C. *The Meanings of Social Life: A Cultural Sociology*. New York: Oxford University Press, 2003.

Alexander, J. C., B. Giesen, R. Munch, and N. Smelser (Eds.) *The Micro-Macro Link*. Berkeley: University of California Press, 1987.

Alexander, J. C., R. Eyerman, B. Giesen, N. J. Smelser, and P. Sztompka. *Cultural Trauma and Collective Identity*. Berkeley: University of California Press, 2004.

Anderson, B. *Imagined Communities: Reflections on the Origin and Spread of Nationalism*. London: Verso, 1983.

Archer, M. S. *Culture and Agency: The Place of Culture in Social Theory*. New York: Cambridge University Press, 1996.

Arendt, H. *The Human Condition*. Chicago: Chicago University Press, 1958.

Arendt, H. *Between Past and Future: Eight Exercises in Political Thought*. New York: Viking Press, 1961.

Aristotle. *The Works of Aristotle*. Two volumes. Translated by W. D. Ross. Chicago: Britannica Press, 1952.

Ascherson, N. "On with the Pooling and Merging. Review of: Tom Nairn, *After Britain: New Labour and the Return of Scotland*." London Review of Books, April 22, 2000, 8–9.

Ash, M. G. *Gestalt Psychology in German Culture, 1890–1967: Holism and the Quest for Objectivity*. Cambridge: Cambridge University Press, 1998.

Asimov, I. "Liar." *Astounding Science Fiction*, May 1941. New York: Street and Smith Publications, Inc., 1941.

Asimov, I. "Runaround." *Astounding Science Fiction*, March 1942. New York: Street and Smith Publications, Inc., 1942.

Asimov, I. *I, Robot: The Evitable Conflict*. New York: Street and Smith Publications, Inc., 1950.

Asimov, I. *Foundation*. New York: Gnome Press, 1951.

Asimov, I. *Foundation and Empire*. New York: Gnome Press, 1952.

Asimov, I. *Second Foundation*. New York: Gnome Press, 1953.

Asimov, I. *Foundation's Edge*. New York: Doubleday, 1982.

Asimov, I. *Foundation and Earth*. New York: Doubleday, 1986.

Asimov, I. *Prelude to Foundation*. New York: Bantham/Doubleday, 1988.

Asimov, I. *Forward the Foundation*. New York: Spectra, 1993.

Asimov, I. *I. Asimov: A Memoir*. New York: Bantam/Doubleday, 1994.

Asplund, J. *Det sociala livets elementära former*. Göteborg: Korpen, 1987.

Auerbach, E. *Dante: Poet of the Secular World*. New York: NYRB Classics, 2007.

Axelrod, R. *The Evolution of Cooperation*. New York: Basic Books, 1984.

Bakhtin, M. *Rabelais and His World*. Bloomington: Indiana University Press, 1965.

Bakhtin, M. *The Dialogic Imagination: Four Essays*. Austin: University of Texas Press, 1981.

Barash, J. A. (Ed.) *The Symbolic Construction of Reality: The Legacy of Ernst Cassirer*. Chicago: University of Chicago Press, 2008.

Barnes, B. *The Elements of Social Theory*. Princeton: Princeton University Press, 1995.

Barnes, B. *Understanding Agency: Social Theory and Responsible Action*. London: Sage Publications, 2000.

Baumann, Z. *Freedom*. Buckingham: Open University Press, 1988.

Bayer, T. I. *Cassirer's Metaphysics of Symbolic Forms: A Philosophical Commentary*. New Haven: Yale University Press, 2001.

Becker, G. S. *A Treatise on the Family*. Cambridge: Harvard University Press, 1991.

Becker, G. S. *Human Capital*. Chicago: University of Chicago Press, 1993.

Becker, H. and H. E. Barnes. *Social Thought From Lore to Science*. Gloucester, MA: Peter Smith, 1978.

Bennett, B. J. 1983. "The Detective Fiction of Poe and Borges." *Comparative Literature*, Vol. 3: 262–275.

Bennett, J. "The Enchanted World of Modernity: Paracelsus, Kant, and Deleuze." *Cultural Values*, Vol. 1(1) (1997): 1–28.

Berger, J., B. P. Cohen, and M. Zelditch, Jr. "Status Characteristics and Expectation States." In *Sociological Theories in Progress*, Vol. 1, edited by J. Berger, M. Zelditch, Jr., and B. Anderson. Boston: Houghton Mifflin, 1966.

Berger, P. L. *Invitation to Sociology; A Humanistic Perspective*. Garden City: Doubleday, 1963.

Berle, A. A. and G. C. Means. *The Modern Corporation and Private Property*. New York: Harcourt, Brace & World, 1968.

Berlin, I. "Two Concepts of Liberty." In *Four Essays on Liberty*. Oxford: Oxford University Press, 1979.

Berman, M. *All That Is Solid Melts Into Air: The Experience of Modernity*. Second Edition. Harmondsworth: Penguin, 1988.

Bernstein, R. "John Dewey." In *The Encyclopedia of Philosophy*, Vol. 1, edited by P. Edwards. New York: Macmillan, 1967, 380–385.

Bertilsson, T. M. *Peirce's Theory of Inquiry and Beyond*. Frankfurt: Peter Lang, 2009.

Binswanger, H. C. *Geld und Magie: Deutung und Kritik der modernen Wirtschaft*. Stuttgart and Wien: Weitbrecht, 1985.

Bloom, Terrie F. "Borrowed Perceptions: Harriot's Maps of the Moon." *Journal for the History of Astronomy*, Vol. IX (1978): 117–122.

Bloor, D. 1997. *Wittgenstein, Rules and Institutions*. London: Routledge.

Blossfeld, H. P., and G. Rohwer, *Techniques of Event History Modelling: New Approaches to Causal Analysis*. Mahwah: Erlbaum, 1995.

Blumer, H. *Symbolic Interactionism: Perspective and Method*. Berkeley: University of California Press, 1969.

Boltanski, L, and E. Chiapello. *Le nouvel esprit du capitalisme*. Paris: Gallimard, 1999.

Booth, Sara Elizabeth, and Albert Van Helden. "The Virgin and the Telescope: The Moons of Cigoli and Galileo." *Science in Context*, Vol. 13, Nos. 3–4 (2000): 463–486.

Borchmeyer, D. *Goethe*. Köln: Dumont, 2005.

Borges, J. L. *Tlön, Uqbar Orbis, Tertius*, in *Ficciones*. New York: Grove Press, 1962.

Borges, J. L. *Ficciones*. New York: Grove Press, 1962.

Borges, J. L. *The House of Asterion*. In *Labyrinths: Selected Stories and Other Writings*, edited by D. A. Yates and J. E. Irby. London: Penguin, 1964.

Borges, J. L. *Other Inquisitions 1937–1952*. Austin: University of Texas Press, 1984.

Borges, J. L. *On Exactitude in Science*. In *Collected Fictions*. New York: Penguin Books, 1998.

Borges, J. L. *The Writing of God*. In *Collected Fictions*. New York: Penguin Books, 1998.

Borges, J. L. His complete works (drawn up by Domenico Porzio, including the introduction Milano, Arnoldo Mondadori (XVIII edition), 2008.

Bourdieu, P. *Outline of a Theory of Practice*. Cambridge: Cambridge University Press, 1977.

Bourdieu, P. *Distinction: A Social Critique of the Judgment of Taste*. London: Routledge, 1984.

Bourdieu, P. "The Forms of Capital." In *Handbook of Theory and Research for the Sociology of Education*, edited by J. G. Richardson. Westport: Greenwood Press, 1986.

Bourdieu, P. *The Logic of Practice*. Cambridge, MA: Polity Press, 1990.

Bourdieu, P. "On Symbolic Power." In *Language and Symbolic Power*. Cambridge, MA: Harvard University Press, 1991.

Bourdieu, P. *Practical Reason: On the Theory of Action*. Stanford: Stanford University Press, 1998.

Bourdieu, Pierre, *Sketch for a Self Analysis*. Chicago: University of Chicago Press, 2007.

Bourdieu, P., and L. Waccquant. *An Invitation to Reflexive Sociology*. Chicago: University of Chicago Press, 1992.

Bowker, G. *Inside George Orwell: A Biography*. New York: Palgrave MacMillan, 2004.

Box, G. E. P., and N. R. Draper. *Empirical Model-Building and Response Surfaces*. New York: Wiley, 1987.

Bramsen, J. "Letter to the Editor." *The Mathematical Sociologist* (newsletter of the Mathematical Sociology Section, American Sociological Association) (1999): 2–4.

Braudel, F. *The Mediterranean and the Mediterranean World in the Age of Philip II*. Vol. 1. Berkeley: University of California Press, 1995.

Breiger, R. L. "Emergent Themes in Social Network Analysis: Results, Challenges, Opportunities." In *Dynamic Social Network Modeling and Analysis: Workshop Summary and Papers*, edited by R. Breiger, K. Carley, and P. Pattison. Washington, DC: National Academies Press, 2003.

Breiger, R. L. "A Tool Kit for Practice Theory." *Poetics*, Vol. 27 (2000): 91–115.

Brent, J. *Charles Sanders Peirce: A Life*. Bloomington, IN: Indiana University Press, 1993.

Brinkmann, S. "Literature as Qualitative Inquiry: The Novelist as Researcher." In *Qualitative Inquiry*, Vol. 15(8): 1376–1394.

Brod, M. "Nachwort zur ersten Ausgabe." In *F. Kafka: Das Schloss*. Frankfurt: Suhrkamp, 2006.

Brown, A. J. "Borges's Scientific Discipline." Hispanic Review, Vol. 4 (2004): 505–522.

Browning, D., and W. T. Myers (Eds.). *Philosophers of Process*. Second Edition. New York: Fordham University Press, 1998.

Buck, P. S. *The Good Earth*. New York: Washington Square Press, 1931.

Buck, P. S. "Easter 1933." *Cosmopolitan*, May 1933, 170.

Buck, P. S. *Dragon Seed*. Wakefield: Moyer Bell, 1941.

Buck, P. S. *My Several Worlds: A Personal Record*. New York: John Day, 1954.

Buck, P. S. *Imperial Woman*. Wakefield: Moyer Bell, 1956.

Buck, P. S. *Pavilion of Women*. Wakefield: Moyer Bell, 1974.

Burgum, E. B. "Freud and Fantasy in Contemporary Fiction." *Science and Society*, Vol. 29/2 (1965): 224–231.

Burke, K. *A Grammar of Motives*. Berkeley: University of California Press, 1945.

Buroker, J. V. *Kant's Critique of Pure Reason: An Introduction*. Cambridge: Cambridge University Press, 2006.

Byrne, D. "Heaven" in *Fear of Music* (album), 1979.

Callaghan, D. (Ed.) *A Feminist Companion to Shakespeare*. Oxford: Blackwell Publishers, 2000.

Callinicos, A. *Social Theory. A Historical Introduction*. Cambridge: Polity Press, 1999.

Capek, K. *R.U.R.* Dover Publications, 1999.

Carley, K. M. "Group Stability: A Socio-Cognitive Approach." In *Advances in Group Processes: Theory & Research*, Vol. VII, edited by E. Lawler, B. Markovsky, C. Ridgeway, and H. Walker. Greenwich, CT: JAI Press, 1990.

Carley, K. M. "A Theory of Group Stability." *American Sociology Review*, Vol. 56(3) (1991): 331–354.

Carley, K. M. "Smart Agents and Organizations of the Future." In *The Handbook of New Media*, edited by L. Lievrouw and S. Livingstone. Thousand Oaks: Sage, 2002.

Carley, K. M., and A. Newell. "The Nature of the Social Agent." *Journal of Mathematical Sociology*, Vol. 19(4) (1994): 221–262.

Carley, K. M., M. K. Martin, and B. Hirshma. "The Etiology of Social Change." *Topics in Cognitive Science*, Vol. 1(4) (2009): 621–650.
Cassirer, E. *Das Erkenntnisproblem in der Philosophie und Wissenschaft der neueren Zeit*, Vol. 1. Berlin: B. Cassirer, 1906.
Cassirer, E. *Das Erkenntnisproblem in der Philosophie und Wissenschaft der neueren Zeit*, Vol. 2. Berlin: B. Cassirer, 1907.
Cassirer, E. "Hermann Cohen, 1842–1918." In *Social Research*, Vol. 10:1(4) (1943): 219–232.
Cassirer, E. *An Essay on Man: An Introduction to a Philosophy of Human Culture*. New Haven: Yale University Press, 1944.
Cassirer, E. "The Concept of Group and the Theory of Perception." In *Philosophy and Phenomenological Research*, Vol. 5(1) (1944): 1–36.
Cassirer, Ernst. *The Myth of the State*. New Haven: Yale University Press, 1946.
Cassirer, E. *Substance and Function. (Substanzbegriff und Funktionsbegriff)*. Translated by W. Collins Swabey and M. Collins Swabey. New York: Dover, 1953 [1910].
Cassirer, E. *The Philosophy of Symbolic Forms. Volume 1: Language*. New Haven: Yale University Press, 1953 [1923].
Cassirer, E. *The Philosophy of Symbolic Forms. Volume 2: Mythical Thought*. New Haven: Yale University Press, 1955 [1925].
Cassirer, E. *The Philosophy of Symbolic Forms. Volume 3: The Phenomenology of Knowledge*. New Haven: Yale University Press, 1957 [1929].
Cassirer, E. *Kant's Life and Thought*. New Haven: Yale University Press, 1981.
Cassirer, E. *Goethe und die geschichtliche Welt*. R. A. Bast (Ed.). Hamburg: Meiner, 1995.
Cassirer, E. *The Philosophy of Symbolic Forms. Volume 4: The Metaphysics of Symbolic Forms*. New Haven: Yale University Press, 1996.
Cassirer, E. *The Logic of the Cultural Sciences*. New Haven: Yale University Press, 2000.
Caws P. *Structuralism: The Art of the Intelligible*. Atlantic Highlands: Humanities Press Int, 1988.
Christakis, N. A., and J.H. Fowler. *Connected: The Surprising Power of Our Social Networks and How They Shape Our Lives*. New York: Little, Brown, 2009.
Cialdini, R. and M.R. Trost. "Social Influence: Social Norms, Conformity, and Compliance." In *The Handbook of Social Psychology*, Fourth Edition, edited by D.T. Gilbert, S.T. Fiske, and G. Lindzey. Boston: McGraw Hill, 1998.
Cicero, M. T. *On Duties (De Officiis)*. Cambridge: Cambridge University Press, 1991.
Cicero, M. T. *On the Commonwealth* and *On the Laws* (*De Re Publica* and *De Legibus*). Cambridge: Cambridge University Press, 1999.
Cicero, M. T. *On Moral Ends* (*De Finibus*). Cambridge: Cambridge University Press, 2001.
Citton, Y., and F. Lordon. *Spinoza et les sciences sociales. De la puissance de la multitudes à l'économie des affects*. Paris: Éditions Amsterdam, 2008.
Cogan, M. *The Design in the Wax: The Structure of the Divine Comedy and Its Meaning*. Note Dame, IN: University of Notre Dame Press, 1999.
Cohan, A. S. *Theories of Revolution. An Introduction*. London: Nelson, 1975.
Coleman, J. S. *Introduction to mathematical sociology*. New York: Free Press of Glencoe, 1964.
Coleman, J. S. "Social Capital in the Creation of Human Capital." *American Journal of Sociology*, Vol. 94(S1) (1988): S95–S121.

Coleman, J. S. *Foundations of Social Theory*. Cambridge: Harvard University Press, 1990.

Collier, M. *Italian Unification*. Oxford: Heinemann, 2003.

Collins, R. *Interaction Ritual Chains*. Princeton: Princeton University Press, 2004.

Conn, P. *Pearl S. Buck: A Cultural Biography*. Cambridge: Cambridge University Press, 1996.

Corino, K. *Robert Musil. Eine Biographie*. Reinbek bei Hamburg: Rowohlt, 2003.

Corngold, S., J. Greenberg, and B. Wagner. 2009. "Preface." In Corngold, S., J. Greenberg, and B. Wagner (Eds.), *F. Kafka: The Office Writings*. Princeton: Princeton University Press.

Coser, L. A. *Sociology Through Literature: An Introductory Reader*. Englewood Cliffs: Prentice-Hall, 1963.

Cosmides, L., and J. Tooby. "Neurocognitive Adaptations Designed for Social Exchange." In *The Handbook of Evolutionary Psychology*, edited by D. M. Buss. Hoboken: Wiley, 2005.

Crossick G., and S. Jaumain. "The world of the department store: distribution, culture and social change." In *Cathedrals of Consumption*, edited by G. Crossick and S. Jaumain. Aldershot: Ashgate, 1999.

Curtis, N. "The Body as Outlaw: Lyotard, Kafka and the Visible Human Project." *Body & Society*. Vol. 5(2–3) (1999): 249–266.

Dante. *The Divine Comedy I: Inferno*. Princeton, NJ: Princeton University Press, 1991.

Dante. *The Divine Comedy II: Purgatorio*. Princeton, NJ: Princeton University Press, 1991.

Dante. *The Divine Comedy III: Paradisio*. Princeton, NJ: Princeton University Press, 1991.

Darwin, C. *On the Origin of Species by Means of Natural Selection*. London: J. Murray, 1859.

Darwin, C. *The Expression of the Emotions in Man and Animals*. London: J. Murray, 1872.

Dawkins, R. *The Selfish Gene*. Oxford: Oxford University Press, 2006.

Della Rocca, M. *Spinoza*. New York: Routledge, 2008.

Dewey, J. *How We Think*. Boston: Heath & Co., 1910.

Dewey, J. *The Middle Works, 1899–1924: Human Nature and Conduct*. Carbondale, IL: Southern Illinois University Press, 1988.

Dewey, J. 1988b. *The Later Works, 1925–1953: 1938–1939 Experience and Education, Freedom and Culture, Theory of Valuation, and Essays*, Vol. 13. Carbondale: Southern Illinois University Press.

Dewey, J. 1998. "The Problem of Truth." In *The Essential John Dewey: Ethics, Logic, Psychology*, edited by L. A. Hickman and T. M. Alexander. Bloomington: Indiana University Press.

Dostoevsky, F. *Demons*. New York: Vintage Classics, 1994.

Dugatkin, L. A. *The Altruism Equation: Seven Scientists Search for the Origins of Goodness*. Princeton: Princeton University Press, 2006.

Duneier, M. *Sidewalk*. New York: Farrar, Straus & Giroux, 1999.

Durkheim, E. *The Rules of Sociological Method* (translated by S. A. Solovay and J. H. Mueller). Glencoe: The Free Press, 1938.

Durkheim, E. "Individual and Collective Representations." In *Sociology and Philosophy*. Glencoe: The Free Press, 1953.

Durkheim, E. *Moral Education*. New York: The Free Press, 1961

Durkheim, E. *The Division of Labor in Society*. Translated by G. Simpson. New York: The Free Press, 1964a.

Durkheim, E. "The Dualism of Human Nature and Its Social Conditions." In *Essays on Sociology and Philosophy*, edited by K. H. Wolff. New York: Harper Torchbooks, 1964b.

Durkheim, E. *Les formes élémentaires de la vie religieuse. Le système totémique en Australie*. Fifth Edition. Paris: Les Presses universitaires de France, 1968.

Durkheim, E. *Le Socialisme: Sa definition, ses Débuts, La Doctrince Saint-Simoienne*. Second Edition. Paris: PUF, 1971.

Durkheim, E. *De la Division du Travail Social*. Tenth Edition. Paris: PUF, 1978.

Durkheim, E. *Suicide*. New York: The Free Press, 1979.

Durkheim, E. *The Rules of the Sociological Method*. Edited by S. Lukes. New York: Free Press, 1982.

Durkheim, E. *The Division of Labour in Society*. Translated by W. D. Halls. Basingstoke: Macmillan, 1984.

Durkheim, E. *The Elementary Forms of Religious Life*. New York: The Free Press, 1995.

Durkheim, E. *Durkheim's Philosophy Lectures*. Cambridge: Cambridge University Press, 2004.

Earl, D. 1967. *The Moral and Political Tradition of Rome*. Ithaca: Cornell University Press.

Edgerton, Samuel Y. Jr. "Galileo, Florentine 'Disegno,' and the 'Strange Spottednesse' of the Moon." *Art Journal*, Vol. 44(3) (1984): 225–232.

Edling, C., and J. Rydgren (Eds.) *Sociala Relationer och Social Handling*. Stockholm: Natur & kultur, 2007.

Ehrenpreis, I. *Swift: The Man, His Works, and the Age, Volume One: Mr. Swift and His Contemporaries*. Cambridge: Harvard University Press, 1962.

Ehrenpreis, I. *Swift: The Man, His Works, and the Age, Volume Two: Dr. Swift*. Cambridge: Harvard University Press, 1967.

Ehrenpreis, I. *Swift: The Man, His Works, and the Age, Volume Three: Dean Swift*. Cambridge: Harvard University Press, 1982.

Elias, N. *Die Gesellschaft der Individuen*. Edited by M. Schröter. Frankfurt: Suhrkamp, 1987.

Elias, N. *The Germans. Power Struggles and the Development of Habitus in the Nineteenth and Twentieth Centuries*. Edited by M. Schröter. Cambridge: Polity, 1996.

Elliott, R. C. *The Power of Satire: Magic, Ritual, Art*. Princeton: Princeton University Press, 1960.

Elster, J. *Alexis de Tocqueville: The First Social Scientist*. Cambridge: Cambridge University Press, 2009.

Elster, J. *Nuts and Bolts for the Social Sciences*. Cambridge: Cambridge University Press, 1989.

Elster, J. "A Plea for Mechanisms." In *Social Mechanisms*, edited by P. Hedström and R. Swedberg. Cambridge: Cambridge University Press, 1998.

Elster, J. *Explaining Social Behavior: More Nuts and Bolts for the Social Sciences*. Cambridge: Cambridge University Press, 2007.

Emirbayer, M., and D. W. Maynard. "Pragmatism and Ethnomethodology." Working paper, 2007.

Etzioni, A. *The Active Society: A Theory of Societal and Political Processes*. New York: The Free Press, 1968.

Eyerman, R. *Cultural Trauma: Slavery and African-American Identity*. Cambridge: Cambridge University Press, 2002.

Fallesen, P. *Modstand og den politiske krop—Konstruktionen af asylansøgeren som biopolitisk subjekt i Danmark*. København: Sociologisk Institut, 2008. (http://pfallesen.files.wordpress.com/2008/06/fallesen–modstand–og–den–politiske–krop–s.pdf).

Fararo, T. J. *The Meaning of General Theoretical Sociology: Tradition and Formalization*. Cambridge: Cambridge University Press, 1989.

Fararo, T. J. *Social Action Systems*. Westport: Praeger, 2001.

Faulkner, R., and H. S. Becker. *Do You Know—?The Jazz Repertoire in Action*. Chicago: University of Chicago Press, 2009.

Febvre, L. *The Problem of Unbelief in the Sixteenth Century: The Religion of Rabelais*. Cambridge: Harvard University Press, 1982.

Feder, B. J. "Ben Leaving as Ben & Jerry's Chief." *The New York Times*, June 14, 1994, D1, D5.

Ferrante, J. *The Political Vision of the "Divine Comedy."* Princeton: Princeton University Press, 1984.

Fine, G. A., and B. Harrington. "Tiny Publics: Small Groups and Civil Society." *Sociological Theory* 22 (2004): 341–356.

Fisch, M. "Peirce's General Theory of Signs." In *Peirce, Semeiotic, and Pragmatism*, edited by K. Laine Ketner and C. Kloesel. Bloomington: Indiana University Press, 1986.

Forde, S. "Gender and Justice in Plato." *American Political Science Review*, Vol. 91 (1997): 657–670.

Foucault, M. *Discipline and Punish: The Birth of the Prison*. New York: Pantheon, 1977.

Foucault, M. "On the Geneaology of Ethics." In *Essential Works of Michel Foucault*, Vol. I, edited by P. Rabinow. New York: The New Press, 1997.

Foucault, M. *Fearless Speech*. Los Angeles: Semiotext(e), 2001.

Foucault, M. *The Order of Things: An Archaeology of the Human Sciences*. New York: Pantheon Books, 1970.

Foucault, M. *Power/Knowledge*. New York: Pantheon Books, 1980.

Foucault, M. *Introduction to Kant's Anthropology*. Los Angeles: Semiotext(e), 2008.

Frank, R. C. *Choosing the Right Pond: Human Behavior and the Quest for Status*. Oxford: Oxford University Press, 1985.

Frankl, V. E. *Man's Search for Ultimate Meaning*. New York: Basic Books, 2000.

Franzosi, R.. "Outside and Inside the Regression Black Box: A New Approach to Data Analysis." *Quality and Quantity*, No. 28 (1994): 21–53.

Franzosi, R.. *The Puzzle of Strikes: Class and State Strategies in Postwar Italy*. Cambridge: Cambridge University Press, 1995.

Friedkin, N. E. "The Interpersonal Systems and Organized Suicides of Death Cults." Mimeo, 2004.

Friedland, R. "Institution, Practice and Ontology: Towards A Religious Sociology." *Research in the Sociology of Organizations*, Vol. 27 (2009): 45–83.

Friedman, M. *A Parting of the Ways: Carnap, Cassirer, and Heidegger*. Chicago: Open Court, 2000.

Frisby, D. *Sociological Impressionism: A Reassessment of Georg Simmel's Social Theory*. Second Edition. New York: Routledge, 1992.

Fry, Jr., W. *Sweet Madness: A Study of Humor*. Palo Alto: Pacific Books, 1963.

Galilei, G. *Le opere di Galileo Galilei*. Edizione nazionale delle Opere di Galileo Galilei sotto gli auspicii di S. M. il Re d'Italia. Twenty volumes, Edited by Antonio Favaro. Florence: G. Barbèra, 1890–1909.

Garfinkel, H. *Studies in Ethnomethodology*. Englewood Cliffs, NJ: Prentice Hall, 1967.

Gambetta, D. "Deceptive Mimicry in Humans." In *Perspectives on Imitation: From Neuroscience to Social Science, Volume 2, Imitation, Human Development, and Culture*, edited by S. Hurley and N. Chater. Cambridge, MA: MIT Press. 2005.

Gawronsky, D. "Cassirer: His Life and His Work." In *The Philosophy of Ernst Cassirer*, edited by P. A. Schilpp. Evanston: The Library of Living Philosophers, 1949, 3–37.

Garfinkel, H. *Studies in Ethnomethodology*. Englewood Cliffs: Prentice Hall, 1967.

Gatens, M., and G. Lloyd. *Collective Imaginings: Spinoza, Past And Present*. New York: Routledge, 1999.

Geertz, C. *The Interpretation of Cultures*. New York: Basic Books, 1973.

Geisthövel, A., and H. Knoch. *Orte der Moderne*. Frankfurt: Campus, 2005.

Gellner, E. *Nations and Nationalism*. Oxford: Blackwell, 1983.

Giddens, A. *Central Problems in Social Theory: Action, Structure, and Contradiction in Social Analysis*. Berkeley: University of California Press, 1979.

Gill, C. "Personhood and Personality: The Four-*Personae* Theory in Cicero, *De Officiis* I." In *Oxford Studies in Ancient Philsophy, IV*, edited by J. Annas. Oxford: Clarendon Press, 1988.

Goethe, J. W. *Faust: Part One*. Oxford and New York: Oxford University Press, 1991.

Goethe, J. W. *Faust: Part Two*. Oxford and New York: Oxford University Press, 1994.

Goethe, J. W. *Faust. Texte und Kommentare*. Two volumes., edited by A. Schöne. Frankfurt and Leipzig: Insel, 2003.

Goethe, J. W. *Sämtliche Werke*. Münchner Ausgabe (MA, 21 in 33 vols.), edited by K. Richter et al. München: btb, 2006.

Goffman, E. "Embarrassment and Social Organization." *American Journal of Sociology*, Vol. 62(3) (1956): 264–271.

Goffman, E. *The Presentation of Self in Everyday Life*. New York: Doubleday, 1959.

Goffman, E. *Behavior in Public Places: Notes on the Social Organization of Gatherings*. New York: The Free Press, 1963.

Goffman, E. *Asylums. Essays on the Social Situation of Mental Patients and Other Inmates*. Harmondsworth: Penguin, 1968.

Goffman, E. *Strategic interaction*. Philadelphia: University of Pennsylvania Press, 1969.

Goffman, E. *Frame Analysis*. Cambridge: Harvard University Press, 1974.

Goldstone, J. A. "Theory Development in the Study of Revolutions." In *New Directions in Contemporary Sociological Theory*, edited by J. Berger and M. Zelditch Jr. Lanham. Lanham: Rowman & Littlefield, 2002.

Goldstone, J. A. "Toward a Fourth Generation of Revolutionary Theory." *Annual Review of Political Science*, Vol. 4: 139–187, 2001.

Goldthorpe, J. H. *On Sociology*. Oxford: Oxford University Press, 2000.

Gouldner, A. "The Norm of Reciprocity: A Preliminary Statement." *American Sociological Review*, Vol. 25 (1960): 161–178.

Greene, J.D. Forthcoming. *The Moral Brain, and What To Do About It*. New York: Penguin.

Griffin, M. T., and E. M. Atkins. "Introduction." In *Cicero: On Duties*. Cambridge: Cambridge University Press, 1991.

Griswold, W. *Bearing Witness: Readers, Writers, and the Nigerian Novel*. Princeton: Princeton University Press, 2000.

Gross, N. "A Pragmatist Theory of Mechanisms." *American Sociological Review*, Vol. 74 (2009): 358–379.

Gross, N. "Pragmatism, Phenomology, and Twentieth-Century American Sociology." In *Sociology in America: a History*, edited by Craig Calhoun. Chicago: University of Chicago Press, 2007.

Grusky, D. B. "The Contours of Social Stratification." In *Social Stratification: Class, Race, and Gender in Sociological Perspective*, edited by D. B. Grusky. Boulder, CO: Westview Press, 1994.

Guillory, J. "Bourdieu's Refusal. " *Modern Language Quarterly*, Vol. 58 (1997): 367–398.

Habermas, J. *The Structural Transformation of the Public Sphere*. Cambridge: MIT Press, 1989.

Hacking, I. *Representing and Intervening: Introductory Topics in the Philosophy of Natural Science*. Cambridge: Cambridge University Press, 1983.

Hacking, I. *Mad Travelers: Reflections on the Reality of Transient Mental Illnesses*. Charlottesville: University Press of Virginia, 1998.

Hadot, P. *Exercices spirituels et philosophie antique*. Paris: Michel Albin, 2002.

Haidt, J. "The Emotional Dog and Its Rational Tail: A Social Intuitionist Approach to Moral Judgment." *Psychological Review*, Vol. 108(4): 814–834, 2001.

Halewood, M. "Introduction to Special Section on Whitehead." *Theory, Culture & Society*, Vol 25(4) (2008): 1–14.

Harrington, A. "Alfred Weber's Essay *'The Civil Servant'* and Kafka's *'In the Penal Colony'*: the Evidence of an Influence." *History of the Human Sciences*, Vol. 20(3) (2007): 41–63.

Hastie, Reid. *Inside the Juror: The Psychology of Juror Decision Making*. Cambridge: Cambridge University Press, 1994.

Hedström, P. *Dissecting the Social. On the Principles of Analytical Sociology*. Cambridge: Cambridge University Press, 2005.

Heer, F. *Der Kampf um die österreichische Identität*. Vienna, Cologne, and Graz: Böhlau, 1981.

Heller, E. "Man Guilty and Man Ashamed–II. Man Ashamed." *Psychiatry*, Vol. 37(2) (1974): 99–108.

Hindus, M. *A Reader's Guide to Marcel Proust*. Syracuse: Syracuse University Press, 1962.

Hobbes, T. *Leviathan*. London: Oxford University Press, 1952.

Hobbes, T. *The English Works of Thomas Hobbes*. Edited by W. Molesworth. Aalen: Scientia, 1839 (reprinted in 1962).

Hobsbawm, E. J. *Nations and Nationalism since 1780*. Cambridge: Cambridge University Press, 1990.

Hofstadter, D. R. *Goedel Escher Bach: An Eternal Golden Braid*. New York: Basic Books, 1979.

Hollis, M. "Of Masks and Men." In *The Category of the Person*, edited by M. Carrithers, S. Collins, and S. Lukes. Cambridge: Cambridge University Press, 1985.

Homans, G. C. *The Human Group*. New York: Harcourt, Brace, Jovanovich, 1950.

Horton, M. "The Literature of Alienation." *The Sociological Review Monograph*, Vol. 26 (1978): 197–220.

Hsueh, Y. " 'He sees the development of children's concepts upon a background of sociology': Jean Piaget's honorary degree at Harvard University in 1936." *History of Psychology*, Vol. 7 (2004): 20–44.

Huber, J. (Ed.) *Macro-Micro Linkages in Sociology*. Newbury Park: Sage Publications, 1991.

Hume, D. "Of the Standard of Taste." In *Essays, Moral, Political and Literary*. Indianapolis: Literary Fund, 1985.

Iacoboni, M. *Mirroring People: The New Science of How We Connect with Others*. New York: Farrar, Straus, and Giroux, 2008.

Iannacone, L. R. "Sacrifice and Stigma: Reducing Free–Riding in Cults, Communes, and Other Collectives." *Journal of Political Economy*, Vol. 100(2) (1992): 271–292.

Ibsen, H. N.d. *The Master Builder and Other Plays*. Translated by U. Ellis-Fermor. Harmondsworth: Penguin, 1958.

Ibsen, H. 1978. Samlede verker 1–6. Oslo: Gyldendal.

Ibsen, H. *Plays: Five. Brand; Emperor and Galilean*. Translated by M. Meyer. London: Methuen, 1986.

Ignatieff, M. *Isaiah Berlin: A Life*. London: Vintage, 2000.

Jaeger, M. *Fausts Kolonie: Goethes kritische Phänomenologie der Moderne*. Würzburg: Königshausen & Neumann, 2004.

Jaeger, M. *Global Player Faust oder das Verschwinden der Gegenwart: Zur Aktualität Goethes*. Berlin: Siedler, 2008.

James, W. *Principles of Psychology*. Two Volumes. New York: Dover Publications, 1950.

James, W. *Pragmatism and the Meaning of Truth*. Cambridge, MA: Harvard University Press, 1975 [1906].

Jasso, G. "Studying Status: An Integrated Framework." *American Sociological Review*, Vol. 66 (2001): 96–124.

Jasso, G. "Comparison Theory." In *Handbook of Sociological Theory*, Chapter 30, edited by J. H. Turner. New York: Kluwer Academic/Plenum Publishers, 2002.

Jasso, G. "A New Unified Theory of Sociobehavioral Forces." *European Sociological Review*, Vol. 24 (2008): 411–434.

Jasso, G., and S. Kotz. "A New Continuous Distribution and Two New Families of Distributions Based on the Exponential." *Statistica Neerlandica*, Vol. 61 (2007): 305–328.

Jasso, G., and S. Kotz. "Two Types of Inequality: Inequality Between Persons and Inequality Between Subgroups." *Sociological Methods and Research*, Vol. 37 (2008): 31–74.

Jencks, C., M. Smith, H. Acland, M. J. Bane, D. Cohen, H. Gintis, B. Heyns, and S. Michelson. *Inequality: A Reassessment of the Effect of Family and Schooling in America*. New York: Basic Books, 1972.

Jerome, St. *Patrologiae Cursus Completus*. Edited by J. P. Migne. Series Latina, Vols. 22–30, 1845–1846.

Joas, H. "Symbolic Interactionism." In *Social Theory Today*, edited by Anthony Giddens and Jonathan H. Turner. Stanford: Stanford University Press, 1987.

Joas, H. *The Creativity of Action*. Cambridge: Polity Press, 1996.

Kafka, F. *Erzählungen*. Leipzig: Reclam, 1978.

Kafka, F. *Brief an den Vater*. Edited by Faksimile. J. Unseld. Frankfurt: Fischer, 1994.

Kafka, F. *The Castle*. Translated by M. Harman. New York: Schocken, 1998a.

Kafka, F. *The Trial*. Translated by M. Harman. New York: Schocken, 1998b.

Kafka, F. *Amerika:The Missing Person*. Translated by M. Harman. New York: Schocken, 2004.

Kant, I. *Grundlegung Zur Metaphysik Der Sitten*. Sämtliche Werke, Fünfter Band. Leipzig: Inselverlag, 1922.

Kant, I. *The Fundamental Principles of the Metaphysic of Ethics*. Translated by O. Mathey-Zorn. New York: D. Appleton-Century Company, 1938.

Kant, I. *Critique of Pure Reason*. Translated by N. Kemp Smith. London: Macmillan and Company, 1950.

Kant, I. *Prolegomena to Any Future Metaphysics That Will Be Able to Present Itself as a Science*. Translated by P. G. Lucas. Manchester: Manchester University Press, 1953.

Kant, I. *Groundwork of the Metaphysic of Morals*. Translated by H. J. Paton. New York: Harper and Row, 1964.

Kant, I. *Critique of Judgment*. Translated by Werner S. Pluhar. Indianapolis: Hackett Publishing Company, 1987.

Kant, I. *The Metaphysic of Morals*. Translated by M.Gregor. Cambridge: Cambridge University Press, 1991.

Kant, I. *Critique of Practical Reason*. Translated by W. S. Pluhar. Indianapolis: Hackett Publishing Company, 2002.

Kant, I. *Anthropology from a Pragmatic Point of View*. Translated by R. B. Louden. Cambridge: Cambridge University Press, 2006.

Katz, D. and F. H. Allport. *Students' Attitudes: A Report of the Syracuse University Reaction Study*. Syracuse, New York: The Craftsman Press, Inc. 1931.

Katz, J. *Seductions of Crime*. New York: Basic Books, 1988.

Katz, J. "Ethnography's Warrants." *Sociological Methods and Research*. Vol. 25 (1997) (4): 391–423.

Keltner, D. "Signs of Appeasement: Evidence for the Distinct Displays of Embarrassment, Amusement, and Shame." *Journal of Personality and Social Psychology*, Vol. 68(3) (1995): 441–454.

Keltner, D., and C. Anderson. "Saving Face for Darwin: The Functions and Uses of Embarrassment." *Current Directions in Psychological Science*, Vol. 9(6) (2000): 187–192.

Kern, S. *The Culture of Time and Space, 1880–1918*. Cambridge: Harvard University Press, 1983.

Khanna, R. "Indignity." *Positions*, Vol. 16(1) (2008): 39–77.

King, G. *Unifying Political Methodology: The Likelihood Theory of Statistical Inference*. Ann Arbor: University of Michigan Press, 1998.

Kitchener, R. F. "Jean Piaget: The Unknown Sociologist?" *The British Journal of Sociology*, Vol. 42 (1991): 421–442.

Kittang, A. *Ibsens heriosme*. Oslo: Gyldendal, 2003.

Kolker, R. "The Madoff Exiles." *New York Magazine*, September 27 2009.

Kopp, R. L. *Marcel Proust as a Social Critic*. Rutherford: Fairleigh Dickinson University Press, 1971.

Koselleck, R. *Goethes unzeitgemäße Geschichte*. Heidelberg: Manutius, 1997.

Krippendorf, E. *Wie die Großen mit den Menschen spielen: Versuch über Goethes Politik*. Frankfurt: Suhrkamp, 1988.

Krogstad, A. and A. Storvik. "Seductive Heroes and Ordinary Human Beings: Charismatic Political Leadership in France and Norway." *Comparative Social Research*, Vol. 23 (2007): 211–245.

Krois, J. M. *Cassirer: Symbolic Forms and History*. New Haven: Yale University Press, 1987.

Krois, J. M. "A Note about Philosophy and History: The Place of Cassirer's Erkenntnisproblem." *Science in Context*, Vol. 9 (1996): 191–194.

Kruglanski, A. W., X. Chen, M. Dechesne, S. Fishman, and E. Orehek. "Fully Committed: Suicide Bombers' Motivation and the Quest for Personal Significance." Political Psychology 30, no. 3 (2009): 331–57.

Kurzman, C. "The Rhetoric of Science." *Berkeley Journal of Sociology*, Vol. 33 (1988): 131–158.

Kuzmics, H., and G. Mozetič. *Literatur als Soziologie: Zum Verhältnis von literarischer und gesellscahftlicher Wirklichkeit*. Konstanz: UVK Verlagsgesellschaft, 2003.

Lagercrantz, O. *August Strindberg*. London: Faber & Faber, 1984.

Lakoff, G. "A Figure of Thought." *Metaphor and Symbolic Activity*, Vol. 1(3) (1986): 215–225.

LaMarre, H., K. Landreville, and M. Beam. "The Irony of Satire: Political Ideology and the Motivation to See What You Want to See in the Colbert Report." *International Journal of Press/Politics*, Vol. 14 (2009): 212–231.

Lancaster, B. *The Department Store*. London: Leicester University Press, 2000 [1995].

Langer, S. *Feeling and Form*. New York: Charles Scribner's Sons, 1953.

Langer, S. *Philosophy in a New Key: A Study in the Symbolism of Reason, Rite, and Art*. Cambridge: Harvard University Press, 1957.

Leerssen, J. "The Allochronic Periphery: Towards a Grammar of Cross-Cultural Representation." In *Beyond Pug's Tour. National and Ethnic Stereotyping in Theory and Literary Practice*, edited by C.C. Barfoot. Amsterdam: Rodopi, 1997.

Lefranc, A. *Les Navigations de Pantagruel, étude sur la géographie Rabelaisienne*. Paris: H. Leclerc, 1905.

Lehnert, G. "Nachwort." In *E. Zola: Das Paradies der Damen*. Frankfurt: Büchergilde Gutenberg, 2002.

Leibow, E. *Tally's Corner*. New York: Little Brown, 1967.

Lepenies, W. *Between Literature and Science: The Rise of Sociology*. Cambridge: Cambridge University Press, 1988.

Levine, D. N. *Visions of the Sociological Tradition*. Chicago: University of Chicago Press, 1995.

Lewin, K. "The Conflict Between Aristotelian and Galileian Modes of Thought in Contemporary Psychology." In *A Dynamic Theory of Personality: Selected Papers of Kurt Lewin*. New York: McGraw, Hill, 1935 [1931].

Lewin, K. "Cassirer's Philosophy of Science and the Social Sciences." In *The Philosophy of Ernst Cassirer*, edited by P. A. Schilpp. Evanston: Library of Living Philosophers, 1949, 269–288.

Lewin, K. *Field Theory in Social Science*. New York: Harper, 1951.

Lewis, D., and R. Smith. *American Sociology and Pragmatism: Mead, Chicago Sociology and Pragmatism*. Chicago: University of Chicago Press, 1980.

Liao, K. *Pearl S. Buck: A Cultural Bridge Across the Pacific*. Westport: Greenwood Press, 1997.

Lin, N. *Social Capital: A Theory of Social Structure and Action*. Cambridge: Cambridge University Press, 2001.

Lizardo, O. "The Cognitive Origins of Bourdieu's Habitus." *Journal for the Theory of Social Behaviour*, Vol. 34(4) (2004): 375–401.

Loetscher, L. A. *The Broadening Church*. Philadelphia: University of Pennsylvania Press, 1954.

Lofts, S. G. *Ernst Cassirer: A Repetition of Modernity*. Albany: State University of New York Press, 2000.

Long, A. A. *From Epicurus to Epictetus*. Oxford: Oxford University Press, 2006.

Lordon, F. *L'intérêt souverain: Essai d'anthropologie économique spinoziste*. Paris: Éditions La Découverte, 2006.

Loury, G. C. *The Anatomy of Racial Inequality*. Cambridge: Harvard University Press, 2002.

Lowe, V. *Alfred North Whitehead: The Man and His Work*. Vol. I: 1861–1910. Baltimore: Johns Hopkins University Press, 1985.

Lowy, M. "The Religion of Liberty in Franz Kafka's Work: Against the Authority of the Guardians of the Law." *Archives de Sciences Sociales des Religions*, Vol. 43(101) (1998): 75–86.

Luhmann, N. *Social Systems*. Stanford: Stanford University Press, 1995.

Lynch, M. "Pictures of Nothing? Visual Construals in Social Theory." *Sociological Theory*, Vol. 1(1991): 1–21.

Löwith, K. *Von Hegel zu Nietzsche: Sämtliche Schriften. Band 4*. Stuttgart: Metzler, 1988.

Machamer, P. K., L. Darden, and C. F. Craver. "Thinking About Mechanisms." *Philosophy of Science*, Vol. 67 (2000) (1): 1–25.

MacIntyre, A. "Spinoza, Benedict (Baruch)." In *The Encyclopedia of Philosophy*, edited by P. Edwards. New York: MacMillan, 1967.

Mahanta, A. "From Politics to Literature: A Consideration of Jonathan Swift and George Orwell." *Economic and Political Weekly*, Vol. 18 (May 1983): 919–930.

Mann, T. "Goethe als Repräsentant des bürgerlichen Zeitalters" (1932). In *Essays*, Vol. 3., edited by H. Kurzke and S. Stachorski. Frankfurt: Fischer, 1994.

Markovsky, B. "Building and Testing Micro-Macro Theories." In *Status, Network, and Structure: Theory Development in Group Processes*, edited by J. Szmatka, J. Skvoretz, and J. Berger. Stanford: Stanford University Press, 1997.

Martin, J. L. "Authoritative Knowledge and Heteronomy in Classical Sociological Theory." *Sociological Theory*, Vol. 16 (1998): 99–131.

Martin, J. L. *Social Structures*. Princeton: Princeton University Press, 2009.

Marx, K. *Capital: A Critique of Political Economy*, Vol. I. Chicago: Charles H. Kerr and Co., 1906.

Maslow, A. H. "A Theory of Human Motivation." *Psychological Review*, Vol. 50(4) (1943): 370–396.

Mauss, M. *The Gift. Forms of Exchange in Archaic Societies*. London: Routledge and Kegan Paul, 1960.

Mauss, M. "A Category of the Human Mind. The Notion of Person; The Notion of Self." In *The Category of the Person*, edited by M. Carrithers, S. Collins, S. Lukes. Cambridge: Cambridge University Press, 1985.

McCall, G. "Symbolic Interaction." In *Contemporary Social Psychological Theories*, edited by Peter J. Burke. Stanford: Stanford University Press, 2006.

McCall, L. "The Complexity of Intersectionality." *Signs*, Vol. 30(3) (2005): 1771–1800.

Mead, G. H. "The Social Self." *The Journal of Philosophy*, Vol. 10(14) (1913): 374–380.

Menand, L. *The Metaphysical Club: A Story of Ideas in America*. New York: Farrar, Straus, and Giroux, 2001.

Meier, R. *Gesellschaftliche Modernisierung in Goethes Alterswerken "Wilhelm Meisters Wanderjahre" und "Faust II."* Freiburg i. Br.: Rombach, 2002.

Menton, S. *Jorge Luis Borges, Magic Realist Author(s)*. *Hispanic Review*, Vol. 4 (1982): 411–426.

Merleau-Ponty, Maurice. *Phenomenology of Perception*. London: Routledge, 1998. [1962].

Merton, R. K. "The Matthew Effect in Science." *Science*, Vol. 159 (1968): 56–63.

Merton, R.K., and E. Barber. *The Travels and Adventures of Serendipity*. Princeton: Princeton University Press, 2004.

Meyersson Milgrom, E. "A Labor Market Analysis of Extreme Political Violence." Mimeo. Stanford University, 2009.

Miller, J. G. *Living Systems*. New York: McGraw-Hill, 1978.

Mills, C. W. *The Sociological Imagination*. London: Oxford University Press, 1959.

Mills, C. W. "Charles Peirce." In *Sociology and Pragmatism: The Higher Learning in America*. New York: Paine-Whitman Publishers. 1964.

Mincer, J. *Schooling, Experience, and Earnings*. New York: Columbia University Press, 1974.

Mohr, J. W. "Implicit Terrains: Meaning, Measurement, and Spatial Metaphors in Organizational Theory." In *The Economic Sociology of Markets and Industries*, edited by M. Ventresca, K. A. Munir, and M. Lounsbury. Cambridge University Press (Forthcoming).

Mohr, J. W., and C. Rawlings. "Formal Models of Culture." In *A Handbook of Cultural Sociology*, edited by J. Hall, L. Grindstaff, and M. Lo. London: Routledge, 2010, 118–128.

Morford, M. P. O. *The Roman Philosophers: From the Time of Cato the Censor to the Death of Marcus Aurelius*. London: Routledge, 2002.

Mozetič, G." 'Der Mann ohne Eigenschaften' und die Zwänge der Moderne. Ein soziologischer Beitrag aus zivilisationstheoretischer Perspektive." In *Der unendliche Prozeß der Zivilisation. Zur Kultursoziologie der Moderne nach Norbert Elias*, edited by H. Kuzmics and I. Mörth. Frankfurt and New York: Campus, 1991.

Murry, J. M. *Jonathan Swift: A Critical Biography*. New York: Farrar, Straus, and Giroux.

Musil, R. *The Man without Qualities*. Translated by Sophie Wilkins. Two Volumes. New York: Vintage Books, 1996.

Müller, H. P. *Max Weber: Eine Einführung*. Köln-Weimar: UTB–Böhlau, 2007.

Müller, Walter, and Wolfgang Karle. "Social Selection in Educational Systems in Europe." *European Sociological Review*, Vol. 9(1) (1993): 1–23.

Negt, O. *Die Faust–Karriere:Vom verzweifelten Intellektuellen zum gescheiterten Unternehmer*. Göttingen: Steidl, 2006.

Nelson B. "Introduction." In *E. Zola: The Ladies' Paradise*. New York: Oxford University Press, 1998.

*New York Times* correspondents. *Class Matters*. New York: Times Books, 2005.

Nielsen, D. A. *Three Faces of God: Society, Religion, and the Categories of Totality in the Philosophy of Emile Durkheim*. Albany: State University of New York Press, 1999.

Nietzsche, F. *On the Genealogy of Morality*. Cambridge: Cambridge University Press, 2006.

Nordenmark, M., and C. Nyman. "Fair or Unfair? Perceived Fairness of Household Division of Labour and Gender Equality Among Women and Men: The Swedish Case." *European Journal of Women's Studies*, Vol. 10(2) (2003): 181–209.

Nussbaum, M. "Duties of Justice, Duties of Material Aid." *Journal of Political Philosophy*, Vol. 8 (2004): 176–206.

Oakleaf, D. 2008. *A Political Biography of Jonathan Swift*. London: Pickering and Chatto.

Ollén, G. 1984. Kommentarer. In *Fadren, Fröken Julie, Fordringsägare* (A. Strindberg, National ed., Vol. 27: 274–339). Stockholm: Almqvist & Wiksell.

Olson, M. 1965. *The Logic of Collective Action*. Cambridge: Harvard University Press.

Orbuch, T. L. 1997. "People's Accounts Count: The Sociology of Accounts." *Annual Review of Sociology*, Vol. 23: 455–478.

Orwell, G. 1946. "Politics *vs*. Literature: An Examination of Gulliver's Travels." *Polemic*, No 5.

Orwell, G. 1961. *Nineteen Eighty–Four*. New York: Harcourt Brace Jovanovich.

Orwell, G. 1996. *Animal Farm. A Fairy Story*. New York and London: Penguin Books.

Osten, M. *"Alles veloziferisch" oder Goethes Entdeckung der Langsamkeit*. Frankfurt and Leipzig: Insel, 2003.

Panchanathan, K., and R. Boyd. "Indirect Reciprocity Can Stabilize Cooperation Without the Second-Order Free Rider Problem." *Nature*, Vol. 432(7016) (2004): 499–502.

Panofsky, E. "Galileo as a Critic of the Arts: Aesthetic Attitude and Scientific Thought." *Isis*, Vol. 47(1) (1956): 3–15.

Panofsky, E. *Perspective as Symbolic Form*. New York: Zone Books, 1991.

Panofsky, E. "Galileo as a Critic of the Arts: Aesthetic Attitude and Scientific Thought." *Isis*, Vol. 47(1) (1956): 3–15.

Parsons, T. *The Structure of Social Action*. New York: The Free Press, 1937.

Parsons, T. *The System of Modern Societies*. Englewood Cliffs: Prentice-Hall, 1971.

Peirce, C. S. "Abduction and Induction" In *Philosophical Writings of Peirce*, edited by Justus Buchler. New York: Dover, 1955 [1901].

Peirce, C. "Critique of Positivism." MS 146: Winter 1867–1868. Downloaded October 30, 2009 from http:/www.iupui.edu/~peirce/writings/v2/w2/w2_11/v2_11.htm.

Peirce, C. *Collected Papers of Charles Sanders Peirce*. Vol. 1. Cambridge, MA: Harvard University Press, 1931.

Peirce, C. *Letters to Lady Welby*. New Haven, CT: Whitlock's, Inc., 1953.

Peirce, C. 1955. *Philosophical Writings*. New York: Dover Publications.

Peirce, C. "Giddings's Inductive Sociology." In C. *Sanders Peirce: Contributions to the Nation*, edited by K. Ketner and J. Cook, Vol. 3. Texas: Graduate Studies Texas Tech University, 1979.

Peirce, C. *Peirce on Signs*, edited by James Hoppes. Bloomington: Indiana University Press, 1991.

Peirce, C. "Herbert Spencer's Philosophy." In *Writings of C S. Peirce*, Vol. 6. Bloomington: Indiana University Press, 2000.

Pentland, A. *Honest Signals: How They Shape Our World*. Cambridge, MA: MIT Press, 2008.

Pequigney, J. "Sodomy in Dante's Inferno and Purgatorio." *Representations*, No. 36 (1991): 22–42.

Pevear, R. "Introduction." In *Dostoevksy: Demons*. Vintage Clasics: New York, 1994.

Piaget, J. *Structuralism*. New York: Basic Books, 1970.

Piaget, J. "A History of Psychology in Autobiography." In *Piaget Sampler: An Introduction to Jean Piaget Through his Own Words*, edited by S. F. Campbell. New York: Jason Aronson, 1977.

Piaget, J. *Sociological Studies*.London: Routledge, 1995.

Pinker, S. *The Blank Slate: The Modern Denial of Human Nature*. Viking Penguin, 2002.

Pinker, S. "The Evolutionary Social Psychology of Off-Record Indirect Speech Acts." *Intercultural Pragmatics*, Vol. 4(4) (2007): 437–461.

Pizzorno, A. "Some Other Kind of Otherness. A Critique of 'Rational Choice' Theories." In *Development, Democracy and the Art of Trespassing: Essays in Honour of Albert O. Hirschman*, edited by A. Foxley et al. Notre Dame: University of Notre Dame Press, 1986.

Pizzorno, A. "On the Individualistic Theory of Social Order." In *Social Theory for a Changing Society*, edited by P. Bourdieu and J. Coleman. Boulder, CO: Westview Press, 1991.

Pizzorno, A. *Il velo della diversità*. Milano: Feltrinelli, 2007.

Plato. *The Dialogues of Plato*. Translated by B. Jowett. Chicago: Britannica, 1952.

Platt, J. *A History of Sociological Research Methods in America: 1920–1960*. Cambridge: Cambridge University Press, 1996.

Pluhar, W. S. "How to Render Zweckmäßigkeit in Kant's Third Critique." In *Interpreting Kant*, edited by M. S. Gram. Iowa City: University of Iowa Press, 1982.

Poletta, F. *It Was Like a Fever: Storytelling in Protest and Politics*. Chicago: University of Chicago Press, 2006.

Pols, E. *Whitehead's Metaphysics: A Critical Examination*. Carbondale: Southern Illinois Press, 1967.

Popper, K. *The Logic of Scientific Discovery*. New York: Basic Books, 1959.

Popper, K. "Plato." In *International Encyclopedia of the Social Sciences*, Vol. 12, edited by D. L. Sills. New York: Macmillan, 1968.

Portes, A. "Social Capital: Its Origins and Applications in Modern Sociology." *Annual Review of Sociology*, Vol. 24 (1997): 1–24.

Powys, J. C. *Rabelais*. London: The Bodley Head, 1948.

Prentice, D. A., and D. T. Miller. "Pluralistic Ignorance and Alcohol Use on Campus: Some Consequences of Misperceiving the Social Norm." *Journal of Personality and Social Psychology* 64(2) (1993): 243–256.

Proust, M. *The Guermantes Way* (*In Search of Lost Times*, Vol. III). New York: The Modern Library, 2003a.

Proust, M. *Sodom and Gomorrah* (*In Search of Lost Times*, Vol. IV). New York: The Modern Library, 2003b.

Proust, M. *The Captive & The Fugitive* (*In Search of Lost Times*, Vol. V). New York: The Modern Library, 2003c.

Quintana, R. *The Mind and Art of Jonathan Swift*. Oxford: Oxford University Press, 1936.

Rabelais, F. *Gargantua and Pantagruel*. New York: Penguin Classics, 1955.

Radkau, J. *Max Weber*. Munich: Carl Hanser Verlag, 2006.

Rawls, J. *A Theory of Justice*. Cambridge: Harvard University Press, 1971.

Reichenbach, H. *Experience and Prediction: An Analysis of the Foundations and the Structure of Knowledge*. Chicago: University of Chicago Press, 1938.

Rescher, N. *Process Philosophy: A Survey of Basic Issues*. Pittsburgh: University of Pittsburgh Press, 2000.

Reynolds, L.T., and N. J. Herman-Kinney, eds. *Handbook of Symbolic Interactionism*. Lanham: Rowman and Littlefield, 2003.

Richerson, P.J., and R. Boyd. *Not By Genes Alone: How Culture Transformed Human Evolution*. Chicago: University of Chicago Press, 2005.

Ricoeur, P. *Freud and Philosophy: An Essay on Interpretation*. New Haven, CT: Yale University Press, 1970.

Riesbrodt, M. "*Charisma* in Max Weber's Sociology of Religion." *Religion*, Vol. 29 (1999): 1–14.

Ringen, S. "Do We Need Self–Knowledge in Order to Live as Free Citizens." In *Knowledge and Democracy, A 21st Century Perspective*, edited by Nico Stehr. New Brunswick: Transaction, 2008.

Ringer, F. K. *The Decline of the German Mandarins: The German Academic Community, 1890–1933*. Hanover: Wesleyan University Press, 1990.

Rousseau, J. J. *The Social Contract or Principles of Political Right* (Translated by G. D. H. Cole, public domain, Rendered into HTML, and text by Jon Roland of the Constitution Society, 1762).

Runciman, W. G. *A Treatise on Social Theory*. Cambridge: Cambridge University Press, 1983.

Russell, B. *Power*. New York: Routledge, 2003.

Ryle, G. *The Concept of Mind*. Chicago: The University of Chicago Press, 1949.

Said, E. *The World, the Text, and the Critic*. London: Faber and Faber, 1984.

Salert, B. *Revolutions and Revolutionaries. Four Theories*. New York: Elsevier, 1976.

Sartre, J. P. *The Critique of Dialectical Reason*. London: NLB, 1976.

Sawyer, R. K. "Emergence in Sociology: Contemporary Philosophy of Mind and Some Implications for Sociological Theory." *American Journal of Sociology*, Vol. 107 (2001): 551–585.

Schilpp, P. A. (Ed.) *The Philosophy of Ernst Cassirer*. Evanston, IL: The Library of Living Philosophers, 1949.

Schmaus, W. *Rethinking Durkheim and his Tradition*. New York: Cambridge University Press, 2004.

Schmidt, J. *Goethes Faust Erster und Zweiter Teil: Grundlagen–Werk–Wirkung*. München: Beck, 1999.

Schoneboom, A. "Diary of a Working Boy." *Ethnography*, Vol. 8(4) (2007): 403–423.

Sen A. "Rational Fools." In *Philosophy and Economic Theory*, edited by F. Hahn and M. Hollis. Oxford: Oxford University Press, 1979.

Sen, A. K. "Description as Choice." *Oxford Economic Papers*, Vol. 32(3) (1980): 353–369.

Sewell, W. H. "Historical Events as Transformations of Structures: Inventing Revolution at the Bastille." *Theory and Society*, Vol. 6 (1996): 841–881.

Sharples, R. W. "The Problem of Sources." In *A Companion to Ancient Philosophy*, edited by M. L. Gill and P. Pellegrin. Oxford: Wiley-Blackwell, 2009.

Sherburne, D. W. *A Key to Whitehead's Process and Reality*. Bloomington: Indiana University Press, 1966.

Simmel, G. *Conflict and the Web of Group-Affiliations*. Glencoe: The Free Press, 1955.

Simmel, G. *On Individuality and Social Forms*, edited by D. Levine. Chicago: University of Chicago Press, 1971a.

Simmel, G. "The Metropolis of Modern Life." In *Simmel: On Individuality and Social Forms*, edited by D. Levine. Chicago: University of Chicago Press, 1971b.

Simmel, G. *The Philosophy of Money*, Second Edition. New York: Routledge, 1990.

Simmel, G. *Die quantitative Bestimmtheit der Gruppe*. In *The Georg Simmel Edition*, Vol. 11, edited by O. Rammstedt. Frankfurt: Suhrkamp, 1992.

Simmel, G. *Essays on Religion*. New Haven: Yale University Press, 1997.

Simmel, G. *Goethe*. In *The Georg Simmel Edition*, Vol. 15, edited by U. Kösser, H. M. Kruckis, and O. Rammstedt. Frankfurt: Suhrkamp, 2003.

Simon, D., L. B. Pham, Q. A. Le., and K. J. Holyoak. "The Emergence of Coherence Over the Course of Decision Making." *Journal of Experimental Psychology-Learning Memory and Cognition* 27 (2001): 1250–1260.

Simon, D. "A Third View of the Black Box: Cognitive Coherence in Legal Decision Making." *University of Chicago Law Review* 71, 2004.

Simon, D, C. J. Snow, and S. J. Read. "The Redux of Cognitive Consistency Theories: Evidence Judgments by Constraint Satisfaction." *Journal of Personality and Social Psychology* 86 (2004): 814–837.

Singer, B. D. "Crazy Systems and Kafka Curcuits." *Social Policy*, Vol. 11(2) (1980): 46–54.

Sizi, F. *Dianoia Astronomica, Optica, Physica*. Venice, 1611. http:/pinakes.imss.fi.it:8080/pinakestext/home.jsf Vol. 3, Part I.

Skidelsky, E. *Ernst Cassirer: The Last Philosopher of Culture*. Princeton, NJ: Princeton University Press, 2008.

Smiley, J. "Nowhere Man. The Man Without Qualities by Robert Musil." *The Guardian*, 17 June, 2006.

Smith, A. D. *The Ethnic Origins of Nations*. Oxford: Blackwell, 1986.

Smith, P. "Marcel Proust as Successor and Precursor to Pierre Bourdieu: A Fragment." *Thesis Eleven*, Vol. 79 (2004): 105–111.

Soentgen, J. "Der Bau. Betrachtungen zu einer Metapher der Luhmannschen Systemtheorie." *Zeitschrift fur Soziologie*, Vol. 21(6) (1992): 456–466.

Sørensen, A. B. "A Model and a Metric for the Analysis of the Intragenerational Status Attainment Process." *American Journal of Sociology*, Vol. 85 (1979): 361–384.

Sørensen, A. B. "The Structural Basis of Social Inequality." *American Journal of Sociology*, Vol. 101 (1996): 1333–1365.

Sorokin, P. A. *Social and Cultural Dynamics*, Vol. I. New York: American Book Company, 1937.

Steiner, P. *Russian Formalism: A Metapoetics*. Ithaca: Cornell University Press, 1984.

Stewart, M. *The Courtier and the Heretic: Leibniz, Spinoza, and the Fate of God in the Modern World*. New York: Norton, 2006.

Stevens, S. S. "Measurement, Psychophysics, and Utility." In *Measurement: Definitions and Theories*. New York: Wiley, 1959.

Strauss, A. *Negotiations: Varieties, Contexts, Process, and Social Order*. San Francisco: Jossey-Bass, 1978.

Strindberg, A. *Miss Julie and Other Plays*. Oxford: Oxford University Press, 1998.

Swedberg, R. "Thinking and Sociology." *Journal of Classical Sociology*, 2010.

Swidler, A. "Culture in Action: Symbols and Strategies." *American Sociological Review*, Vol. 51 (1986): 273–286.

Swift, J. *Gulliver's Travels and Other Writings*. New York: Modern Library, 1958.

Taylor, C. "What Is Wrong with Negative Liberty?" In *The Idea of Freedom*, edited by A. Ryan. Oxford: Oxford University Press, 1979.

Thoits, P. A, and L. N. Hewitt. 2001. "Volunteer Work and Well-Being." *Journal of Health and Social Behavior*, Vol. 42(2): 115–131.

Tilly, C. 1998. *Durable Inequality*. Berkeley: University of California Press.

Toren, C. 1999. *Mind, Materiality and History: Explorations in Fijian Historiography*. London: Routledge.

Toth, M. A. "Figures of Thought: The Use of Diagrams in Teaching Sociology." *Teaching Sociology*, Vol. 7(4) (1980): 409–424.

Treiman, D.J., and K.B. Yip. "Educational and Occupational Attainment in 21 Countries." In *Cross-National Research in Sociology*, edited by M L. Kohn. Beverly Hills, CA: Sage, 1989.

Trivers, R. L. "The Evolution of Reciprocal Altruism." *The Quarterly Review of Biology*, Vol. 46(1) (1971): 35–57.

Turner, J., and B. Markovsky. "Micro and Macro Links." In *Encyclopedia of Sociology*, edited by G. S. Ritzer. Malden: Blackwell, 2006.

Turner, R. H. "Sponsored and Contest Mobility and the School System." *American Sociological Review*, Vol. 25 (1960): 855–867.

Turner, S. P. "Defining a Discipline: Sociology and Its Philosophical Problems from Its Classics to 1945." In *The Handbook of Philosophy of Anthropology and Sociology*, edited by S. Turner and M. Risjord. Amsterdam: Elsevier, 2007.

van den Berghe, P. L. "Why Most Sociologists Don't (and Won't) Think Evolutionarily." *Sociological Forum*, Vol. 5(2) (1990): 173–185.

Van Helden, A. "The Invention of the Telescope." *Transactions of the American Philosophical Society*, New Series, Vol. 67(4) (1977): 1–67.

Van Helden, A. "Galileo and the Telescope." In *Novità celesti e crisi del sapere*, edited by P. Galluzzi. Florence: Annali dell'Istituto e Museo di Storia della Scienza di Firenze, 1983.

Varela, F., E. Thompson, and E. Rosch. *The Embodied Mind: Cognitive Science and Human Experience*. Cambridge, MA: MIT Press, 1991.

Verene, D. P. "Cassirer's View of Myth and Symbol." *The Monist*, Vol. 50(4) (1966): 553–564.

Verene, D. P. P. "Foreword." In *Ernst Cassirer, The Logic of the Cultural Sciences*. New Haven, CT: Yale University Press, 2000.

Verene, D. P. "Cassirer's Metaphysics." In *The Symbolic Construction of Reality: the Legacy of Ernst Cassirer*, edited by J. A. Barash. Chicago: University of Chicago Press, 2008.

Vidmar, N., and M. Rokeach. "Archie Bunker's Bigotry: A Study in Selective Perception and Exposure." *Journal of Communication*, Vol. 24 (1974): 36–47.

Vives, J. L. *Opera Omnia*, edited by G. Mayans y Siscár. Valencia: Montfort. Reprinted London, UK: Gregg, 1964.

Vogl, J. *Kalkül und Leidenschaft: Poetik des ökonomischen Menschen*. München: Sequenzia, 2002.

Vonnegut, K., Jr. *Cat's Cradle*. New York: Holt, Rinehart and Winston, 1963.

Vonnegut, K., Jr. "Deer in the Works." In *Welcome to the Monkey House*. New York: Delacorte Press, 1968.

Vonnegut, K., Jr. *Slaughterhouse Five*. New York: Delacorte Press, 1969.

Vonnegut, K., Jr. *Slapstick*. New York: Delacorte Press, 1976.

Vonnegut, K., Jr. *A Man Without a Country*. New York: Seven Stories Press, 2005.

Wagner B. "Kafka's Office Writings: Historical Background and Institutional Setting." In *Franz Kafka: The Office Writings*, edited by S. Corngold, J. Greenberg, and B. Wagner. Princeton, NJ: Princeton University Press, 2009.

Walsh C. "The Newness of the Department Store: A View from the Eighteenth Century." In *Cathedrals of Consumption*, edited by G. Crossick and S. Jaumain. Aldershot: Ashgate.

Walster, E., E. Berscheid, and G. W. Walster. "New Directions in Equity Research." In *Equity Theory: Toward a General Theory of Social Interaction*, edited by L. Berkowitz and E. Walster. New York: Academic, 1976.

Weber, M. *The Protestant Ethic and the Spirit of Capitalism*. London: Unwin & Allen, 1930.

Weber, M. *The Methodology of the Social Sciences*. New York: The Free Press, 1949.

Weber, M. "Science as a Vocation." In *From Max Weber: Essays in Sociology*, edited by H. H. Gerth and C. Wright Mills. New York: Oxford University Press, 1946.

Weber, M. "Politics as a Vocation." In *From Max Weber: Essays in Sociology*, edited by H. H. Gerth and C. W. Mills. London: Kegan Paul, 1947.

Weber, M. *Gesammelte Aufsätze zur Religionssoziologie*, Vol. 1. Tübingen: Mohr-Siebeck, 1972.

Weber, M. *Economy and Society*. Berkeley and Los Angeles: University of California Press, 1978.

Weber, M. *Political Writings*. Cambridge: Cambridge University Press, 1994.

Weber, Marianne. *Max Weber. A Biography*. New Brunswick: Transaction Books, 1988.

Weeks, A. *The Paradox of the Employee*. Berne: Land, 1980.

Weinberg, G. *A World at Arms: A Global History of World War II*. New York: Cambridge University Press, 1993.

West, S. A., A. S. Griffin, and A. Gardner. "Social Semantics: Altruism, Cooperation, Mutualism, Strong Reciprocity, and Group Selection." *Journal of Evolutionary Biology*, Vol. 20(2) (2007): 415–432.

West, S. A., A. S. Griffin, and A. Gardner. "Social Semantics: How Useful Has Group Selection Been?" *Journal of Evolutionary Biology*, Vol. 21(1) (2008): 374–385.

Westbrook, R. B. *John Dewey and American Democracy*. Ithaca: Cornell University Press, 1993.

Western, B. "Bayesian Thinking about Macrosociology." *American Journal of Sociology*, Vol. 107(2) (2001): 353–378.

White, H. "Foucault Decoded: Notes from Underground." *History and Theory*, Vol. 12(1) (1973): 23–54.

White, H. C. "Can Mathematics Be Social? Flexible Representations for Interaction Process and Its Sociocultural Constructions." In *Sociological Forum*, Vol. 12(1) (1997): 53–71.

White, H. *Identity and Control*. Princeton, NJ: Princeton University Press, 2008.

Whitehead, A. N. *A Treatise on Universal Algebra*. Cambridge: Cambridge University Press, 1898.

Whitehead, A. N. *An Enquiry Concerning the Principles of Natural Knowledge*. Cambridge: Cambridge University Press, 1925.

Whitehead, A. N. *Religion in the Making*. New York: Macmillan, 1926a.

Whitehead, A. N. *Science and the Modern World*. New York: Macmillan, 1926b.

Whitehead, A. N. *Symbolism: Its Meaning and Effect*. New York: Macmillan, 1927.

Whitehead, A. N. *Adventures of Ideas*. New York: Macmillan, 1933.

Whitehead, A. N. *Process and Reality*. Corrected Edition. New York: Free Press, 1978.

Whitehead, A. N. and B. Russell. *Principia Mathematica*. Vols. I–III. Cambridge: Cambridge University Press, 1910–1913.

Whitford, Josh. "Pragmatism and the Untenable Dualism of Means and Ends: Why Rational Choice Theory Does Not Deserve Paradigmatic Privilege." *Theory and Society* 31 (2002): 325–363.

Wiley, N. "Early American Sociology and the Polish Peasant." *Sociological Theory*, Vol. 4(1) (1986): 20–40.

Wiley, N. *The Semiotic Self*. Chicago: University of Chicago Press, 1994.

Wiley, N. "Peirce and the Founding of American Sociology." *Journal of Classical Sociology*. Vol. 6(1) (2009): 23–50.

Willer, D. 1987. *Theory and the Experimental Investigation of Social Structures*. New York: Gordon and Breach.

Willer, D. (Ed.) *Network Exchange Theory*. Westport: Praeger, 1999.

Winship, Christopher. "Policy Analysis as Puzzle Solving," Volume 10 of the *Oxford Handbooks of Political Science*, edited by Robert E. Goodin. *Oxford Handbook of Public Policy*, edited by Michael Moran, Robert E. Goodin, and Martin Rein. Chapter 5, 2006.

Wittgenstein, L. *Philosophical Investigations*. Third Edition. New York: Macmillan, 1958.

Wolf, N. C. "Verkünder des Terrors, Propheten der Erlösung: Hans Sepp und Meingast." In *Terror und Erlösung. Robert Musil und der Gewaltdiskurs der Zwischenkriegszeit*, edited by H. Feger, H. G. Pott, and N. C. Wolf. Munich: Fink, 2009: 93–140.

Wood, N. *Cicero's Social and Political Thought*. Berkeley: University of California Press, 1988.

Yeats, W. B. "The Second Coming." *The Dial*, 1920.

Young, M. *The Rise of Meritocracy*. London: Thames and Hudson, 1958.

Yovel, Y. *Spinoza and Other Heretics: The Marrano of Reason*. Princeton, NJ: Princeton University Press, 1989a.

Yovel, Y. *Spinoza and Other Heretics: The Adventures of Immanence*. Princeton, NJ: Princeton University Press, 1989b.

Zola, E. *The Ladies' Paradise*. New York: Oxford University Press, 1998.

# Index

('n' indicates a note; 't' indicates a table)


*A Guess at the Riddle* (Peirce), 301
*A Modest Proposal* (Swift), 247, 249
*A Tale of the Tub* (Swift), 247
*Á la Recherche du Temps Perdu* (Proust), 55
Abacus, 202
Abbott, Andrew, 211
Abduction, 303
"Abstract sociality," 264
Abu Ghraib, 50
Accademia del Disegno, 202
Achebe, Chinua: on anomie, 14–15, 106, 107–108; 109; works of, 105
Achieved freedom, 264
Achievement, 26, 27
Action, 303, 305–306
Action theory: Dewey, 19, 291–295; Kant, 19; shortcomings, 295–296
Actual entity, 230, 234–235
Actual occasion, 234
Actual world, 230
Addison, Joseph, 247
Adorno, Theodore W.: on freedom, 268; Kafka's influence, 52; on mass consumption, 157
*Adventures of Ideas* (AI) (Whitehead), 232, 235
Advertising, 151, 152–153, 154
Aesthetics, 284–286
Afterworlds, 190–191
Agamben, Giorgio, 268
Agency: Dostoevsky, 161–162; Asimov, 224
*Aleph, The* (Borges), 208
Alexander, Jeffrey, 107
Algebraic geometry, 228
Alighieri, Dante: as ethnographer, 189–190, 194–195; structure of hell, 17, 191–194
"All in the Family," 246
Allende, Salvador, 74
Alter, 89, 90
Altruism: Cicero, 128; Darwin, 15, 134; defined, 135; explanations, 135–137
American Humanist Association, 217

American pragmatism: Dewey, 19, 294; Peirce, 20, 300, 301, 302; strengths, 289
American Sociological Association, 239
*Among French Peasants* (Strindberg), 88
*An American in Paris*, 240
Analytical interactionism, 321
Analytical realism, 229–230
Anamalism, 68, 69
*Ancien régime*, 171
Anglo-Irish causes, 246, 247, 248, 249
*Animal Farm* (Orwell): published work, 14, 65; theoretical model, 66–73
*Annales d'Histoire Economique et Sociale*, 144
Anne, Queen of England, 247
Anomie, 14–15, 105, 106–109
"Anschauung," 170, 171
*Anthills of the Savannah* (Achebe), 108, 109
Arbuthnot, John, 247
Archetypes, 170
Arendt, Hannah: on "banality of evil,"50; on Kafka, 49
Aristotle: and Cicero, 123; on marital inequality, 38; substantialism, 115
Arranged marriages, 181, 184–185
*Arrow of God* (Achebe), 107
Art, 239
As if" models, 8, 13
*As You Like It* (Shakespeare), 28
Asimov, Isaac: biography, 217; computational modeling, 18, 219–226; psychohistory, 217, 219–222, 225, 226n.3; robotics, 18, 217, 218–219, 226n.4
Asplund, Johan (sociologist), 264
Assens, Rafael Cansinos, 208
Assigned freedom, 264
Austria-Hungarian Empire, 75–81, 82–83
Austrian Workmen's Accident Insurance Law (1887), 47
Authoritarian rule, 71–72
Autobiography, 8

Bacon, Sir Francis, 308
Bakhtin, Mikhail: on laughter, 15–16; on Rabelais's work, 143, 145–147
Balzac, Honoré de, 48
"Banality of evil," 50
Barber, Elinor, 204
Barbera, Filippo, 17, 207–215
Barnes, Barry, 292
*Battle of the Books, The* (Swift), 247
Bauman, Zygmunt, 50, 52, 263
"Bearing witness," 105, 109n.2
Bearman, Peter, 17, 189–195
"Beasts of England," 70
Beauty, 284–286
Beckett, Samuel, 52
"Before the Law"(Kafka), 49, 50
Behavior, 136
Belief, 302–303, 304–305, 306
Benjamin, Walter, 52
Bentham, Jeremy, 312
Berger, Peter,
Berlin, Isaiah: biography, 263–264; defender of freedom, 19, 263; *Two Concepts of Liberty*, 264
Bertilsson, Margareta: on I Berlin, 19, 263–270; on C. S. Peirce, 301
Biography, 8
Birth control, 271
Bloch, Marc, 144
Blushing, 137
Bodily techniques, 318
Bonaparte, Napoleon, 169
Borges, Jorge Luis: biography, 207–208; on "senseless completeness," 17, 208, 209, 211, 213–213
Bourdieu, Pierre: and Cassirer, 115, 118, 120, 121, 122n.8; on habits, 289, 293, 294–295; and Kant, 286–289; and Levin, 118; "ontological complicity," 285; and Proust, 56, 57–58; theories of, 13, 19, 214
Bradbury, Ray, 217
*Brand* (Ibsen), 96, 98–99
Braudel, Fernand, 144
Breiger, Ronald, 19, 255–262
Brenzoni, Ottavio, 198, 199
Brevity, 28
*British Journal of Sociology*, Piaget, 315
Brod, Max, 48, 51
Buck, Pearl Sydenstricker: advise from, 10; biography, 179–181;

problematizing deviance, 181–185; and social change, 185–187; social worlds, 17; sociological relevance, 181, 187–188
Bureaucracy: in Kafka's work, 13, 49–52; and power, 278
Burke, Edmund, 123
Burke, Kenneth, 28
Byrne, David, 191

Calling, Ibsen, 96, 97
Camus, Albert, 52
Cantor, Georg, 117
Capitalism: and Cicero, 124; luxury goods, 152; triple revolutions, 171–172
Carley, Kathleen, 18, 217–226
Carlyle, Thomas, 208
Carnetti, Elias, 48
Carroll, Lewis, 287
Cassirer, Ernst: biography, 113–114; influence, 113, 121; sociological ideas, 15, 113–122
*Castle, The* (Kafka): bureaucracy, 45, 47, 48, 49, 50–51; citations, 52
*Cat's Cradle* (Vonnegut), 241–242
Causality, 317
Cavendish, William, 307
Cerulo, Karen A., 17, 179–188
Cervantes, Miguel, 48
Cesi, Federico, 201, 202, 204n.1
Charisma: in Ibsen's works, 96, 97–103; as ideational power, 14, 95–96;
"Charismatic authority," 95, 96
Charles I, King of England, 307
Charles II, King of England, 308
Cherkaoui, Mohammed, 20, 307–314
Chiaroscuro, 203
China, 186–187
Christianity, 180
Cicero, Marcus Tullius: on economic exchange, 127–129; ideas of, 15; on social relations, 124–127; on social roles, 129–132
Cigoli, Ludovico, 203
"Circle of recognition," 213
Cities, 37, 41
Civilization, 267
Civilized society, 232–233, 235
Clarity, 302–303
Clarke, Arthur C., 217
Class: in capitalism, 152; and *grand magasins*, 153–154; in *Miss Julie*, 92
Class conflict, 187
*Class Matters* (New York Times), 29n.3
"Classic social analysis," 2
Clinton, Gervase, 307
Coetzee, J. M., 52
Cohen, Hermann, 114, 121, 122n.6
Colbert Report, 246
Collective action theory, 68–69
"Collective epistemology," 319
"Collective representation," 317
Colonialism, 106
Columbia University: Cassirer, 114; Dewey, 290
Commodities, 152
*Commonwealth* (Cicero), 125, 127
Communicability, 286
"Communist Manifesto," 169
"Community of feeling," 125
Comparison, NUT goal, 43
Complementarity, 19, 255, 257, 258
Computational modeling, 18, 219–226
Comte, Auguste: "collective epistemology,"319; sociology profession, 301
"Concrete experience," 295
Concubinage, 181, 182–183, 185
"Conduct of the Allies, The," 248
Conflict, 88
Conformity: Orwell, 72; Proust, 62–63
Consumer desire, 154
Consumption: and department stores, 150–151, 152; Zola, 16, 149, 154
Containment level, 240
Context, 292–293
Contract: Hobbes, 313; Locke, 313–314;
Cooperation: costly, 133; in Darwin's work, 15; defined, 133; evolutionary origin, 133, 134, 140; and scorekeeping, 138–140, 139
Coquetry, 90
Corporations: public control, 277; Vonnegut, 238

Coser, Lewis: on Kafka, 45, 49; on removed observation, 181
"Creatio ex nihilo," 172–173
"Creative advance," 228
*Crime and Punishment* (Dostoevsky), 163
Critical events, 69
*Critique of Practical Reason*, (Kant), 281
*Critique of Pure Reason* (Kant), 281
"Crypto-Jewish" life, 256
Cultural analysis, 15, 113
Cultural capital, 14, 56, 57, 58, 59
Cultural sociology, 16
"Cultural trauma," 107

Da Vinci, Leonardo, 203
*Daemons* (Dostoevsky): group leadership, 166–168; individual motivation, 161–163; Russian social structures, 163–166; and sociological inquiry, 16, 160–161; title translations, 164
Dante. *See* Alighieri, Dante
Darwin, Charles: on altruistic behavior, 15; citation ranking, 11, 12t; evolutionary theory, 133–134; Goethe's influence, 170
Davis, Natalie Zemon, 146
Dawkins, Richard, 125
*De Cive* (Hobbes), 309
*De Corpore, on the Body* (Hobbes), 309
*De Divina Proportione* (Pacioli), 203
*De Homine, On Man* (Hobbes), 309
*De Prospectiva Pingendi* (Piero della Francesca), 202
De Quincey, Thomas, 208
Deductive methodology, 309
*Deer in the Works* (Vonnegut), 238
Definitional bridge, 240
Degradation work, 266
Del Monte, Guidobaldo, 203
Delayed reciprocity, 138–139
Department stores, 150–153
*Der Beamte* (A. Weber), 50
Derrida, Jacques, 52
Descartes, René: dualist ideas, 257; and Hobbes, 309
Desire, 312
"Deus ex machina," 172–173
*Deus sive natura*, 256, 257–259
Dewey Decimal System, 217
Dewey, John: action theory, 19, 289, 291–294; biography, 290–291; citation ranking, 11, 12t; critiques, 294–295; theoretical pluralism, 20, 289–290; theory's shortcomings, 295–296
*Dialogue Concerning the Two Chief Systems of the World - Ptolemaic and Copernican* (Galileo), 200
*Dialogues* (Plato), 35–37
*Dianoia Astronomica, Optica, Physica* (Sizi), 199–200
"Dichterfürst," 169
Dictatorship: efforts to continue, 72–73; opposition to, 72; revolutionary, 70–71
"Dictatorship of the proletariat," 67–68
Differentiation, 171
Dilthey, Wilhelm, 114
*Discourses and Mathematical Demonstrations Concerning Two New Sciences* (Galileo), 201
Discovery, 4
*Dissecting the Social* (Hedström), 6–7
Distinct idea, 302
Distributive justice, 13
*Divine Comedy* (Dante), 190
*Division of Labor* (Durkheim), 171
Documentation, 150
Domination: interaction forms, 88; in *Miss Julie*, 90, 91
*Dominatum maritorum*, 39–40
Dostoevsky, Fyodor: Berlin's reference, 268; biography, 159; citation ranking, 11, 12t; as cultural theorist, 160–168; on political violence, 16
Doubt, 302, 304, 305, 306
*Dragon Seed* (Buck): arranged marriage, 184; social change, 186–187
Dramaturgy, 28
*Drapier's Letters, The* (Swift), 247, 248
Dreyfus Affair: Proust's view, 56; Zola's view, 149
Dualism: Descartes, 257; sociological explanation, 317

Durkheim, Emile: on anomie, 105–106, 108, 109, 312; on economic exchange, 127, 129; as founding father, 55, 62; and Hobbes, 310; and Kant, 279–280, 281–282, 283, 284; on knowledge, 319; moral order, 127; ritual interaction theory, 236; social bonds, 14–15; society, 320–321; sociological explanation, 316, 317; and Spinoza, 19, 255, 260–261; "Vergesellschaftung," 171
Dyad: in *Miss Julie*, 91, 92–93; as social form, 88, 91
"Easter" 1933, 180

Economic exchange, 127–129
Economic power, 276–277
Edling, Christofer, 14, 85–93
Education, 277
Ego, 89, 90
Ehrenpreis, Irwin, 246
*Eichmann in Jerusalem* (Arendt), 50
Einstein, Albert, 117, 118, 122n.4, 229
"Elective affinity," 50
"Electromagnetic Society," 231
*Elementary Forms of the Religious Life* (Durkheim), 281–282
*Elements of Law, Natural and Public* (Hobbes), 309–310
*Elements, The* (Euclidides), 308–309
Elias, Norbert, 81–82
Eliot, T. S., 48, 51
Elster, Jon, 291
Embarrassment, 137–138
*Embarrassment and Social Organization* (Goffman), 137
Emergence, 321, 322
Emigration, 37
*Emperor and Galilean* (Ibsen), 96, 99–100
"Emperor of Peace," 77
Empirical evidence, 200
Endowment: and achievement, 26; formulations, 29n.2; in Shakespeare's work, 24, 26
Enduring objects, 232
Engels, Frederick, 169
Engelstad, Fredrik, 14
"Enigma of the universe," 208
Enlightenment: Cicero's influence, 15, 123–124; and the *philosophes*, 280; philosophy, 119
Epicureanism, 123, 125, 126, 128
Equality: in Buck's work, 180; in Hobbes's work, 311; and Platonic ideas, 13, 33, 38
Erasmus, Desiderius, 141
Erikson, Emily, 15–16, 141–147
"Eternal object," 231
"Ethic of self," 270
Ethics: Berlin, 266, 268, Cicero, 126
*Ethics* (Spinoza), 257, 310
Ethnocentrism, 187
Ethnography, 17, 189
Event, 228
Event-history analysis, 211
Evolution: costly cooperation, 133; Darwin's theory, 133–134
*Examiner, The*, 247
"Excessive recognition," 213
Exchange, 88
"Exchange of services," 127
Existential ethics, Berlin, 266, 268
Existentialism, 48, 52
Experimentation, 291–292, 293–295
"Expert interviews," 150
*Expressions of the Emotions in Man and Animals* (Darwin), 137
External shock, 214
Eyerman, Ron, 107

Fallibilism, 289
Family, 125
"Fantasy novels," 48
Fararo, Thomas, 18, 227–236
"Farbenlehre," 170
Fate, 194
Father Mersenne circle, 307, 308, 309, 310
*Faust* (Goethe): genealogy, 172; modernity of, 16, 171, 172–173; self-creation/social creation, 173–174; as "Übermensch" 173
*Faust II* (Goethe), career building, 174–176

Febvre, Lucian: historian, 144; on laughter, 15–16; on Rabelais's work, 143, 144–145, 146, 147
Federal Republic of Germany, 74
Female infanticide, 181, 183, 185
Feminism, 180
Fernandez, Macedonio, 208
*Ficciones* (Borges), 208, 209–210
"Field space," 118
Figures of speech, 6–7
"Figures of thought," 7
"Final interpretation," 227, 235
Fine, Gary Alan, 18, 245–252
"Fixation of Belief, The" (Peirce), 302
Flam, Helena, 16, 149–157
Flaubert, Gustave, 52
Flirtation, 89–90
"Fortune's fool," 28
Foucault, Michel: on freedom, 268; knowledge/power link, 270; logical forms, 115, 122n.2; Panopticon, 265
*Foundation* series (Asimov): and computational model, 221; Hugo Award, 218; and individualism, 224–225; landmark series, 217; and prime radiant, 222; and psychohistory, 219, 225
Framing, 248–250
Francesca, Piero della, 202–203
Francis Ferdinand, Archduke of Austria, 81
Francis-Joseph, Emperor of Austria, 77
Franco, Francisco, 74
Frank, Robert, 56
Frankl, Viktor, 165
Franzosi, Roberto, 17, 197–205
"Free rider" problem, 68–69
"Free space," 265, 266
Freedom: Adorno, 268; assigned, 264; Berlin, 19, 263, 267–268; Foucault, 268; and Liberalism, 266, 268–269, 270, negative, 19, 264–269; positive, 19, 264, 269, 270; Rousseau, 263
Freud, Sigmund: fantasy novels, 48; and Kafka, 52
Friends, 125, 128
*Fröken Julie*, 85
Fukayama, Francis, 52
"Fürstenknecht" (prince's servant), 169

Galilei, Galileo: Cassirer's view, 116; experiential science legacy, 200; and Hobbes, 309, 310; mathematical knowledge, 203; microscopes, 201–202; and scientific innovation, 17, 201, 202–204; telescopes, 197–198, 204n.1
Galileo. *See* Galilei, Galileo
Gans, Herbert, 50
*Gargantua* (Rabelais), 15, 142, 143, 144–147
Gay, John, 247
*Gedankenbilder*, 7
"Gedankenexperimente" (thought experiments), 311
Gellner, E.: ethnic nationalism, 82; reconstructive histories, 79
Gender: bias: 187; consumer desire, 154–156; *in Miss Julie*, 92; in *Taming of the Shrew*, 25; Platonic ideas, 13, 39–40
*Genealogy of Morals* (Nietzsche), 96
"Generative structuralism," 316
Geocentrism, 198
Geographic unity, 231–232
Germany, 76
*Germinal* (Zola), 149
Gershwin, George, 240
Giddens, Anthony, 131
Giddings, Franklin, 301
Gill, Christopher, 130
Ginzburg, Carlo, 146
Glorious Revolution, 247
Göbbels, Joseph, 72
Goethe, Johann Wolfgang von: citation ranking, 11, 12t; "kairos" philosophy,176; on modernity, 16, 171, 172–175; significance, 169–170; sociological relevance, 171
"Goethe-Institut," 169
Goffman, Erving: "circle of recognition," 213; on context, 289; on degradation work, 266; on dramaturgy, 28, 85; on facial

expressions, 137; and "free space,"265; ritual interaction theory, 236; "rule-following," 265–266; on situational cues, 293; on social roles, 129; "strategic interaction," 89
Goldthorpe, John, 211
*Good Earth, The* (Buck): concubinage, 182; female infanticide, 183–184; social change, 185–186
*Gorgias* (Plato), 33
*Grand magasins* (department stores), architecture, 150–151; and class, 153–154, 156–157; consumption, 149–153; gender discourses, 154–156
*Grapes of Wrath, The* (Steinbeck), 239–240
"Graph theory," 118
*Great and Inestimable Chronicles of the Great and Enormous Giant Gargantua* (Rabelais), 145
"Great chain of being," 170
Great thinkers: citation ranking, 10, 11, 12t; term, 5–6
Greatness elements, 24–28
"Greatness generating equation," 24, 25, 28, 29n.1
Griswold, Wendy, 14, 105–110
Gross, Neil, 296
*Groundwork for the Metaphysics of Morals* (Kant), 281
Group leadership, 166–168
Group selection, 136, 137
*Gulliver's Travels* (Swift), 247, 249, 250

Habermas, Jürgen, 247
Habit formation, 293–294
Habitus, 13, 19, 286–287
Hacking, 289
Hall, G. S., 290
*Hamlet* (Shakespeare): achievement, 27; brevity, 28; endowments, 26; "mole of nature," 25
Happiness: NUT goal, 43; Plato, 31
*Happy Prince, The* (Wilde), 207
Hapsburg Empire, 75–81, 82–83
Harley, Robert, 247
Harriot, Thomas: early telescope, 198; telescopic observations, 17, 197, 202
Harvard University: Benjamin Peirce, 299; Charles Sanders Peirce, 300
Hatfield principle, 33
Heaven: Dante's worlds, 190–191; morally exceptional individuals, 194
Hedonism, 126
Heer, Friedrich, 81
Heine, Heinrich, 208
Heinlein, Robert, 217
Hell: Dante's worlds, 190–191; morally exceptional individuals, 194; structure of, 191–194
Herbert, Frank, 217
Herzen, Alexander, 268
Historical materialism, 68–69
History of culture, 141, 143
History of science, 116
Hitler, Adolf, 71
*HMS Beagle*, 134
Hobbes, Thomas: biography, 307–308; citation ranking, 11, 12t; power, 273, 312–314; social order, 20, 311–312
Hobsbawm, Eric: ethnic nationalism, 82; reconstructive histories, 79
"Hodological space," 118
Homans, George, 18, 229, 230
"Homo sacer," 266
Homosexuality, 56
Horkheimer, Max, 157
Horky, Martin, 199, 204
*House of Asterion, The* (Borges), 212–213
"How to Make Our Ideas Clear" (Peirce), 302, 303
*How We Think* (Dewey), 306
Hugo Award, 218
Hull House, 290
Human fellowship, 125
*Human Group, The* (Homans), 230
Human nature, 312
Human needs, 160
Hume, David: aesthetic judgements, 284; and Cicero, 123
Huygens, Christian, 257
Hypothesis: "as if" models, 8; discovery context, 4
Hypothetico-deductive methodology, 308–309, 310–311

*I, Robot* (Asimov), 219, 223
Ibsen, Henrik: on charisma, 14, 96, 97–103; citation ranking, 11, 12t; critique of, 8–9
Icon sign, 304
Idea types, 281
Identity, 43
*Identity and Control* (White), 224
*Il Saggiatore* (Galileo), 197–198, 200, 201
Imagination, 2–3
*Imperial Woman* (Buck), 182
*In the Penal Colony*, (Kafka), 48, 50, 52
Index sign, 304
Indian Imperial Police, 65
Indirect reciprocity, 136
"Individual and Collective Representation,"320–321
Individualism: Asimov, 224; triple revolutions, 171–172
Individualization, 171
Individuals, power, 273
*Inductive Sociology* (Giddings), 301
Inequality: historical, 44n.2; measurements, 32; parallel worlds, 32; Platonic ideas, 13, 34, 39; in Shakespeare's work, 28; and sociological inquiry, 23
Inequality equation, 24, 25, 27, 29n.1
Inferences, 4
Inferno Crisis, 87
Information, 208–210
"Infrastructure," 317
"Inside the skin," 213
Institutional logic, 15, 113
Instrumental power, 312
Interaction, 320
Interest, 311
Intersubjectivity, 287
*Invitation to Sociology* (Berger), 85
Iron cage of bureaucracy, 13, 45, 49–52
Iron cage of rationalization, 14, 95
Ivanov, I. I., 163
"J'accuse," 149

James, William, 306
Jane Addams, 290
Jasso, Guillermina, on Plato, 13, 31–44
Jews: expulsion of, 256; in Proust's work, 56
Joas, Hans, 289
*John Gabriel Borkman* (Ibsen), 96, 101–102
Johns Hopkins University, 290
*Journal of Philosophy, The*, 291
Joyce, James: fantasy novels, 48; and Kafka, 52; and Mansil, 75
Judgement, 19, 280
*Judgement, The* (Kafka), 48
*Jugend*,, 260
Just inequality, 34
Just maximum, 34
Just minimum, 34
Just wage, 34
Justice: Cicero, 127; Platonic ideas, 33–34
Justification, 4
"Kafka circuits," 50

Kafka, Franz: biography, 46–48; on bureaucracy, 13, 45, 47, 49–51; published works, 48; *Sociological Abstracts* citations, 46; insights, 48–49, 51–52
"Kairos," 176
"Kakania," 76, 79–81
Kant, Immanuel: aesthetic judgements, 284–286; citation ranking, 11, 12t; communicability, 286; judgements, 283–284; practical reason, 282–283; pure reason, 281–282; significance, 279; structure of mind, 305; trinity of faculties, 280–281
Katz, Jack, 194
Keltner, Dacher, 137–138
Kepler, Johann, 199, 203
Kierkegaard, Søren, 52
*King Lear* (Shakespeare), 27
Kinship, 135
Kitchener, Richard, 315–316
Knowledge: Durkheim, 319; and information, 208, 209–210; Piaget, 316; 319
Königgrätz, Battle of, 77
Kruglanski, Arie, 162
Kuzmics, Helmut, 14, 75–83

*Ladies' Paradise, The* (Zola), 16, 149, 150, 152, 157
Langer, Suzanne, 120–121
Language: in Austria-Hungarian Empire, 78–79; Cassirer, 120
Laughter, 15–16, 146
Law, Kafka, 49–52
*Laws* (Plato): on friendship, 38; on inequality, 32, 33; subdivision of cities, 37; urban planning, 41
Leibniz, Gottfried Wilhelm, 257
*Lese-und Redehalle der Deutschen Studenten*, 46
*Leviathan* (Hobbes), 308, 309, 310, 311, 312
Levy-Bruhl, Lucien, 319
Lewin, Kurt, 117–118, 121, 122n.5
Lexicographic preferences, 126
*Libellus de Quinque Corporibus Regularibus* (Piero della Francesca), 202
Liberalism: and freedom , 266, 268–269, 270; sociological critique, 263
*Life of a Great Sinner, The* (Dostoevsky), 161
Limbo, 191–192
Lindgren, Astrid, 88
Lipperhey, Hans, 204n.1
Literature: Buck's place, 180–181; as qualitative simulation, 8, 13; and sociological texts, 1–2
*Lives of the Artists* (Piero della Francesca), 202
"Living systems," 232
Lizardo, Omar, 20, 315–322
Locke, John: and Borges, 209–210; and Cicero, 123
Logics, 116–117
Long, A. A., 130
Lorentz, Edward, 117
Louis XIV, King of France, 308
Loury, Glenn, 293
Love, 274
Lower, William 198
Loyalty, 28
Lukacs, Georg, 52
Lyotard, Jean-François: and Kafka, 52; on violence, 50
Macaulay, Thomas, 250–251
"Machine, the," 152
*Macro-Micro Linkages in Sociology* (Huber), 239
Macrojustice, 33, 34
*Magic Mountain* (Mann), 82
"Magic realism:" Borges, 214–215; as precursor, 48
Magini, Antonio, 199
Man Booker International Prize, 105
*Man of the People*, A (Achebe), 108
*Man Without Qualities, The* (Musil), 14, 75, 83n.1
Mann, Thomas: and Musil, 75, 82; Protestantism thesis, 48
Marburg School of Neo-Kantianism, 114, 122n.6
"Marginal man," 46
Marital inequality, 38–39, 39t, 44n.3
Markovsky, Barry, 18, 237–244
Marranos, 256
Marriage: Cicero, 125; in *King Lear*, 27; and Platonic ideas, 37–39
Martin, John Levi, 19, 279–288
Marx, Karl: "Communist Manifesto," 169; on economic power, 274–275; fetishism of commodities, 152; on inequality, 23; on power, 19; on praxis, 318; on public ownership; 277; and Simmel, 259, 262n.2
Marxism, 317–318
Masks, 129
Mathematics: Galileo, 201; Renaissance Florence, 202–203; Whitehead, 227–228
Matthew effect, 26
Mauss, Marcel: bodily techniques, 318; "collective epistemology," 319; economic exchange, 129; moral individualism, 130
Maxwell, James Clerk, 229
Mayer, Robert, 116
McCall, George, 294
Mead, George Herbert: and Dewey, 290, 294; reciprocal modification, 320; social psychology, 129
"Means of reasoning," 201
*Mediterranean* (Braudel), 144

Mendeleyev, Dimitri, 117
*Meno* (Plato), 39
*Merchant of Venice* (Shakespeare), 25
Merton, Robert K.: bureaucratic rules, 45; "circle of recognition," 213; on serendipity, 204
Meta-sociology: brief descriptions, 16–18; new insights, 3, 9, 10
"Metamorphosis," 170
Metaphors, 6–7
*Metaphysical Meditations* (Descartes), 309
Methodology: choices, 290; deductive, 309; empirical observations, 4; hypothetic deductive, 308–311; sociological debates, 1; Zola, 149–150
*Micro-Macro Link, The* (Alexander et al.), 239
Microjustice, 33–34
Microscopes, 201–202
Milgrom, Eva Meyersson, 16, 159–168
Mill, John Stuart: and Berlin, 266, 267–268; education of, 300; and C. S. Peirce, 301
Miller, James G., 232
Mills, C. Wright: and Peirce, 301; sociological imagination, 2, 181
Mind: 305
*Miss Julie* (Strindberg), drama, 14, 85–87, 88, 93n.1; social forms, 88–92
"Models of man," 8
*Modern Corporation and Private Property, The* (Berle/Means), 271–272
Modernism, 86
Modernity: in *Faust*, 172–176; and Goethe, 16, 171, 172, 176; moral crisis, 75; triple revolutions, 171–172
Mohr, John, on Cassirer, 15, 113–122
"Mole of nature," 25
*Molestias nuptiarum*, 40
Mommsen, Theodor, 123
Monism, 257–258
"Monster, the," 152, 155
Montesquieu, Baron de, 123
Moon observations, 197–198
Moral action, 282–283
Moral order, 126, 127, 128
Morris, G. S., 290
Mozart, Wolfgang Amadeus, 26
"Mule, The," 224, 225, 226
Muller, Christopher, 19, 289–297
Müller, Hans-Peter, 16, 169–178
"Multitude of motives," 89, 92
Music, 120
Musil, Robert: on Austrian-Hungarian Empire, 76–81, 82–83; and Kafka, 52; on patriotic emotions, 82; on state-formation, 81–82
*Myth of the State, The* (Cassirer), 122n.7

Naked power, 276
Nanking, 187
*Nation, The*, 301
Nation-state: emotional attachment, 76–77; triple revolutions, 171–172
Nationalism: attachments, 14, 76–77, 80; Musil's analysis, 82; reconstructive histories, 79
"Nationalities," Musil, 79, 80
Natural law: Cicero, 124, 126; Hobbes, 312
Natural power, 312
Natural rights, 312
Natural selection: Darwin, 134; genetic inheritance, 135
Naturalism, 85
Nature: Goethe, 170; Hobbes, 313
Nechaev, Sergei, 163
Negative assortative mating, 38–39, 39t, 44n.3
Negative freedom: Berlin, 19, 264–265, 267, 268–269; sociological consequences, 265–266
*New Republic, The*, 291
New unified theory (NUT), 43–44
Newton, Isaac, 170
Nexus, 230, 231
*Nicomachean Ethics* (Aristotle), 38
Nielsen, Donald, 260, 261
Nietzsche, Friedrich: and Borges, 208; and Dostoevsky, 159; and Ibsen, 96; sociological foundations, 62 and Spinoza, 255; and M. Weber, 96

"Nihilism," 159, 160, 166
*Nineteen Eighty-Four* (Orwell), 65
*No Longer at Ease* (Achebe), 106, 107, 108
Nobel Prize for Literature: Buck, 179; Soyinka, 105
Non-interference, 264–266
Non-participatory observation, 150
"Novel-pamphlet," 161, 163, 166
Numerical equality, 13, 32, 33

Objective relations, 115
Observations: empirical, 4; non-participatory, 150; removed, 181; systematic, 4; telescopic, 197–198, 199
*On Duties* (Cicero): economic exchange, 128; social relations. 123–127; social roles, 129–132
*On Friendship* (Cicero), 125, 127, 128
*On Government* (Cicero), 126, 127
*On Moral Ends* (Cicero): social relations, 124–125, 126, 128; social roles, 129
"On Rigor in Science,"(Borges), 210
*On the Law* (Cicero), 125, 126
*On the Origin of Species* (Darwin), 134
Ono, Hiroshi, 13, 23–29
"Ontological complicity," 285
Operation, 320
Opp, Karl-Dieter, 14, 65–74
Oppression, 67
Orwell, George: biography, 65–66; and Swift, 251; revolutionary stages, 14, 66–74
*Othello* (Shakespeare), 25
Oxford University: Cassirer, 114; Hobbes, 307; I. Berlin, 264

Pacioli, Luca, 203
Palestine, 271
Panaetius, 124, 129
Panofsky, Erwin, 120, 203
*Pantagruel* (Rabelais), 15, 142–143, 144–147
"Parallel Campaign," 76, 77, 80–81, 82
Pareto, Vilfredo, 318
Park, Robert, 46
Parsons, Talcott: modern parliamentarianism, 79; social values, 235; societal pattern maintenance, 232; and Whitehead, 18, 229
*Partido Obrero de Unificación* (POUM), 65
*Pavillion of Women* (Buck), 182–183
Peirce, Benjamin, 299–200
Peirce, Charles Sanders: analysis of thinking, 20, 301–304; biography, 299–300; and pragmatism, 20, 300, 301, 302, 303; semiotics, 20, 300, 303–304, 305
*Peloponnesian War, The* (Thucydides), 308
Person, 129
*Persona (personae)*, 129–132
Personality: NUT, 43–44; Plato's five types, 43, 44
Perspective, 202, 203
Pevear, Richard, 164
"Philosophical anarchist," 207
*Philosophy of Money, The* (Simmel), 259
"Philosophy of organism, the," 229
*Philosophy of Symbolic Forms, The* (Cassirer), 114, 119–120, 122n.8
Piaget, Jean: citation ranking, 11, 12t, 20; individual/society, 320–321; location of the social, 318–320; social ontology, 20, 316; sociological explanation, 316–318
Pinochet, Augusto, 74
Plato: ideas, 13, 31–44; influence of, 31, 123; and Whitehead, 234–235
Plato's Paradox: inequality, 39; Platonic love, 41
Plato's ratio: inequality, 32, 33, 34–37, 35t, 36t; status distribution, 41–43, 42t
Platonism,, 123
Pneumatology, 301
Poe, Edgar Allan, 209
Pohl, Frederick, 217
Political commonwealth, 125
Political entrepreneur, 67
Political power, 274–275, 276–277
Political satire, 18

Political violence: Berlin, 263–264; Dostoevsky, 16, 162, 166, 167–168
*Politics as Vocation* (M. Weber), 95
*Politikon*, 124–125
Pope, Alexander, 247
Popper, Karl Raimund, 31
Portugal, 256
Positive assortative mating, 38
Positive freedom, 19, 264, 269, 270
Positronics, 18, 217, 226n.2
Poverty, 180
Power: Hobbes, 273, 312–314; Ibsen, 96; Kafka, 47–48; NUT goal, 43
*Power* (Russell), 19, 271–278
*Practical Reason* (Kant), 282
Practical reasoning, 280–281, 282–283
*Practice and Reason* (Bourdieu), 115
Pragmatism: defined, 303; definitional deficit, 295; Dewey, 19, 294; Peirce, 20, 300, 301, 302, 305; strengths, 289
Prague Circle, 46–47
Praxis, 318
*Presentation of Self in Everyday Life* (Goffman), 129
*Pretenders, The* (Ibsen), 96, 97–98
Prime radiant, 222
Princip, Gavrilo, 81
*Principia Mathematica* (Russell/Whitehead), 271
*Principles of Natural Knowledge* (Whitehead), 228
Private property, 124, 127
*Problem of Unbelief in the Sixteenth Century, The* (Febvre), 144
*Process and Reality* (*P&R*) (Whitehead), 229, 230, 231–232, 234, 235
*Process Studies* journal: *P&R*, 229; Whitehead studies, 235
"Process theology," 235
"Prodigious birth," 26
*Prolegomena to an Future Metaphysics that Will be Able to Present Itself as a Science* (Kant), 281
Property rights, 275
Proportional equality, 13, 33
Propositional bridge, 240
Propositions, 240–241
Prosocial behavior, 133, 134
*Prosopon*, 129
Prostitution, 156
"Protestant Ethic," 173
*Protestant Ethic and the Spirit of Capitalism* (M. Weber), 95
Protestantism thesis, 48
Proust, Marcel: biography, 52; citations of, 12t, 56; on conformity, 62–63; hereditary status groups, 57 and Musil,75; sociological ideas, 13–14, 55; status distinctions, 56–62
Proximate cause, 136, 138
Prussia, 76, 77
Psychohistory, 18, 217, 219–222, 225, 226n.3
Public discourse: literary role, 245, 251; in public sphere, 247
"Public goods," 125–126
"Public Poet," 208
Public sphere, 247
"Public woman," 156
Public writers, 245
Pulitzer Prize, 179
Purgatory, 190–191
Purposiveness, 285–286

Qualitative simulation: defined, 7–8; and literature, 13

Rabelais, François: biography, 141–142; contextual perception, 15–16; significance of, 15–16, 141
Race, 25
Racial inequality, 180, 187
Ratified fact, 139
Rational choice, 124, 174
Rationality: Hobbes, 311; role of, 124
Realism, 48
"Realizing philosophy," 305
Reciprocal modification, 320
Reciprocity: Cicero, 128; and selfish genes, 135–136
*Red Room, The* (Strindberg), 88
Reference group,168n.1
Reflexive power, 284
Refraction theory, 201
Regularity, 285
Reich, Wendelin, 15, 133–140

Relationalism, 113, 115–118, 121
Religion: in *Merchant of Venice*, 25; and priestly power, 276; and ritual, 236; Simmel, 258, 259; Spinoza, 256
*Religion in the Making* (Whitehead), 236
*Remembrance of Things Past* (Proust), 13–14, 55, 56–63
*Report to an Academy*, A (Kafka), 48
*Republic* (Plato), 40
Revolutions: ideology, 67; stages, 14, 73; starting stage, 66–68
Ricci, Ostilio, 203
Richardson, Samuel, 250–251
Ricoeur, Paul, 119, 120
Ritual, 236
Robotics, 18, 217, 218–219, 226n.4
Roddenberry, Gene, 219
Roffeni, Antonio, 199
Romanticism, 80–81
*Romeo and Juliet* (Shakespeare): family feuds, 26; "fortune's fool," 28
"Room of one's own," 266
*Rosmersholm* (Ibsen), 96, 100–101
Rousseau, Jean-Jacques: and Cicero, 123; shackles of freedom, 263; social contract, 313
Ruane, Janet M., 17, 179–188
Rudolph Macon College, 180
*Rules, The* (Durkheim), 282, 316
*Runaround* (Asimov), 218
Rushdie, Salman, 52
Russell, Bertrand Arthur William: activities, 271; on power, 19, 271, 273–278; qualifications, 272–273
Russell, Frank, 272
Russia: Berlin's observations, 263–264; Dostoevsky's portrait, 159–161, 163;
Russian Revolution, 66, 73
Rydgren, Jens, on Proust, 13–14, 55–63

"Sacred individual," 19
Sadowa, Battle of, 77
Said, Edward, 246, 251
Saint-Simon, Claude de, 174–175, 319
Sarton, George, on invention, 204
Sartre, Jean-Paul: and Kafka, 52; social/non-social action, 265–266
Satire: author's stance, 246, 248–249; Swift's works, 247, 248, 250–251
Saussure, Ferdinand de, 119, 120
Savelsberg, Joachim, 13, 45–53
Scapegoats, 71–72
Schopenhauer, Arthur, 208
Science: Cassirer's ideas, 15; experiential, 200; sociological discipline, 4 and sociological texts, 1–2
*Science and the Modern World* (SMW) (Whitehead), 229, 230–231
Science fiction: major contributors, 217; Swift, 250
Scientific innovation, Galileo, 17, 201, 202–203; lessons, 203–204
Scientific materialism, 230–231, 235
Scriblerus club, 247
*Second Foundation* (Asimov), 221
*Second treatise of government* (Locke), 313–314
Self: dual nature, 269–270; in *Faust*, 172; Proust/Bourdieu, 57–58; reflexive modernity, 131
"Self-fulfilling prophecy,"48
Self-interest: Cicero, 126–127; role of, 124
"Self-organized," 11
"Selfish altruism," 136
Selfish genes, altruism, 135–136; and embarrassment, 137–138; as prosocial behavior, 134–137
Semiotics, 20, 300, 303–304, 305
"Senseless completeness," 17, 208, 209, 211, 213–213
*Serving Maid's Son, The* (Strindberg), 87
Shakespeare, William: citation ranking, 11, 12t; influence, 23–24; in sociology texts, 1; on social stratification, 13, 24–28
Shame, 137
"Shopping list," 198
*Short Tract on First Principles* (Hobbes), 309
*Sidereus Nuncius* (Starry Messenger) (Galileo), 197–198, 199, 201, 203
Signs, 20, 304

Simmel, Georg: on agency, 162; and Cassirer, 113–114, 121; on Cohen's work, 114; on coquetry, 90; fetishism of commodities, 152; forms of social interactions, 88, 89, 91; founding fathers, 55, 62; influence of, 14; and Spinoza 19, 255, 258–256, 261; "stranger," 46; "Vergesellschaftung," 171
Simulations, 8
Singularity, 19, 255
Sizi, Francesco, 199–200
*Slapstick* (Vonnegut), 238
*Slaughterhouse Five* (Vonnegut), 242–243
Slavery, 181, 183, 185
Smith, A. D., 79
Smith, Philip, 57
Social behavior, 224
Social capital: Cicero, 129; Proust, 14, 56, 57, 58, 60, 61
Social codes, 59
Social contract, 25
*Social Contract* (Rousseau), 313
Social distinction theory, 13
Social dynamics, 274, 275
"Social environment," 231
Social forms, 88
Social mobility: assumptions, 26–27, 29n.4; *Class Matters*, 29n.3; Shakespeare, 23
Social networks: Asimov, 222; Roman republic, 128
Social norms, 124
Social ontology, 20, 316, 320
Social order: Hobbes, 20, 311–312; Whitehead, 230, 231
Social organization, 20
Social power, 273–275
Social reality, 5
"Social responsivity," 264
Social roles, 129, 130–132
Social science: computational models, 222–226; power concept, 274
Social Science Citation Index (SSCI): general list, 11, 12t, 46, 56; Kafka, 12t, 46; Piaget, 12t, 20; Proust, 12t, 56
Social sciences, 209
Social scorekeeping, 139–140
Social stratification, 13, 24–28
Social structures: Cicero, 131; Dostoevsky, 160
Social worlds, 17
Sociality, 124–126
Socially ratified fact, 139–140
Society: Faust II, 174–176; Plato's five types, 43; Whitehead, 230, 231
Sociobehavioral forces, 43–44
*Sociological Abstracts*, 46, 51–52
Sociological concepts: brief descriptions, 15–16; new insights, 3, 9, 10; terms, 239
Sociological explanation, 316–317
Sociological foundations: brief descriptions, 18–20; new insights, 3, 9, 10
Sociological illustrations: brief descriptions, 13–15; new insights, 3, 9–10; value of, 11, 13
Sociological imagination: Buck's promotion, 181; classic task, 2; new sources, 3
Sociological inquiry, 160
Sociological insights: Asimov, 217, 219; macro/micro links, 238–240; outside discipline, 4, 5–6, 9
Sociological theory: Homans, 230; Parsons, 229–230
Sociology: central issues, 124; characteristics, 4; contextualized analysis, 211–212;defined, 3–4; descriptive analysis, 211; evolution of society, 301; founding fathers, 55; and Kant, 279–280, 282–283, 287; methodological choice, 290; as multilevel analysis, 18, 239, 243–244; new insights, 3; and "non-sociological" originators, 1–2, 9; and Peirce, 301–302, 304–306; and Piaget, 315–316; process-oriented, 18; as the science of non-freedom, 263; and social reality, 5; social roles, 129; social stratification, 23
Socrates: 31, 39–40
Sohm, Rudolf, 96

*Soldaten-Zeitung*, Musil, 82
Sombart, Werner, 152
Sophists, 125
Sorokin, Pitirim, 316, 317
Sovereign power, 312–314
Soviet Union, 73
Soyinka, Wole, 105
Spain: expulsion of Jews, 256; transition to democracy, 74
Spanish Civil War, 65
Spencer, Herbert, 232, 301
Spinozə, Baruch: biography, 256–257; influence, 19; philosophical ideas, 257–261
St. Antoninus, 34
St. Jerome, 40–41
St. Paul, 40
*Stahlhartes Gehäuse*, 45
Standard Oil Trust, 275
*Starry Night, The*, painting, 240
"State-character," 76
Statistics, 150
Status: NUT goal, 43; Platonic Athens, 37, 41–43, 42t: Proust, 13–14, 56–62
"Steel-hard casing," 45
Steele, Richard, 247
Steffen, Gustaf, 88
Stirner, Max, 208
Stoicism, 123, 124, 130
Storytelling, 108–109
"Stranger," 46
Strauss, Anselm, 294
"Stream of consciousness," 306
Strindberg, August: biography, 87–88, 90; citation ranking, 11, 12t; on *Miss Julie*, 89; social structure, 14
Structuralism, 15, 119, 120
*Structure of Social Action, The* (Parsons, 229
Structure societies, 232
"Structured composition," 322
"Strum and Drang," 172
*Sub species aeternitatis*, 260
*Substance and Function* (Cassirer), 115, 117
Substantialism, 113, 115–118
"Superstructure," 317
"Survival units," 81
Swedberg, Richard, 20, 299–306
Swift, Jonathan: biography, 246–247; political satire, 18, 246, 248, 249; as public writer, 245–246, 251; reputation, 250–251, 252; sociological insights, 251–252; works, 247, 248, 249
Sydenstricker, Absalom and Caroline, 179–180
Symbol sign, 304
Symbolic forms, 15, 113, 119–121
Symbolic interactionism, 294
Symbolism, 231–232
Symbols, 71
*System of Logic* (J. S. Mill), 301
Systems theory, 18, 232
"Tabula rasa," 172

*Taming of the Shrew* (Shakespeare): gender, 25; marriage, 27
Tarbell, Ida, 275
Taste: Kant, 285, 286; theory of, 13, 19
*Tatler*, Swift, 247
Technology of change, 67
Telescope: early European, 198; invention of, 17, 197; planetary observations, 199; term, 204n.1
Temple, William, 247
Thackeray, William, 250–251
Theater: Cicero's metaphor, 129; as "disclosure," 85; Strindberg's modernism, 85–86
Theoretical pluralism, 20, 289–290
Theory: evaluating multilevel, 240; pertinence, 4
*Things Fall Apart* (Achebe), 105, 106–107, 108–109
Thought experiments, 311
Thucydides, 308
Thurston-Milgrom, Joshua, 16, 159–168
Tilly, Charles, 296
Time: Borges, 208; macro/micro links, 240
"Tiny publics," 247
*Tlön, Uqbar, Orbis Tertius* (Borges), 208–209
Tolstoy, Lev, 268

Tönnies, Ferdinand, 309
Tory (Conservative) party, 245, 247, 248, 249
*Tractus Theologico-politicus* (Spinoza), 257
*Trattato d'Abaco* (Piero della Francesca), 202
Triads, *Miss Julie*, 91, 92, 93
*Trial, The* (Kafka): bureaucracy, 45, 47, 48, 49, 50; citations, 52
Trust, 127
Twain, Mark, 1
*Twelfth Night* (Shakespeare), 13, 24–28
*Two Concepts of Liberty* (Berlin), 264

U.S. Coastal Service, 300
*Übermensch* (super-man), 173
Udehn, Lars, 15, 123–132
"Ukania," 76
Ultimate cause, 136, 138
Understanding, 280
*Universal Algebra* (Whitehead), 228, 234
Universal sociology: unique elements, 233–235; Whitehead's influence, 18, 230–233
University of Berlin: Cassirer, 114; Lewin, 117
University of Chicago Laboratory School, 290
University of Goeteborg, 114
University of Hamburg, 114, 119
University of Michigan, 290
University of Vermont, 290
"Unredeemed nationalities," 79–81
"Urban Villagers," 50

Values, 37
Van Gogh, Vincent, 240
Vasari, Giorgio, 202–203
Veblen, Thorstein, 157
"Velociferity," 171, 176
"Vergesellschaftung," 171
"Vita activa," 176
"Vita contemplativa," 176
Vives, Juan Luis, 41
Volokhonsky, Larissa, 164
Voltaire, 123
Vonnegut, Kurt: body of work, 237–238, 243–244; *Cat's Cradle*, 241–242; macro/micro links, 238–240; multilevel analysis, 18, 238, 241; *Slaughterhouse Five*, 242–243
Vygotsky, Lev, 319

"Wanderjahre" 171
"War on terrorism," 50
Wars: as raw power, 277; Russell's opposition, 271
Ward, Lester, 299
Weber, Alfred, 50, 52
Weber, Marianne, 96, 103n.2
Weber, Max: charismatic power, 14, 95–96, 97, 102–103; existential ethics, 268;founding fathers, 55, 62; *Gedankenbilder*, 7; and Ibsen, 96; on inequality, 23;iron cage of bureaucracy, 13, 45, 49; iron cage of rationalization, 14, 95; and Kafka, 52; and Kant, 279–280, 281, 282–283, 284; and Mommsen, 123; on power, 19; "Protestant Ethic," 173; on the Puritans, 175, 267; on social power, 273; on social situations, 3–4; spiritual sources of capitalism, 151; on status groups, 56; "Vergesellschaftung," 171
Weimar Republic, 74
Welles, Orson, 49
Western, Bruce, 295
Whig party, 245
White, Harrison, 213
Whitehead, Alfred North: applied mathematics, 228; ideas, 18, 227; mathematician, 227–228; philosopher, 229, 230–234; and Plato, 234–235; on religion, 235–236; sociological relevance, 229–230
Whitman, Walt, 208
*Why I Write* (Orwell), 65
Wilde, Oscar, 207
Wiley, Norbert, 301
"Wilhelm Meister" novels (Goethe), 171
Will, 273
Willer, David: on power, 10; on Russell, 19

William II, King of Germany, 77
Winship, Christopher, 19, 289–297
Wittgenstein, Ludwig, 287
Women: and capitalism, 152; and consumerism, 154–156, 157n.2
Women's rights, 271
Wood, Neal, 131
Workmen's Accident Insurance Institute for the Kingdom of Bohemia, 47
"World-literature," 169
*Wrath of Khan* (Roddenberry), 219
*Writing of God, The* (Borges), 213

Yale University, 114
Yeats, William Butler, 106
Youth movements, 81

Zola, Émile: citation ranking, 11, 12t; on consumption, 16; on grand magasins (department stores), 149–157; sociological methods, 149–150; and Strindberg, 85

# About the Editors and Contributors

## THE EDITORS

**Christofer Edling** is Professor of Sociology at Jacobs University, Bremen. His main research and teaching interests are in social network analysis and sociological theory and methods. In 2002, he was awarded the Pro Futura Fellowship from the Bank of Sweden Tercentenary Foundation. His many research papers have appeared in leading journals, including the *Annual Review of Sociology*, *Nature*, and *Social Networks*.

**Jens Rydgren** is a Professor at Stockholm University, where he holds the Chair in Sociology. His major research interests include political sociology, the sociology of ethnic relations, and sociological theory. He is the author and editor of several books within these fields and publishes regularly in leading journals. Among his recent publications are "Beliefs" in The Handbook of Analytical Sociology (2009), and "The Power of the Past: Towards a Cognitive Sociology of Ethnic Conflict" (2007).

## THE CONTRIBUTORS

**Filippo Barbera** is Researcher in Economic Sociology at the University of Torino and affiliated to the Real Collegio Carlo Alberto. He is interested in analytical approaches to sociological theory and in the study of local development and in the sociological analysis of production markets. Recent publications include "Realism, Social Structure and the Theory of Action," in M. Cherkaoui and P. Hamilton (eds.), *Raymond Boudon: A Life in Sociology* (2009); and "Narratives, Temporality, and Sociology, An Introduction" with M. Santoro in *Sociologica* (2007).

**Peter Bearman** is the Cole Professor of the Social Sciences and Director of the Paul F. Lazarsfeld Center for the Social Sciences at Columbia University. His research cuts across multiple sub-disciplines within sociology, from historical sociology, collective action, social networks, ethnography, and social theory to problems in population and health. Bearman is the author of *Doormen* (2005), *Relations into Rhetorics* (1993), and the co-editor of the *Handbook of Analytical Sociology* (2009). He is a 2008 NIH Pioneer Award Winner in support of research focusing on the rising prevalence of autism. Among other honors, Bearman is a fellow of the AAAS.

**Margareta Bertilsson** is Professor of Sociology at Copenhagen University. Her main research interests are in the areas of social theory and philosophy, sociology of science and knowledge, legal profession and socio-legal studies. Recent publications include the articles "On the accumulation of cosmopolitan capitalism—a comment on Bourdieu and law" (2006), "Two Concepts of Freedom: Implications for the Question of Knowledge" in Stehr, N. (ed.), *Is Freedom the Daughter of Knowledge* (2007) and a volume on pragmatism titled *Peirce's Theory of Inquiry and Beyond* (2009).

**Ronald L. Breiger** is Professor of Sociology at the University of Arizona. He has edited *Dynamic Social Network Modeling and Analysis: Workshop Summary and Papers* with K. Carley and P. Pattison (2003) and *Contexts of Social Capital: Social Networks in Markets, Communities, and Families* with R. M. Hsung and N. Lin (2009). Recent articles include "Cultural Holes: Beyond Relationality in Social Networks and Culture" with M. Pachucki in *Annual Review of Sociology* (2010) and "The Strength of Weak Culture" with J. Schultz in *Poetics* (2010).

**Kathleen M. Carley** is Professor of Computation, Organizations and Society in the Institute for Software Research Department in School of Computer Science at Carnegie Mellon University and the Director of the Center for Computational Analysis of Social and Organizational Systems (CASOS). Her research blends computer science and sociology to address issues of information diffusion, belief formation, social change, organizational design, and social influence. She is the founding editor of the journal *Computational and Mathematical Organization Theory*. She and the members of her center have developed software, widely used through the world for Dynamic network analysis

(ORA), extraction of social networks from texts (AutoMap), network evolution and beliefs (Construct), and organizational design (OrgAhead).

**Karen A. Cerulo** is Professor of Sociology at Rutgers University. Her research addresses culture, communication, and cognition. She is the author of *Never Saw It Coming: Cultural Challenges to Envisioning the Worst* (2006), *Deciphering Violence: The Cognitive Order of Right and Wrong* (1998), and *Identity Designs: The Sights and Sounds of a Nation* (1995). She co-authored *Second Thoughts: Seeing Conventional Wisdom Through the Sociological Eye* with J. M. Ruane (2008), and edited *Culture in Mind: Toward a Sociology of Culture and Cognition* (2002). She has chaired the American Sociological Association's Culture Section and served as the Vice President of the Eastern Sociological Society.

**Mohammed Cherkaoui** is Distinguished Research Director, National Centre for Scientific Research and University of Paris Sorbonne. He is an expert and consultant for public and private institutions. Among his recent publications are *Le Suicide. Un siècle après Durkheim*, (2000), *Ecole et société : les paradoxes de la démocratie* (2001), *Sociologie de l'éducation* (7th ed., 2008), *Histoire et théorie des sciences sociales* (2003), *Invisible Codes* (2005), *Good Intentions* (2006), *Morocco and the Sahara: Social Bonds and Geopolitical Issues*, (2007), *Durkheim and the Puzzle of Social Complexity* (2008). Cherkaoui is a member of the Academia Europeae and European Academy of Sociology.

**Fredrik Engelstad** is Professor of Sociology at Oslo University. His main research interests are in the areas of power, social distribution patterns and processes, sociology of literature, and the philosophy of science. He is the author of many articles and books, including *Comparative Studies of Social and Political Elites* with T. Gulbrandsen (2007); *Power and Democracy; Critical Interventions* with Ø. Østerud (2004); *Social Time and Social Change*; and *Perspectives on Sociology and History* with R. Kalleberg (1999).

**Emily Erikson** is Assistant Professor of Sociology and the School of Management at Yale University. She is interested in the historical development of markets. Recent publications include "Anarchy, Hierarchy and Order" with J. Parent (2009), "Central Authority and Order," with J. Parent (2007), and "Malfeasance and the Foundations for Global Trade" with P. Bearman (2006). She sits on the editorial boards of Sociological Theory and Social Science History and has completed a manuscript on the English-East Indies trade of the eighteenth century.

**Thomas J. Fararo** is Emeritus Distinguished Service Professor of Sociology at the University of Pittsburgh. His articles and books deal with theoretical and mathematical sociology and include *Mathematical Sociology* (1973), *The Meaning of General Theoretical Sociology* (1989), *Social Action Systems* (2001), and *Generating Images of Stratification* with K. Kosaka (2003). He also co-edited *Rational Choice Theory: Advocacy and Critique* with J. Coleman (1992), *The Problem of Solidarity: Theories and Models* with P. Doreian (1998), and *Purpose, Meaning and Action: Control Systems Theories in Sociology* with K. McClelland (2006).

**Gary Alan Fine** is John Evans Professor of Sociology at Northwestern University. Among his recent publications are *Difficult Reputations: Collective Memories of the Evil, Inept and Controversial* (2001), *Gifted Tongues: High School Debate and Adolescent Culture* (2001), *Everyday Genius: Self-Taught Art and the Politics of Authenticity* (2004), and *Authors of the Storm: Meteorology and the Production of the Future* (2007). He will be a Guggenheim Fellow during 2010–2011.

**Helena Flam** is Professor of Sociology at the University of Leipzig. She belongs to the pioneering sociologists of emotions and co-founded the Emotions Network within the European Sociological Association. Her many publications include *Theorizing Emotions: Sociological Explorations and Applications*, co-edited with D. Hopkins, J. Kleres, and H. Kuzmics (2009), *Emotions and Social Movements*, edited with D. King (2005), *The Emotional 'Man' and the Problem of Collective Action* (2000), and *The Shaping of Social Organization* with T. Burns (1990).

**Roberto Franzosi** is Professor of Sociology and Linguistics at Emory University. His main interests have been in social protest (e.g., *The Puzzle of Strikes: Class and State Strategies in Postwar Italy*, Cambridge University Press, 1994). He has had a long-standing interest in issues of language and measurement of text and narrative, with several articles published and three books *From Words to Number: Narrative, Data, and Social Science* (Cambridge University Press, 2005), *Content Analysis* (Sage, 2008), and *Quantitative Narrative Analysis* (Sage, 2010). Using his quantitative approach to narrative, Franzosi has just completed data collection from three newspapers (some 50,000 newspaper articles coded) on the rise of Italian fascism (1919–22). He has also started a new project for the analysis of narratives of lynching (Georgia, 1875–1930).

**Wendy Griswold** is Professor of Sociology and Bergen Evans Professor in the Humanities at Northwestern University and Professor II of Sociology, University of Oslo, Norway. Her books include *Regionalism and the Reading Class* (2008), *Cultures and Societies in a Changing World*, Third Edition (2008), and *Bearing Witness: Readers, Writers, and the Novel in Nigeria* (2000). She was a Guggenheim Fellow in 2008–2009.

**Guillermina Jasso** is Silver Professor and Professor of Sociology at New York University. Her main research interests are basic theory and international migration, together with inequality, probability distributions, and factorial survey methods. Recent articles include "Estimating the Previous Illegal Experience of New Legal Immigrants" (2008), "A New Model of Wage Determination and Wage Inequality" (2009), "How Many Highly Skilled Persons Are Waiting in Line for U.S. Legal Permanent Residence?" (2010), and Linking Individuals and Societies" (2010). Jasso is a fellow of the Hopkins Society of Scholars and of the AAAS..

**Helmut Kuzmics** is Professor of Sociology at the University of Graz. His books include: *Der Preis der Zivilisation. Die Zwänge der Moderne im theoretischen Vergleich* (1989), *Literatur als Soziologie. Zum Verhältnis von literarischer und gesellschaftlicher Wirklichkeit* with G. Mozetic (2003), *Authority, State and National Character: The Civilizing Process in Austria and England 1700–1900* with R. Axtmann (2007). He is also co-editor of *Der unendliche Prozeß der Zivilisation. Zur Kultursoziologie der Moderne nach Norbert Elias* with I. Mörth (1991), *Transformationen des Wir-Gefühls. Studien zum nationalen Habitus* with R. Blomert and A. Treibel (1993); *Zivilisationstheorie in der Bilanz. Beiträge zum 100. Geburtstag von Norbert Elias* with A. Treibel und R. Blomert (2000).

**Omar Lizardo** is Assistant Professor in the Department of Sociology at University of Notre Dame. His primary research interests are cultural and cognitive sociology, the sociology of organizations, the sociology of media and the arts, globalization and transnational processes, and the sociology of emotions. Some of his recent publications include "The Cognitive Origins of Bourdieu's Habitus" (2004), "How Cultural Tastes Shape Personal Networks" (2006), and "Defining and Theorizing Terrorism: A Global Actor-Centered Approach" (2008).

**Barry Markovsky** is Professor of Sociology at the University of South Carolina. His research interests are in the areas of social psychology and theory construction. Currently he is engaged in NSF-sponsored projects investigating fairness perceptions in public goods settings, and the interaction of status, influence and social identity. He is also collaborating with computer scientists on a Web-based system for the collective development and evaluation of "modular" sociological theories. Forthcoming publications include "Modularizing Small Group Theories in Sociology" in *Small Group Research*, and the entries "Theory" and "Theory Construction" in *The Blackwell Concise Encyclopedia of Sociology*.

**John Levi Martin** is a Professor at the University of Chicago. He is the author of *Social Structures* (2009). Other work has dealt with the formal properties of belief systems and social structures, the Constitutional Convention of 1787, field theory, the rationalization of infantry war, the use of race as a conceptual category in American sociology, and the gendered evolution of power structures among adolescents and adults.

**Eva M. Meyersson Milgrom** is a senior scholar at SIEPR and a visiting associate professor at Department of Sociology, Stanford University. Her research lies at the interface of economics and sociology, applying research from areas such as Comparison Theories, Labor Markets, and Organization Theory. Her many research articles include "Distributive Justice and CEO Compensation" with G. Jasso (2008) and "Are Female Workers Less Productive Than Male Workers?" with T. Petersen and V. Snartland. Her most recent work is "Working for Female Managers: Gender Hierarchy in the Workplace" together with I. Kwon, and "The Dispossessed: A Labor Market Analysis of Extreme Political Violence."

**John W. Mohr** is Professor of Sociology and Director of the Survey Research Center at the University of California, Santa Barbara. He has a longstanding interest in using formal network methods to analyze cultural meaning systems. He has also written on: the history of the welfare state, diversity policies in higher education, the role of institutional logics in organizational fields and methods of textual analysis. Along with R. Friedland he is the co-editor of *Matters of Culture* (2004).

**Christopher Muller** is a graduate student in the Department of Sociology at Harvard University. His research interests include incarceration, racial inequality, economic history, political sociology, and philosophy of science. He is a Doctoral Fellow with the Multidisciplinary Program in Inequality and Social Policy, a National Science Foundation Graduate Research Fellow, and an affiliate of the Institute for Quantitative Social Science.

**Hans-Peter Müller** is Professor of sociology at Humboldt University Berlin. His main areas of research are social theory, social structure, and social inequality, economic and political sociology, and sociology of culture. Major publications include *Sozialstruktur und Lebensstile* (Second edition, 1993), *Sozialer Wandel*, edited with M.Schmid (1995), *Hauptwerke sozialer Ungleichheitsforschung*, edited with M Schmid (2003), *Encyclopedia of Social Theory* edited with A. Harrington and B. Marshall (2006), *Die europäische Gesellschaft* edited with Robert Hettlage (2006), and *Max Weber* (2007).

**Hiroshi Ono** is Associate Professor of Sociology at Texas A&M University. His research integrates sociology and microeconomics to study the causes and consequences of inequality, with particular focus on labor market inequality. He is interested in studying the organizational conditions that motivate employee commitment, performance, and trust and the extent to which education and training enhances earnings and mobility. His publications have appeared in the *American Sociological Review*, *Economics of Education Review*, *Social Forces*, *Social Science Quarterly*, *Social Science Research*, and *Sociological Perspectives*, among others.

**Karl-Dieter Opp** is Emeritus Professor at the University of Leipzig and Affiliate Professor at the University of Washington. His research focuses on collective action and, in particular, political protest, national and regional identification, and norms and institutions. He is the author of numerous research articles and books, including *Social Institutions. Their Emergence, Maintenance and Effects* edited with M. Hechter and R. Wippler (1990), *Social Norms*, edited with M. Hechter (2001), and most recently *Political Protest and Social Movements. A Multidisciplinary Introduction, Critique and Synthesis* (2009).

**Wendelin Reich** is a fellow at the Swedish Collegium for Advanced Study (SCAS) and Associate Professor in Sociology at Uppsala University. His interests focus on the social psychology of communicative interaction, including its evolutionary origins. Among his recent works are "Three Problems of Intersubjectivity—And One Solution" (2010) and "A Theory of Respect" with W. Schirmer (forthcoming).

**Janet M. Ruane** is Professor of Sociology at Montclair State University. Her research interests include formal and informal mechanisms of social control. She is author of a brief introduction to research methods: *Essentials of Research Methods* (2004) and co-author of *Second Thoughts: Seeing Conventional Wisdom Through the Sociological Eye* with K. A. Cerulo (fifth edition, forthcoming). She has over 20 years of classroom experience assisting undergraduates in developing their sociological vision.

**Joachim J. Savelsberg** is Professor of Sociology at the University of Minnesota. His work focuses on the impact of institutions on knowledge and practice in the area of crime and punishment. Recent publications include *Crime and Human Rights: Criminology of Genocide and Atrocities* (2010) and "Institutionalizing Collective Memories of Hate" with R. D. King (AJS 2005). His latest book, titled *Atrocities, Law and Collective Memory*, is forthcoming with the Russell Sage Foundation Press (with King). His current National Science Foundation-funded research addresses "Collective Representations and Memories of Atrocities after Judicial Intervention: The Case of Darfur in International Comparison."

**Richard Swedberg** is Professor of Sociology at Cornell University. His two main areas of research are economic sociology and social theory. He is currently working on a study of economic analysis and the division of intellectual labor during the early nineteenth century. His books include *The Handbook of Economic Sociology* co-edited with N. Smelser (1994, 2005), *Max Weber and the Idea of Economic Sociology* (1998), and *Principles of Economic Sociology* (2003).

**Joshua Thurston-Milgrom**, graduated from the University of Chicago, where his theoretical study of West African rhythms was awarded the 2007 Meyer Prize for the best undergraduate music thesis. He lives in Berlin and works as a freelance jazz musician and writer.

**Lars Udehn** is Professor of Sociology at Stockholm University. He is a leading expert on Methodological Individualism. Among his books are *The History and Meaning of Methodological Individualism* (2001) and *The Limits of Public Choice* (1995).

**David Willer** is Scudder Professor of Sociology, University of South Carolina. He founded Elementary Theory, a scientific research program that investigates the effects of social structures on human behavior. His *Network Exchange Theory* (1999) received the Coleman award from the American Sociological Association. Since then he has published *Building Experiments: Testing Social Theory* with H. Walker (2007) as well as a series of papers, including "Testing Ten Theories" with P. Emanuelson (2008), "Power, Embedded Games and Coalition Formation" with C. Borch (2006), "The Embeddedness of Collective Goods" with B. Simpson (2005), and "Theory Programs and Theoretical Problems" with J. Berger and M. Zelditch Jr (2005).

**Christopher Winship** is the Diker-Tishman Professor of Sociology at Harvard University and a member of the senior faculty of the Kennedy School. He is a research associate at the Hauser Center for Nonprofit Organizations, the Criminal Justice Program, the Institute for Quantitative Social Science. Prior to coming to Harvard in 1992, he was Professor of Sociology, Statistics, and Economics at Northwestern University. He has published widely on social stratification, policy analysis, and sociological methods. Together with S. L. Morgan he is the author of *Counterfactuals and Causal Inference: Methods and Principles for Social Research* (2007).